THE HINDU GĪTĀ

THE HINDU GĪTĀ

Ancient and Classical Interpretations of the Bhagavadgītā

Arvind Sharma

OPEN COURT
La Salle, Illinois

Open Court and the above logo are registered in the U.S. Patent and Trademark Office.

Published by arrangement with Gerald Duckworth & Co. Ltd., London.

OC 885 10 9 8 7 6 5 4 3 2 1

ISBN 0-8126-9013-3

Library of Congress Cataloging in Publication Data

Sharma, Arvind.
The Hindu Gītā.
Bibliography: p.
Includes index.
1. Bhagavad-gītā—criticism, interpretation etc.—
History. I. Title
BL1138.6.S495 1985 294.5'924 85-21520
ISBN 0-8126-9013-3

Printed and bound in the United Kingdom.

Contents

For

Eric J. Sharpe

Preface

The Bhagavadgītā has attracted so much scholarly attention that most prefatory notes to new books tend to be apologetic in tone under pressure of the need to justify yet one more. This book, however, which deals with the ancient Hindu tradition of commentary, requires no such justification, for the following reasons.

Chapter One adopts the novel approach that insights may be gained into the Gītā's role in the Hindu religious tradition by treating the Anugītā for all practical purposes as the first 'commentary'.

Chapter Two explores another possibility that the various *Gītāmāhātmyas*, or verses glorifying the Gītā as found in the Purāṇas, may be treated as a further body of source-material for assessing current interpretations.

Chapter Three offers, perhaps for the first time in English in any detail, material from Bhāskara's commentary, of which a full English translation has yet to appear.

Chapters Four and Five are harder to justify in terms of novelty, but Śaṅkara's and Rāmānuja's commentaries have been subjected to a close scrutiny in relation to the text, and what has often been stated is here documented and demonstrated in detail: namely, that these scholiasts tend to bend the meaning of the text to suit the context of their own philosophical systems. At the same time their positive exegetical contributions are also noted.

Chapter Six offers, perhaps for the first time in English in any detail, material from the commentary of Madhva. A full English translation of this commentary, as of Bhāskara's, has yet to be published.

The reason for the subtitle should therefore be clear, for the book deals with ancient and classical Hindu interpretations, not with *all* Hindu interpretations. Medieval and modern views, such as those of

Jñānadeva and Tilak, among others, would require volumes in their own right. Even in dealing with ancient and classical interpretations I have concentrated on Hindu and Sanskrit sources and the main scholiasts. This is the primary need.

Material included in some the chapters has appeared earlier, as follows: in the *Journal of Religious Studies* (Introduction); in *Religious Studies* (Chapter One); in *Textual Studies in Hinduism* (Chapter Four); and in *Viśiṣṭādvaita Vedānta: A Study* (Chapter Five).

Sydney, 1985 A.S.

Introduction

1. *The Bhagavadgītā: what is it?*

The Bhagavadgītā is a text of Eighteen Chapters[1] which is found in the Bhīṣmaparvan of the Hindu epic known as the Mahābhārata, one of the two *itihāsas*[2] of the Hindu religious tradition. Within the Bhīṣmaparvan it constitutes Chapters 23-40. The Bhīṣmaparvan is the sixth of the eighteen *Parvans* which constitute the Mahābhārata and in itself consists of 117 chapters (6.1.1 – 6.117.34).[3]

This description is based on the critical or Poona edition of the Mahābhārata.

The Bhagavadgītā is also referred to as Gītā,[4] as Īśvaragītā,[5] as Anantagītā,[6] as Harigītā,[7] and as Vyāsagītā.[8]

[1] The Bhagavadgītā is on this account referred to as *aṣṭādaśādyāyinī* (cf. *aṣṭādhyāyī* of Pāṇini).

[2] T.M.P. Mahadevan, *Outlines of Hinduism* (Bombay: Chetana, 1971), p.33.

[3] See Shripad Krishna Belvalkar (ed.), *The Bhīṣmaparvan* (Poona: Bhandarkar Oriental Research Institute, 1947).

[4] e.g. by Śaṅkara; also in the plural, see K.T. Telang (tr.), *The Bhagavadgītā with the Santasujātīya and the Anugītā* (Delhi: Motilal Banarsidass, 1965 [first published by Clarendon Press, 1882]), p.2.

[5] ibid. 'Śaṅkarācārya, indeed, sometimes calls it the Īśvara Gītā, which I believe, is the specific title of a different work altogether.'

[6] e.g. by Bāṇa; see ibid., p.28. Telang maintains that in the expression *anantagītākarṇanānanditanaram*, which appears in Bāṇa's *Kādambarī*, 'Anantagītā is evidently only another name here for Bhagavadgītā'.

[7] Hemachandra Raychaudhuri, *Materials for the Study of the Early History of the Vaishnava Sect* (New Delhi: Oriental Books Reprint Corporation, 1975 [first published in 1920 by the University of Calcutta]), p.13.

[8] Haridas Bhattacharyya (ed.), *The Cultural Heritage of India*, Vol.II (Calcutta: Ramakrishna Mission Institute of Culture, 1962 [first published 1937]), p.205.

This poem of 18 cantos appears as an inset in the Mahābhārata, where it describes the two rival armies of the Pāṇḍava and the Kauravas as ranged against each other on the battlefield. Arjuna who, taken all in all, is the most notable of the five Pāṇḍava brothers, is suddenly overtaken by despair; and he refuses to fight. The thought uppermost in his mind at the moment is that he should not kill his kith and kin but should withdraw from the contest, *whatever* the consequences of such withdrawal may be. He is far from sure that he and his brothers will win the battle; and, even if they do, the kingdom which they will gain, he feels, will be one that has been denuded of almost everything that they care for. In his despondency, he prefers to turn an anchorite. Then Śrī Krishna, who has undertaken to guide his chariot, advises him to begin the fight which it is his duty as a prince to do; and it is that advice which is believed to be embodied in the poem.[9]

2. *The Bhagavadgītā: a coat of many colours?*

There is a primary issue which must be faced before we can begin to talk of the interpretation of any scripture: is the scripture univalent or multivalent? In other words does it possess one or many meanings? To pose this question in this fashion, however, is to sound the bugle for hermeneutical warfare, in which it is not my intention to engage, notwithstanding the temptation, especially since we are dealing with a text with such an explicitly martial context as the Gītā. We may perhaps ask: is the Bhagavadgītā univalent or multivalent? Even in this more cautious formulation the way is left open for a general exegetical eruption, for the issue can be debated endlessly. In a third attempt we may narrow the question further: Does the Bhagavadgītā *consciously* set out to be univalent or multivalent?

This is not an unfair question to ask of a text. For instance, the same question can be asked of the Qur'ān, and the answer provided by Islamic orthodoxy is that the Qur'ān is to be understood literally except where it is obviously metaphorical, e.g. 'hang on to the rope of faith'. But the Qur'ān was variously interpreted[10] and is itself less sanguine on the point, admitting that there are clear as well as opaque verses.[11] The same question can be asked of the well-known

[9] M. Hiriyanna, *The Essentials of Indian Philosophy* (London: Allen & Unwin, 1978), pp. 52-3. Also S. Radhakrishnan, *Indian Philosophy* (New York: Macmillan, 1962) I, p.520.

[10] H.A.R. Gibb, *Islam: A Historical Survey* (Oxford University Press, 1978), pp.34-5, 65, 67, 101 etc.

[11] H.A.R. Gibb and J.H. Kramers (eds.), *Shorter Encyclopedia of Islam* (Leiden: E.J. Brill, 1974), p.275.

Hindu text the Brahmasūtra, which tries to systematise the teachings of the Upaniṣads. It clearly states that the various statements are to be understood harmoniously.

> I.1.4. This section declares that *Brahman* is the meaning of all scriptural passages. Their differences are only apparent and are capable of reconciliation. The many passages have one purport.
>
> *tat tu samanvayāt:* 'But that is the result of the harmony (of the different scriptural statements).
> *tat:* that; *tu:* but; *samanvayāt:* being the result of the harmony of the different texts.[12]

Indeed the general temper of the tradition known as Vedānta, of which the Gītā, along with the Upaniṣads and the Brahmasūtras, is considered as a basic text, is that 'the Vedānta, in its later forms, stands for the teaching not merely of the Upanishads, together with the earlier portions of the Veda, but also of other parts of the sacred literature such as the Bhagavadgītā and the Viṣṇu Purāṇa which are regarded as reiterating and amplifying the Upanishadic doctrine. The doctrine thus combines in one harmonious whole the results attained by all previous orthodox thinkers, and is therefore looked upon as the most perfect expression of Indian thought.'[13]

But what does the Gītā say about itself: is it univalent or multivalent?

It seems to be ambivalent. While it exhorts Arjuna to be of one resolve (II:41), it offers him so many points of view that he confesses to being confused (III:2). Even if we put this down to his own mental fecklessness, what are we to make of such verses as IX:14-15:

14. *satataṃ kīrtayanto māṃ*
yatantaś ca dṛḍhavratāḥ
namasyantaś ca māṃ bhaktyā
nityayuktā upāsate

15. *jñānayanjñena cā 'py anye*
yajanto māṃ upāsate
ekatvena pṛthaktvena
bahudhā viśvatomukham

[12] S. Radhakrishnan, *The Brahma Sūtra: The Philosophy of Spiritual Life* (London: Allen & Unwin, 1971), p.246.

[13] Hiriyanna, op.cit., p.151. S.N. Dasgupta, *A History of Indian Philosophy* (Cambridge University Press, 1922), passim.

Ever glorifying Me,
  And striving with firm resolve,
And paying homage to Me with devotion,
  Constantly disciplined, they wait upon Me.

With knowledge-worship also others
  Worshipping wait upon Me,
In My unique and manifold forms,
  (Me as) variously (manifested), facing in all directions.[14]

It could be argued, however, that these verses only provide for a multiplicity of approaches, though directed only towards Kṛṣṇa, and are therefore ultimately univalent.

This implied univalency becomes harder to sustain, however, if the various contradictions in which the Gītā is involved are taken into account, which at the moment may be charitably regarded as only apparent.

3. *The Bhagavadgītā: do the colours blend?*

The Gītā contains many apparent contradictions.[15] They are so numerous that it is best to sort them out in different bags and label these bags for convenience.

Theological contradictions

These show up clearly if we try to find the answer in the Gītā to these four questions: (1) Is God Personal or Impersonal? (2) Is God or the Ultimate Reality active or passive? (3) Is God or the Ultimate Reality immanent or transcendent? (4) What is the relation of God to Man? Is He indifferent to Man? Is He his well-wisher? Is He his chastiser?

In several passages in the Gītā God is described as Personal.[16] In others, He is described as Impersonal.[17] He is even described in terms of the neuter Brahman. One of the epithets Arjuna lavishes on Kṛṣṇa in the Tenth Chapter is that of the 'Supreme Brahman'.[18]

[14] Franklin Edgerton, *The Bhagavad Gītā* (Cambridge, Massachusetts; Harvard University Press, 1944), Part I, pp.90, 91.

[15] The Gītā itself is conscious of some apparent contradictions, see III:1, IV:4, V:1, V:4, XVIII:3 etc. See below, Appendix I.

[16] XV:17-18, X:20-42 (note use of first person), etc.

[17] XIII:12.

[18] X:12. All the other epithets used in the first line of the verse are neuter, though not in the next.

Salvation is described as attaining Brahma-Nirvāṇa[19] or as 'having become Brahman'.[20]

The Ultimate Reality is described as intervening in the universe in the famous Avatāra verses;[21] but it is also described elsewhere as not merely neuter but also neutral.[22]

Similarly, God is sometimes described as immanent,[23] sometimes as transcendent.[24]

Different answers are given in different passages to the question of the nature of relationship between God and Man. Sometimes one finds signs of an indifference to Man.[25] Yet, at other places, we have hints of an emotional relationship, loving,[26] or vengeful.[27]

Soteriological ambiguity

Let a question be posed: does man achieve the Perfect State of Union with God while alive or only after his death?

What is the Gītā's answer to this question? It has two answers, and the door is left open to both possibilities. At one place it suggests that the Union is posthumous,[28] at another that it can be attained here and now.[29]

Metaphysical antinomy

The question is: is the world real or unreal? Again the Gītā seems to have two apparently contradictory answers. At places it treats of the world as real,[30] and yet in the concepts of Māyā (a veil to go beyond),[31] Ajñāna (darkness to be penetrated),[32] and Aśvattha (etymologically, that which is not there tomorrow),[33] we find hints of the unreality of the world.

Liturgical inconsistencies

On the mode of worship Kṛṣṇa (etymologically the 'attractor')[34] seems to pull in two directions: both towards, and away from, ritual.

[19] V:24-6 and II:72. These are the three places where the expression Brahma-Nirvāṇa occurs in the Gītā. If Nirvāṇa is to be 'blown out' the implication is that one is blown out into Brahman.

[20] XVIII:54. [21] IV:7-8. [22] IX:9.

[23] VII:7-8, X:34, IX:6, XV:12-15. [24] XV:6, 18 etc.

[25] IX:29 (first line). [26] XVIII:64. [27] XVI:19.

[28] VIII:5, 13. [29] V:19.

[30] VII:4-5. [31] VII:14. [32] V:15-16, X:11.

[33] XV:1-3. See Swami Swarupananda, *Shrimad Bhagavad Gītā* (Calcutta: Advaita Ashrama, 1967), p.323.

[34] E.O. Martin, *The Gods of India* (London: Dent, 1914), p.130.

Some statements strongly favour sacrificial ritual,[35] while in others ritualism is sharply criticised.[36] Moreover, sometimes He comes out in favour of Homa[37] and sometimes of Pūjā.[38]

Canonical ambivalence

The position of the Gītā on the role of Scriptural authority is apparently ambivalent. At times Arjuna is exhorted by Kṛṣṇa to free himself from Vedic bonds.[39] The Vedas are no more than 'a water tank, When on all sides there is a flood of water'.[40] And yet, later, the Sixteenth Chapter concludes with a heavy emphasis on the necessity of abiding by Śāstric injunctions.[41] And the Vedas are the Śāstras *par excellence.*[42] Hence one spots a contradiction: an exhortation to go beyond the Vedas, simultaneously with a warning to abide by them.

Franklin Edgerton has enlarged this ambivalence to indicate an inconsistency in the Gītā's attitude to established religion, by which he means the system of traditional sacrifices and observance.[43] Says he:

> The curious many-sidedness, tolerance or inconsistency – whichever one may choose to call it – of the Bhagavad Gītā ... is shown nowhere more strikingly than in its attitude towards what we may call orthodox established religion.

Now it seems to opt for the orthodox established religion,[44] now against it.

Ethical dilemma

A moral issue lies at the very heart of the Gītā: indeed the Gītā may be viewed as an effort to resolve it. The issue is: is it morally proper to kill? That the question is posed in a martial context etches it even more deeply.

The answer given is quite clear: Arjuna should do his duty, which is to fight.[45] But it immediately raises the question: how could

[35] IV:31. [36] II:42-3. [37] IV:31.

[38] IX:26. See R.C. Majumdar (ed.), *The Vedic Age* (Bombay: Bharatiya Vidya Bhavan, 1965), pp.163-4.

[39] II:45. [40] II:46. Edgerton's translation. [41] XVI:23-4.

[42] See Vishva Bandhu, *The Vedas and Sastras* (Hoshiarpur: Vishveshvarananda Institute, 1966), passim.

[43] Edgerton, op.cit., Part II, p.77. [44] III:9, 12, 13; IV:23.

[45] Dasgupta, op.cit., pp.502, 506, 513. Also the text II:33, XVIII:45-7 etc.

Kṛṣṇa ask Arjuna to kill?[46]

The problem is that along with exhortations to Arjuna to fight[47] there are verses extolling *ahiṁsā*, or non-violence. *Ahiṁsā* is lauded as a quality of him who 'to the divine lot, Is born'.[48] And Arjuna is then told quite explicitly that 'to the divine lot Thou art born'.[49] *Ahiṁsā* is also mentioned by Kṛṣṇa as one of the conditions of beings arising from Him alone.[50]

The force of this contradiction can be seen from the fact that Mahatma Gandhi pitted himself non-violently against the British on the strength of the Bhagavadgītā, with which he fought the Indian Penal Code,[51] and N. Godse drew his inspiration to assassinate Mahatma Gandhi from the self-same Gītā[52] and was hanged under the Indian Penal Code. Thus Gandhi and Godse personify the ethical dilemma of the Gītā.

Yogic embarras de richesses

The Gītā espouses several Yogas. The colophons of the Eighteen Chapters yield a rich harvest of about seventeen Yogas.[53] To these may be added references to Buddhi Yoga,[54] Abhyāsa Yoga,[55] Jñāna Yoga,[56] Karma Yoga,[57] etc.

At a simpler level, the Gītā distinguishes between the two schools of Sāṁkhya and Yoga,[58] or more generally, between Jñāna and Karma Yoga.[59] That even these two approaches are mutually contradictory can be seen from Arjuna's uneasiness at the beginning of the Third Chapter.[60] At the end of the Second Chapter Kṛṣṇa seemed to be plumping for Jñāna.[61] When Arjuna then asks: 'Then why to violent action Dost Thou enjoin me, Keśava',[62] Kṛṣṇa comes out for Karma in the Third Chapter.[63] Towards the end of the Fourth Chapter He starts swinging towards Jñāna again[64] and finally exhorts Arjuna to cut the Gordian knot of doubts with the Alexandrian sword of Knowledge![65]

[46] Nataraj Guru, *The Bhagavad Gītā* (New York: Asia Publishing House, 1961), p.ix.
[47] II:3, 18, 37; III:30 etc.
[48] XVI:3. Edgerton, op.cit., Part I, p.149.
[49] XVI:5. ibid.
[50] X:5. ibid., p.97. *Ahiṁsā* is also regarded as a virtue in XIII:7, XVI:2, XVII:14.
[51] D.P. Karmarkar, *Bal Gangadhar Tilak: A Study* (Bombay, 1956), pp.107-8.
[52] See Robert Payne, *The Life and Death of Mahatma Gandhi* (New York: Dutton, 1969), pp.635-47.
[53] With the sole exception of Chapter XI sometimes.
[54] X:10. [55] VIII:8. [56] III:3. [57] III:3.
[58] II:39. [59] III:3. See Dasgupta, op.cit., p.455.
[60] III:1-2. [61] II:54-72. [62] III:1.
[63] III:4-5, 8, 10-26. [64] IV:33-9. [65] IV:42.

But Arjuna is still on his knees, more confused than ever, requesting Kṛṣṇa to make up his mind.[66] Arjuna has good reasons to be bewildered. For the Gītā contains strong[67] as well as tepid endorsements of Karma, and strong[68] as well as tepid[69] endorsements of Jñāna. The picture becomes even more complicated when Bhakti Yoga enters the scene, and by the beginning of the Twelfth Chapter Arjuna has fresh doubts.[70]

These instances amply indicate the contradictory potential of the Yogas.

Interpretative differences

It has already been shown how the Gītā has been used either as a base or as a supporting column by commentators to raise the superstructure of their own philosophies.[71] It has also been shown how the Gītā has been used by modern scholars to formulate different theories.[72] The strongest proof of the apparent contradictoriness of the Gītā seems to lie in this: that it has been associated with so many ancient philosophies and so many modern scholarly conjectures. From the raw material of the Gītā have been manufactured such philosophies and theories as make one wonder: Is the Gītā the word of God Incarnate as the pious Bhāgavata believes? Is it an *advaita*, a *viśiṣṭādvaita*, a *dvaita* or a *śuddhādvaita* work? Does it propound Karma Yoga, Jñāna Yoga or Bhakti Yoga, or all of them, or all of the various other Yogas enumerated? Is it a Vedantic revision of a theistic poem? Is it a Viṣṇuite remodelling of a pantheistic poem? Is it a Kṛṣṇaite version of a Viṣṇuite poem? Is it an Upaniṣad of the 'Svetāśvatara' type adopted by the Kṛṣṇa cult? Is it a late product of the degeneration of Upaniṣadic monistic thought in the transitional period from theism to realistic atheism? Is it an old verse Upaniṣad, later than Śvetāśvatara, worked into the Gītā by Kṛṣṇaism? Does it merely reflect different streams of tradition flowing through a confused mind? Is it the application of the Upaniṣadic ideal to the Mahābhārata reality?[73]

Will the real Gītā please stand up?

The existing literature on the subject offers two divergent explanations to account for the apparent contradictoriness. The first

[66] V:1. [67] IV:1-32. [68] IV:34-8. [69] VI:46.
[70] XII:1.
[71] See above, n.15 and below, Appendix 1, pp.xxvii-xxviii.
[72] ibid.
[73] R.C. Majumdar (ed.), *The Age of Imperial Unity* (Bombary: Bharatiya Vidya Bhavan, 1953), p.447; Radhakrishnan, op.cit., p.530.

is to regard it as an interpolated work, the second as a mystic poem.

The first approach was developed by a whole train of scholars from Richard Garbe onwards, and is well-articulated by Hopkins. According to him, the Gītā

> has shared the fact of most Hindu works in being interpolated injudiciously, so that many of the puzzling anomalies, which astound no less the reader than the hero to whom it was revealed are probably later additions.

Elsewhere Garbe talks of the Gītā's 'patchwork origin, which again would help to explain its philosophical inconsistencies'.[74]

Thus, on this view, the Gītā is replete with contradictions because of interpolations. It is patchy because patches have been put on it from time to time.[75]

This approach bases itself on two grounds: one linguistic and literary, the other philosophical. E.H. Johnston's position is a case in point. Johnston regards the last six chapters as interpolated, partly because 'elevation of thought and language are markedly absent from the last six cantos', and partly because the Sāṁkhya expressions used in them correspond, according to him, to the later strata of the Mahābhārata.[76] For the purpose of this chapter, these two aspects – the linguistic-literary and the philosophical – must be disentangled. The non-philosophical issues are recounted elsewhere.[77] It appears that the interpolationistic viewpoint is based quite substantially on philosophical grounds also.[78] And here, in our view, the approach suffers from a serious limitation. It identifies unity with uniformity, the continuity of a text with the consistency of its content or philosophy. This is a particularly doubtful assumption to make when handling as rich and diverse a tradition as the Hindu.

Philological insights and semantic investigations may clarify some apparent contradictions; historical circumstances shed some light on them, but the contributions of such an approach remain peripheral, for in essence the contradictions are philosophical. This leads us to the second approach, which regards the Gītā as a mystic poem or song.

[74] Quoted by Hill, op.cit., p.15.

[75] See below, Appendix 2, pp.xxviii-xxx.

[76] Johnston, *Early Sāṁkhya*, p.7.

[77] See above, nn.61, 62.

[78] See Roy, *The Bhagavadgītā and Modern Scholarship*, pp.10-11; D.D. Vadekar, *Bhagavad-Gītā* (Poona: Oriental Book Agency, 1928) seems to underplay the philosophical grounds *vis-à-vis* philological.

A few scholars tend to emphasise the poetic aspect,[79] but most focus on the mystic element. Franklin Edgerton's approach typifies the mystic kind of explanation of the apparent contradictions. In his opinion, the Gītā must be thought of as a poem, and to understand the apparent inconsistencies one 'must be able and willing to adopt the poet's attitude'.[80] This attitude is mystical. Hence, if the points of view are intuitional, the fact that they are not logical, that they are apparently contradictory, becomes less significant. 'To the mystic they are above reason; to the rationalist below it.'[81] Thus according to Edgerton the explanation of apparent contradictions lies in the mystical nature of the work.

This is a widely shared view. Hence D.S. Sarma regards it as 'a song or a series of songs. It is not, therefore, a theological or a philosophical treatise';[82] it is 'rather irregular'.[83] And he adds somewhat eloquently: 'It is irregular as the mountains are irregular, as the forests are irregular, as the ocean is irregular.'[84] Surendranath Dasgupta has shown how the Gītā 'combines different conceptions of God without feeling the necessity of reconciling the oppositions or contradictions involved in them'.[85] This is indicative of its mystical aproach. It is obvious, therefore, that the mystical explanation of the apparent contradictions in the Gītā has a great measure of plausibility.

At this point, however, some questions may be raised. Can the Gītā properly be called a mystical poem? Would it not be more accurate to say that it is the description of the Reality in the Gītā that is mystical? Could not the Gītā then be viewed as a practical, even a martial, poem with the cut-and-dried aim of urging a nervous Arjuna to rejoin the fight?

After all, the moment Arjuna expresses his readiness to fight all discussion ceases. And during the course of that discussion some remarkably unmystical and unspiritual reasons have been advanced for Arjuna's contemplation by Kṛṣṇa, along with all that is said for his edification. Thus Arjuna is asked to fight to avoid the ridicule of being considered a coward;[86] to escape ignominy;[87] and because if he perishes he goes to heaven, and if he wins he rules the earth, and thus has the best of both worlds![88]

[79] See J. Cockburn Thomson, *The Bhagavad-Gītā* (Hartford: Stephen Austin, 1855) p.xi; C.C. Caleb, *The Song Divine* (London: Luzac, 1911), Preface.

[80] Edgerton, op.cit., Part II, p.4. [81] ibid.

[82] D.S. Sarma, *Lecturers on the Bhagavad Gītā*, p.2.

[83] ibid. p.19. [84] ibid.

[85] Dasgupta, op.cit., p.533.

[86] II:35. [87] II:34. [88] II:37.

A third approach to explain the apparent contradictions is to regard the Gītā neither as a corrupt text nor as a mystical poem, but primarily as a practical work. This approach seems to change the complexion of the whole controversy. For, whereas from a philosophical point of view several apparent contradictions in the Gītā may be identified, 'so far as the practical teaching is concerned, there is no ambiguity. The reason for this is the setting of the poem.'[89] In a nutshell, this is that Arjuna loses nerve on the eve of battle, and after an invigorating pep-talk with liberal draughts of philosophy and mysticism he rises ready to fight. 'This important element in the conception of the poem would lose its entire significance if we did not regard action as its essential lesson.'[90]

It is significant that before Edgerton could treat the Gītā as a mystic poem he had to abstract it from the setting. Thus he chose imperatively to 'think of the Gītā as a unit complete in itself, without reference to its surroundings'.[91] In other words he chose to look at the text without the *con*text.

The reason he chose to do so was the 'dramatic absurdity'[92] of the situation in which the Gītā is believed to have been revealed. The dialogue is set in the midst of the battlefield with armies arrayed in mortal combat. To visualise Arjuna and Kṛṣṇa bandying Anuṣṭubh metres[93] for over an hour does strain one's credulity, to say the least. The point, however, is not the feasibility of the setting, nor its historicity: the point is its relevance to understanding the Gītā. Whether, on a literary view, the context was created for the text or, on a mystical view, the text for the context, the view advocated here is that the text should not be read apart from the context. To use the old cliché, in dismissing the context outright wasn't Edgerton throwing out the baby with the bathwater?[94]

From this point of view, although the Gītā is 'one foot of the triple base on which Vedānta is founded', it stands on a different footing from the rest. The other two are the Upaniṣads and the Brahmasūtra. The Upaniṣads explicitly concern themselves with the spiritual quest, as does the very first Brahmasūtra,[95] but the Gītā has

[89] M. Hiriyanna, *Outlines of Indian Philosophy* (London: Allen and Unwin, 1964), p.118.

[90] ibid.

[91] Edgerton, op.cit., Part II, p.4. [92] ibid., p.3.

[93] The entire Gītā is not in the same metre, though; e.g. XI:15-50, II:5-8, etc.

[94] On the close connection of the Gītā with the Mahābhārata, see S. Radhakrishnan, op.cit., p.523.

[95] See Bādarāyaṇa, *Brahmasūtra* I. 1. Also see, among other Upaniṣads, *Kena-Upaniṣad* I. 1.

a backdrop of martial conflict. Small wonder that, within the space of twenty pages, S.N. Dasgupta twice identifies the 'fundamental idea'[96] and the 'fundamental teaching'[97] of the Gītā, not as the identity of God and Godhead, or of Ātman-Brahman, but that a man should 'always follow his own caste duties'[98] 'without any motive of self-interest or gratification of sense-desires'.[99] Unlike the other two works, the Gītā did not set out to crack the riddle of the universe. Its main goal was to get Arjuna going. In trying to resolve Arjuna's moral dilemma, Kṛṣṇa was drawn into a discussion about philosophical and metaphysical issues. He was drawn in all the more deeply when Arjuna was baffled by the apparent contradictions of His statements. When the explanations began to become too involved, Kṛṣṇa asked Arjuna to put his faith in Him – and fight, which he did.

The third approach, then, suggests that the apparent contradictions in the Gītā may not be all due to its assessment as a mystical poem. They arise because Kṛṣṇa uses as many points of view as he can to convince Arjuna to fight, and in such a situation these points of view may be contradictory. What is required is that they should all converge (on the issue at hand), not that they should merge. Kṛṣṇa has to be persuasive, not consistent.

Three possible explanations of apparent contradictions were examined in this section. The philological approach was abandoned as inadequate. The philosophical approach seemed more fruitful. It was further suggested that the practical approach may supplement the philosophical, if not supplant it.

We said that the context of the Gītā only requires the various points of view to converge, not to merge. But the question may be asked: even if not intended to, *do* they merge? Can the various apparent contradictions be resolved within the framework of the Gītā? Can the 'inconsistencies' be reconciled?

Theological contradictions

It has been shown that the Gītā regards God as both Personal and Impersonal. An effort is made to reconcile the two aspects through what Ranade calls Super-personalism – by merging the two aspects in a single description.[100] A reconciliation could also be achieved through the concepts of Saguṇa and Nirguṇa Brahman, which are two ways of describing God, just as 'both waves and particles may be

[96] Dasgupta, op.cit., Part II, p.502. [97] ibid., p.513.
[98] ibid., p.502. [99] ibid., p.513.
[100] IX:17-18.

equally accurate heuristic devices for describing the nature of light'.[101]

The activity and passivity of God, his Actor versus Spectator roles, may be reconciled through what has been called Emanationism – 'It is on account of the force of the magnet that motion is imparted to the iron filings.' Thus can God be the prime mover without moving.[102]

The compatibility of immanence with transcendence can be shown by analysing the concept of Hindu theism in the manner of Sir R.G. Bhandarkar. God is regarded as expressing himself through the cosmos but is not exhausted by it[103] – this leaves room for transcendence even when God is immanent.[104]

So far as the relation of God to Man is concerned, the possibility of this emerges in the context of a Personal God. Then God's attitude is governed by the nature of actions and degree of devotion of man.[105]

Soteriological ambiguity

The position of the Gītā seems to be that Salvation can be attained here and everywhere;[106] and that if the Perfect State of Union with God is achieved even on one's deathbed, one is saved. Hence there is no ambiguity here – the point being that even if that state is achieved with the last breath, one is saved.[107]

Metaphysical antinomy

The Gītā tries to bridge the gulf between the two notions of the world as real and unreal by saying that it is ephemeral, that we don't see the whole show, only a part of it.[108] The phenomenal world is, so to speak, not entirely unreal, but it is too fleeting to be fully real either.

Liturgical inconsistency

The Gītā can be seen here as helping to perform the great feat of synthesis which merged the Āgamic and Nigamic traditions of India. S.K. Chatterji remarks that the 'first conscious attempt to give the imprimatur to Pūjā as a rite, which is to be taken sympathetically, we find in that great work of synthesis in Hindu thought and life, the

[101] Huston Smith, *The Religions of Man* (New York: Harper and Row, 1958), p.66.
[102] IX:10.
[103] Vishwas G. Bhat, *The Bhagavadgītā* (Poona: Arya Sanskrit Press, 1932), p.39.
[104] X:42.
[105] IX:22; X:9-11; XVI:19-20, etc.
[106] V:26. [107] II:71. [108] II:28.

Bhagavad Gītā ...'.[109] The Gītā also tries to reconcile ritualism with spiritualism by internalising the concept of Yajña,[110] and by linking it with Brahman.[111]

Canonical ambivalence

The attitude of the Gītā to the Vedas is like that of a wayfarer towards a raft – which is to be used while crossing but is to be abandoned after the crossing has been made. For one who has had self-realisation the Vedas are not binding, but for one like Arjuna who is not a realised soul they are.[112] Hence there is no contradiction. Attitudes appropriate to two different stages of spiritual development are involved.

Ethical dilemma

The Gītā tries to reconcile the ethical dilemma by reinterpreting the notion of moral responsibility. According to the Gītā, acts which are performed selflessly are free from any taint.[113] With selflessness, ruthlessness is no sin. Real violence lies in killing out of personal motives.[114] 'Kṛṣṇa advises Arjuna to fight without passion or ill-will, without anger or attachment, and if we develop such a frame of mind violence becomes impossible.'[115]

Yogic embarras de richesses and interpretative differences

It has been recognised earlier that the Gītā refers to several Yogas and is associated with diverse philosophical systems. But it is not the ultimate goal of the Gītā to reconcile the several Yogas or to synthesise the systems. Its manifest goal is simple and proximate – to induce Arjuna to get on with the fight.[116] A conscious effort is indeed made in the Gītā to reconcile Karma and Jñāna;[117] but this is done, not out of a general integral consciousness, but because Arjuna is confused and a man beset with doubt is liable to be destroyed.[118] Hence Kṛṣṇa's keenness to dispel Arjuna's doubts. Arjuna is finally satisfied.[119] The question is: are *we*?

[109] See R.C. Majumdar (ed.), *The Vedic Age*, p.163.
[110] IV:26-7. [111] IV:24.
[112] This attitude is not unique to the Gītā, and is shared by several other works, e.g. Śaṅkarācārya (putative author), *Viveka-cūḍāmaṇi*, verses 26, 60, 61, 72 etc.
[113] XVIII:17. [114] XVI:13-16.
[115] Paul Arthur Schilapp (ed.), *The Philosophy of Sarvepalli Radhakrishnan* (New York: Tudor Publishing, 1952), p.532.
[116] II:18, 31-8; VIII:7; XI:32-4; XVIII:59-60.
[117] V:1-5. [118] IV:40. [119] XVIII:73.

Karma and Jñāna can be reconciled in four ways. Thus (1) Karma can be shown as superior to Jñāna and Jñāna inferior; (2) Jñāna can be shown as superior to Karma and Karma inferior; (3) each can be shown as leading to the other; and (4) both can be shown as identical. The Gītā seems to attempt all four approaches.[120] The main aim appears to be to make Arjuna see the light, whichever way he sees it.

After Bhakti enters the discussion an effort is made to reconcile Karma, Jñāna and Bhakti, though this time not so explicitly.[121] The synthetic patterns pointed out earlier come into play again. Sometimes the Gītā seems to opt for Jñāna,[122] sometimes for Bhakti,[123] and sometimes for Karma.[124] Then, at times, it seems to blend Jñāna and Bhakti,[125] at times Jñāna and Karma,[126] and at times Bhakti and Karma.[127] Sometimes Jñāna is shown as leading to Bhakti,[128] and sometimes to Karma,[129] Bhakti as sometimes leading to Jñāna[130] and sometimes to Karma.[131] The same applies to Karma *vis-à-vis* Bhakti and Jñāna.[132] Yet again, sometimes Bhakti and Karma are treated as ancillary to Jñāna,[133] sometimes Jñāna and Karma as ancillary to Bhakti,[134] and sometimes Jñāna and Bhakti as ancillary to Karma.[135] Finally, according to Yāmuna, 'all these three paths mutually lead to one another'.[136]

The second half of the last chapter of the Gītā – the Eighteenth – is a particularly interesting study in the shifting emphasis among the three Yogas of Jñāna, Bhakti and Karma. There is first an emphasis on Karma;[137] soon it shifts to Jñāna,[138] and then it moves on to Bhakti, until finally Arjuna declares himself free of delusion, by Kṛṣṇa's grace, and ready to act, in the last verse that he utters in the Gītā.[139] Freedom from delusion corresponds to Jñāna, the grace of Kṛṣṇa to Bhakti and the resolve to act (according to Kṛṣṇa's bidding) to Karma.

In the light of this analysis the exegetical corpus on the Gītā alluded to earlier seems to fall into place. The difference in the various approaches can be viewed as differences in emphasis. Thus, among the early Hindu commentators of whom we know,

[120] e.g. for (1) V:2; for (2) II:49; III:1; for (3) IV:33, read with III:21-4; and for (4) V:4, 5.

[121] XI:55; XII:9-11. [122] IV:36. [123] XVIII:65, 66.

[124] III:20. [125] VI:14-15. [126] XVIII:63. [127] XVIII:56.

[128] XVIII:54. [129] II:19-30. [130] XIV:26. [131] XII:10.

[132] IX:27-8, III:19. [133] XII:4. [134] XVIII:63-5.

[135] XVIII:45-6.

[136] Dasgupta, op.cit., p.441.

[137] XVIII:41-7. [138] XVIII:49-53. [139] XVIII:73.

Śaṁkarācārya emphasised Jñāna[140] and Yāmuna, Rāmānuja and Vallabhācārya Bhakti.[141] None of the known early commentators seem to show particular enthusiasm for Karma. Among the moderns, Swami Rāmakṛṣṇa Paramahaṁsa regarded Jñāna as the quintessence of the Gītā,[142] and Vivekānanda[143] shared the same view, though in his case it was tempered with a liberal dash of Karma.[144] Śrī Aurobindo[145] emphasised Bhakti, supported by Jñāna and Karma as the message of the Gītā,[146] whereas in the Hare-Krishna movement of Swami Bhaktivedānta the Gītā has been epitomised even more along the Bhakti line.[147] From the hands of B.G. Tilak[148] the Gītā emerged as a gospel of Karma;[149] and it was interpreted primarily along the lines of Karma-Yoga also by Mahatma Gandhi.[150] The same tendency to distil the essence of the Gītā through one of the three Yogic funnels manifests itself also in the various selections from the Gītā that modern Hindu leaders have made from time to time. Thus, whereas Mahatma Gandhi's selection[151] centred on the Second Chapter, with its marked emphasis on disinterested action, the selection made by Maharishi Ramaṇa of Aruṇācalam[152] comes through as primarily concerned with Jñāna;[153] and Swami Śivānanda's octet has a strong devotional flavour.[154]

[140] Hill, op.cit., p.273; Dasgupta, op.cit., pp.437-8.

[141] Hill, op.cit., p.274; Dasgupta, op.cit., pp.439-44.

[142] See Swami Nikhilananda (tr.), *The Gospel of Sri Ramakrishna* (New York: Ramakrishna Vivekananda Centre, 1942), p.255.

[143] Swami Vivekananda, *The Complete Works of Swami Vivekananda* (Almora, 1948), Vol.V, pp.353-9.

[144] D. Mackenzie Brown, 'The philosophy of Bal Gangadhar Tilak', *Journal of Asian Studies* XVII (2), p.202ff.

[145] Sri Aurobindo, *Essays on the Gita*, (Pondicherry: Sri Ashram, 1959).

[146] Mackenzie Brown, op.cit., p.202.

[147] A.C. Bhaktivedanta Swami, *The Bhagavad Gītā As It Is* (London: Collier Macmillan, 1968).

[148] B.G. Tilak, *Gita Rahasya* (tr. B.S. Sukthankar) (Poona: J.S. & S.S. Tilak, 1965 [Second edition in English]).

[149] Mackenzie Brown, op.cit., p.202.

[150] M.K. Gandhi, *Discourses on the Gita* (Ahmedabad: Navajivan Publishing House, 1948), *Gita – My Mother* (Bombay: Bharatiya Vidya Bhavan, 1965), p.47 etc.

[151] M.K. Gandhi, *Ashram Observances in Action* (Ahmedabad: Navjivan Publishing House, 1955), p.33.

[152] For a life sketch see Aksharajna, *Sri Ramana* (Tiruvannamalai: Niranjanananda Swami, 1948); for an encounter, Paul Brunton, *A Search in Secret India* (London: Rider, 1954), Ch.9.

[153] *The Song Celestial*, selected and reset by Sri Raman Maharshi (Tiruvannamalai: Sri Niranjanananda Swami, 1951).

[154] Sri Swami Sivananda, *Srimad Bhagavad Gītā* (Rishikesh: The Yoga-Vedanta Forest University, 1949), pp.879-81.

Modern Hindu scholars also appear to take up corresponding positions. Professor Chandradhar Sharma of Benaras Hindu University regards Jñāna, seconded by Karma and Bhakti, as the central message of the Gītā.[155] Sir Ramakrishna Gopal Bhandarkar earlier, however, was inclined to give pride of place to Bhakti.[156] But Professor M. Hiriyanna holds a strong brief for Karma as the essential message,[157] and in this he is supported by Professor U.M. Apte, though the latter accords greater recognition to Bhakti and Jñāna as supplements to Karma.[158]

It must be borne in mind, however, that whenever a scholar, ancient or modern, has attempted to interpret the Gītā exclusively in terms of one Yoga he has run into difficulties. This has happened, for instance, on occasion, with Śaṁkara,[159] with Rāmānuja[160] and with Tilak.[161] Any attempt to straightjacket the Gītā leads to odd excesses, so that there is also something to be said for the view that the Gītā places equal and balanced emphasis on all three Yogas. On this view 'knowledge, devotion and work are complementary both when we seek the goal and after we attain it. We may climb the mountain from different paths, but the view from the summit is identical for all.'[162] This view has also been felicitously articulated by Dr Belvalkar, for whom the essence of the Gītā lies not in Jñāna or Bhakti or Karma but in Jñāna-Bhakti-Karma-samuccaya; that is to say, not in the differences between Jñāna, Bhakti and Karma but in their 'triune unity'.[163]

Apparent contradictions are present in a fair measure in the Gītā. According to some scholars they are real rather than apparent, according to others more apparent than real. Thus the Gītā has been assessed on the one hand as 'an ill-assorted cabinet of primitive philosophical opinions',[164] and on the other as 'the most systematic scriptural statement of the Perennial Philosophy'.[165] But both these

[155] Chandradhar Sharma, op.cit., Ch.2.

[156] Sri Ramakrishna Gopal Bhandarkar, *Vaiṣṇavism, Śaivism and Minor Religious Systems* (Strassburg: K.J. Trubner, 1913).

[157] Hiriyanna, op.cit., Ch.IV.

[158] Majumdar, op.cit., pp.440-6.

[159] e.g. Hill, op.cit., p.273

[160] e.g. J.A.B. van Buitenen, *Rāmānuja on the Bhagavad Gītā* (New Delhi: Motilal Banarsidas, 1968), pp.20-1; Hill, op.cit., p.274.

[161] e.g. Mackenzie Brown, op.cit., n.12.

[162] Sarvepalli Radhakrishnan and Charles A. Moore, *A Source Book in Indian Philosophy* (Princeton University Press, 1957), p.102.

[163] Ranade, op.cit., pp.149-50.

[164] E.W. Hopkins as quoted in Hill, op.cit., p.15.

[165] Aldous Huxley in Introduction to Swami Prabhavananda and Christopher Isherwood's *The Bhagavad Gītā* (Hollywood: Marcel Rodd, 1945), p.19.

views seem to overlook the fact that the Gītā is a text with a definite context. That context is the live situation, which consisted of Arjuna wavering in his duty. When Arjuna argued against fighting on ethical grounds, Kṛṣṇa countered on metaphysical grounds, and this produced a dialogue about the ultimate ground of the universe. In the course of this dialogue, which centred heavily on spiritual and philosophical issues, Kṛṣṇa used several approaches to drive home the point that Arjuna should fight no matter from which angle the issue was viewed – whether of Jñāna, Bhakti or Karma – and no matter what the nature of Reality – Personal or Impersonal, theistic or pantheistic. It is this intensity of aim which, to our mind, really constitutes the unity of content of the Gītā.

If such be the case, various apparently contradictory opinions expressed cannot be debunked as confused, because they are purposive. Nor, on the other hand, can they be extolled as a synthesis, since no such grand formal synthesis is aimed at.[166] For we have often shown how apparent contradictions within the Gītā can be reconciled either by material contained in the work or by interpretative insights. Yet, the Gītā itself makes such a deliberate effort only in a few cases. If anything, because of its setting the Gītā may be described as achieving a kind of spontaneous synthesis. Thus it is neither a patchwork quilt nor a variegated tapestry. It is rather of a stuff like unto fine yarn from which different patterns may be woven from time to time, and which spiritual aspirants have woven into the very texture of their lives.

4. *The Bhagavadgītā: a coat of many colours but one fitting?*

The foregoing discussion suggests a simple but vital conclusion – that we should distinguish between the theoretical and practical teaching of the Bhagavadgītā.

> The teaching, when taken in its details, is full of perplexity because the work shares the heterogeneous character, previously mentioned, of the epic to which it belongs. We have already referred by the way to one aspect of it, viz. that while it is based in some places on the Upanishads, it presupposes in others a theistic view of the type designated as Bhāgavata religion. But whatever these perplexities may be, there is absolutely no doubt as regards the central point of its practical teaching.[167]

[166] See Nicol Macnicol, *Indian Theism* (London: Oxford University Press, 1915), p.79.

[167] Hiriyanna, op.cit., p.53.

So far as its practical teaching is concerned, the Gītā is univocal: Arjuna must fight. But so far as its theoretical or spiritual teaching is concerned it is multivalent. Now the classical Hindu tradition has regarded the work as a spiritual manual, and this is why it has had to come face-to-face with the multivalent character of the text, and has felt the need to understand it. But in order to understand the work, the tradition has been forced to interpret it, for while at the practical level it serves as a guide to the perplexed, at the spiritual level, as many Hindu Masters discovered, it can be perplexing to one seeking guidance.

Appendix 1

That the Gītā contains several apparent contradictions is recognised by several scholars. Yet to the best of our knowledge, no collection of all the alleged contradictions in the Gītā has been compiled by any scholar. Apparent contradictions have, however, been recognised or identified by John A. Hardon, *Religions of the World* (Maryland: New Man Press, 1963), pp.52-3; R.E. Hume, *The World's Living Religions* (New York: Scribner's, 1959), pp.28-31; D.S. Sarma, *Lectures on the Bhagavad Gītā* (Rajamundry: N. Subbarau Pantulu, 1937), pp.3-5; P.S. Mathai, *A Christian Approach to the Bhagavad Gītā* (Calcutta: YMCA, 1956), pp.206, 11, 13-14 etc.; Chandradhar Sharma, *Indian Philosophy*, Vol.1 (New York: Macmillan, 1962), pp.529-33: Franklin Edgerton, *The Bhagavad-Gītā* (Cambridge: Harvard University Press, 1944), Part I, pp.xii-xiv, Part II, p.77 etc.: K.T. Telang, *The Bhagavadgītā with the Sanatsujātīya and the Anugītā* (Oxford: Clarendon Press, 1882), pp.11-13; W.D.P. Hill, *The Bhagavadgītā* (London: Humphrey Milford, 1928), pp.14-16: L.D. Barnett, *Bhagavadgītā* (Boston: Beacon Press, 1951), pp.79-80; T.E. Slater, *The Higher Hinduism in Relation to Christianity* (London: Elliot Stock, 1906), Ch.IX; Nicol Macnicol, *Indian Theism* (Oxford University Press, 1915), Ch.V; R.D. Ranade, *The Bhagavadgītā* (Nagpur: M.S. Modak, 1959), Chs.6, 15; Richard Garbe, *India and Christendom* (La Salle: Open Court, 1959), Ch.X; Rudolph Otto, *The Original Gītā* (London: Allen and Unwin, 1939), pp.10-14, passim: E.H. Johnston, *Early Sāṁkhya* (London: Royal Asiatic Society, 1937), pp.6-7; S.C. Roy, *The Bhagavadgītā and Modern Scholarship* (London: Luzac, 1941), passim; etc.

Scholars can be broadly classified in three groups according to their perception of apparent contradictions in the Gītā:

(1) In the first group may be placed almost all ancient Hindu commentators and some modern ones. Already Śaṅkara (788-820 A.D.) is conscious of the conflicting interpretations the Gītā is capable of: see Swami Nikhilananda, *The Gītā* (New York: Ramakrishna Vivekananda Centre, 1944), p.53. The fact that Śaṅkara, Rāmānuja, Madhvācārya and

Vallabhācārya could interpret the Gītā along *advaita, viśiṣṭādvaita, dvaita* and *śuddhādvaita* lines: Rājānka and Rāmakaṇṭha along Śaiva lines (see S. Dasgupta, op.cit., pp.437-43); Jñānadeva and B.G. Tilak along their own lines (see W.D.P. Hill, op.cit., pp.274, 278) and Swami Vivekananda, Sri Aurobindo and Mahatma Gandhi along their own in our own times indicates that the Hindu intellectual tradition has been conscious of the apparent contradictoriness of the Gītā at the interpretative level.

(2) In the second group may be placed scholars who have shown a consciousness of the contradictoriness of the Gītā at the textual level. To this group belongs a long line of German scholars: Richard Garbe, Rudolph Otto, Holtzmann, Winternitz, etc. (see S.C. Roy, op.cit., Chs.I & II; also R.D. Ranade, op.cit., Ch.6). Certain other Western scholars, such as E.W. Hopkins, J.N. Farquhar and E.H. Johnston could also be placed in this group, which has carried textual analysis in the light of the apparent contradictions to the point of textual dissection.

(3) In the third group fall most Western scholars of the pre-1900 period, such as Charles Wilkins, J. Cockburn Thomson, John Davies, Mrs Annie Besant, Edwin Arnold etc. (see W.D.P. Hill, op.cit., pp.272-8). These scholars do not show any marked consciousness of apparent contradictions in the Gītā. With them may also be placed some modern Indian scholars such as Dr Radhakrishnan, Chandradhar Sharma, etc. who, though conscious of the presence of contradictions in the Gītā, are inclined to regard them as merely apparent and superficial. They approach the Gītā in a mood more sophisticated than, but reminiscent of, those earlier scholars, who wrote before critical German scholarship got into the act at the turn of the century, perhaps under the influence of the Protestant principle of 'sola scriptura'.

Appendix 2

The view that the apparent contradictions in the Gītā are due to interpolation is built around the following questions:

(1) Is the Gītā itself an interpolation in the Mahābhārata?

(2) If there have been interpolations in the Gītā, then what was the primitive or original Gītā like?

(3) When was the Gītā interpolated into the Mahābhārata (if it was) and when were the 'foreign' materials interpolated into the Gītā (if they were), and who interpolated them?

(4) When was the 'original Gītā' originally composed, if there was an 'original Gītā'?

(5) When did the Gītā achieve the form in which we have it today?

(6) Was the Gītā, in its original conception, a sectarian or an eclectic work?

Obviously the various questions are interconnected, and the same would hold for answers too. For instance, if the Gītā is held to be comprehensive in its very conception (as W.D.P. Hill holds, see op.cit., pp.16-17) then theories which argue for interpolation by contrasting, say, monistic with theistic passages go overboard.

Each one of these questions bristles with controversy. Is the Gītā an interpolation in the Mahābhārata? S.C. Roy says yes (op.cit., p.66); K.T. Telang says no (op.cit., p.6). Rudolf Otto says that what he identified as the epic kernel of the Gītā was a part of the Mahābhārata, not the Gītā as we know it (see op.cit., pp.10, 14). There is a bewildering variety of opinions on this issue, see S.C. Roy, op.cit., Part Two; R.C. Majumdar (ed.), op.cit., pp.245-6, 249, etc.

What was the original Gītā like? According to Garbe it had 630 verses, according to his disciple Otto 133, as against the present 700. Winternitz first adopted, and then abandoned Garbe's approach (see F. Edgerton, op.cit., Part I, p.xii, n.1). According to Oldenberg, the original Gītā consisted only of the first twelve chapters, see R.D. Ranade, op.cit., pp.10, 90, 92, etc.

Who interpolated what, when and where? J.N. Farquhar thought a Kṛṣṇaite poet interpolated an old verse Upaniṣad after the Christian era, giving us the Gītā (op.cit., p.389). Garbe thought a Vedantin worked over an original Sāṁkhya Yoga Gītā (200-150 B.C.) in the second century A.D. to give us the present Gītā (see W.D.P. Hill, op.cit., p.14). But before one goes into all that another question must be asked: has the Gītā undergone interpolation? Garbe, Otto, Hopkins, Farquhar, Oldenberg, Johnston say yes; Lassen, Schleget, Humboldt, Edgerton and perhaps also Zaehner say no (see S.C. Roy, op.cit., p.55; F. Edgerton, op.cit., Part I, pp.xii; R.C. Zaehner, *The Bhagavad-Gītā* (Oxford University Press, 1969) p.5).

K.T. Telang believes that 'the text of the Gītā is now exactly in the condition in which it left the hands of the author' (quoted by S.C. Roy, op.cit., p.61).

The date of the Gītā or parts thereof, is a complicated issue. It has been shown how Garbe split-dates it – some sections to around 200 B.C., some to 200 A.D. W.D.P. Hill indicates 'second century B.C. as the period when the Gītā in its present form appeared' (op.cit., p.11). Dr. S. Radhakrishnan assigns it to the fifth century B.C. (op.cit., p.524) and R.C. Zaehner steers a middle course. In his opinion it could be dated 'at some time between the fifth and second centuries B.C.' (op.cit., p.7), but Lorinser stretches the other end into the post-Christian era (see S. Dasgupta, op.cit., p.549). The crux of the problem is that, external evidence on the question being 'tantalisingly meagre', attention is primarily focused on internal evidence which opens the Pandora's box of all the questions mentioned at the beginning.

There is hardly any settled body of knowledge when it comes to interpolationism, to use Ranade's term (op.cit., Ch.VI). The contradictions in the Gītā, however, have an important bearing on the issues raised. Nevertheless it is not possible to establish interpolations on the ground of contradictions alone, and even on other grounds this approach is now out of favour: see Hill, op.cit., pp.15-17; Chandradhar Sharma, op.cit., p.27; Edgerton, op.cit., Part I, p.xiv; Roy, op.cit., pp.49-55; etc.

CHAPTER ONE

The Anugītā

1.

Some time after the famous fratricidal battle among the Bharatas known as the Mahābhārata[1] war was over (on the eve of which the Bhagavadgītā had been revealed to Arjuna by Kṛṣṇa),[2] Arjuna

> requested Kṛṣṇa ... to repeat the instruction which has already been conveyed to him on 'the holy field of Kurukṣetra' but which has gone out of his 'degenerate mind'. Kṛṣṇa thereupon protests that he is not equal to a verbatim recapitulation of the Bhagavadgītā but agrees in lieu of that to impart to Arjuna the same instruction in other words, through the medium of a certain ancient story – or *purātana itihāsa*. And the instruction thus conveyed constitutes what is called the Anugītā, a name which is in itself an embodiment of this anecdote.[3]

[1] Pāṇini IV.2.56.

[2] See Bhagavadgītā I:20-47.

[3] K.T. Telang (tr.), *The Bhagavadgītā with the Sanatsujātīyā and the Anugītā* (Delhi: Motilal Banarsidass, 1965 [first published 1882]), p.198. Sometimes the Anugītā is selected for separate treatment not only with (1) Sanatsujātīya but also with (2) Mokṣadharma or the Nārāyaṇīya section of the Mahābhārata (see J.N. Farquhar, *An Outline of the Religious Literature of India* [Delhi: Motilal Banarsidass, 1967] (original edition 1920), p.96). It is sometimes also coupled with the Harigītā (see Surendranath Dasgupta, *A History of Indian Philosophy* [Cambridge University Press, 1952], p.545) and could be coupled, being a direct imitation of the Gītā, with the Iśvara-Gītā (see Mariasusai Dhavamony, *Love of God According to Śaiva Siddhānta* [Oxford: Clarendon Press, 1971], p.89). When it is placed along with such tracts, however, notwithstanding the similarities, a crucial difference tends to be overlooked. Unlike any of the other works, the Anugītā claims to be in direct connection with, and a direct and self-conscious descendant of, the Bhagavadgītā. This fact puts it in a class apart from all the other comparable works.

This chapter contends that the significance of the Anugītā has been overlooked by much current scholarship on the Gītā.[4] My purpose is to remedy the neglect and to show that, once remedied, the situation calls for a reassessment of some current ideas about the history of the interpretation of the Gītā in India.

2.

Some scholars who show an awareness of the Anugītā dismiss it with innocuous[5] or critical[6] remarks. No one after K.T. Telang seems to have taken serious interest in it, especially in its relation to the Bhagavadgītā. The crucial point which needs to be borne in mind is this: if the Anugītā is what it claims to be – the re-presentation of the Bhagavadgītā – then it can be looked upon as the first comment, if not commentary, on the Bhagavadgītā within the Hindu tradition. For according to current historical criticism, 'Śaṅkara's bhāṣya is probably the earliest commentary now available', though 'from references and discussions found therein there seems to be little doubt that there were previous commentators which he wished to

[4] See Franklin Edgerton, *The Bhagavad Gītā* (New York: Harper & Row, 1964); W. Douglas, P. Hill, *The Bhagavadgītā* (Oxford University Press, 1928); S. Radhakrishnan, *The Bhagavadgītā* (London: Allen & Unwin, 1948); Nataraja Guru, *The Bhagavadgītā* (London: Asia Publishing House, 1961); Jan Honda, *Die Religionen Indiens* I (Stuttgart: W. Kohlhammer, 1960), p.267ff. etc.

[5] Thus Mircea Eliade: 'The Anugītā (Mahābhārata, XIV:16-51) forms a sort of an appendix to the Bhagavad Gītā, the amalgamation of Sāṃkhya-Yoga and Vedānta is carried even further' (*Yoga Immortality and Freedom* [New York: Pantheon, 1954], p.394).

[6] Thus R.C. Zaehner: 'There is plenty of didactic matter in the *Mahābhārata* – almost the whole of books twelve and thirteen and much of books three and five, but in none of these is Krishna the teacher. Only in book fourteen does he condescend to teach Arjuna again – in the so-called *Anugītā* or "Gītā Recapitulated", which, in fact, is no recapitulation at all for it omits all that teaching in the Gītā which, because it was new, was described by Krishna as being "most mysterious" – the revelation of the love of God. This is no accident, for Arjuna had proved himself unworthy of receiving the divine mystery: in the heat of battle he had forgotten every word Krishna had said! In the Anugītā he is merely treated to a rehash of what his far more religious-minded brother had been told by the dying "grandsire", Bhīshma, at enormous and wearisome length throughout those mammoth books twelve and thirteen of by far the longest epic in the world' (*The Bhagavad-Gītā* [Oxford: Clarendon Press, 1969], pp.6-7). Elsewhere, though, Zaehner does raise the important issue: 'Why is it that Krishna's second discourse, the *Anugītā* or "Supplementary Gītā", remains neglected, and almost unknown?' (*Discordant Concord* [Oxford: Clarendon Press, 1970], p.118).

refute'.[7] Thus our first clear understanding of the Bhagavadgītā from within the tradition dates from around the ninth century A.D.[8] But if we may, though on the basis of a calculation 'avowedly a very rough one', 'fix the third century of the Christian era as the latest year at which the Anugītā can have been composed',[9] then our understanding of the Gītā within the tradition is advanced by five centuries. In any case, a pre-Śaṅkaran point is established as 'the Anugītā must have been some few centuries old in the time of Śaṅkarācārya'.[10] And if we accept the generally accepted view that the Gītā belongs to the second century B.C.,[11] we are in a position to assess a stage in its interpretation within the tradition within a period of five centuries since its composition.

But in order to draw any conclusions about the evolution of the Hindu understanding of the Gītā in the light of the Anugītā we must be convinced that the Anugītā does in fact claim to recapitulate the Bhagavadgītā. Then the omissions of certain themes, and the expansion of others, could be taken as indicative of the kind of interpretation the Gītā was being given within the tradition of the time.

There can be little doubt that the Anugītā sets out to recapitulate the Gītā. It may even be described as the Bhagavadgītā 'recollected in tranquillity'. It commences in the post-bellum era, with Kṛṣṇa and Arjuna 'in a certain portion of the palace which resembled heaven':

> Then Arjuna, the son of Pāṇdu, having surveyed with delight that lovely palace, in the company of Kṛṣṇa, spoke these words: 'O you of mighty arms! O you whose mother is Devakī! when the battle was about to commence, I became aware of your greatness, and that divine form of yours. But that, O Keśava, which through affection (for me) you explained before, has all disappeared, O tiger-like man! from my degenerate mind. Again and again, however, I feel a curiosity about those topics. But (now), O Mādhava! you will be going at no distant date to Dvārakā.'[12]

[7] Dasgupta, op.cit., Vol.II, p.437. Also see F. Otto Schrader, 'Ancient Gītā commentaries', *The Indian Historical Quarterly*, Vol.X, No.2 (June 1934), pp.348-57; Mahendra Nath Sarkar, 'The Bhagavadgītā: its early commentaries' in Haridas Bhattacharyya (ed.), *The Cultural Heritage of India* (Calcutta: Ramakrishna Mission Institute of Culture, 1962), Vol. II, p.195n. For the authenticity of the Bhagavadgītā Śaṅkara-bhāṣya on the Gītā, see Sengaku Mayeda, 'The authenticity of the Bhagavadgītā bhāṣya ascribed to Śaṅkara', *Wiener Zeitschrift für die Kunde Süd- und Ostasiens und Archiv für Indische Philosophie*, Band IX, 1965, pp.155-97.

[8] Eliot Deutsch and J.A.B. van Buitenen, *A Source Book of Advaita Vedānta* (Honolulu: University Press of Hawaii, 1971), p.122.

[9] Telang, op.cit., p.207. [10] ibid., p.206. [11] Hill, op.cit., p.23.

[12] Telang, op.cit., pp.229-30.

Thus, Kṛṣṇa's imminent departure precipitates Arjuna's request. But Kṛṣṇa rebukes Arjuna for having forgotten what he was told earlier, for at that time Kṛṣṇa was inspired (*yogayukta*)[13] but now

> it is not possible for me to repeat in full (what I said before). For that doctrine was perfectly adequate for understanding the seat of the Brahman. It is not possible for me to state it again in full in that way. For then accompanied by my mystic power, I declared to you the Supreme Brahman. But I shall relate an ancient story upon that subject, so that adhering to this knowledge, you may attain the highest goal. O best of the supporters of piety! listen to all that I say.[14]

Actually several stories are related, but after the first major disquisition Kṛṣṇa asks Arjuna:

> Have you listened to this, O son of Pṛthā! with a mind (fixed) on (this) one point only? For on that occasion too, sitting in the chariot you heard this same instruction.[15]

The careful reader of the Gītā is immediately struck by the near-identity of the first line (*kaccid etat tvayā pārtha śrutam ekāgracetasā*)[16] with a line in the terminal section of the Gītā:

> Has this been heard, son of Pṛthā
> By thee with concentrated thought?[17]

Not only that: there is a clear reference to the chariot.[18]

The Anugītā essentially consists of three extended dialogues: (1) one between the Siddha and his disciple Kāśyapa; (2) another between Brāhmaṇa and his spouse; and (3) another between a Master and his *śisya* or disciple. What Kṛṣṇa said above at the end of the first dialogue he repeats at the end of the third and final dialogue.

[13] Mahābhārata 14.16.12; for the entire Sanskrit text see V.S. Sukthankar and S.K. Belvalkar (eds.), *The Āśvamedhikaparvan* [Poona: Bhandarkar Oriental Research Institute, 1960], pp.58-194.

[14] Telang, op.cit., p.231. [15] ibid., p.254.

[16] Mahābhārata 14.19.50 ab.

[17] Edgerton, op.cit., p.91. Although Telang remarks that 'the original words here are identical with those in the Gītā' (op.cit., p.254, n.2), this is true only in translation: The comparable verse (Bhagavadgītā XVIII:72 ab) runs: *kaccid etac śrutam pārtha tvayaikāgreṇa cetasā* (see Sukthankar and Belvalkar (eds.), *The Bhīsmaparvan*, op.cit., p.188).

[18] According to some versions the Anugītā ends here, but as Telang has shown this is an erroneous view (op.cit., pp.198-206).

> I have related this mystery to you out of love for you. If you have love for me, O supporter of the family of the Kauravas! then having heard this (instruction) relating to the self, always duly act (according to it). Then when this piety is duly practised, you will attain the absolute final emancipation, getting rid of all sins. It was this thing I stated to you before when the time for battle had come, O you of mighty arms! Therefore fix your mind on this.[19]

And soon thereafter Kṛṣṇa leaves for *dvārkā*.

It is thus clear that the Anugītā claims to be a recapitulation of the Bhagavadgītā. Hence we may feel justified in asking the next question: what kind of an interpretation of the Gītā does this recapitulation suggest?

3.

The most striking feature of the recapitulation consists not of what it does, but of what it does not, recapitulate. It does not recapitulate the devotional elements of the Bhagavadgītā, even though Arjuna begins by saying that 'when the battle was about to commence I became aware of your greatness and that divine form of yours'.[20] There is *no further mention* of the divine form of the theophany. The themes of the Gītā which are elaborated are those of the movement of the soul and its passage to the *lokas*,[21] only briefly touched on in the Gītā;[22] of the winds (*apāna*, etc.)[23] which are not even fully mentioned in the Gītā;[24] a detailed discussion of sense control on the sacrificial metaphor,[25] briefly touched on in the Gītā,[26] and a discussion of the interrelation of the senses, and the interdependence of the mind[27] and the senses, and the elaboration of Sāṅkhyan ideas, like those of the *gūṇas*.[28] The threefold separation of *karaṇa, kartā* and *karma*, again only briefly mentioned in the Gītā, is elaborated, and a new theme of the relation of thought and speech is introduced. But what is conspicuous by its absence is any glorification of Kṛṣṇa; the word

[19] ibid., p.394. [20] ibid., pp.230-1. [21] ibid., pp.235-54.

[22] Bhagavadgītā VIII:24-6, IX:21, XV:9-10 etc.

[23] Telang, op.cit., pp.271-7; see Dasgupta, op.cit., pp.256-64, 448-9; Paul Deussen, *The Philosophy of the Upanishads* (New York: Dover, 1966), p.276ff.

[24] Bhagavadgītā IV:20-9, V:27, IV:29 etc.

[25] Telang, op.cit., pp.261ff. 267ff.

[26] Bhagavadgītā IV:24-33.

[27] Telang, op.cit., p.268ff. [28] ibid., p.317ff.

Nārāyaṇa[29] barely occurs. The other themes of the Gītā expatiated on are (1) the knowledge of *brahman* through the *yoga* of sense control,[30] and (2) the *yoga* of action, based on knowledge so that action is not really action.[31]

In sharp contrast to the Bhagavadgītā, which ends with Arjuna seeking refuge in Kṛṣṇa, so that XVIII:66 is hailed as the *carama śloka* among the Śrīvaiṣṇavas, the Anugītā ends on a rather *jñāna*-oriented note.[32]

Two further facts tend to underscore the gnostic rather than *bhaktic* orientation of the Anugītā. There is the famous verse in the Bhagavadgītā (IX:32) which offers salvation to all through *bhakti*:

> For if they take refuge in Me, son of Pṛthā,
> Even those who may be of base origin,
> Women, men of the artisan caste, and serfs too,
> Even they go to the highest goal.[33]

A similar verse occurs in the Anugītā,[34] but it substitutes '*māṁ hi pārtha vyapāśritya*' (taking refuge in me) in the first *pāda* of the verse with the expression '*evaṁ hi dharmamāsthāya*' (adopting the

[29] When it does occur it is often either along with *brahman* (ibid. 280-1, etc.) or with other gods (ibid., p.347).

[30] ibid., pp.285-7. [31] ibid., p.289ff.

[32] 'Some men of dull understandings extol action. But as to the high-souled ancients they do not extol action. By action a creature is born with a body and made up of the sixteen. Knowledge brings forth the being, and that is acceptable and constitutes immortality. Therefore those who are far-sighted have not attachment to actions. This being is stated to be full of knowledge, not full of action. The self-restrained man who thus understands the immortal, changeless, incomprehensible, and ever indestructible and unattached (principle), he dies not. He who thus understands the self to which there is nothing prior, which is uncreated, changeless, unmoving, which is incomprehensible (even) to those who feed on nectar, he certainly becomes immortal and not to be restrained, in consequence of these means. Expelling all impressions, and restraining the self in the self, he understands that holy Brahman, than which nothing greater exists. And when the understanding is clear, he attains tranquillity. And the nature of tranquillity is as when one sees a dream. This is the goal of those emancipated ones who are intent on knowledge. And they see all the movements which are produced by development. This is the goal of those who are indifferent (to the world). This is the eternal piety. This is what is acquired by men of knowledge. This is the uncensured (mode of) conduct. This goal can be reached by one who is alike to all beings, who is without attachment, who is without expectations, and who looks alike on everything. I have now declared everything to you, O best of Brahmana sages! Act thus forthwith; then you will acquire perfection' (ibid., pp.391-3).

[33] Edgerton, op.cit., p.49.

[34] Mahābhārata 14.19.56.

doctrine).[35] And that doctrine turns out to be one of regarding the eternal Brahman as the highest goal.[36]

Thus the fruits of *bhakti* offered by the Bhagavadgītā are offered as the fruits of *jñāna* in the Anugītā. The second fact should not come as a surprise now – that in Śaṅkara's Introduction to his commentary on the Gītā the first few quotations are *not* from the Bhagavadgītā, the text he is going to comment on, but from the Anugītā.[37] This may be contrasted with Rāmānuja, in whose commentary citations from the Anugītā seem to be conspicuous by their absence.[38]

4.

If the Anugītā represents a recapitulation of the Bhagavadgītā and may therefore be looked upon as one of the first interpretations of it available to us within the tradition, and further, if it be true, as we have tried to show, that this interpretation is *jñāna*- rather than *bhakti*- or *karma*- oriented, then some of the prevailing views in the field call for a reassessment. Two such views may be identified.

The first is represented by the statement that 'the Bhagavadgītā is somewhat of an embarrassment for Advaita Vedānta ... the Gītā exhibits a strong if not dominant "theistic" dimension: it emphasises a *karma-yoga*, or way of action, and *bhakti*, devotion to a "personal" deity. Śaṅkara, accordingly, must strain the text rather considerably in order to bring it into harmony with his advaitic principles.'[39] It is clear that already in the Anugītā the 'theistic' dimension of the Bhagavadgītā is de-emphasised and the path of *jñāna* emphasised, so that the process of which Śaṅkara's interpretation of the Gītā may be regarded as a culmination may be seen as having been in motion for quite some centuries.[40] What to us appears to be a straining of the

[35] Telang, op.cit., p.255. [36] ibid.

[37] See *Śrīśāṅkarangranthāvaliḥ* Saṁpuṭa 8 (Śrīraṅgam: Śrīvāṇīvilāsamudrāyantrālayaḥ), p.3; also see A. Mahadeva Sastri, *The Bhagavadgītā with the Commentary of Sri Śankaracharya* (sic) (Madras: V. Ramaswamy Sastruly & Sons, 1961), p.5.

[38] See Śrī Mahāvana Śāstrī (ed.), *Śrīmadbhagavadgītā Śrīmadrāmānujācāryakṛtabhāṣyasametā* (Bombay: Lakṣmīvenkaṭeśvara Press, 1959).

[39] Deutsch and van Buitenen, op.cit., p.213.

[40] One may note here a point concerning the Bhagavadgītābhāṣya, to which Otto Schrader calls attention. 'If Śaṅkara's *praguru*, or, as some would have it, his direct teacher, was Gauḍapāda, how can it be accounted for that in this juvenile work of his, the Gītābhāṣya, he appears to be even less affected by Gauḍapāda's extreme idealism than in the Brahmasūtrabhāṣya which rejects the Buddhist *vijñānavāda* and has but two quotations from the Māṇḍukyākārikās (III:15 and I:16)? The Gītābhāṣya professes in its very introduction a standpoint widely different from Gauḍapāda's by

text may, in the light of that tradition, be a reasonable understanding. In other words, the tradition of the *jñāna*-oriented interpretation of the Gītā can no longer be seen as originating from Śaṅkara and therefore must be seen as having deeper roots in the tradition which antedates Śaṅkara.[41]

The second point which calls for reassessment is the view that, compared with Śaṅkara for instance, 'Rāmānuja's bhāṣya does full justice to the intentions of the author of the Gītā ...'.[42] The problem which such a statement raises is methodological. The statement could certainly be true – but in a theological not a historical sense. For the critical modern scholar 'the texts are determined by their place in history, their date, their relations to other texts of the same age, their connections with older and younger texts, etc.',[43] so that if chronological rather than purely logical considerations are taken into account the whole question of a Hindu tradition of a largely non-theistic interpretation of an avowedly theistic text such as the Gītā has to be taken far more seriously. For if the 'connections between younger and older texts' are considered, Śaṅkara can be seen as doing full justice to the Gītā as well, though by *other* standards Rāmānuja may be judged as more successful in this respect.

To conclude: the role of the Anugītā needs to be given its proper place in the exegetical history of the Bhagavadgītā, and when this is done it becomes clear that the *jñāna*-oriented interpretation of the Bhagavadgītā needs to be given greater weight in that history than seems to have been allowed hitherto.

---

declaring that the Lord, "ever possessed of *jñāna, aiśvarya, śakti, bala, vīrya* and *tejas* (which are the six *aprākṛta guṇas* of God in the Pāñcarātra!) and keeping control of the *mūlaprakṛti*, viz., his *vaiṣṇavī māyā* consisting of the three *guṇas*", condescended to be born, with a part of his (*aṁśena*) as Kṛṣṇa, son of Devakī by Vasudeva. This is hardly what one would expect from an enthusiastic young pupil of Gauḍapāda! And would not such a one have felt irresistibly tempted to quote his guru's *kārikā* or at least to refer to him with one or two words at such passages as *Bhag. Gītā* II:16 (comp. Gaud. Kar. IV:31)? This complete silence is suspicious, and the sole explanation of it I can think of is that Śaṅkara wrote his Gītābhāṣya *before* being acquainted with the work of Gauḍapāda' (op.cit., pp.356-7). If this is true, there is all the more reason to assume that Śaṅkara was led to a *jñāna*-oriented interpretation of the Gītā by a pre-existing tradition of the kind reflected in the Anugītā.

[41] 'It is but a cheap tribute to Śaṅkara's genius to credit him with having been the first to introduce the *Gītā* into the Advaita-Vedānta' (Schrader, op.cit., p.349).

[42] J.A.B. van Buitenen, *Rāmānuja on the Bhagavadgītā* [Ś-Gravenhage: H.L. Smits 1953 (?)], p.39. Also see R.C. Zaehner, *The Bhagavadgītā*, pp.8-9.

[43] van Buitenen, op.cit., p.29.

5.

Nevertheless, the Anugītā 'professes to be a sort of continuation, or rather recapitulation, of the Bhagavadgītā'.[44] Our purpose now is to contrast the circumstances of the recapitulation with those of the original event, in the hope that it may contribute towards a better understanding of both.

The general situation in the Bhagavadgītā and the Anugītā differs quite a bit.

> The *Gītā* opens with Arjuna standing in the forefront of the Pāṇḍava forces surveying friends, relatives, and teachers in both armies. Krishna stands with him as his charioteer, known to Arjuna only as a prince who has volunteered to aid him in battle. Looking at the armies and hearing conch-trumpets sounding the call to battle, Arjuna is suddenly paralysed by indecision. Should he go into battle and slay his own kinsmen, bringing the family to ruin? Would it not be better, he asks Krishna, to let himself be killed than to kill his kinsmen, for the sake of a mere kingdom.[45]

In the Anugītā, however, the situation is post-bellum rather than ante-bellum. The comparison of the two situations may now be carried out in more detail.

(1) In the Bhagavadgītā, Arjuna is uncertain whether he will win the war or not.[46] In the Anugītā the war has been won.[47] The tense uncertainty of the former moments contrasts with the relaxed enjoyment of victory and the attainment of sole sovereignty.

(2) In the Bhagavadgītā Arjuna says that his grief will not be dispelled 'though I should win on earth broad sovereignty unrivalled, and lordship even of Heaven's Lords'.[48] In the Anugītā such unrivalled lordship has been attained,[49] and although heaven's lordship has not been won the references in the initial portions of the Anugītā to heaven have a more positive air about them. Thus, before

[44] Telang, op.cit., p.197.

[45] Thomas J. Hopkins, *The Hindu Religious Tradition* (Belmont, California: Dickenson, 1971), p.90.

[46] Bhagavadgītā II:6.

[47] Mahābhārata 14.16.2.

[48] Bhagavadgītā II:8.

[49] Mahābhārata 14.16.2.

the actual dialogue constitutive of the Anugītā, Arjuna is shown as rejoicing in 'a certain portion of the palace, which resembled heaven'.[50] And Arjuna's grief has been dispelled, for both he and Kṛṣṇa are shown in a cheerful mood.

(3) There are references to *svajana* – one's people – both in the Bhagavadgītā and in the Anugītā in the initial portions. But in the Bhagavadgītā the sight of his kinsmen[51] precipitates Arjuna's crisis; in the Anugītā both Arjuna and Kṛṣṇa are shown as enjoying themselves in the company of their kinsmen.[52]

(4) In the Bhagavadgītā, Arjuna adopts the attitude of a disciple[53] and later of a devotee,[54] though there are clear references to 'friendship' with Kṛṣṇa by both of them.[55] In the Anugītā the mood and attitude of friendship seems to preponderate,[56] and the original revelation is also recalled as being vouchsafed out of friendship.[57]

(5) In the Bhagavadgītā the theophany of Chapter Eleven constitutes, according to some scholars,[58] the high point of the text. In the Anugītā it is briefly referred to in the beginning and passed over – not to be mentioned again.[59]

(6) The Bhagavadgītā develops as a narration within a narration. Thus Sañjaya is reporting the battle to Dhṛtarāṣṭra through the gift of clairvoyance, and the Bhagavadgītā then becomes the report of the dialogue between Kṛṣṇa and Arjuna. The Anugītā develops similarly, but this time it is Kṛṣṇa who reports to Arjuna various pieces of dialogue between others. So there is a one-tier difference.[60]

[50] Mahābhārata 14.16.3. K.T. Telang translates an earlier verse as depicting them 'full of delight in that heavenly place' as well (op.cit., p.229).

[51] Bhagavadgītā I:28, 31, 37, 45.

[52] Mahābhārata 14.16.3.

[53] Bhagavadgītā II:7. [54] ibid., XI:39-40. [55] ibid., IV:3, XI:41.

[56] Mahābhārata 14.16.1-4.8. [57] ibid., 14.16.6.

[58] See Zaehner, *The Bhagavad-Gītā*, op.cit., p.303.

[59] Mahābhārata 14.16.5.

[60] One may also contrast the sense of distance from Kṛṣṇa which Arjuna feels in the Bhagavadgītā (Chapter Eleven, passim) with the mention of his being embraced by Kṛṣṇa in the early section of the Anugītā (Mahābhārata 14.16.8). The contrast can be pushed even further if Kṛṣṇa's theophany in the Gītā is taken into account. As S.C. Roy points out: 'It is interesting to note that the Anugītā is immediately succeeded by a much inferior imitation of Viśvarūpa or the revelation of the Divine Form (now styled Vaiṣṇava-rūpa) showing that it was composed with other wild growth of Purānic legends after Kṛṣṇa had been elevated to the rank of God or recognised as an incarnation of God, and at the time when the Gītā, too, was made a Vaiṣṇava scripture. Anugītā might be a title given to this work in jest by a Brahminical opponent of Vaiṣṇavism, who wanted to bring into ridicule the theory of Kṛṣṇa's divine birth, by showing that he was no more than an ordinary mortal who forgot all about his teachings in the Gītā as soon as the war was finished, because there was no longer any motive for inducing the hero Arjuna to that ghastly undertaking. If Kṛṣṇa confesses

The differences between the starting points of the Bhagavadgītā and the Anugītā are quite marked, and one wonders how far the way they start affects the way they run their course. Is the initial tension of the Bhagavadgītā to be associated with its accent, at times at least, on devotion, and is the initial lack of tension, or rather the atmosphere of relaxation with which the Anugītā begins to be associated with its comparatively greater accent on knowledge and meditation?

---

that he was *yogastha* (in a state of perfect unison with God or mystic ecstasy and inspiration) at the time of preaching the Gītā, it only shows that he is at present *yogabhraṣta*, i.e. fallen from the height of his divine vision, implying that he was just like other men, subject to periodical lapses of memory or downward fall, and therefore not fit to be ranked as an incarnation. The same impression is confirmed by the fact that Kṛṣṇa is shortly afterwards made to reveal the cosmic form against his will, out of fear of Utaṅkas's curse, as if the display of the Divine Form were a mere fun, and could be made to order like a pantomimic show before anybody and everybody. Moreover, it is inconceivable how this revelation of Divine Form to the sage Utaṅka could be made by Kṛṣṇa, who on his own confession is now fallen from *Yoga*' (*The Bhagavad-Gītā and Modern Scholarship* [London: Luzac, 1941], p.78).

CHAPTER TWO

The Gītāmāhātmyas

1.

It was shown in the last chapter that once we learn to treat the Anugītā, which like the Bhagavadgītā is itself a part of the Mahābhārata, as a commentary on the Bhagavadgītā, we can detect the emergence of the tradition of the interpretation of the Gītā within the Mahābhārata itself. It will now be suggested that by taking a fresh look at a genre of literature associated with the Gītā we can further chart the development of the tradition of the interpretation of the Gītā within the Hindu religious tradition.

This genre consists of the Gītāmāhātmyas, or verses glorifying the virtues of the Gītā as a religious text. These verses appear regularly in the Purāṇas. For instance, the Varāha Purāṇa contains a section devoted to the glories of the Bhagavadgītā, and the Padma Purāṇa contains verses glorifying each of the Eighteen Chapters of the Bhagavadgītā.[1]

The existence of the Gītāmāhātmyas in the Purāṇas also enables us to chart the development of the tradition of the interpretation of the Gītā in terms of the now generally accepted chronology of the Hindu religious tradition. The Mahābhārata is generally seen as assuming its final form around 400 A.D., and the entire text is broadly seen as spanning a period stretching from the fourth century B.C. to the fourth century A.D.[2] The Anugītā may, therefore, be seen as representing a trend in the interpretation of the Bhagavadgītā, around, say, the third to fourth century A.D.

This and the subsequent centuries witnessed the flowering of

[1] See G.S. Sadhale (ed.), *The Bhagavad-Gītā with Eleven Commentaries* (Bombay: 'Gujarati' Printing Press, 1935), pp.13, 58-9, etc.

[2] R.C. Majumdar (ed.), *The Age of Imperial Unity* (Bombay: Bharatiya Vidya Bhavan, 1960), p.251.

Hindu culture under the Guptas, and it was under the Guptas that the Purāṇas are said to have been redacted. There are, to be sure, passages in the Purāṇas which seem to have been interpolated later, but there is a broad consensus among scholars that the Purāṇas are, by and large, in their present form the product of the Gupta age.[3]

Now these *māhātmyas* occur in the Purāṇas. It stands to reason, therefore, that they may well represent trends in the interpretation of the Gītā in the Hindu religious tradition during the sixth and seventh centuries A.D. As Dr Hazra has shown, there seem to have been 'two main stages in the development of puranic smṛiti material': (1) the stage in which the Purāṇas dealt with the concerns of the classical *smṛtis*, such as those of Manu and Yājñavalkya; (2) the stage in which they 'dealt with topics relating to gifts, glorification of holy places, *vrata* (vows), *pūjā* (popular worship)', etc.[4] Now although Hazra does not specifically mention the glorification of the Gītā,[5] it seems to belong to the same genre as the glorification of holy places. The first stage is assigned by him to the 'third and fifth century A.D.' and the second to 'about the sixth century'. Hence we may not be far wrong in assigning the interpretation of the Gītā as represented by the Gītāmāhātmyas to the sixth and seventh centuries A.D.

2.

What interpretation of the Gītā do these glorificatory verses seem to suggest? A representative survey of this material reveals some interesting features, which may be listed numerically for convenience:

(1) The connection between the Bhagavadgītā and the Upaniṣads is clearly recognised by tradition. The Gītā, of course, calls itself an Upaniṣad, but in popular estimation it is seen more as providing the distilled essence of the Upaniṣads than as being an Upaniṣad in itself. The 'popular verse' which 'compares the Upaniṣads to the cows, Śri Kṛṣṇa to the cowherd, Arjuna to the calf, *Gītā* to the milk and the wise men to those who drink the milk' seems to appear in at least one Gītāmāhātmya.[6]

[3] R.C. Majumdar (ed.), *The Classical Age* (Bombay: Bharatiya Vidya Bhavan, 1962), p.298.

[4] ibid.

[5] R.C. Hazra, *Studies in the Purāṇic Records on Hindu Rites and Customs* (Delhi: Motilal Banarsidass, 1975 [first edition: Dacca, 1940]), passim.

[6] Sadhale (ed.), op.cit., p.35.

(2) The egalitarian spirit of the Gītā is again recognised in the same Gītāmāhātmyas whose source is cited as Puranic though the Purāṇa is not specified.[7] It is clearly stated that a person being born among the four *varṇas*, or 'castes', obtains *mokṣa* through the Gītā; that the fabled kings of yore obtained it; and that the Gītā does not distinguish between the high and the low. It is also said to remove pollution of any kind.[8]

(3) These very glorificatory verses cry fie on the householder and the ascetic alike who is ignorant of the Gītā. This seems to imply that the Gītā cut across not only the *varṇas*, or the organisation of Hindu society into classes and castes, but also its organisation into *āśramas*, or the various stages of life – those of the celibate student, householder, hermit and renunciant.

(4) The metaphysical statement in these verses is as intriguing as the sociological, for it is by the knowledge of the Gītā imparted by Kṛṣṇa to Arjuna that one attains to *mokṣa*, whether it be *saguṇa* or *nirguṇa*. In view of the subsequent debate within the Hindu religious tradition, whether Brahman is ultimately *saguṇa* (with qualifying attributes) or *nirguṇa* (without qualifying attributes), this is an extremely significant statement. Its implications ramify through the philosophical systems of Hinduism – *nirguṇa mokṣa* being associated with *jñāna* or knowledge and *saguṇa mokṣa* with *bhakti* or devotion. The matter also goes to the very root of the Hindu philosophical tradition, for the 'seeds of theism and absolutism' or the *saguṇa* and *nirguṇa* approaches to Brahman, the ultimate reality, which 'are to be found in the Vedas germinate and grow to huge proportions in later Hinduism, and get embellished in great detail'.[9] Both the theistic and absolutistic traditions lay claim to the Gītā later as a bright jewel in their own crown!

(5) The glorificatory verses referred to hitherto, and the ones in the Varāha Purāṇa also, suggest the conclusion that at least by the time of the Gupta age the Hindu tradition was not identifying the Gītā with any particular Yoga within Hinduism. Thus it is clearly stated that the Gītā produces 'unswerving devotion', 'impeccable action' and 'living liberation', the last being associated with knowledge or *jñāna*, as the first two are with *bhakti* and *karma yoga*.

(6) Another interesting feature in the interpretation of the Gītā at this stage is its non-sectarian character. Although it is generally considered, and to all appearances is, a Vaiṣṇavite work, its glories

[7] ibid., p.12. [8] ibid.
[9] T.M.P. Mahadevan, *Outlines of Hinduism* (Bombay: Chetana, 1971), p.251.

are expounded in the Padma Purāṇa, for instance, by Śiva to Indra.[10] The reciters of a certain chapter of the Gītā are said to go to the world of Rudra.[11]

(7) Finally, the Gītā is seen as effective for securing the good both here and in the hereafter. It has already been shown how it confers liberation (*mokṣa*). In some of the glorificatory verses it is shown as affording protection against demons, ghosts, theft, imprecations, etc.,[12] and even as leading to the attainment of the status of the lordship of the gods (*Indrapada*).

3.

No account of the Gītāmāhātmyas can be complete without a reference to the role of specific devotion to Kṛṣṇa and/or Viṣṇu in them. Such devotion is clearly mentioned. Thus it is stated that 'Kṛṣṇa, the son of Devakī, is pleased with the recitation of the Gītā'.[13] Kṛṣṇa is also mentioned as describing the Gītā as his excellent station (*uttamaṁ gṛham*), supreme abode (*paramaṁ padam*), supreme secret (*paramaṁ guhyam*), and the supreme Guru (*paramo guruḥ*). Kṛṣṇa proceeds to describe the Gītā as his 'heart', 'supreme essence', and 'intense' and 'inexhaustible' knowledge.

In these descriptions, that of the Gītā as Kṛṣṇa's supreme Guru holds our attention for the role-reversal it involves. Kṛṣṇa is the *guru* in the Gītā, and Arjuna is the *śiṣya*; but in these glorificatory verses Kṛṣṇa is describing the Gītā as his own Guru. Is it that in communicating it to Arjuna in a state of exaltation he had indeed surpassed himself, as he suggests in the Anugītā? A similar reversal occurs in some other verses. In the Gītā Kṛṣṇa is shown as supporting the world (VII:24), but in the Varāha Purāṇa Viṣṇu states that he supports the three worlds relying on the knowledge of the Gītā. Thus the glorificatory verses indicate the emergence of a symbiotic relationship between the 'author' and the text which is not itself testified to within the Gītā. This seems to indicate the emergence of the Gītā as a text *in its own right*. Viṣṇu does not say that where I am there is the Gītā, rather that 'where the reading, recitation, hearing and reflection on the Gītā is to be found, O earth!, I, to be sure, reside there for good'.[14] The Gītā has come a long way over those last few centuries: it is not just sacred because it was recited by Kṛṣṇa, it now sacralises by its mere recitation.

[10] Sadhale (ed.), op.cit., p.444. [11] ibid., p.13.
[12] ibid., p.11. [13] ibid. [14] ibid., p.13.

CHAPTER THREE

Bhāskara

1.

The date of Bhāskara is uncertain; some place him before the famous Śaṅkara (eighth century A.D.) and others after him.[1] Our reasons for discussing him before Śaṅkara are logical rather than chronological. First, the extant commentary of Bhāskara covers only half the chapters of the Gītā, the first nine.[2] Secondly, Śaṅkara belongs to the famous triad of the *ācāryas*, along with Rāmānuja and Madhva, and it seems best to treat him alongside them.[3]

With the commentary of Bhāskara our discussion of the interpretation of the Bhagavadgītā within the Hindu religious tradition emerges into the light of the commentarial tradition as such. In the last two chapters attention was drawn to

[1] See Daniel H.H. Ingalls, 'Bhāskara the Vedāntin', *Philosophy East and West* XVII (1967), p.61, n.2; Subhadra Upadhyaya (ed.), *Śrīmadbhagavadgītāyāḥ Bhagavadāśayānusaraṇābhidhānabhāṣyam Bhagavadbhāskaraviracitam* (Varanaseya Sanskrit Vishvavidyalaya, 1965), Preface.

[2] ibid., passim.

[3] For other references to and treatment of Bhāskara and his commentary, see: J.A.B. van Buitenen 'The relative dates of Śaṅkara and Bhāskara', *The Adyar Library Bulletin* XXV (1962), pp.268-73; and also his references to him in 'On the archaism of the Bhāgavata Purāṇa' in Milton Singer (ed.), *Krishna: Myths, Rites, and Attitudes* (Honolulu: East-West Center Press, 1966); B.N. Krishnamurti Sarma, 'Bhāskara: a forgotten commentator on the Gītā', *Indian Historical Quarterly* IX (1933), pp.663-77; V. Raghavan, 'Bhāskara's Gītābhāṣya', *Weiner Zeitschrift für die Kunde Süd- und Ostasiens und Archiv für Indische Philosophie* XII/XIII (1968/1969), pp.281-94. Professor J. Patrick Olivelle has drawn my attention to the following references to Bhāskara: (1) In Yatiliṅgasamarthana Varada's *Prameyamālā* (10th Chapter); (2) Vedāntadeśika's *Śatadūṣaṇī* (Chapter 64 and 65); and (3) Ānandānubhava's *Nyāyaratnadīpāvalī* (pp.311-35 of Sastrigal (ed.) [Madras: Government Oriental Manuscript Library, 1961]).

source-material within the tradition which could be used, so to speak, as a proxy for commentary. But with Bhāskara we enter the realm of commentary proper. As no English translation of this commentary has appeared in print, I shall be providing my own renderings of the relevant sections.

It will be analytically useful to discuss Bhāskara's interpretation under different rubrics, rather than verse by verse. An overview of his commentary suggests that the relevant material could be usefully organised under the following headings: textual, polemical, liturgical, philosophical, hermeneutical and social.

Textual aspects

Bhāskara is usually placed some centuries after Śaṅkara, though his date is a matter of some controversy, as mentioned earlier. There is little doubt, however, that he is an early commentator on the Bhagavadgītā. This makes any variant readings he may give of the text of the Bhagavadgītā particularly interesting. Moreover, Bhāskara himself refers to variant readings,[4] so that this textual aspect of his commentary must claim our attention first.

A variant reading is offered of the very first line:

dharmakṣetre kurukṣetre sarvakṣatrasamāgame

for

dharmakṣetre kurukṣetre samvetā yuyutsavaḥ.[5]

Now the same reading is also found in Rāmakaṇṭha's Gītābhāṣya from Kashmir, which means either that this was the reading current in that region or that Rāmakaṇṭha followed Bhāskara.[6] It is commented on by van Buitenen,[7] who 'notes the advantage in *kṣetre-kṣetre-kṣatra-*'.[8]

More significant is the reading of I:10. The vulgate text runs as follows:

[4] He is not the only one to do so. Śaṅkara notes and dismisses a variant construction if not reading in his gloss on VII:22.

[5] Upadhyaya (ed.), op.cit., p.1. Also noted by T.K. Gopalaswamy Aiyengar, 'Bhāskara on the Gītā' in E.R. Sreekrishna Sarma (ed.), *Gītā Samīkṣā* (Tirupati: Sri Ventateswara University, 1971), p.53.

[6] ibid., p.53.

[7] See J.A.B. van Buitenen, 'A Contribution to the Critical Edition of the Bhagavadgītā', *Journal of the American Oriental Society* 85 (1) (March 1965), pp.99-109.

[8] Robert N. Minor, *Bhagavadgītā: An Exegetical Commentary* (Delhi: Heritage Publishers, 1982), p.3.

aparyāptaṃ tad asmākaṃ
balaṃ bhīṣmābhirakṣitam
paryāptaṃ tv idam eteṣāṃ
balaṃ bhīmābhirakṣitam

(Altho) insufficient (in number) this our
Host is protected by (the wise) *Bhīṣma*;
On the other hand, (while) sufficient, this their
Host is protected by (the unskilled) *Bhīma.*[9]

Bhāskara has the following:

aparyāptam tad asmākaṃ
balaṃ bhīmābhirakṣitam
paryāptam tv idam eteṣām
balaṃ bhīṣmābhirakṣitam[10]

The importance of this reading can be judged from the fact that, while Kees Bolle used the critical edition throughout as the text for his translation of the Bhagavadgītā, he makes a single exception in the case of this verse (I:10).[11] The verse is problemetical. 'The words are spoken by Duryodhana who is much given to boasting and come somewhat unnaturally from his lips. Hence, Rk., following some ancient and modern commentators, translates *aparyāptam* as "unlimited" and *paryāptam* as "limited". He does not, however, quote any parallel for such a use of the word. Some MSS. reverse the order of *Bhīṣma*, thus giving the required sense.'[12] Bhāskara's text does just that.

Not all scholars share Bolle's optimism regarding the solution to the problem,[13] but there can be no doubt regarding the significance of the reading.

Three questions may be raised at this point in relation to the variant readings. (1) Do they represent a separate recension? (2) Was Bhāskara aware of variant readings himself? And (3) do commentators, including Bhāskara, tend to choose the reading

[9] Franklin Edgerton, *The Bhagavad Gītā*, Part I (Cambridge: Massachusetts: Harvard University Press, 1944), pp.4, 5.
[10] Upadhyaya (ed.), op. cit., p.21.
[11] Kees W. Bolle, *The Bhagavadgītā: A New Translation* (Berkeley: University of California Press, 1979), pp.257-8.
[12] R.C. Zaehner, *The Bhagavad-Gītā* (Oxford: Clarendon Press, 1969), p.114. Rk = Radhakrishnan.
[13] Gopalaswamy Aiyengar, op.cit., pp.53-4.

which best suits their understanding of the Gītā?

It is difficult to say whether Bhāskara's text represents a separate recension, for several reasons. First, his extant commentary only covers the first nine chapters of the Gītā, although references to some other glosses survive. Secondly, while to some extent his text corresponds to Kāśmīrī readings, we do not know whether Bhāskara was a Kāśmīrī, which would enhance the probability of his having followed the Kāśmīrī recension.

The possibility that he followed the Kāśmīrī recension, however, is diminished by instances of variations from it, unless it be argued that his case is a particular version of the recension, which no one seems to have done. In this context it is important that Bhāskara's text of what is now Gītā XVIII:61(a) (b) differs *both* from the critical text *and* from the reading of Rāmakaṇṭha, who follows the Kāśmīrī recension. They vary as follows:

Īśvaraḥ sarvabhūtānām hṛddeśe'rjuna tiṣṭhati[14] (critical)
Īśvaraḥ sarvabhūtānām hṛddeśe vasate'rjuna (Bhāskara)
Īśvaraḥ sarvabhūtānām hṛddyeṣa vasate'rjuna[15] (Rāmakaṇṭha)

The question of Bhāskara's awareness of different readings has to be discussed at two levels. At one level he is silent about variant readings in relation to certain verses. This is particularly intriguing as they are significant verses doctrinally or textually and differ from the vulgate, but he gives his own reading as if it were the only one. Two examples may be cited. I:10, cited earlier, is one of them. Another is III:35:

śreyān svadharmo viguṇaḥ
paradharmāt svanuṣṭhitāt
svadharme nidhanaṃ śreyaḥ
paradharmodayād api

The last *pāda* replaces the vulgate and critical: *paradharmo bhayāvahaḥ*.[16]

At another level, Bhāskara is quite aware that different readings of the text exist, and he even charges some commentators with having altered (*pāṭhāntaraṁ kurvanto*) some readings to suit their

[14] S.K. Belvalkar (ed.), The *Bhīṣmaparvan* (Poona: Bhandarkar Oriental Research Institute, 1947), p.187.
[15] Gopalaswamy Aiyengar, op.cit., p.54.
[16] ibid., p.54.

philosophical inclinations.

In answer to the third question, it might be pointed out that philosophical preferences do seem to affect choice of readings. Bhāskara implies this in the case of others.[17] In his own case he discusses the variant readings in the light of their philosophical implications. A good example is II:18 (II:19 in Bhāskara's text). The critical/vulgate runs as follows:

antavanta ime dehā
nityasyo 'ktāḥ śarīriṇaḥ
anāśino 'prameyasya
tasmād yudhyasva bhārata

These bodies come to an end,
It is declared, of the eternal embodied (soul),
Which is indestructible and unfathomable.
Therefore fight, son of Bharata![18]

Bhāskara's text, however, runs:

antavanta ime dehā
nityasy'oktāḥ śrīriṇaḥ
vinaśino' prameyasya
tasmād yudhyasva bhārata[19]

Bhāskara discusses the two variants in (c): *vināśino* and *avināśino.* The former he takes as nominative plural qualifying *antavantaḥ* and raises the point whether it is not tautological to refer to *dehāḥ* as both *vināśino* and *antavantaḥ* when they could be seen as meaning more or less the same thing. But if it is read as *avināśino* (critical and vulgate: *anāśino*), the problem of tautology again arises, since it qualifies the genitive singular *śarīriṇaḥ*, which has already been called *nitya*, and *nitya* and *avināśino* carry more or less the same meaning! As will be shown later, he plumps for *vināśino*, seeing a fine distinction between it and *antavantaḥ*.

Before we conclude this section it may be useful to point out the overall place of Bhāskara's text in the study of the Gītā. 'From the current state of textual studies on the *Gītā*, van Buitenen's reconstruction of the textual history of the *Gītā* sums up the current state of the evidence. From the "original" text, two branches have

[17] Upadhyaya (ed.), op.cit., p.54; etc
[18] Edgerton, op.cit., Part I, pp.18, 19.
[19] Upadhyaya (ed.), op.cit., p.51.

resulted: (1) the "Vulgate" of Śaṁkara; (2) the text of Bhāskara. The Kashmir recension, then, is a further development of Bhāskara's version.'[20] There is no way of proving this point of view, but it may be considered as good a conjecture as any.

Polemical aspects

Another respect in which Bhāskara's commentary is remarkable is its polemical nature. Almost all commentators on the Gītā refer to, if not challenge or claim to refute, the views of other scholars and commentators, but Bhāskara does so with particular frequency and vehemence. His glosses on II:16-18, II:20-1, 29, III:3-4 and VII:19-20 provide good examples.

Bhagavadgītā II:16, which is II:17 in Bhāskara's text,[21] runs as follows:

nā 'sato vidyate bhāvo
na 'bhāvo vidyate sataḥ
ubhayor api dṛṣṭo 'ntas tv
anayos tattvadarśibhiḥ

Of what is not, no coming to be occurs;
No coming not to be occurs of what is;
But the dividing-line of both is seen,
Of these two, by those who see the truth.[22]

In his gloss on this verse Bhāskara refers to (1) Vaiśeṣikas; (2) Māyāvādins;[23] (3) *pramāṇakuśalas.*[24] The last two have been identified with the Advaitins and the Buddhists.[25] He criticises the views of the last two schools,[26] but it is interesting to note the extent of his philosophical sophistication – he distinguishes between *māyāvāda* and *śūnyavāda* and then proceeds to attack both:

> Others who uphold the doctrine of *māyā* explain extraneously (thus). Henceforth not indulging in grief or delusion it is meet that you should tolerate cold, heat, etc. Why? Because on account of their non-being, cold and heat, etc., do not really exist. Being consists of 'isness'. Why (do heat and cold not exist)? Because they are

[20] Minor, op.cit., p.111.
[21] Upadhyaya (ed.), op.cit., p.47.
[22] Edgerton, op.cit., Part I, pp.16, 17.
[23] Upadhyaya (ed.), op.cit., p.47. [24] ibid. [25] ibid.
[26] Gopalaswamy Aiyengar, op.cit., p.57.

modifications. That modification which is preceived by means of valid knowledge (such as *pratyakṣa*, etc.) cannot attain (the status of) true existence ('isness'). The pot, etc., will not be objects of apprehension without their cause (which brings them into 'existence'). The same holds true of all forms of being (*vikāras*). Now (it may be said that) this leads to the doctrine of emptiness (*śūnyavāda*). But no logical defect is involved here. Two forms of *Buddhi* ('Intelligence') are well-known in regard to all living beings – *viśesyabuddhi* and *viśeṣaṇabuddhi*. 'This is a pot', 'This is a piece of cloth' (it knows thus). In this respect this *viśesyabuddhi* which has the pot, etc., as its object is false because it deviates into the piece of cloth, etc. (changes with the objects). Now that *buddhi* (which may be called *viśeṣaṇabuddhi*), which has the qualification as its object is not false, being ever present in all modes of perception (*vṛtti*). Therefore it is 'real in the only true sense of the term' (*pārmārthika*). All of this, pots, etc., and physical bodies, etc., are a web (of falsehood) – merely *māyā* and untrue. Thus do they believe.

Others possessing expertise in epistemology, refute this view. Now it had been said modification such as pots, etc., being perceived by means of knowledge become devoid of their own being. This is not true. Light, the visual sense and the mind being properly present, the knowledge directly arises that 'this is a pot' 'this is a piece of cloth'. That *buddhi* which perceives an object, that very (*buddhi*) perceives its absence – will a logician speak otherwise? The existence of a thing is determined by the five means of valid knowledge – (*pramāṇas*) *pratyakṣa, anumāna, upamāna, arthāpatti* and *āgama* (*śabda*). In the case in which the five don't operate, in that case, on account of the lack of the operation of the *pramāṇas* it is concluded that the object of the valid knowledge is not present.[27]

Bhagavadgītā II:17, which is II:18 in Bhāskara's text,[28] runs as follows:

avināśi tu tad viddhi
yena sarvam idaṃ tatam
vināśam avyayasyā 'sya
na kaścit kartum arhati

But know that that is indestructible,
By which this all is pervaded;
Destruction of this imperishable one
No one can cause.[29]

[27] Upadhyaya (ed.), op.cit., pp.48-9. [28] ibid., p.51.
[29] Edgerton, op.cit., Part I, pp.16, 17.

Bhāskara argues that 'the context refers only to the *jīva* of the form of *paramātman*' – *paramātmarūpeṇa kṣetrajño* – 'in the original form and that the interpretation with reference to meditation will be discussed only in the sixth chapter' and 'that it is out of context here'.[30]

The question is in a sense particular to Bhāskara's own school of philosophy of *bhedābheda*. Herein as elsewhere in Hindu philosophy, the question arises of whether the worlds and the souls are different from *brahman* or identical with it?

> Bhāskara's answer to such a question is that 'difference' (*bheda*) has in it the characteristic of identity (*abhedadharmaś ca*) – the waves are different from the sea, but are also identical with it. The waves are manifestations of the sea's own powers, and so the same identical sea appears to be different when viewed with reference to the manifestations of its powers. So the same identical fire is different in its powers as it burns or illuminates. So all that is one is also many, and the one is neither absolute identity nor absolute difference.[31]

In relation to the verse in question the doubt arises as to whether it is the *jīvātman* which is referred to, or *brahman*, for the expression *yena sarvam idaṃ tatam* (by which all this is pervaded)[32] could be applied to both *ātman* and *brahman*. Bhāskara clarifies that here it applies to the *ātman*, for *brahman* is not being invoked here and worship in accordance with *jñāna* (*brahmajñāna*) will be pursued in a later chapter. The polemics are below the surface; the Advaitins take the reference as pertaining to *brahma*.[33]

Bhagavadgītā II:18, which is II:19 in Bhāskara's text, has been cited earlier. Bhāskara makes two interesting polemical points in this connection: one textual, the other contextual. The textual one has been hinted at before. It remains to be justified why Bhāskara prefers *vināśino* in the third *pāda*. He does so basically for two reasons. First, according to him, the reading *avisnāśino* does not improve matters, since calling the embodied soul both *nitya* and *avināśī* is tautological.[34] He prefers, therefore, to read it with *dehāḥ*, or bodies. But the body has also been called *antavat* (that which comes to an end); so calling it *vināśī* (perishable) raises the same problem of redundancy. Bhāskara resolves the problem by distinguishing

[30] Gopalaswamy Aiyengar, op.cit., p.57.

[31] Surendranath Dasgupta, *A History of Indian Philosophy*, Vol.III (Cambridge University Press, 1922), p.6.

[32] Bhagavadgītā XVIII:46.

[33] *Śrīśāṅkaragranthāvaliḥ*, Sampuṭa 8, p.24.

[34] Upadhyaya (ed.), op.cit., p.51.

semantically between *antavat* and *vināśī*. The body comes to an end, but this leaves room for the following possibility: smell disappears from the earth when it dries up but reappears when it rains. The epithet *vināśī* rules out the possibility of the same body arising again. In modern parlance the end of the body leaves two eschatological possibilities open: (1) resurrection, and (2) rebirth. According to Bhāskara the use of *vināśī* denies resurrection.

The contextual point made in his gloss here by Bhāskara is also significant. 'Bhāskara refutes the comments of some Bhāsyakāras, who hold that the *Gītā śāstra* is meant only to remove *śoka* and *moha* and not to instigate Arjuna to do his own duty (*svadharma*). Bhāskara reminds the opponent that it is futile to advise the removal of *śoka* and *moha* after the commencement of the war. Lord Kṛṣṇa might as well have stayed at Dvārakā and composed the *Gītā* to teach *jñāna*, conducing to *mokṣa*. The very intention of teaching in the battlefield is to teach *jñāna* and *karma* in full concordance for the attainment of salvation.'[35]

Gītā II:20 (II:21 in Bhāskara's text)[36] runs as follows:

na jāyate mriyate vā kadācin
na 'yaṃ bhūtvā bhavitā vā na bhūyaḥ
ajo nityaḥ śāśvato 'yam purāṇo
na hanyate hanyamāne śarīre

He is not born, nor does he ever die;
Nor, having come to be, will he ever more come not to be.
Unborn, eternal, everlasting, this ancient one
Is not slain when the body is slain.[37]

It should be noted that the critical text, the vulgate text and Bhāskara's text are identical. This is important because Bhāskara indulges in polemics here against those who choose to read the text as: *nāyaṃ bhūto bhavitā vā na bhūyaḥ* for *nāyaṃ bhūtvā bhavitā vā na bhūyaḥ*. Bhāskara argues that, by changing *bhūtvā* to *bhūto*, those who wish to read the worship of *parabrahma* in the Gītā can argue that the *brahma* is not *bhūta* or past cause, like clay, or *bhavitā*, that is, future effect, like a pot. Thus causality is denied with respect to it in its absolute (*pāramārthika*), as opposed to the conditioned (*aupādhika*), aspect. In this respect T.K. Gopalaswamy Aiyengar presents Bhāskara's views forcefully:

[35] Gopalaswamy Aiyengar, op.cit., p.59.
[36] Upadhyaya (ed.), op.cit., p.53.
[37] Edgerton, op.cit., Part I, p.18, 19.

Bhāskara holds that the change in reading is not consistent with the context. The commentators who change the reading mean to incorporate the sense of meditation on *Parabrahman* into the context. The opponents argue that the terms *bhūta* (past) and *bhavitā* (future becoming) of Brahman are negated in the stanza, whereby Brahman is neither a cause nor an effect like clay or pot. The opponents ultimately contend that the cause-effect relationship of Brahman is apparent and not real. Bhāskara is vehement in his criticism to fling the charge of wrongly directing their faith and interest towards meditation instead towards the contextual considerations and topical sequences based on the principles of *Mīmāṃsā* such as *śruti, liṅga, prakaraṇa*, etc. Bhāskara justifies his reading as correct and holds the view that the dispelling of Arjuna's ignorance is imminent and that a sudden jump to meditation without contextual sanction is unwarranted and illogical. To thrust meditation on to the context by changing the reading is named by Bhāskara as *āhopuruṣikā* which means the bragging of a person arbitrarily prompted by extreme vanity, self-conceit and high-handedness. The views of such persons are liable to cause confusion in the minds of those who are real seekers after truth.[38]

What is intriguing about the whole situation is that, while Bhāskara does not say so, we can see him suspecting that an Advaitic invisible hand has tampered with the text. Yet the interpretation of this verse by Bhāskara and Śaṅkara runs on parallel lines. Śaṅkara says that the verse denies the six modifications of being (*ṣaḍ bhāvavikārāḥ*) in relation to the *ātman*,[39] and Bhāskara says the same (*ṣaḍ bhāvavikāranivṛttiparāṇi na jāyata ityādīny akṣarāṇi*).[40] These modifications are mentioned by Yāska as follows: (i) the birth of the physical body (*deho jāyate*); (ii) its existence (*asti*); (iii) its growth (*vardhate*); (iv) its changes or metamorphosis (*vipariṇamate*); (v) its decline (*apakṣīyate*); and (vi) its death (*vinaśyati*). These are respectively negated by the following units of the verse: (i) *na jāyate*; (ii) *na bhūtvā bhavitā*; (iii) *nityaḥ*; (iv) *purāṇaḥ*; (v) *śāśvataḥ*; and (vi) (*na*) *mriyate*.[41]

So what is going on? Is Bhāskara barking up the wrong tree, or is the tree lost in some forest of Hindu philosophical schools?

Gītā II:21 (II:22 in Bhāskara) runs:

[38] Gopalaswamy Aiyengar, op.cit., p.58.

[39] *Śrīśāṅkagranthāvalih*, Sampuṭa 8, p.28.

[40] Upadhyaya (ed.), op.cit., p.55.

[41] Swami Vireswarananda, *Srimad-Bhagavad-Gītā* (Mylapore, Madras: Sri Ramakrishna Math, 1948), pp.41-2.

vedā 'vināśinaṃ nityaṃ
ya enam ajam avyayam
kathaṃ sa puruṣaḥ pārtha
kaṃ ghātayati hanti kam

Who knows as indestructible and eternal
This unborn, imperishable one,
That man, son of Pṛthā, how
Can he slay or cause to slay – whom?[42]

In his gloss on this verse, according to T.K. Gopalaswamy Aiyengar, Bhāskara 'directs his attack on Śaṅkara who strains and twists the words in the context to convey the sense of total renunciation of all *karma* and attributes the same as the central teaching of Lord Kṛṣṇa. He disproves the theory of Śaṅkara that *karma* is the path to be resorted to by the unwise or *avidvān* alone who are incompetent to take up to the path of *jñāna*. Bhāskara criticises this view that the categorical and assertive imperatives *yudhyasva, karma kuru*, etc., become futile, had the Lord meant the total renunciation of all *karmas*.'[43]

Śaṅkara here cites the view, held by some sapient scholars (*paṇḍitaṁ manyamānāḥ*)[44] that, as it is not possible for anyone to be free from the six modifications discussed earlier, the renunciation of all actions is not possible. This is denied by Śaṅkara, who holds out for total abandonment of action. This position, in turn, is challenged by Bhāskara. The relevant text of his gloss is as follows:

In this matter some, afraid of undertaking the (intellectual) effort (required to arrive at a correct understanding), explain the meaning by imposing their own sense on (the words of) the Lord: that the meaning the Lord wishes to convey in this context is the prohibition of all works on the part of the wise. Killing has been used as an example. Those actions which are prescribed in the scriptures are laid down for those lacking in wisdom: this, it is said, is the conclusion of the Lord.

Such an explanation of the intended meaning does not take into account the relation with the words already uttered. Why is it that, in order to induce (Arjuna) to fight, the potency of the *ātman* is being described? Having said (to Arjuna): 'Therefore, O descendant of

[42] Edgerton, op.cit., Part I, pp.18, 19.
[43] Gopalaswamy Aiyengar, op.cit., p.59.
[44] *Srīśāṅkaragranthāvaliḥ*, Sampuṭa 8, p.31.

Bharata, fight', (such description) is meant for its successful accomplishment. If the abandonment of all action was intended right from the beginning, then this verse would not have been spoken to Arjuna. The *ātman* is free from the six modifications of being as stated by the Lord. If it is impossible for the wise to act then non-action on his part would be like it (that of the *ātman*). All the later verses (however) are not in harmony (with this conclusion). One should not hope in vain thus: that with our minds captivated by the (idea of the) abandonment of one's *dharma* may we attain salvation by remaining seated at ease. Later on we shall expound (the doctrine which emphasises) the combination of *jñāna* and *karma* logically and skilfully.

The indestructibility (of the *ātman*) was stated on account of it being impossible to kill it.

Bhagavadgītā II:29 (II:30 in Bhāskara's text)[45] runs:

āścaryavat paśyati kaścid enam
āścaryavad vadati tathai 'va cā 'nyaḥ
āścaryavac cai 'nam anyaḥ śṛṇoti
śrutvā 'py enaṃ veda na cai 'va kaścit

By a rare chance one may see him,
And by a rare chance likewise may another declare him,
And by a rare chance may another hear (of) him;
(But) even having heard (of) him, no one whatsoever knows him.[46]

It has been pointed out that this verse is often connected by exegetes with a similar verse in the Kaṭha Upaniṣad (I.2.7). This is exactly what Bhāskara does, like many modern commentators.[47] However, in the process he attacks those who rather imaginatively connect the verse not with the one from Kaṭha Upaniṣad just cited but with the Bṛhadāraṇyaka passage 2.4.5 (also 4.5.6) *ātmā vā are draṣṭavyaḥ śrotavyo mantavyo nididyāsayitavaḥ*: 'It is the self that should be seen, heard of, reflected on and meditated upon.'[48]

Bhāskara's point is well-taken, but does create room for two observations.[49] First, Śaṅkara quotes neither the Kaṭha nor the Bṛhadāraṇyaka passage; so once again we must ask who are these

[45] Upadhyaya (ed.), op.cit., p.60.
[46] Edgerton, op.cit., Part I, pp.19, 20
[47] Zaehner, op.cit., p.136; S. Radhakrishnan, op.cit., p.111.
[48] S. Radhakrishnan (ed.), *The Principal Upaniṣads* (London: Allen & Unwin, 1953), p.197.
[49] Gopalaswamy Aiyengar, op.cit., pp.59-60.

people Bhāskara is referring to who describe the meaning of the verse according to their own fancy (*kecid asya ślokasya arthaṁ svamatikalpanayā varṇayanti*).[50] Secondly, it is worth noting that Bhāskara's blow may have to be softened in the case of those who take *āścaryavat* as applying to the *ātman*, for then the Bṛhadāraṇyaka passage gains a greater semblance of relevance.[51]

III:3 runs as follows:

loke 'smin dvividhā niṣṭhā
purā proktā mayā 'nagha
jñānayogena sāṃkhyānāṃ
karmayogena yoginām

In this world a two-fold basis (or religion)
Has been declared by Me of old, blameless one:
By the disciple of knowledge of the followers of reason-method,
And by the discipline of action of the followers of discipline-method.[52]

Bhāskara's gloss on this verse is extensive and full of interest, both polemically and philosophically. His polemics are directed towards both the exegetical procedures and the conclusions of those who hold that liberation is possible through *jñāna* alone. By contrast, Bhāskara upholds the view of *jñānakarmasamuccaya*: that liberation results from the combined pursuit of *jñāna* and *karma*. This major philosophical point we shall turn to later.

At this stage of the game we must consider Bhāskara's charge that the upholders of the *jñāna*-alone view misconstrue Upaniṣadic passages. He refers to two passages specifically, and shows how in his opinion they have been misinterpreted. Both are from the Mahānārāyaṇa Upaniṣad;[53] though one also occurs in the Kaivalya Upaniṣad. The passage runs (Kaivalya, Mahānārāyaṇa 10.5):

na karmaṇā na prajayā dhanena
tyāgenaike amṛtatvam ānaśuḥ

[50] Upadhyaya (ed.), op.cit., p.60.

[51] In view of the above, Surendranath Dasgupta's use of the Bṛhadaraṇyaka quotation in explicating Bhāskara's position must generate a modicum of scepticism (see Surendranath Dasgupta, op.cit., Vol.III, p.8).

[52] Edgerton, op.cit., Part I, pp.32, 33.

[53] Bhāskara's text runs *na karmaṇā prajayā* for *na karmaṇā na prajayā* (Gopalaswamy Aiyengar, op.cit., p.60, n.36).

Not by work, not by offspring, nor wealth; only by renunciation does one reach life eternal.[54]

The second one runs as follows (Mahānārāyaṇa 24.1):

nyāsam eṣām tapasā atiriktam āhuḥ

According to Bhāskara *tyāga* in the first citation only means *kāmyakarmatyāga*, or the abandonment of optional duties;[55] and in the second citation *nyāsa* means *brahma*, and not *karmatyāga.*[56] Perhaps he has Mahānārāyaṇa 23.1 in mind: *nyāsa ity āhur manīṣiṇo brahmāṇam* or 21.2: *nyāsa iti brahmā.* Be that as it may, Bhāskara's warning against homonymous and homophonous confusion is well-taken:

He states that similarity of sounds with some modification will always mislead one towards a wrong interpretation. He cites an example from *Mimāmṣa śāstra* where the Vedic passage '*ājyaiḥ stuvate*' does not convey the meaning ghee by similarity of syllables but a collection of *sāmans* known as *ājya sāmans*. In this connection he quotes a *kārikā*, warning one to guard oneself from being carried away by the mere similarity of syllables while interpreting the word and its meaning in a particular context. There shall be an efficient scrutiny as to the complete concordance in respect of the words and their meaning in the context (*paurvāparya*).[57]

Bhāskara's position with respect to the non-abandonment of action even by those who are *jñānins*, or would-be *jñānins*, is quite firm.[58]

Bhagavadgītā III:4 runs as follows:

na karmaṇām anārambhān
naiṣkarmyam puruṣo 'śnute
na ca samnyasanād eva
siddhim samadhigacchati

Not by not starting actions
Does a man attain actionlessness,
And not by renunciation alone
Does he go to perfection.[59]

[54] S. Radhakrishnan (ed.), *The Principal Upaniṣads*, p.927.
[55] Upadhyaya (ed.), op.cit., p.81. [56] ibid.
[57] Gopalaswamy Aiyengar, op.cit., p.61.
[58] Upadhyaya (ed.), op.cit., p.80.
[59] Edgerton, op.cit., Part I, pp.32, 33.

Even more than III:3, this verse seems to challenge the position that literal abandonment of action is recommended by the Gītā. Bhāskara makes good use of it to strengthen his position, as when he states: Liberation results from knowledge along with karma and not by knowledge alone – this is the purport (*karmasāpekṣāj jñānān muktir na kevalād ity abhiprāyaḥ*).[60]

On the other hand, while the positions of Bhāskara and the Gītā in regard to III:4 do overlap to a certain extent, Bhāskara gives the verse an exegetical twist of his own. As a matter of fact, he does it right at the start of his gloss, which he begins with the following remark: Naiṣkarmya is the abstract noun of the absence of action. By the word *karma*, good and bad deeds are to be understood. Their absence is *mokṣa* (*niṣkarmaṇo bhāvo naiṣkarmyam karmaśabdena puṇyāpuṇyayor grahaṇam. Tad rahitam mokṣam ity arthaḥ*). His point may be elaborated thus.[61] Action here means ritual action, and the performance of Vedic ritual is the 'only way to attain release. This is what they teach: *mokṣa* is the pure state of the self. In that state there is neither merit nor demerit for the soul. How can this be achieved? By performing *nitya-karmas* and by refraining from *niṣiddha-karmas* (prohibited deeds), one avoids demerit; and by not performing *kāmya-karmas*, one does not acquire merit.'[62] Thus one becomes free from both merit and demerit – and thereby liberated.

But is this the teaching of the Gītā?

Liturgical aspects

Viṣṇu is the primary god according to Bhāskara. It is the foolish who think that he is just like any god for he is not.[63] In point of fact he is the root cause of the entire universe and the overlord of such gods as Brahmā, Rudra, Indra, etc. (*samastasya jagato mūlakāraṇam īśvarāṇām brahmarudrendrādīnām apy adhīśvaro'yam*).[64]

Devotion to such a god leads to salvation; devotion to other gods does not produce the same result (*devāntarabhaktānām ca tad vāsitacetasām ca tato nivṛttir nāsti*).[65] In his commentary on VII:20-3, which deal with the worship of other gods, Bhāskara makes a few interesting comments. He remarks that people worship gods other than Viṣṇu on account of the mental impressions of past lives (*pūrvajanmavāsanayā*);[66] he seems to be referring to the worship of the images of such gods (*tanuṃ devatā-mūrtim ity arthaḥ*),[67] and he

[60] Upadhyaya (ed.), op.cit., p.83. [61] ibid., p.3.
[62] T.M.P. Mahadevan, *Outlines of Hinduism* (Bombay: Chetana, 1971), pp.137-8.
[63] Upadhyaya (ed.), op.cit., p.177. [64] ibid.
[65] ibid., p.175. [66] ibid. [67] ibid., p.176.

emphasises the role of God as the dispenser of *karma*. Thus, when in VII:22 Kṛṣṇa says that the devotees obtain the desires granted by him, Bhāskara notes that this is so because God is the dispenser of *karma* (*yasmād īśvaraḥ sarvatra phaladātā karmānurūpeṇa*).[68]

Viṣṇu then must be the focus of true devotion. In his gloss on VII:19 Bhāskara offers a 'twofold etymology of the word *vāsudeva* and thereby brings to light the cardinal metaphysical truths regarding Brahman as *jagatkāraṇa* and as *antaryāmin*'. Moreover, 'in relation to the same etymological explanation, he says specifically that Brahman assumes both the states as cause and effect'.[69] It should be noted that Brahman is to be identified with Viṣṇu and that salvation consists in repairing to the abode of Kṛṣṇa (VII:21).

One interesting detail relates to the offering of *bilva* (wood-apple) leaves in the worship of Viṣṇu. These are referred to by Bhāskara in his gloss on IX:26. The normal association of *bilva* is with Śiva not Viṣṇu, and while some scholars like K. Gopalaswamy Aiyengar have tried to resolve the paradox[70] it once again emerges as a point of interest that the boundaries between Śaivism and Vaiṣṇavism often seem to hold barely or not at all in the context of the Gītā.

Philosophical aspects

The philosophical position of Bhāskara can be specified neatly: metaphysically he belongs to the *bhedābheda* school; soteriologically he is an advocate of *jñānakarma-samuccaya*; cosmologically he is a *pariṇāmavādī*, eschatologically he believes in *videhamukti*; and epistemologically he is a *svataḥ-prāmāṇyavādī*. It is in his commentary on the Brahmasūtra that these philosophical positions are fully explicated.[71]

In the context of the Gītā, as pointed out earlier, his doctrine of *jñāna-karma-samuccaya* is prominently presented. Whenever a verse seems to imply that *karma* by itself may suffice for liberation, Bhāskara uses his gloss to redress the balance. Two examples should suffice. Gītā III:20 runs:

karmaṇai 'va hi saṃsiddhim
āsthitā janakādayaḥ
lokasaṃgraham evā 'pi
sampaśyan kartum arhasi

[68] ibid.
[69] Gopalaswamy Aiyengar, op.cit., p.62.
[70] ibid., p.64.
[71] Dasgupta, op.cit., Vol.III, Ch.XB.

For only thru action, perfection
  Attained Janaka and others.
Also for the mere control of the world
  Having regard, thou shouldst act.[72]

The verse obviously tilts towards *karma.* Bhāskara immediately comments that the verse is intended, in effect, to prevent inaction and not to slight *jñāna.*[73] Let IV:38 be now considered:

na hi jñānena sadṛśam
  pavitram iha vidyate
tat svayaṃ yogasaṃsiddhaḥ
  kālenā 'tmani vindati

For not like unto knowledge
  Is any purifier found in this world.
This the man perfected in discipline himself
  In time finds in himself.[74]

The verse obviously tilts towards *jñāna.* Bhāskara is quick to add that *yogasaṁsiddhaḥ* here means *karmayogena saṁsiddhaḥ.*[75]

Bhāskara's commentary on one of the verses of the Gītā seems to create some difficulty in relation to the view that Bhāskara believed in post-mortem salvation. This obviously seems to be the position he takes in his commentary on the Brahmasūtra. S. Dasgupta writes:

> Bhāskara denies the possibility of liberation during lifetime (*jīvan-mukti*); for so long as the body remains as a result of the previous *karmas,* the duties assigned to the particular stage of life (*āśrama*) to which the man belongs have to be performed; but his difference from the ordinary man is that, while the ordinary man thinks himself to be the agent or the doer of all actions, the wise man never thinks himself to be so. If a man could attain liberation during lifetime, then he might even know the minds of other people. Whether in *mukti* one becomes absolutely relationless (*niḥsambandhaḥ*), or whether one becomes omniscient and omnipotent (as Bhāskara himself urges), it is not possible for one to attain *mukti* during one's lifetime, so it is certain that so long as a man lives he must perform his duties and try to comprehend the nature of God and attend on Him through meditation, since these can only lead to liberation after death.[76]

[72] Edgerton, op.cit., Part I, p.36, 37.
[73] Upadhyaya (ed.), op.cit., p.93.
[74] Edgerton, op.cit., Part I, pp.50, 51.
[75] Upadhyaya (ed.), op.cit., p.132.
[76] Dasgupta, op.cit., Vol.III, pp.10-11.

As against this, V:19 needs to be taken into account. It runs as follows:

inhai 'va tair jitaḥ sargo
yeṣāṃ sāmye sthitaṃ manaḥ
nirdoṣaṃ hi samaṃ brahma
tasmād brahmaṇi te sthitāḥ

Right in this world they have overcome birth,
Whose mind is fixed in indifference:
For Brahman is flawless and indifferent;
Therefore they are fixed in Brahman.[77]

In his gloss on this verse Bhāskara seems to concede the possibility of *jīvanmukti*:

By them here even in the body rebirth has been won over, destroyed, whose minds are established in the undifferentiated nature of Brahman. Brahman is flawless and equal. Seen by that point of view everything becomes Brahman just as whatever falls on a saline field turns to salt. In such a Brahman are they established therefore has (victory over rebirth) been won, this is the connection.[78]

Similarly, V:23 must also be considered:

śaknotī 'hai 'va yaḥ soḍhuṃ
prāk śarīravimokṣaṇāt
kāmakrodhodbhavaṃ vegaṃ
sa yuktaḥ sa sukhī naraḥ

Who can control right in this life,
Before being freed from the body,
The excitement that springs from desire and wrath,
He is disciplined, he the happy man.[79]

Here again the gloss translates:

Now the verse beginning *śaknoti*. He who is able to endure, that is control, while possessing a body not just for a moment but as long as

[77] Edgerton, op.cit., Part I, pp.56, 57.
[78] Upadhyaya (ed.), op.cit., p.148.
[79] Edgerton, op.cit., Part I, pp.56, 57.

> not liberated from the body, that is, till the body fall off. (And what does he endure?) The access (of emotion) arising out of passion and anger. *Kāma* consists of desiring to obtain what one does not have. The mental modification instigated by it is *kāmavega*. The control of passion (*kāmodvega*) consists of the cessation of the mental modification tinged by it, as characterised by changes of ocular and facial expression. And (by control of anger) is meant the control of the impetuosity arising out of wrath. The person who holds back these impulses, he is intent on *yoga* and is happy.
>
> He, who, having overcome desire and anger abides in the *ātman* is indeed said to be liberated.[80]

The gloss does not say that the person is *as if* (*iva*) liberated, but that he *is*, though initially it seems to support *videhamukti*.

Hermeneutical aspects

The distinction between the two categories of sacred literature, the *śruti* and the *smṛti*, is fairly well-established in Hinduism.

> The foundational Scriptures of the Hindus are the Vedas. They are usually designated '*Śruti*', while all the other scriptural texts go under the omnibus term '*Smṛti*'. The authority of the *Śruti* is primary, while that of the *Smṛti* is secondary. *Śruti* literally means what is heard, and *Smṛti* means what is remembered. *Śruti* is revelation; *Smṛti* is tradition. As between the two, *Śruti* is primary because it is a form of direct experience, whereas *Smṛti* is secondary, since it is a recollection of that experience.[81]

To these trite, if true, observations must be added another commonplace in Indological circles: that the Mahābhārata and therefore the Gītā, which forms a part of it, is a *smṛti* and not a *śruti*. Notwithstanding its tremendous popularity, the Gītā does not technically enjoy the status of *śruti*, or revelation, in Hinduism, a fact which some students of Hinduism find intriguing.[82]

One remarkable aspect of Bhāskara's commentary on the Gītā is that he regards the Mahābhārata, and by implication the Gītā, as on a par with the Vedas. This assertion is made in the rather unexpected

[80] Upadhyaya (ed.), op.cit., p.150.
[81] Mahadevan, op.cit., p.28.
[82] S. Radhakrishnan, *Indian Philosophy*, Vol. I (London: Allen & Unwin, 1923), p.519.

context of his gloss on I:19, a verse whose cacophonous din usually stops commentators from saying anything at all. The verse runs as follows in the vulgate:

sa ghoṣo dhārtarāṣṭrāṇāṃ
hṛdayāni vyadārayat
nabhaś ca pṛthivīṃ cai 'va
tumulo vyanunādayan

That sound Dhṛtarāṣṭra's men's
Hearts did rend;
And both sky and earth
It made to resound, swelling aloft.[83]

Bhāskara's text reads *vyanunādayat* for *vyanunādayan*.[84] He glosses the verse as follows:

> The tumult, the sound of the conches as described, rent the hearts of Duryodhana, etc. The expression reverberation has been used because (that tumult) filled the sky and the earth, all of it with echoes. In the expression *vyanunādayat*, the grammatical interpretation of the nominal and verbal forms present herein is not offered out of the fear of the glorious nature of the text (i.e. that by so doing its sanctity will be compromised). Those words which herein do not appear to be grammatically correct should not be objected to. For the supreme sage Vyāsa has himself said (the Mahābhārata) is adorned with auspicious words (so they should not be questioned). Therefore when their auspiciousness has been established by the canon itself and there exist numerous systems of grammar how is it proper to raise an objection on the basis of Pāṇini alone? For the historical accounts, etc., are to be considered on a par with the *chandas* (Vedic literature) because they expound the meaning of the Vedas. And as he (i.e. Vyāsa) has himself said: 'This (Mahābhārata) is consistent with the Vedas, hallowed and peerless'; 'This is the sacred Veda of Kṛṣṇa.' And elsewhere too it has been said: 'Vyāsa, on regarding the Mahābhārata as not different from the Vedas, first duly composed a hymn for the Aśvins using Vedic sentences and will repeatedly employ the remaining Vedic usages.'[85]

Bhāskara not only uses linguistic arguments to bridge the

[83] Edgerton, op.cit., Part I, pp.6, 7. [84] Upadhyaya (ed.), op.cit., p.24.
[85] ibid. According to standard grammar it should be *vi+anu+anādayat*.

revelatory gulf between the Vedas and the Mahābhārata, he refines the general linguistic argument into a specifically textual argument in relation to the Gītā. He takes to task those scholars who wish to classicise the language of the Gītā by introducing suitable changes in the texts, and remarks that the variation in reading carried out by them serves to destroy the 'Vedic' nature of the text of the Gītā, a nature which is Vedic on account of the Gītā's being (a part) of the Fifth Veda and full of Vedic usages. The remarks are occasioned by the occurrence in Bhāskara's reading of III:22 of the form *vartāmi*. Bhāskara states that some read *varte* here because the root *vṛt* is *ātmanepada*. In this he sees a misguided effort to *pāṇinize* the Gītā, as this only detracts from its *ārṣa* (Vedic) character.

A more likely place where one meets with similar sentiments is towards the end of Bhāskara's Introduction to the commentary where he maintains that sages such as Vyāsa enjoy the same status as the *ṛṣis* to whom the Vedas were revealed. He writes:

> The traditional precepts of the blessed sage Vyāsa and others possess their own authority. On account of having had a direct vision of *dharma* they see the entire Vedic message like the fruit of emblic myrobalan on the palm of their hand (i.e. clearly) perceiving it directly, as it were. For it has been said – the seers possessed a direct vision of *dharma*. Therefore we cannot say that sages like Vyāsa do not perceive the suprasensible goal as (was done) in the beginning (by the seers). No blame attaches to saying that suprasensible perception on their part is possible because they had shaken off sin, received the grace of God and had written about the meaning of the Vedas.[86]

Thus Bhāskara used linguistic,[87] textual and mystical arguments together to establish parity between *śruti* and *smṛti*. All this seems to indicate a very progressive outlook. There are hints of a progressive view of revelation,[88] and even echoes of Jayanta.[89] A closer scrutiny of Bhāskara's writing, however, suggests the opposite conclusion that, far from being hermeneutically progressive as he seems to be, he is really socially quite regressive. It seems that one of the reasons why he wishes to impart a Vedic character to the Gītā is to make it

[86] Upadhyaya (ed.), op.cit., p.17.
[87] Gopalaswamy Aiyengar, op.cit., p.55.
[88] K. Satchidananda Murty, *Revelation and Reason in Advaita Vedānta* (New York: Columbia University Press, 1959), pp.301ff.
[89] ibid., pp.232ff.

inaccessible to the *śūdras*. Thus he writes in his Introduction to the Gītā:

> Thus it is settled that the *śūdra*, etc., may only listen to historical narratives. And moreover they can listen to only historical narratives if it is recalled that they are forbidden from those places where the esoteric Vedantic doctrines are being propounded, and the Sanatsujātīya, Gītā and the *mokṣadharma* (section of the Mahābhārata) as well; and are also forbidden from studying or hearing the Vedas and from knowing about them and what (courses of study) are grounded in them. As has been said in the Manusmṛti:
>
> > Do not offer (spiritual) opinion to a Śūdra; neither what has been left over nor what is offered in oblation. Do not instruct him in dharma nor prescribe observances.
>
> Thus the debarment from explaining what pertains to the unseen (divine), from offering opinion, charity and instruction in *dharma*. Nor is it the case that disregarding the instruction of the Brahmins he may study the books, etc., on his own initiative or having them described understand their purport and acting accordingly may obtain the desired results. On the contrary the knowledge acquired by one not invested with the sacred thread and debarred by the scriptures results in disaster. For the true import of the scripture consists of that sense which does not contradict logic, the *smṛtis* and norms of conduct. Herein the following logic applies: just as the *karma* of the superior and inferior *varṇas* are not comparable, so also is it not meet that their *dharmas* be comparable as has been said:
>
> > If even women and *śūdras* have a right to liberation then the superiority of the twice-borns becomes meaningless.[90]

In other words while Bhāskara narrows the hermeneutical gap between *śruti* and *smṛti*; he does so as a part of the process of widening the religio-social gap between the *divjātis* and the *śūdras*. This last point is further developed in the next section.

Social aspects

Hinduism is essentially hierarchical, on account of the *varṇa* system; but, given that fact, the Bhagavadgītā is generally commended for its egalitarian outlook, especially in its devotional orientation. In this context verses IX:32-3 are often cited:

[90] Upadhyaya (ed.), op.cit., pp.2-3.

māṃ hi pārtha vyapāśritya
ye 'pi syuḥ pāpayonayaḥ
striyo vaiśyās tathā śūdrās
te 'pi yānti parāṃ gatim

kiṃ punar brāhmaṇāḥ puṇyā
bkaktā rājarṣayas tathā
anityam asukhaṃ lokam
imaṃ prāpya bhajasva mām

For if they take refuge in Me, son of Pṛthā,
Even those who may be of base origin,
Women, men of the artisan caste, and serfs too,
Even they go to the highest goal.

How much more virtuous brahmans,
And devout royal seers, too!
A fleeting and joyless world
This; having attained it, devote thyself to Me.[91]

The general interpretation of these verses is represented by such comments as those made by Abhinavagupta in the eleventh century A.D., for example, and by S. Radhakrishnan in the twentieth. Abhinavagupta writes:

> Now the verse beginning *māṁ hi*: [In this verse by the expression] *pāpayonayaḥ* ('those born in wicked wombs') are meant animals, birds and reptiles; by *striyaḥ* (women) those that are ignorant, by *vaiśyas* (merchants, etc.) those engaged in the occupation of farming, etc., and by *śūdras* (serfs, etc.) all of those who are excluded from Vedic ritual and dependent on others for a living; even they, resorting to me, worship me indeed. When the (marvellous) deeds of the supremely compassionate God, such as the freeing of the elephant (from the jaws of the crocodile) are heard by the thousand, then what doubt can there be (of the salvation) of those of perverse conduct? Some say that this statement is meant to glorify the *brāhmaṇas* and the *kṣatriyas* and it is not intended to indicate the accessibility of salvation on the part of women, etc. They (who say so), denying the all-embracing power of God with their narrow intellects; being unable to bear the supreme kindheartedness of the supreme lord, going against sentences which clearly state the intending meaning such as 'I hate none and love

[91] Edgerton, op.cit., Part I, pp.94, 95.

> none', 'even if one be terribly depraved' and others; not accepting, on the strength of dualism the non-duality of the essence of God established through a host of irrefutable arguments; not noticing other scriptural contradictions (of theirs); joining issue repeatedly 'How can you say this', 'How can you say this'; with their hearts penetrated and possessed by the supreme prejudice of birth, etc., which has been completely accepted; turning askance their lowered face and eyes because of enmity, dissimulation and embarrassment, prating nonsense before all, – make themselves the butt of ridicule among the people – which serves to explain everything in advance.[92]

And S. Radhakrishnan observes:

> The message of the Gītā is open to all without distinction of race, sex or caste. This verse is not to be regarded as supporting the social customs debarring women and Śūdras from Vedic study. It refers to the view prevalent at the time of the composition of the Gītā. The Gītā does not sanction these social rules. The Gītā gets beyond racial distinctions in its emphasis on spiritual values. Its gospel of love is open to all men and women, persons of all castes as well as those outside caste.[93]

Bhāskara violently disagrees with such an obvious liberal interpretation of the verse.[94] His comments are reproduced at length on account of the extent of departure they represent both from the text and from the traditional exegesis of the text:

> IX:32. Now the verse beginning *mām.* O Arjuna, resorting to me, that is, specially seeking my refuge, even those who are *pāpayoni* or of sinful birth (attain liberation). (The compound *pāpayoni*) means those who are born on account of sin; these of reprehensible origin like women, etc., who are totally debarred from attaining salvation, when (their behaviour is) characterised by following their *svakarma* and carrying out my orders they achieve the supreme, that is, the exalted and excellent state characterised by residence in heaven. This is possible. Contact with me purifies them, just as contact with fire purifies iron. Serve me by following *svadharma* (one's own allotted duties in life). For it has been laid down that one should follow only

[92] Arvind Sharma (tr.), *Abhinavagupta Gitārthasangraha* (Leiden: Brill, 1983), pp.172-3..

[93] S. Radhakrishnan, *The Bhagavadgītā* (New Delhi: Blackie [India], 1974), pp.252-3.

[94] Upadhyaya (ed.), op.cit., pp.205-6.

one's own duties. For the *śūdra* serving others is his natural duty. By serving others and following one's own natural duty a person attains the desired goal by *svakarma.* For the accomplishment of the *puruṣārthas* it is the performance alone which has been laid down (as the means).

Now bringing the laudatory statements (*arthavāda*) to a conclusion it is said:

X:33. The verse beginning with *kim.* Women, etc., who are not eligible, attain to excellent states on seeking refuge in God. Then will the Brahmins and royal sages, of impeccable birth, not attain (those states)? By the word *api* (even) a favourable description of the knowledge of the Brahmins, etc., is instituted through exaggeration by generating the possibility (of even those of sinful birth attaining excellent states). The meaning is not to be taken literally. For example, in expressions such as 'split even the mountain with the head', 'eat even a cooked crow', it is the strength of the person who is asserted; not the (literal) splitting of the mountain. For this is impossible ... Just because (it has been said: 'eat even cooked crow') to glorify what is meant to be done (eaten) does not mean that the forbidden reprehensible cooked crow is not to be condemned. It is not declared to be the meaning that one should consume poison. That is why Jaimini composed the *sūtras* dealing with *arthavāda* (exaggeration). Because *vidhi* (or injunctions) is the one purport (of the Vedas) the exaggerations are meant to laud or to condemn what is recommended or forbidden. That is what is meant, because the sentences expressing *arthavāda* make syntactical sense but in themselves possess no meaning and refer to something else. And as the revered (Kumārila?) Bhaṭṭa has said:

> Explain as *guṇavāda* (praise) that statement not directly applicable – if you wish to understand its meaning – how could it be literally true?

The Vedas declare: 'At an animal sacrifice offer fat as oblation.' In order to establish the obligatory nature of this injunction there is the following explanation: 'Prajāpati extracted (his own) fat, etc.' This is the meaning of the statement: so indeed should the one offering sacrifice offer fat in the fire. When it is said that in the absence of another animal Prajāpati extracted his own fat and performed the sacrifice-offering of fat, the extraction of (his own) fat is imputed to Prajāpati in order to commend the necessity of doing so (i.e. offering fat) at an animal sacrifice. (What of Vedic usage) even in the course of ordinary usage someone sometimes says in order to dissuade someone from eating at the house of an undesirable and wicked fellow 'eat poison but do not eat in his house'. From this exaggeration in ordinary usage it is clear that the eating of poison which is the literal sense is not intended, but rather that through exaggeration one is dissuaded from dining at someone's house.

2.

Bhāskara's commentary affords an interesting preview of what follows. The exegetical manoeuvres employed by him are typical of the classical tradition of Gītā commentary. The role of etymological ingenuity, polemical sparring, textual variation, philosophical predispositions, social horizons, violent exegeses, as well as interpretative felicities, to which we have been introduced in this chapter serve as earnest of what is to come. Yet underlying all this is the abiding conviction that he is offering the 'correct' interpretation of a great religious text, obfuscated by lesser or smaller minds.

CHAPTER FOUR
Śaṅkara

1.

Śaṅkara's commentary on the Gītā is the oldest of which the full text is available.[1] In that sense the scholastic tradition dates from Śaṅkara, who is usually placed in the eighth/ninth century A.D.[2] Because of the eminent position he was to occupy in the philosophical history of India, he is regarded as the putative author of numerous works, but his commentary – the Gītābhāṣya – has generally been accepted by scholars as his own genuine work.[3]

Now Śaṅkara is also the most famous representative of a school of Hindu thought which remained pre-eminent in India for centuries and which continues to be one of the most influential schools of Hindu philosophy even today – namely, that of Advaita Vedānta.[4] His commentary tries to reconcile the tenets of his own school with the teachings of the Gītā – a situation which arose repeatedly in the course of the history of Hinduism. That his is the oldest extant commentary and that he is the first formulator of a philosophical system naturally inspires the question: did he use the Gītā, to some extent, as a building block for his system, along with the Upaniṣads and the Brahmasūtra, or did he merely use it as a vehicle to propagate his preconceived ideas? The Hindu philosophical tradition inclines towards the first view,[5] modern critical scholarship towards

[1] S. Radhakrishnan, *The Gītā* (New Delhi: Blackie [India], 1974 [first published 1948]), p.16.

[2] T.M.P. Mahadevan, *Outlines of Hinduism* (Bombay: Chetana, 1971), p.141.

[3] See above, Chapter One, note 7.

[4] F. Coppleston, *Religion and the One: Philosophies East and West* (New York: Crossroad, 1982), p.72.

[5] Maharishi Mahesh Yogi, *Bhagavad-Gītā* (Harmondsworth: Penguin, 1969) Preface.

the second.[6] The question will need to be reopened at the end of this chapter after we have examined the commentary in some detail.

Before we embark on such an investigation, however, it might be useful to outline the system of thought Śaṅkara upheld, namely that of Advaita Vedānta. Briefly, his system postulates that the ultimate reality, Brahman, is the whole and sole reality and is free from any distinguishing attributes. 'Śaṅkara puts the entire philosophy of Advaita in half a verse where he says: *Brahman* is real: the world is an illusory appearance; the individual soul (*jīva*) is *Brahman* alone, not other. The non-duality of *Brahman*, the non-reality of the world, and the non-difference of the soul from *Brahman* – these constitute the teaching of Advaita."[7] To this may be added the fact that the empirical world does represent an order of reality,[8] though not the ultimate one, and the realisation of the identity of one's self, or *ātman*, with *Brahman* confers salvation right here in this life (*jīvanmukti*).[9]

The manner in which Śaṅkara's philosophical position tends to influence his interpretation of the Gītā may be summarised thus to provide an initial point of illumination:

> Śaṅkara holds that, while action is essential as a means for the purification of the mind, when wisdom is attained action falls away. Wisdom and action are mutually opposed as light and darkness. He rejects the view of *jñānakarmasamuccaya*. He believes that Vedic rites are meant for those who are lost in ignorance and desire. The aspirants for salvation should renounce the performance of ritual works. The aim of the *Gītā*, according to Śaṅkara, is the complete suppression of the world of becoming in which all action occurs though his own life is an illustration of activity carried on, after the attainment of wisdom.[10]

2.

We may now turn to a detailed examination of Śaṅkara's commentary. So great has been its influence that it has led R.C. Zaehner to lament that modern commentators are 'conditioned by

[6] Eliot Deutsch and J.A.B. van Buitenen, *A Source Book of Advaita Vedānta* (Honolulu: University Press of Hawaii, 1971), p.213.

[7] Mahadevan, op.cit., p.141. [8] ibid., p.147.

[9] ibid., pp.149-50. (For a concise summary of Advaitic teachings, see Deutsch and van Buitenen, op.cit., Chapter 20).

[10] Radhakrishnan, op.cit., p.17.

the most ancient and the most authoritative of the medieval commentaries, that of the founder of the extreme school of Vedāntin non-dualism, Śaṅkara. Meanwhile the commentaries of the "modified non-dualist" Rāmānuja, so much nearer in spirit to the Gītā, and of the dualist Madhva and his successors had largely fallen into neglect.'[11]

The commentary deserves serious study for its influence, if for no other reason. Therefore the present section will offer a critical synopsis of the commentary; in the next section the commentary will be examined in the light of certain ideas typical of Śaṅkara's thought, and in the final section an assessment will be offered.

We may now turn to an examination of those parts of Śaṅkara's commentary where he enriches, or seems to depart from, the plain meaning of the text, or where he seems to bend the semantics to suit his own philosophical predispositions or, contrariwise, alerts us to the philosophical depth of a verse which may have gone unnoticed.

Śaṅkara shows his hand early in his commentarial enterprise, in his gloss on II:21:

vedāvināśinaṃ nityaṃ
ya enam ajam avyayam
kathaṃ sa puruṣaḥ pārtha
kaṃ ghātayati hanti kam[12]

Who knows as indestructible and eternal
This unborn, imperishable one,
That man, son of Pṛthā, how
Can he slay or cause to slay – whom?[13]

In trying to explain 'Can he slay or cause to slay – whom?', Śaṅkara resorts to his favourite philosophical position that 'the enlightened man is identical with the Self and is therefore incapable of any action whatsoever'.[14] It is true that the Gītā subsequently does make a statement to this effect (V:8, 13), but not in the context of slaying and not yet. Śaṅkara has clearly over-interpreted the verse. The 'meaning is simply that when a man understands the invulnerable nature of the Self he knows that he cannot slay it'.[15]

[11] R.C. Zaehner, *The Bhagavad-Gītā* (Oxford: Clarendon Press, 1969), p.3.

[12] Kees Bolle, *The Bhagavadgītā: a New Translation* (Berkeley: University of California Press, 1979), p.22.

[13] Franklin Edgerton, *The Bhagavad Gītā*, Part I (Cambridge, Massachusetts: Harvard University Press, 1944), p.19.

[14] W. Douglas, P. Hill, *The Bhagavadgītā* (Oxford University Press, 1969), p.86 n.5.

[15] ibid.

Similarly, Śaṅkara's commitment to the concept of the pure *ātman* seems to lead him into under-interpreting the word *ātman* in III:27:

prakṛteḥ kriyamāṇāni
guṇaiḥ karmāṇi sarvaśaḥ
ahaṃkāravimūḍhātmā
kartāham iti manyate[16]

Performed by material nature's
Strands are actions, altogether;
He whose soul is deluded by the I-faculty
Imagines 'I am the agent'.[17]

Zaehner notes here that Śaṅkara 'unnecessarily glosses – *ātmā* as *antaḥ-karaṇa*, "The internal sense", that is, the mind. In the Sāṃkhya system and in the Gītā the [individual] self or "person" may and does experience anything and everything so long as it is in contact with material Nature (13.20). Self and psychosomatic organism are according to the *Sāṃkhya-kārikā* (21) like a lame man mounted on the shoulders of a blind man – the one sees and the other acts; spirit sees and experiences, but it is the psychosomatic organism which is a microcosm of material Nature that alone acts.'[18]

In viewing the Gītā as a harmonious whole in the light of one's philosophy, one may tend to overlook thematic transitions which occur within the text. Śaṅkara seems to do that when the theme of incarnation is introduced in the Fourth Chapter. It is true that in his Preface to his commentary on the Gītā he comments on Kṛṣṇa's status as an *avatāra*,[19] like Rāmānuja.[20] But when the key text[21] appears and is followed by IV:9:

My wondrous births and actions
Whoso knows thus as they truly are,
On leaving the body, to rebirth
He goes not; to Me he goes, Arjuna![22]

[16] Bolle, op.cit., p.44.
[17] Edgerton, op.cit., Part I, p.39.
[18] Zaehner, op.cit., p.171.
[19] *Śrīśāṅkaragranthāvaliḥ*, Samputa 8 (Śrīraṅgam: Śrīvāṇīvilāsamudrāyantrālayaḥ, no date), p.2.
[20] J.A.B. van Buitenen, *Rāmānuja on the Bhagavadgītā* (Delhi: Motilal Barnarsidass, 1968 [first reprint]), p.47.
[21] *Bhagavadgītā* IV:7-8.
[22] Edgerton, op.cit., p.185.

Śaṅkara treats the point rather skimpily. As Zaehner notes:

> Just as in the last chapter (3:17) the ascetic ideal of the man 'in self alone content' suddenly obtrudes itself into Krishna's discourse on the desirability of leading an active life, presumably to serve as a reminder that action must always be balanced by contemplation, so too here, *pace* Śaṅkara, a new idea (or rather two) is introduced. By meditating on Krishna's incarnation and his deeds both as God and as man, one comes to know Him as the God who acts, the Lord of history as Protestant theologians would put it. Secondly in 4.10, as if to restore the balance, the ascetic ideal of detachment and contemplative wisdom is once again proclaimed: as in 2.55-72 and 3.37-43 desire and anger, passion and hatred must be put aside. The result, however, is not the Buddhist Nirvāna 'which is Brahman too' of 2.72 but access to Krishna's 'mode of being' as yet undefined. Finally, in 4.11 the idea of *bhakti* is introduced for the first time (for in 4.3 the word *bhakta* means little more than a loyal friend) meaning here the love which God returns to his devotees. Thus by contemplating God's activity one knows God as agent, by assimilating oneself to Him one participates in his mode of being which, though at present undefined, must surely mean his timeless Being which is in fact Nirvāna, and by humbly aproaching Him, one wins his love. This, in three stanzas, may be said to sum up the whole teaching of the Gītā.[23]

It is interesting how both ancient and modern commentators claim to be able to reduce the teachings of the Gītā to a few key verses.

Śaṅkara's preference for *jñāna-yoga* affects his glosses in the Fourth Chapter as well. We may begin with IV:24:

brahmārpaṇaṃ brahma havir
   brahmāgnau brahmaṇā hutam
brahmaiva tena gantavyaṃ
   brahmakarmasamādhinā[24]

The (sacrificial) presentation is Brahman; Brahman is the oblation;
   In the (sacrificial) fire of Brahman it is poured by Brahman;
Just to Brahman must he go,
   Being concentrated upon the (sacrificial) action that is Brahman.[25]

[23] Zaehner, op.cit., p.185.
[24] Bolle, op.cit., p.56.
[25] Edgerton, op.cit., Part I, p.47.

This is a problematical verse, but one's exegetical skill can be seen in how well one's interpretation of it is sustained by the succeeding verses. According to Śaṅkara, 'the knowledge of one who has given up all rites and renounced all action is represented as a sacrifice; to such a man everything connected with his "sacrifice" is Brahman; the idea of Brahman has replaced all idea of accessories. After 24, which simply represents *jñāna* as a *yajña*, Kṛṣṇa proceeds to enumerate other kinds of sacrifice with a view to extol *jñāna*.'[26] But this 'forced interpretation of Śaṅkara breaks down' when we consider verses 25 and 31. The second half of IV:25 runs as follows: *brahmāgnāv apare yajñaṁ yajñenaivopajuhvati*[27] ('In the [sacrificial] fire of Brahman, others the sacrifice offer up by the sacrifice itself').[28] Now Śaṅkara explains thus: ' "In the fire of Brahman others offer the self by the self", making *yajña*=*ātman*; i.e. "know their conditioned self as identical with the unconditioned Brahman". But he has already explained this list of *yajñas* as material, in contrast to *jñānayajña*; so he has to add that this *jñānayajña* is placed here "with a view to extol it"; which means nothing.'[29]

The fact that sacrifice is being offered by sacrifice into the sacrifice tends to lend a certain monistic colour to the verse. But the entire statement can be clearly understood purely in terms of the ritual fire sacrifice thus:

> As the messenger to the gods, Agni linked the worlds of gods and men. He also linked these worlds with nature by the various physical forms of fire. Agni was often compared to the sun, kindled by the gods in heaven as by men on earth. Agni was present in the heavenly waters, from which he was brought down by lightning, and in the aerial or atmospheric waters, where he was referred to as the shining thunder. Brought down from his high abode in rain, Agni was latent in stream and ponds until he passed into plants, from which fire again could be kindled. Completing the cycle, Agni in plants was seen as offering himself to himself in fire, rising again in smoke to the clouds.[30]

[26] Hill, op.cit., p.106, n.3. Zaehner notes that Śaṅkara 'is unusually obscure on this passage. What he seems to be saying is that everything *is* Brahman in so far as it *is*, but in so far as anything shows diversity of any sort it is as non-existent as the silver for which a man may mistake mother-of-pearl. On his realising the mistake the "silver" is simply annihilated. So with the phenomenal world, once one has realised Brahman, the One, it is seen to be simply nothing. All this is very far from the thought of the Gītā.'

[27] Bolle, op.cit., p.56. [28] Edgerton, op.cit., Part I, p.47.

[29] Hill, op.cit., p.107, n.2.

[30] Thomas J. Hopkins, *The Hindu Religious Tradition* (Belmond, Cal.: Dickinson, 1971), p.18.

The first line of IV:31 provides another example of the difficulties Śaṅkara gets into by plugging *jñāna* excessively. The line runs: *yajñaśiṣṭāmṛtabhujo yānti brahma sanātanam*[31] ('Those who eat the nectar of the leavings of the sacrifice go to the eternal Brahman').[32] Here the ritual content is obvious; it cannot be spiritualised; in any case it is not *jñānised* by Śaṅkara, which then leaves him stuck with the statement that the performance of ritual sacrifice leads to the eternal Brahman – a position which violates his philosophical presuppositions. So he is compelled to comment 'in course of time, not at once, as we should understand for the sake of consistency',[33] Śaṅkara's, not the Gītā's; and the 'weakness of his interpretation' is revealed.[34]

The first line of IV:32 has been exegetically somewhat problematical. The whole verse is cited for convenience before it is analysed:

evaṃ bahuvidhā yajñā
vitatā brahmaṇo mukhe
karmajān viddhi tān sarvān
evaṃ jñātvā vimoksyase[35]

Thus many kinds of sacrifice
Are spread out in the face of Brahman
Know that they all spring from action!
Knowing this thou shalt be freed.[36]

The expression *vitatā brahmaṇo mukhe* ('are spread out in the face of Brahman') is the part that causes the difficulties. Śaṅkara takes *brahman* to mean the Veda, so that the expression, according to him, means known through the Vedas (*vedadvāreṇa avagamyamānāḥ*).[37] Almost all modern commentators are united in rejecting Śaṅkara's interpretation. Edgerton regards it as 'most implausible',[38] while Hill thinks it 'may be definitely rejected'.[39] Zaehner recounts various suggestions and comments that 'all these interpretations are plausible enough except, perhaps, Śaṅkara's.[40] He also notes that

[31] Edgerton, op.cit., Part I, p.48. [32] ibid., p.49.
[33] Hill, op.cit., p.106, n.3. [34] ibid.
[35] Bolle, op.cit., p.58.
[36] Edgerton, op.cit., Part I, p.49.
[37] *Śrīśaṅkaragranthāvaliḥ*, Sampuṭa 8, p.122.
[38] Edgerton, op.cit., Part I, p.182.
[39] Hill, op.cit., p.109, n.4.
[40] Zaehner, op.cit., p.195.

Śaṅkara takes *evaṁ jñātvā vimoksyase* 'to mean that once you realise that sacrifice, works, and everything to do with them are wholly foreign to the Self, you will win release from the bondage of phenomenal existence (*saṁsāra*). This is very far indeed from what the Gītā says. Rather, Brahman which both is the source of the sacrifice and *is* the sacrifice acts as a link between "this world" of time and "the other" world of timelessness.'[41]

Before we take leave of Chapter Four two parting comments may be made. IV:13 is regarded as a fairly simple if significant verse. It runs as follows:

cāturvarnyaṇ mayā sṛṣṭaṃ
guṇakarmavibhāgaśaḥ
tasya kartāram api māṃ
viddhy akartāram avyayam[42]

The four-caste-system was created by Me
With distinction of Strands and actions (appropriate to each);
Altho I am the doer of this,
Know Me as one that eternally does no act.[43]

Notwithstanding its simplicity, some interesting points emerge in the light of Śaṅkara's gloss. First, he does not cite the Puruṣasūkta in the context, as he might be expected to.[44] Secondly, he glosses the compound *guṇakarma-vibhāga* elaborately, establishing definite connections between the three *guṇas* and the four *varṇas*; as he would do again in glossing XVIII:41. But in XVIII:41 he also detaches *svabhāva* from the *guṇas* but retains its link with *karma*, which is curious. Thirdly, he seems to imply that the *varṇa* system obtains only among humans.[45] Now this comment raises two points: already the Buddha is said to have indicated in the Pali canon that there was no *varṇa* system among the Greeks, and by the time of Śaṅkara there must have been enough evidence for him to wonder if *varṇa* was a universal human institution. The other point moves in an opposite direction: in some circles it was believed that even superhuman beings and subhuman objects have *varṇa*. So why is Śaṅkara so restrictive? The points are indeed contradictory, and they seem to expose a certain vulnerability in Śaṅkara's position. Finally Kṛṣṇa,

[41] ibid. [42] Bolle, op.cit., p.52.
[43] Edgerton, op.cit., Part I, p.45.
[44] See *Ṛg Veda* X:90.12.
[45] *Śrīśaṅkaragranthāvaliḥ*, Sampuṭa 8, p.102.

after claiming to have created the four *varṇas*, adds that even though he is the doer he is not the doer. This, of course, is an excellent opportunity for Śaṅkara to press the two levels of truth doctrine to advantage, which he does. Zaehner's comment here is interesting:

> From the empirical point of view – the point of view of *māyā* – God is the only true agent and therefore, in accordance with the law of *karma* which 'binds' the agent to and by what He does, He must himself be 'bound', that is, limited (since to define is to make finite); He must be associated with the result of what He does. All this is true enough (I am paraphrasing Śaṅkara), but from the absolute point of view God, being by definition changeless, cannot be regarded as an agent: He does not act because in eternity there is no such thing as action. This is how Śaṅkara interprets the passage. It is an over-simplification as any purely logical and philosophical explanation of religious truth is bound to be; for religion is of its very nature paradoxical and cannot be expressed in any logical formula. Hinduism in particular resists any 'either/or' approach, it is essentially a religion of 'both/and'.[46]

The other parting comment concerns IV:33:

śreyān dravyamayād yajñāj
jñānayajñaḥ paraṃtapa
sarvaṃ karmākhilaṃ pārtha
jñāne parisamāpyate[47]

Better than sacrifice that consists of substance
Is the sacrifice of knowledge, scorcher of the foe.
All action without remainder, son of Pṛthā,
Is completely ended in knowledge.[48]

It seems only fair to point out that sometimes Śaṅkara may have been unduly criticised. For instance, Hill refers to Śaṅkara here as classing all aforementioned sacrifices as material (except those which he interpreted gnostically) and then saying that '*jñāna* is extolled as compared with these'.[49] He adds: 'But the "sacrifice as knowledge" here means "any one of these forms of sacrifice, provided it be performed with knowledge", and such sacrifice is said to be superior

[46] Zaehner, op.cit., p.187.
[47] Bolle, op.cit., p.58.
[48] Edgerton, op.cit., Part I, p.49.
[49] Hill, op.cit., p.110, n.1.

to "mere material sacrifice" that is nothing else; because "every work comes to complete fulfilment, if it be performed with knowledge".'[50]

A look at the text of the verse suggests that Śaṅkara's interpretation flows naturally from the text and Hill's seems forced.

The Fifth Chapter of the Gītā is a relatively short one and need not detain us long, but even here Śaṅkara's own pet ideas influence his interpretation. This is apparent from his gloss on the very first verse of the chapter which runs:

saṃnyāsaṃ karmaṇāṃ Kṛṣṇa
punar yogaṃ ca śaṃsasi
yac chreya etayor ekaṃ
tan me brūhi suniścitam[51]

Renunciation of actions, Kṛṣṇa
And again discipline Thou approvest;
Which one is the better of these two,
That tell me definitely.[52]

Śaṅkara is 'unwilling to allow any slight to be put on the *saṁnyāsa* of the *jñānayogin*'[53] and 'argues that the word', namely, *saṁnyāsa* 'in this chapter means no more than a partial renunciation of certain works, applicable only to the unenlightened man'.[54]

The same situation arises in Śaṅkara's gloss on *yogayukto munir brahma nacireṇādhigacchati* in V:6 ('Disciplined in discipline, to Brahman the sage Goes in no long time').[55] Zaehner notes that Śaṅkara glosses the phrase *brahma adhigacchati* 'oddly' thus:

> 'Brahman means renunciation because it is characterised by the attainment of intuitive apprehension (*jñāna*) of the highest Self.' The phrase, however, can scarcely be separated from the *brahma* ... *gantavyam*, 'to Brahman must he go', of 4.24 where, as we have seen, Brahman is the eternal seen as present in the sacrifice. Sacrifice is based on works (*karma*, 3.15) and hence it is only natural that the *yoga-yukta*, the 'man integrated, etc. by the Yoga *of works*' should go to the Brahman which is the link between works and 'imperishable

[50] ibid.
[51] Bolle, op.cit., p.62.
[52] Edgerton, op.cit., Part I, p.53.
[53] Hill, op.cit., p.112, n.1. [54] ibid.
[55] Edgerton, op.cit., Part I, p.53.

wisdom', before he finally expires in the 'Nirvāna which is Brahman too' (5.24-26 where this concept which we had already encountered in 2.72 is more fully elaborted). That 'Brahman' does not here mean the 'highest Self' of Ś. or even the 'self' of R. seems clear not only from 4.24 (the last time the word was used) but also from 5.10 (q.v.) where it clearly means the divine *in operation*, not the 'fixed, still state of Brahman' of 2.72. This will only be reached later.[56]

Two verses of the Fifth Chapter are slightly problematical because they use words usually applied to God as applying to the individual soul. 'Certainly the use of the word *prabhu* for the individual self is unusual but far less shocking than *īśvara* used in the same sense in 15:8.'[57] What *is* unusual, however, is the use of words which normally stand for God in the sense of soul in successive verses (V:14-15):

na kartṛtvaṃ na karmāṇi
lokasya sṛjati prabhuḥ
na karmaphalasaṃyogaṃ
svabhāvas tu pravartate

nādatte kasyacit pāpaṃ
na caiva sukṛtaṃ vibhuḥ
ajñānenāvṛtaṃ jñānaṃ
tena muhyanti jantavaḥ[58]

Neither agency nor actions
Of the (people of the) world does the Lord (soul) instigate,
Nor the conjunction of actions with their fruits;
But inherent nature operates (in all this).

He does not receive (the effect of) any one's sin,
Nor yet (of) good deeds, the Lord (soul);
Knowledge is obscured by ignorance;
By that creatures are deluded.[59]

Śaṅkara seems to take the word *prabhu* in the sense of the individual soul and *vibhu* in the sense of God in the text. He seems to be right in the first case and probably wrong in the second. In V:14

[56] Zaehner, op.cit., p.204. Ś=Śaṅkara; R=Rāmānuja.
[57] ibid., p.208.
[58] Bolle, op.cit., p.66. [59] Edgerton, op.cit., Part I, p.55.

he 'identifies the self with the "embodied [self]" by which he presumably means the empirical self viewed from the empirical point of view. This fits in with his commentary on the previous line where he compares the self to a monarch and the bodily faculties to his subjects. R. also interprets *prabhuḥ* as meaning the individual self.'[60] But in V:15, in glossing *vibhuḥ* Śaṅkara switches from one level to another and 'attacks devotional religion as being ultimately pointless',[61] taking *vibhuḥ* in the sense of God. So although 'commentators differ in their interpretation of these words *prabhu* and *vibhu*' and some take them to refer 'to the Supreme Lord of the world; some to the individual self already spoken in 13', 'it seems clear from the context that' Rāmānuja is 'right in referring the words to the individual self (*jīvātman*)'.[62]

As with the beginning of the Fifth Chapter, Śaṅkara finds himself having to think his way through the beginning-verse of the Sixth Chapter to accommodate it within his own philosophical perimeter. The verse runs as follows (VI:1):

anāśritaḥ karmaphalaṃ
kāryaṃ karma karoti yaḥ
sa saṃnyāsī ca yogī ca
na niragnir na cākriyaḥ.[63]

Not interested in the fruit of action,
Who does action that is required (by religion),
He is the possessor of both renunciation and discipline (of action);
Not he who builds no sacred fires and does no (ritual) acts.[64]

Śaṅkara 'finds difficulty in reconciling this very plain statement with his own doctrine. He compels the verse to mean that the terms *saṁnyāsin* and *yogin* may be applied to the *karmayogin* by way of courtesy or praise, and not *only* to the "fireless man who does no work".'[65]

Like the previous verse, the sixth verse of the Sixth Chapter is quite straightforward (VI:6):

[60] Zaehner, op.cit., p.208. R=Rāmānuja.
[61] ibid., p.209.
[62] Hill, op.cit., p.114.
[63] Bolle, op.cit., p.70.
[64] Edgerton, op.cit., Part I, p.61.
[65] Hill, op.cit., p.117, n.1. Hill also adds that the Manusmṛti 'forbids the *saṁnyāsin* to perform any sacrifice or ceremonial act, or even to keep a fire for the purpose of cooking food' (ibid.).

bandhur ātmātmanas tasya
yenātmaivātmanā jitaḥ
anātmanas tu śatrutve
vartetātmaiva śatruvat[66]

The self is a friend to that self
By which self the very self is subdued;
But to him that does not possess the self, in enmity
Will abide his very self, like an enemy.[67]

The fact, however, that several *ātmans* are mentioned, or, perhaps more accurately, that the word *ātman* is mentioned several times, creates what Hill calls 'this riddle of *ātman*' which 'leaves room for a variety of interpretations'.[68] The question then is to decide which of the various interpretations best clarifies the meaning of the verse. Now Śaṅkara 'does not especially distinguish between the higher Self and the lower Self, but emphasises the fact that every man is his own friend or enemy and is independent of other men'.[69] This is a fine sentiment but not the one, it seems, intended here. Śaṅkara also glosses *anātmanas* as 'those who have not subdued themselves'[70] and Zaehner sees 'no reason why it should not be taken literally'[71] as meaning 'bereft of self'.[72]

> The 'carnal' self which includes what we would call 'soul', which is conditioned by its works in this and previous lives, and which transmigrates, can be 'lost' or 'destroyed' (2.63) by the combined assaults of desire, anger, and greed (16.21) – an eternal alienation from the centre of its being and therefore from God (16.20). Such a person is literally *anātman*, 'Bereft of self'. In Christian terms he is damned. 'Hell', as the modern American Trappist monk, Thomas Merton, puts it in what must be one of the most pregnant footnotes of all time – ' "Hell" can be described as a perpetual alienation from our true being, our true self, which is in God' (*New Seeds of Contemplation*, London, Burns and Oates, 1962, p.6).[73]

The thirteenth verse of the Sixth Chapter contains an expression which has caused some difference of opinion among commentators. It is: *saṁprekṣya nāsikāgram svam*[74] ('gazing at the tip of his own

[66] Bolle, op.cit., p.70.
[67] Edgerton, op.cit., Part I, p.61.
[68] Hill, op.cit., p.118, n.1.
[69] ibid., p.118, n.1.
[70] Zaehner, op.cit., p.221.
[71] ibid.
[72] ibid.
[73] ibid.
[74] Bolle, op.cit., p.72.

nose').[75] The question is: is this fixing of the gaze on the tip of the nose to be taken literally or metaphorically? Śaṅkara seems to favour the latter view, for he 'supplies "as it were", and says that the phrase means only "fixing the eyesight within" '.[76] Hill, however, thinks that 'there is no doubt that the physical posture was literally recommended'.[77] Zaehner goes on to elaborate that 'by giving his gaze at the tip of his nose or between the eyebrows (5.27) the Yogin matches one-pointedness of mind with one-pointedness of vision'.[78] Although Śaṅkara could still be right, and is certainly within his rights in sugesting a metaphorical understanding, it seems that the use of the word *svam* (own) tilts the scale in favour of the literal interpretation.

There is a quartet of verses in the Sixth Chapter which may next claim our attention. They are religiously inspired but philosophically difficult to handle (VI:29-32):

sarvabhūtastham ātmānaṃ
sarvabhūtāni cātmani
īkṣate yogayuktātmā
sarvatra samadarśanaḥ

yo māṃ paśyati sarvatra
sarvaṃ ca mavi paśyati
tasyahaṃ na praṇaśyami
sa ca me na praṇaśyati

sarvabhūtasthitaṃ yo māṃ
bhajaty ekatvam āsthitaḥ
sarvathā vartamāno 'pi
sa yogī mayi vartate

ātmaupamyena sarvatra
samaṃ paśyati yo 'rjuna
sukhaṃ vā yadi vā duḥkhaṃ
sa yogī paramo mataḥ[79]

Himself as in all beings,
And all beings in himself,
Sees he whose self is disciplined in discipline,
Who sees the same in all things.

[75] Edgerton, op.cit., Part I, p.63.
[76] Hill, op.cit., p.119, n.2. [77] ibid.
[78] Zaehner, op.cit., p.225.
[79] Bolle, op.cit., pp.76, 78.

Who sees Me in all,
And sees all in Me,
For him I am not lost,
And he is not lost for Me.

Me as abiding in all beings whoso
Reveres, adopting (the belief in) one-ness,
Tho abiding in any possible condition,
That disciplined man abides in Me.

By comparison with himself, in all (beings)
Whoso sees the same, Arjuna,
Whether it be pleasure or pain,
He is deemed the supreme disciplined man.[80]

Here the difficulties they cause for Śaṅkara may be noted first. Verse 30 states how neither God nor the devotee are lost to each other. 'This, as Ś(aṅkara) himself points out, means that neither God "disappears" from the sight of the integrated self nor does the integrated self disappear from the sight of God "because He and I are one Self and one's self is always dear to [one] self". But if that is so, how can one speak of "vision" which implies duality?'.[81] Zaehner goes on to cite Rāmānuja, adding his comments:

> But if that is so, how can one speak of 'vision' which implies duality? R. comments: 'He sees that all self-stuff as it is in itself (*svarūpeṇa*) and after it has shaken off good and evil, is the same in Me', that is, 'untrammelled wisdom' (on 6.31). This seems to me to miss the point: 'all beings' are not obliterated in God, nor is God obliterated in 'the All'; hence neither is 'lost' or 'destroyed'. That is what the Gītā says, and it is the great divide between the 'pantheistic' and 'theistic' portions of the poem.[82]

Verse 32 is of some interest for assessing Śaṅkara as an exegete. The verse speaks of the Gītā's version of the golden and silver rule, if by the golden rule is meant the exhortation that we should do unto others as we would have done unto ourselves and by the silver rule is meant the exhortation that we should not do unto others what we would not have done to us. The Gītā here offers the platinum rule: use yourself as the yardstick, whichever way you would. Treat others the same way as you would yourself. Now Zaehner remarks:

[80] Edgerton, op.cit., Part I, p.67.
[81] Zaehner, op.cit., p.235. [82] ibid., p.235.

> This 'sameness' the integrated man no longer receives on trust from authority, but sees to be true with his own spiritual eyes. Both Ś. and R. give this a humanitarian twist (oddly perhaps in the case of Ś. who never tires of telling us that both good and evil actions, both righteousness and unrighteousness, bind), and say that by analogy with oneself one sees that what is pleasant or painful to oneself must also be pleasant or painful to others, and that one should therefore refrain from harming them. This scarcely seems to fit in with the doctrine that Krishna had preached from the very beginning, namely, that it is impossible to hurt the embodied self since it is of its very nature inviolate (2.12-30).[83]

Zaehner here seems to be off the mark in treating Śaṅkara's comments as odd. For Bhagavadgītā XIII:28 is similar in spirit and more explicit. It speaks of one who 'harms not himself (in others) by himself', a good paraphrase of *ātmaupamya* here. Edgerton's remarks (see note 83) regarding that verse seem more apropos than Zaehner's.

There are two verses in the Seventh Chapter on which Śaṅkara's glosses have invited comment. The first is VII:4:

bhūmir āpo 'nalo vāyuḥ
khaṃ mano buddhir eva ca
ahaṃkāra itīyaṃ me
bhinnā prakṛtir aṣṭadhā[84]

Earth, water, fire, wind,
Ether, thought-organ, and consciousness,
And I-faculty: thus My
Nature is divided eight-fold.[85]

[83] Zaehner, op.cit., p.237. Ś=Śaṅkara; R=Rāmānuja. Edgerton writes: 'In this verse, which I think most interpreters have failed to understand (Paul Deussen has it right), we have in my opinion the clearest evidence that the "Golden Rule" was not only fully accepted in Hinduism, but provided with a metaphysical proof (which it seems to lack in Christianity). It is a logical deduction from the Upaniṣad doctrine mentioned above, which has always been widely accepted in India, that the soul or real self of every man is identical with that of the universe ("that art thou", *tat tvam asi*). It follows, since things which are equal to the same thing are equal to each other, that one must identify his own self with all other selves. If he harms others, he harms himself. This conclusion seems inevitable, if one accepts the premises. That is why the supremely moral man, even while he lives by the ordinary norm, "identifies his self with the self of all beings" and "delights in the welfare of all beings" (Gītā 5.7, 24). Note also that in higher forms of Hinduism, animals are included under the Golden Rule. The law of *ahiṃsā*, "non-injury" to any living thing, is mentioned several times in the Gītā.' (Franklin Edgerton, *The Beginnings of Indian Philosophy* [Cambridge, Massachusetts: Harvard University Press, 1965] p.242, n.1).

[84] Bolle, op.cit., p.84.

[85] Edgerton, op.cit., Part I, p.73.

The verse deals with the eight-fold nature of Kṛṣṇa.[86] These are enumerated as (1) *bhūmi* (earth); (2) *ap* (water); (3) *anala* (fire); (4) *vāyu* (air); (5) *kha* (space); (6) *manas* (mind); (7) *buddhi* (intellect) and (8) *ahaṁkāra* (egoity). The fact that my translations diverge from those cited above serves to alert the reader to the problem. Now according to Hill 'this eight-fold division corresponds to the ordinary Sāṁkhya diversion of *vyaktā prakṛtī*. The five elements here mentioned stand for the subtle and the gross elements; mind stands for itself and all the organs of sense and action.'[87]

SĀṄKHYA PSYCHOLOGY[88]

PRAKṚTI
(undifferentiated primal matter)
↓
Buddhi/Mahat
(the suprapersonal potentiality of experiences)
↓
Ahaṅkāra
(egoity: a function appropriating the data of consciousness and wrongly assigning them to *puruṣa*)
↓

the five jñānendriya (the faculties of sense)	*manas* (the faculty of thought)	*the five jñānendriya* (the faculties of sense)	*the five-tan-mātra* (the subtle, primary elements: realised as the inner, subtle counterparts of the five sense experiences, viz., sound, touch, colour-shape, flavour, smell: *śabda, sparśa, rūpa, rāsa, gandha*); *parama-aṇu* (subtle atoms: realised in the experiences of the subtle body); *sthūla-bhūtāni* (the five gross elements, ether, air, fire, water, earth, constituting the gross body and the visible tangible world: realised in sense experiences)

[86] It may be compared with the eight-fold nature of Śiva; see M.R. Kale (ed.), *The Abhijñānaśākuntalam of Kālidāsa* (Delhi: Motilal Banarsidass, 1980), pp.3-5.

[87] Hill, op.cit., p.126, n.1.

[88] Joseph Campbell (ed.), *Philosophies of India* by Heinrich Zimmer (New York: Meridian Books, 1964), p.327.

In terms of this chart, according to Hill, the following elements are covered by the Gītā: the five subtle and gross elements (the list standing for both), the five faculties of action and the five faculties of sense – both subsumed under mind – the faculty of thought, *manas*; plus Reason (*buddhi*) and Individuation (*ahaṅkāra*). Thus, with the mention of *prakṛti*, the whole chart is covered. According to Hill Śaṅkara 'compels *manas* to stand for *ahaṁkāra* and *ahaṁkāra* for *avyakta* together with *avidyā*; he explains "my Nature" as the *māyā* of *īśvara*'.[89] It is difficult to avoid the impression, in reading Śaṅkara's gloss,[90] that he is going one step ahead in the identification. But why is he doing it? It is hard to say, but we may be able to hazard an informed guess by examining the concept of the 'eight-fold *prakṛti*'. Dasgupta relates the twenty-four categories to the eight thus. 'From other points of view, the categories may be said to be twenty-four only, viz. the ten senses (five cognitive and five conative), *manas*, the five objects of senses and the eight-fold *prakṛti* (*prakṛti, mahat, ahamkāra* and the five elements)'.[91] The following reduced-to-size diagram may help sum up the situation:[92]

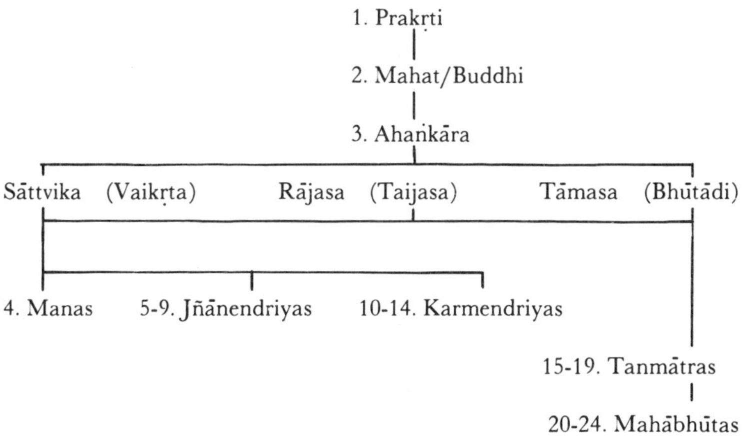

It is now clear what is happening. By identifying *manas* with *ahaṅkāra*, Śaṅkara is making the eight-fold pattern as mentioned in

[89] Hill, op.cit., p.126, n.1. Zaehner seems to be of little help here (op.cit., p.245).
[90] *Śrīśāṅkaragranthāvaliḥ*, Samputa 8, p.184.
[91] Surendranath Dasgupta, *A History of Indian Philosophy*, Vol.I (Cambridge University Press, 1922), p.213.
[92] Mahadevan, op.cit., p.121. I have added the term *buddhi* after *mahat*.

the verse correspond to the standard description of eight-fold *prakṛti*. There are two complications, however, even after we recognise that '*prakṛti* is regarded as containing eight elements (*prakṛtiścāṣṭādhātukī*), viz. *avyakta, mahat, ahaṁkāra*, and five other elements'.[93] First, are the eight forms inclusive or exclusive of *prakṛti*? Śaṅkara makes *prakṛti* stand outside them, as *ayakta* is given a separate status. We could, however, maintain that *avyakta* is 'manifested *prakṛti*',[94] but Śaṅkara clearly distinguishes between the *ayakta* and *prakṛti* in the gloss. Secondly, the five elements are normally identified with the gross elements, whereas Śaṅkara identifies them with the *tanmātras*, or subtle elements. Caraka, in his generally neglected treatment of Sāṅkhya philosophy 'does not mention the *tanmātras* at all'.[95]

It may not be out of place to reflect on why these Śāṅkhyan lists cause so much trouble. M. Hiriyanna's explanation here seems to be fairly persuasive. He thinks that the Upaniṣads take an integral view of nature and spirit in as much as they see matter or nature evolving out of spirt (*brahma-pariṇāmavāda*). But with regard to Śāṅkhyan dualism:

> Is there any explanation of this glaring discrepancy? It appears possible to explain it in two ways: The first is to assume a spiritual element immanent in *prakṛti* as a whole, which prompts and completely guides its evolutionary course from within. It would not then be nature that 'wills' the salvation of *puruṣa* but spirit or, if we like to put it so, spirit together with nature that does so. This assumption would satisfactorily account for the rational order discoverable in nature. Life is a struggle to attain true freedom eventually; and, if man pursues lower values at first, it is due to his ignorance of the ultimate truth. But that would be the teaching of the Upanishads in one of its two forms (*Brahma-pariṇāma-vada*); and the doctrine in its present form would then have to be explained as derived from it. The Svetāśvatara Upanishad, in fact, describes God as 'hidden in his own *guṇas*'. This integral view of ultimate reality found in the Upanishads, we must take it, has been meddled with here as a result of dualistic bias; and spirit has been separated from nature, rendering the whole doctrine unintelligible. Its failure to account satisfactorily for the cooperation between *puruṣa* and *prakṛti* is the natural consequence of this forced separation of the two. Such an explanation also throws light on the names given to some of the evolutes of Prakṛti like 'intellect' (*mahat*), 'egoism' (*ahaṁkāra*), etc. As cosmic entities, they would then represent the psychic organs of the *universal* self which is immanent in

[93] Dasgupta, op.cit., p.214, n.1. [94] ibid., p.214. [95] ibid.

prakṛti as a whole. But as the notion of such a self was dropped when the doctrine emerged from the Upanishadic teaching, their designations naturally came to be quite arbitrary and perplexing. The other explanation is to suppose that the system was originally purely naturalistic, and that the notion of *puruṣa* or spirit, for which there is really no need by the side of self-evolving and self-regulating *prakṛti*, was imported into it on the analogy of other doctrines.[96]

This verse detained us longer than expected. We may now move on to the next, which Śaṅkara, perhaps under the influence of the ascetic ideal, under-interprets just as he seems to over-interpret the previous one. The verse now under discussion runs as follows (VII:11):

balaṃ balavatāṃ cāhaṃ
kāmarāgavivarjitam
dharmāviruddho bhūteṣu
kāmo 'smi bharatarṣabha[97]

Might of the mighty am I, too,
(Such as is) free from desire and passion;
(So far as it is) not inconsistent with right, in creatures
I am desire, O best of Bharatas.[98]

Śaṅkara quite consistently under-interprets the verse. He glosses the powerful word *balam* as ' "only such power as is needed to sustain the body etc.": similarly he confines desire to the craving for what one does not possess'[99] (distinguishing it 'from *rāga*, as affection for what has been obtained').[100] We have to agree with Zaehner that this is 'plainly to whittle away at Kṛṣṇa's words',[101] and hardly consistent with Kṛṣṇa's displays of divine power. Śaṅkara also confines *kāma* to the 'desire for eating and drinking for the bare support of the body',[102] and Hill almost apologetically adds: 'Probably the phrase is meant to include the desire which results in the legitimate procreation of children'.[103] This is clearly an understatement of the intention of the text. Zaehner has shown that

[96] M. Hiriyanna, *The Essentials of Indian Philosophy*, pp.127-8.
[97] Bolle, op.cit., p.86.
[98] Edgerton, op.cit., Part I, p.75.
[99] Zaehner, op.cit., p.248.
[100] Hill, op.cit., p.127, n.1.
[101] Zaehner, op.cit., p.248.
[102] Hill, op.cit., p.127, n.2. [103] ibid., p.127, n.2.

elsewhere in the Mahābhārata (14.13.9-17) Kṛṣṇa explains to Yudhiṣṭhira, 'a natural *sannyāsin* if ever there was one', the significance of *kāma*, 'just how he is desire'.[104]

We now turn to Chapter Eight of the Gītā and may confine our discussion to one well-known verse therein (VIII:6):

yaṃ yaṃ vāpi smaran bhāvaṃ
tyajaty ante kalevaram
taṃ tam evaiti kaunteya
sadā tadbhāvabhāvitaḥ[105]

Whatsoever state (of being) meditating upon
He leaves the body at death,
To just that he goes, son of Kuntī,
Always, being made to be in the condition of that.[106]

The key expression here is *tadbhavābhāvitaḥ*. Śaṅkara glosses it as 'projecting himself (or rather "being projected") by bearing it in mind into that state'.[107] Zaehner seems to be quite right in pointing out that

> *bhāvitaḥ*: past part, pass. caus. of *bhu-*, 'to become': this word (in the causative) frequently means 'train'. Ś. glosses, 'projecting himself (or rather, "being projected") by bearing it in mind into that state'. This is not quite right, as it is the state or mode of being (*bhāva*) that does the projecting. The word-play on *bhāva* and *bhāvita* is difficult to render into English, but the sense of 'growing into' another form of being is clearly there. What you worship and what you believe in exercise a powerful fascination over you and make you grow into them. The same idea is expressed in 7.23 where the worshippers of the gods are said to go to the gods and the worshippers of Krishna to go to Krishna, and again in 9.25. Even more striking is the assertion in 17.3: 'Man is instinct with faith: as is his faith, so too must he be.'[108]

The sparseness of the critique of Śaṅkara's commentary on Chapter Eight of the Gītā gives way now to a fuller examination of his comments in the somewhat longer Ninth Chapter. The second verse of the chapter contains the apparently harmless statement that the doctrines expounded therein are *sasukhaṃ kartum* ('easy to carry out'). But Śaṅkara refers in this context to *brahmajñāna*[109] and 'takes the

[104] Zaehner, op.cit., p.248.
[105] Bolle, op.cit., p.85. [106] Edgerton, op.cit., Part I, p.00.
[107] Zaehner, op.cit., p.262. [108] ibid. Ś=Śaṅkara.
[109] *Śrīśāṅkaragranthāvaliḥ*, Samputa 8, pp.214-14.

jñāna here taught to be simply *brahmajñāna*. But to call *brahmajñāna* "very easy to practise", without special reference to the incarnation, would be to contradict the teaching of XII:5.'[110]

A philosophical problem also appears in the case of IX:5:

na ca matsthāni bhūtāni
paśya me yogam aiśvaram
bhutabhṛn na ca bhūtastho
mamātmā bhūtabhāvanaḥ[111]

And (yet) being do not rest in Me:
Behold My divine mystery (or magic)!
Supporter of beings, and not resting in beings,
Is My Self, that causes beings to be.[112]

The problem arises when the verse is read in the light of the preceding statements on *adhyātma* (VIII:4) for 'in view of the fact that Kṛiṣṇa as *adhyātma* is said to dwell in the heart of every being, it is strange to find the statement that the Self (*ātman*) dwells not in beings.'[113] Now Śaṅkara 'tries to meet this difficulty by saying that *ātman* is here used popularly – the physical and material nature of Brahman as apart from the true *ātman*.'[114] But Hill thinks that Kṛṣṇa 'is probably emphasising the fact of atman's real isolation, in spite of an apparent indwelling, as explained by the simile in the following śloka'.[115]

IX:6 *yathākāśasthito nityaṃ*
vāyuḥ sarvatrago mahān
tathā sarvāṇi bhūtāni
matsthānīty upadhāraya[116]

As constantly abides in the ether
The great wind, that penetrates everywhere,
So all beings
Abide in Me; make sure of that.[117]

[110] Hill, op.cit., p.139, n.4.
[111] Bolle, op.cit., p.102.
[112] Edgerton, op.cit., Part I, p.89.
[113] Hill, op.cit., p.140, n.1. [114] ibid. [115] ibid.
[116] Bolle, op.cit., p.102.
[117] Edgerton, op.cit., Part I, p.89.

Here Hill, following Śaṅkara, comments: 'The point in this simile seems to be that though in a sense the wind rests and moves in the all-pervading ether, yet there is no real contact between them.'[118]

Now we come to a verse which is partly responsible for the association with the spirit of religious tolerance said to be characteristic of Hinduism:

jñānayajñena cāpy anye
yajanto mām upāsate
ekatvena pṛthaktvena
bahudhā viśvatomukham[119]

With knowledge-worship also others
Worshipping wait upon Me,
In My unique and manifold forms,
(Me as) variously (manifested), facing in all directions.[120]

Hill notes that Śaṅkara[121] and other commentators 'interpret: "either as one or as many *devas* & c." '[122] He goes on to observe:

> But there is no alternative conjunction, and certainly to fix the mind on God's manifoldness is not a mark of the 'sacrifice of knowledge'. We have already seen (4-10) how Kṛṣṇa claims to be one with all beings, and at the same time free from contact with them. It is with this knowledge that these men worship him, both 'with the idea of his oneness' with all existences, and at the same time 'with the idea of his separateness' from them.[123]

Zaehner's exposition here is closer to the text, in the sense that he sees the implied tolerance of the verse as really internal to the Gītā:

> 'As One and yet as Manifold': unity in multiplicity is the consistent doctrine of the Gītā. First, the unity of the self-in-itself must be recognised, realised, experienced (6.31), then comes participation and communion (*bhakti*) with the whole and through the whole with God (ibid.). God is One, yet really present everywhere (II.13:13.16:18.20) and eminently present in the human heart (18.61:cf.13.17) even

[118] Hill, op.cit., p.140, n.2.
[119] Bolle, op.cit., p.106.
[120] Edgerton, op.cit., Part I, p.91.
[121] *Śrīśāṅkaragranthāvaliḥ*, Sampuṭa 8, p.223.
[122] Hill, op.cit., p.142, n.1. [123] ibid., p.142.

though the owner of that heart may hate Him (16.18). For R. the universe of unconscious matter, conscious beings still dependent on matter, and selves as they are eternally in themselves together form the one infinitely varied body of God who is Himself the One Great Self of the whole universe.[124]

In the twenty-second verse of the Ninth Chapter the expression *ananyāḥ* occurs which means 'with no other thought'.[125] Śaṅkara glosses it as *apṛthagbhūtāḥ*,[126] i.e. 'as not separate from me'. Hill thinks this interpretation is 'due to his monistic bias'.[127] But the whole verse runs as follows:

ananyāś cintayanto māṃ
ye janāḥ paryupāsate
teṣāṃ nityābhiyuktānāṃ
yogakṣemaṃ vahāmy aham[128]

Thinking on Me, with no other thought,
What folk wait upon Me,
To them, when they are constant in perseverance,
I bring acquisition and peaceful possession (of their aim).[129]

What Śaṅkara has said till now is unexceptionable, *pace* Hill, for Śaṅkara's bias is not apparent in the expression cited by Hill. But it emerges in what he says subsequently: *paraṃ devaṃ nārāyaṇam ātmatvena gatāḥ santaḥ cintayantaḥ*[130] – who regard the supreme god Nārāyaṇa as their own *ātman.*

We next cite a verse about which there is some difference of opinion regarding Śaṅkara's understanding of it (IX:29):

samo 'haṃ sarvabhūteṣu
na me dveṣyo 'sti na priyaḥ
ye bhajanti tu māṃ bhaktyā
mayi te teṣu cāpy aham[131]

[124] Zaehner, op.cit., p.280. R = Rāmānuja.
[125] Edgerton, op.cit., Part I, p.93.
[126] *Śrīśāṅkaragranthāvaliḥ*, Sampuṭa 8, p.227.
[127] Hill, op.cit., p.143, n.4.
[128] Bolle, op.cit., p.108.
[129] Edgerton, op.cit., Part I, p.93.
[130] *Śrīśāṅkaragranthāvaliḥ*, Sampuṭa 8, p.227.
[131] Bolle, op.cit., p.110.

I am the same to all beings,
No one is hateful or dear to Me;
But those who revere Me with devotion,
They are in Me and I too am in them.[132]

Zaehner is appreciative of Śaṅkara's comments.[133] Hill also points out, like Zaehner, that Śaṅkara compares Kṛṣṇa 'to a fire, which does not choose on whom to shed its warmth; he who draws near to it will be warmed; he who remains aloof will be cold. Ānadagiri speaks of the sun, whose light is reflected in a clean mirror, but not in a dirty one. B.'s translation of *sama*: "I am *indifferent* to all born beings" – is misleading. The doctrine of the śloka is not consistent with the teachings of such passages as Kaṭh. Up. ii. 12: "He is to be obtained only by the one whom he chooses".'[134] But Hill himself notes that Kaṭha Upaniṣad ii.24 says: 'He cannot be obtained by knowledge by one who has not ceased from evil conduct.'[135] This raises the question that it may be possible to know the Self apart from its self-disclosure, and that for this moral purity is required. The issue is a contentious one. Perhaps the best we can do is to let the reader ponder over the two successive verses, I.2.23 and I.2.24, from Kaṭha Upaniṣad:

23. *nāyam ātma pravacanena labhyo na medhayā, na bahunā śrutena:*
yamevaiṣa vṛṇute, tena labhyas tasyaiṣa ātmā vivṛṇute tanūṁ svām.

23. This self cannot be attained by instruction, nor by intellectual power, nor even through much hearing. He is to be attained only by the one whom the (self) chooses. To such a one the self reveals his own nature.

24. *nāvirato duścaritān nāśānto nāsamāhitaḥ*
nāśānta-mānaso vāpi prajñānenainam āpnuyāt.

24. Not he who has not desisted from evil ways, not he who is not tranquil, not he who has not a concentrated mind, not even he whose mind is not composed can reach this (self) through right knowledge.[136]

[132] Edgerton, op.cit., Part I, p.110.
[133] Zaehner, op.cit., p.285.
[134] Hill, op.cit., p.145, n.1. B=L.D. Barnett. [135] ibid., n.2.
[136] S. Radhakrishnan, *The Principal Upaniṣads* (London: Allen & Unwin, 1953), pp.619,620.

It should also be noted that what Śaṅkara says may be contrary to Kaṭha ii.23; but not as it is interpreted by Śaṅkara, though Śaṅkara's interpretation is generally acknowledged as forced. As Radhakrishnan says, Śaṅkara 'gives a different interpretation by an ingenious exegesis. "Him alone whom he chooses by that same self is his own self obtainable." The self reveals its true character to one that seeks it exclusively.'[137]

The last verse of the Ninth Chapter has led Zaehner to criticise Śaṅkara's syntactical understanding of it. But before we come to the criticism we may take a look at what is being criticised (IX:34):

manmanā bhava madbhakto
madyājī māṃ namaskuru
māṃ evaisyasi yuktvaivam
ātmānaṃ matparāyaṇaḥ[138]

Be Me-minded, devoted to Me;
Worshipping Me, pay homage to Me;
Just to Me shalt thou go, having thus disciplined
Thyself, fully intent on Me.[139]

The key expression is *yuktvaivam* (*yuktvā* + *evam*). Zaehner remarks:

> *yuktv'aivam*, 'now that you have thus integrated self': once again 'integration' is seen as an indispensable condition for the pursuit of what Krishna will call the 'highest' *bhakti*' (18.54). So little is this to Śankara's taste that his interpretation violates the perfectly straightforward grammar of the last sentence.
>
> *yuktvā* which obviously governs *ātmānāṁ*, 'having integrated self', he takes to mean *samādhāya cittam*, 'having integrated [your] thought', *evam*, 'so', *esyasi*, 'you will come', *ātmānaṃ*, 'to the Self, (for I am the Self of all beings, the highest Way, the highest path, that is,) to Me as Self'.[140]

Let us look at the entire line: *māṃ evaisyasi yuktvaivam ātmānaṃ matparāyaṇah*. Zaehner reads it as: *yaktvaivam ātmānam, matyparāyaṇaḥ mām evaisyasi*.[141] Śaṅkara reads it thus: *yuktvā, evaṁ ātmānam mām*

[137] ibid., p.620.
[138] Bolle, op.cit., p.110.
[139] Edgerton, op.cit., Part I, p.95.
[140] Zaehner, op.cit., p.286.
[141] As per English translation: 'Now that you have thus integrated self, your striving bent on Me, to Me you will [surely] come.'

esyasi. It is strange that Śaṅkara, who is accused of having an Advaitic bias, interprets *ātmānam* theistically by identifying *ātman* with Kṛṣṇa, and that too in a somewhat forced way!

The Tenth Chapter of the Gītā need not detain us long. It is the famous chapter in which Kṛṣṇa describes his *vibhūtis*, or glorious manifestations, when 'he speaks of himself (a) as the chief of each class of beings, e.g. as the sun among the lights, and (b) as that without participation in which each member of the class could not exist as it is; for example, all lights owe their possession of light to the sun'.[142]

As Kṛṣṇa proceeds to speak of himself as the chief of a class he declares (X:31): *rāmaḥ śastrabhṛtām aham*[143] ('I am ... Rāma of warriors').[144] Śaṅkara identifies Rāma here with Rāma, the son of Daśaratha (*dāśarathiḥ rāmaḥ*),[145] as do most scholars. But Zaehner comments:

> 'Rāma': either Rāma ... who is Vishnu's seventh incarnation, or Paraśu-Rāma, 'Rāma with the axe', his sixth incarnation. The purpose of Vishnu's incarnation as Paraśu-Rāma was to extirpate the princely or warrior class. Since this is largely the purpose of his incarnation as Krishna too, it is quite likely that it is this Rāma who is referred to here.[146]

D.H.H. Ingalls also favours such an identification.[147] The possibility does not seem to have crossed Śaṅkara's mind at all.

The Eleventh Chapter may be passed over, as it does not seem to have generated discernible exegetical differences. Its significance is devotional and religious rather than philosophical. But with the Twelfth Chapter we are back on philosophical turf, although the first point we run into is philological. It appears in XII:3:

ye tv akṣaram anirdeśyam
avyaktaṃ paryupāsate
sarvatragam acintyaṃ ca
kūṭastham acalaṃ dhruvam[148]

[142] Hill, op.cit., p.148, n.4.
[143] Bolle, op.cit., p.120.
[144] Edgerton, op.cit., Part I, p.103.
[145] *Śrīśāṅkaragranthāvaliḥ*, Sampuṭa 8, p.247.
[146] Zaehner, op.cit., p.300.
[147] See *Journal of Asian Studies* XLII (1) (1982), p.209.
[148] Bolle, op.cit., p.146.

But those who the imperishable, undefinable,
Unmanifest, revere,
The omnipresent and unthinkable,
The immovable, unchanging, fixed[149]

The word involved is *kūṭṣtha*. Śaṅkara's comment on it is rather puzzling: 'There is no doubt at all about the meaning of this word.'[150]

> It is, then, all the more surprising that Śaṅkara, usually so careful in matters of philology and semantics, should interpret the word in the following way: 'standing in *kūṭa* (the crooked), that is, something that has the quality of being visible and has an internal defect, that is to say, the seed of repeated reincarnation originating in [cosmic] ignorance ... also known as *māyā*: ... [the Self] abides in this as an onlooker (*adhyakṣa*).' alternatively he suggests 'standing like a heap'. These extraordinary interpretations he repeats at 15.16, though at 6.8 he rightly glosses 'unshakable'.[151]

Śaṅkara has simply missed the mark here; perhaps he was misled by the use of the word in such forms as *kūṭanīti* (diplomacy) or *kūṭayantra* (trap).[152]

The next verse is of considerable interest in the context of the dispute between a monistic and a theistic interpretation of the Gītā. It runs as follows (XII:5):

kelśo 'dhikataras teṣām
avyaktāsaktacetasām
avyaktā hi gatir duḥkhaṃ
dehavadbhir avāpyate[153]

Greater is the toil of them
That have their hearts fixed on the unmanifest;
For with difficulty is the unmanifest goal
Attained by embodied (souls).[154]

[149] Edgerton, op.cit., Part I, p.121.
[150] Zaehner, op.cit., p.324. [151] ibid.
[152] Monier Monier-Williams, *A Sanskrit-English Dictionary* (Oxford: Clarendon Press, repr. 1970), p.299.
[153] Bolle, op.cit. p.146.
[154] Edgerton, op.cit., Part I, p.121.

The verse obviously seems to favour the theistic over the absolutistic way, especially when read in the context of the previous verses. How Śaṅkara, the confirmed absolutist, would exegetically handle such a verse naturally piques one's intellectual curiosity. Surprisingly little attention has been paid to it. His gloss is reproduced below *in toto*:

> Great indeed is the trouble of those who are engaged in doing works for My sake, and so on; but greater still is the trouble of those who identify themselves with the Imperishable and contemplate the Supreme Reality, – the trouble arising from the necessity of having to abandon their attachment for the body. The Goal, the Imperishable, is very hard for the embodied to reach, – for those who are attached to their bodies. Therefore their trouble is greater.[155]

In assessing Śaṅkara's commentary on the Twelfth Chapter we must bear in mind his understanding of the term *ayakta*. This helps to solve some riddles. *Ayakta*, for Śaṅkara, is *not* to be equated with Brahman, but rather with unmanifest *prakṛti*. Once this is realised it becomes clear why he cannot take *kūṭastha* to stand for the transcendental, and why he considers verses XII:13-20 as describing 'those who follow the *ayaktā gati*' and not the path which leads directly to Brahman. 'His preference for "contemplation of the Supreme" leads him to defy the context and reverse the teaching of the Reading'.[156]

The Thirteenth Chapter furnishes several minor examples of the ways in which Śaṅkara either restricts or enlarges the semantic scope of the statements therein. This need not automatically be the result of bias; actually in a few cases the immediate sense of the expression is more monistic than he takes it to be. An example is provided by the expression *sa ca yo yat prabhāvaś ca tat samasena me śṛṇu* (XII:3).[157] 'And who He (the Field-knower) is, and what His powers are, That hear from Me in brief.'[158] Śaṅkara refers to the *prabhāvās*, or powers, as *upādhikṛtāḥ śaktayaḥ*,[159] or phenomenally conditioned powers. Hill thinks that the 'term is probably more general'.[160] In XIII:6 the

[155] Alladi Mahadeva Sastry (tr.), *The Bhagavad Gītā with the Commentary of Sri Sankaracharya* (Madras: Samata Books, 1979), pp.305-6. Zaehner, in his comment on XII:5: ' "Greater is the toil of those whose thinking clings to the Unmanifest": obviously, for how can you think of the "unthinkable" and "indeterminate" ' (op.cit., p.327) reflects the usual understanding of the verse which Śaṅkara does not follow.

[156] Hill, op.cit., p.171.

[157] Edgerton, op.cit., Part I, p.126. [158] ibid., p.127.

[159] *Śrīśāṅkaragranthāvaliḥ*, Sampuṭa 8, p.311.

[160] It is not entirely clear why Hill remarks that Śaṅkara 'refers the *prabhāvas* or *śaktis* to the "power of seeing & c". mentioned in 13,14' (op.cit., p.172, n.6).

term *saṅghāta* occurs in the list of what comprises the Field and its modifications. No one is quite sure what it means, and 'the appearance of this word' with associations of a physical assemblage 'among the modifidations of the mind is not easy to explain'.[161] Zaehner follows Śaṅkara in taking it to mean 'the bringing together of the bodily senses'[162] (*dehendriyāṇām saṁhatiḥ*).[163] It seems that *saṅghāta* here could have the meaning of *saṁskāra*, which would seem to fit the context.

In XIII:10 occurs the expression *ananyayoga*. Hill claims that Śaṅkara 'explains *ananyayoga* as *apṛithaksamādhi*, i.e. contemplation of the non-separate.'[164] He adds: 'The meaning is, more probably, work for me alone.'[165] Śaṅkara seems to have been misrepresented here, for the full gloss runs: *ananyayogena apṛthaksamādhinā 'na anyo bhagavato vāsudevāt paraḥ asti, ataḥ sa eva naḥ gatiḥ' ity evam ...*[166] That is to say: '*Yoga of non-separation: apṛithak-samādhi*, a steady unflinching meditation on the One with the idea that there is no Being higher than the Lord, Vāsudeva, and that therefore He is our sole Refuge. And this devotion is (conducive to) knowledge.'[167]

More curious are Śaṅkara's glosses on two expressions occurring in XIII:15:

babir antaś can bhūtānām
acaraṃ caram eva ca
sūkṣmatvāt tadavijñeyam
dūrasthaṃ cāntike ca tat[168]

Outside beings, and within them,
Unmoving, and yet moving;
Because of its subtleness it cannot be comprehended:
Both far away and near it is.[169]

Śaṅkara explains *bhūtānām acaram caram eva ca* in the context of that which is to be known – Brahman – thus: ' "it appears as bodies moving and unmoving." But this explanation destroys the paradox; Brahman, as Supreme, is "unmoving"; as individual Self, it appears to move with body'.[170] Similarly Śaṅkara explains *dūrastham cāntike ca*

[161] ibid., p.174, n.7.
[162] Zaehner, op.cit., p.336.
[163] Hill, op.cit., p.174. [164] ibid., p.175, n.3. [165] ibid.
[166] *Śrīśāṅkaragranthāvaliḥ*, Samputa 8, p.316.
[167] Alladi Mahadeva Sastry (tr.), op.cit., p.342. Diacritics supplied.
[168] Bolle, op.cit., p.156.
[169] Edgerton, op.cit., Part I, p.129.
[170] Hill, op.cit., p.176, n.4.

tat in relation to Brahman as 'far away (to the ignorant); near (to the enlightened)' but the 'meaning is practically "transcendent" and "immanent" '.[171] In these cases Śaṅkara opts for the less impressive resolutions of the paradoxical descriptions of Brahman. But his bias soon reappears. In XIII:26 it is stated that any creature 'stationary or moving' is produced from the 'union of Field and Field-knower'.[172] Śaṅkara informs us that this union is 'purely illusory'[173] (*mithyājñānalakṣaṇaḥ*). The text does not say so; Śaṅkara brings his philosophical views on *adhyāsa* into full play. We may also note in passing that XIII:12 contains the expression *anādimat param* in relation to Brahman. The reading *anādi matparam* is also noticed by Śaṅkara, but rejected.[174] This rejection, inasmuch as it may be based on philosophical and not text-critical considerations, would reflect Śaṅkara's monistic leanings, for *anādimat param* would mean 'beginningless highest' and *anādi matparam* 'beginningless, dependent on Me', i.e. Kṛṣṇa. The critical edition has the form *anā dimatparam*![175]

We turn now to the Fourteenth Chapter. The second verse arrests attention by itself and also by reason of Śaṅkara's gloss on it. It runs (XIV:2):

idaṃ jñāam upāśritya
mama sādharmyam āgatāḥ
sarge 'pi nopajāyante
pralaye na vyathanti ca[176]

Having resorted to this knowledge,
Come to a state of likeness with Me,
Evan at a world-creation they do not come to birth,
Nor at a dissolution are they disturbed.[177]

The interesting point here is that the Gītā, perhaps for the first time, employs a term to indicate the nature of the relationship of God to the released souls. The term is *sādharmya*, which does not, it seems, become a technical word unless such terms as express different

[171] ibid., p.176, n.5.
[172] Edgerton, op.cit., p.131.
[173] Hill, op.cit., p.178, n.3.
[174] *Śrīśāṅkaragranthāvaliḥ*, Sampuṭa 8, p.336.
[175] S.K. Belvalkar, *The Bhīṣmaparvan* (Poona: Bhandarkar Oriental Research Institute, 1947), p.167.
[176] Bolle, op.cit., p.162.
[177] Edgerton, op.cit., Part I, p.135.

degrees of association with God such as '*sārūpya* (same appearance as that of Nārāyaṇa), *sāmīpya* (vicinity of Nārāyaṇa), *sālokya* (residence at the same abode as Nārāyaṇa), *sārṣṭi* (*aiśvarya* similar to that of Nārāyaṇa)'[178] and perhaps *sāyujya*, if taken in the sense of intimate communion with Nārāyaṇa rather than union with *nirguṇa brahman*, are treated as various forms of *sādharmya*. In any case, Śaṅkara 'says that *sādharmya* here means, not *samānadharmatā* (mere similarity of quality) but *svarūptā* (identity)'.[179] He also goes on to state the reason for saying so: because in the Gītā no distinction is drawn between the *kṣetrajña* (the *ātman*) and *īśvara* (God).[180] Śaṅkara does not say that *sārūpya* is involved, but rather *svarūpya*. Not all these fine gradations are found in the Gītā; it only mentions *sādharmya*. Zaehner's rendering of *sādharmya* 'reached a rank [in order of existence] equivalent to my own'[181] places far greater distance between God and the sages than Śaṅkara does.

The sixth verse of the chapter is also of interest from the point of view of Śaṅkara as an exegete. Thus XIV:6 refers to the bondage caused by attachment to *jñāna* (*jñānasaṅgena ... badhnāti*).[182] It is easy to see why Śaṅkara must take *jñāna* here as not of the *ātman* (for that liberates rather than binds) but of the *antaḥkaraṇa*, or (roughly) the mind.[183] Zaehner is not convinced:

> *jñāna-*, 'wisdom': according to Ś. the wisdom referred to is the pursuit of happiness, not the intuitive wisdom of the self. H. and Rk. follow him in this, but it is doubtful whether the author of the Gītā made any such distinction, for it is legitimate to attach oneself to God (7.1) or to the Unmanifest Brahman (12.5) which is synonymous with the 'highest wisdom'. In MBh. 12.240.19-22 'Goodness' and the 'knower of the field' can only be distinguished in thought: in practice they are always interfused ... Attachment to wisdom and joy, however, is wrong if, once having experienced their 'radiance', one sorrows when the ecstatic state passes (14.22).[184]

The other verse of interest is XIV:20 which speaks of the

[178] Haridas Bhattacharyya (ed.), *The Cultural Heritage of India*, Vol. III (Calcutta: Ramakrishna Mission Institute of Culture, 1963 [first published 1937]), pp.376-7.

[179] Hill, op.cit., p.180, n.1. Thus Edgerton's 'come to a state of likeness with Me' (op.cit., Part I, p.135) is rejected by Śaṅkara.

[180] *Śrīśāṅkaragranthāvaliḥ*, Sampuṭa 8, p.345.

[181] Zaehner, op.cit., p.351.

[182] Bolle, op.cit., p.162.

[183] *Śrīśāṅkaragranthāvaliḥ*, Sampuṭa 8, p.348.

[184] Zaehner, op.cit., p.353. H=Hill; Rk=Radhakrishnan.

association of the three *guṇas* with the embodied soul through the expression *dehī dehasamudbhavān*,[185] which occurs in the context of transcending the three *guṇas* 'that spring from the body, the embodied (soul) ...'[186] 'Most commentators and translators have found the compound *dehasamudbhavān* difficult, because it seems to imply that *guṇas* are caused by the body, whereas the body is rather caused by the *guṇas*.'[187] Śaṅkara explains: 'which are the seed out of which body is evolved (*dehotpattibījabhūtān*)'.[188]

Śaṅkara has not succeeded in resolving the issue. Hill is far more convincing: 'which owe their being to the body', i.e. 'which exist in relation to the Self because it is embodied'.[189] Or perhaps better still, 'which arise in the body'.

The last verse of the chapter is of considerable interest, for in it, in apparently direct opposition to the Advaitic position, Kṛṣṇa declares himself to be the foundation of Brahman itself. Zaehner recognises the full significance of this and remarks that the 'unqualified claim of the personal God Krishna, to be the "base supporting Brahman" confirms everything'.[190] He later adds that Kṛṣṇa's 'present statement, then, coming where it does, can only mean that He, as personal God, transcends even the absolutely transcendent'.[191] It is interesting that not even Rāmānuja exploits the full theistic potential of the verse, for he 'seems to take Brahman as the individual *ātman*; Kṛṣṇa is that *ātman's* support'[192] – that is what it means to him. Now the verse XIV:27:

brahmaṇo hi pratiṣṭhāham
amṛtasyāvyayasya ca
śāśvatasya ca dharmasya
sukhasyaikāntikasya ca[193]

For I am the foundation of Brahman,
The immortal and imperishable,
And of the eternal right,
And of absolute bliss.[194]

As one would expect, Śaṅkara tones down the exaltation of the Personal Brahman (*saguṇa*) over the Impersonal (*nirguṇa*): 'Brahman

[185] Edgerton, op.cit., Part I, p.138. [186] ibid., p.139.
[187] Hill, op.cit., p.183, n.1. [188] ibid. [189] ibid., p.183.
[190] Zaehner, op.cit., p.358. [191] ibid.
[192] Hill, op.cit., p.184, n.1.
[193] Bolle, op.cit., p.168.
[194] Edgerton, op.cit., Part I, p.141.

is *paramātman*, immortal and indestructible that abides in me, who am *pratyagātman* ... that being so, one sees by right knowledge the identity of the two ... it is through the power that Brahman has to manifest itself as Lord (*īśvaraśakti*) that Brahman shows grace to devotees. I am that power in manifestation, and therefore Brahman itself.' He then gives an alternative: 'Brahman is the conditioned (*savikalpa*) Brahman; I am the abode, or ground, of that Brahman, and am myself unconditioned (*nirvikalpa*).'[195]

Śaṅkara's line of reasoning is ingenious, but is it convincing? It might have been more to the point to refer to the unequivocal exaltation of Impersonal Brahman in the Gītā as the ultimate reality. But is there any such unequivocal passage in the text?

We now turn to a small but significant chapter – the Fifteenth. We must begin our exegetical analysis of Śaṅkara's interpretation with the very first, and famous, verse (XV:1):

ūrdhvamūlam adhaḥśākham
aśvatthaṃ prāhur avyayam
chandāṃsi yasya parṇāni
yas taṃ veda sa vedavit[196]

With roots aloft and branches below,
The eternal peepal-tree, they say
Whose leaves are the (Vedic) hymns,
Who knows it, he knows the Veda.[197]

Two points stand out in Śaṅkara's commentary: what he and many others do, and what he and many others do not. Śaṅkara derives the word *aśvattha* 'from *a-śvaḥ-sthā-*(*na śvo 'pi sthātā*), because, though it is *avyaya* as without beginning or end, the world is in a constant state of change or flux'.[198] In point of fact the word is probably to be 'derived from *aśva-sthā* – the tree under which horses stand'.[199]

What neither Śaṅkara nor other commentators explain is the inverted nature of the tree. Why is it said to have roots above, we may ask, and branches below? Hill has come closest to providing a satisfactory answer:

[195] Hill, op.cit., p.184, n.1.
[196] Bolle, op.cit., p.170.
[197] Edgerton, op.cit., Part I, p.143.
[198] Hill, op.cit., p.3. [199] ibid., p.4.

'roots above and branches below'; it is noticeable that commentators neglect this point altogether. The following tentative explanation endeavours to account for the choice of this tree.

The *aśvattha* (probably derived from *aśva-sthā* – the tree under which horses stand) is the Ficus Religiosa, or *pīpal* tree, well known to those who live in India as a tree held in great reverence among Hindus. It does not, like its cousin the banyan, drop aerial rootlets to take fresh root in the earth. Why, then, is it said to have roots above and branches below? The formation of the tree is peculiar, in that its roots (which often stand in part above the ground) do not altogether, as in other trees, lose themselves in a central rounded trunk, but to a great extent retaining their separate form, climb up in a cluster, each to spread out into a separate branch. Each root is thus continuous with its own branch, and therefore, root and branch being inseparably one, it is possible to speak of the branch as descending to the earth, and of the root as rising aloft. This interpretation of the phrase not only explains the choice of the *aśvattha* as a symbol, but is an aid to the understanding of the figure.

'Above' then, means 'above the ground in the visible world'; 'below' means 'down to the hidden places below ground'. Root, and branch, as one, are *prakṛiti*; below ground, *avyakta*; above ground, *vyakta*. There is no need to distinguish between the *mūla* of 1 and the *mūlāni* of 2. Cf. Kaṭh. Up.vi.1.[200]

Another verse in the chapter we may now deal with is XV:15:

sarvasya cāhaṃ hṛdi saṃniviṣṭo
mattaḥ smṛtir jñānam apohanaṃ ca
vedaiś ca sarvair aham eva vedyo
vedāntakṛd vedavid eva cāham[201]

I am entered into the heart of every one;
From Me come memory, knowledge, and disputation;
I alone am that which is to be known by all the Vedas;
And I am the author of the Upaniṣads and the Vedas' knower.[202]

The exegesis of the word *vedāntakṛt* is what concerns us. Śaṅkara glosses it as *vedāntārthasampradāyakṛt*;[203] that is to say, Kṛṣṇa is the founder of the sects which expound the meaning of Vedānta. But the

[200] ibid., pp.184-5.
[201] Bolle, op.cit., p.170.
[202] Edgerton, op.cit., Part I, p.145.
[203] *Śrīśāṅkaragranthāvaliḥ*, Sampuṭa 8, p.371.

word itself literally means the 'author of Vedānta'. We should note the fascinating distinction between the two words *vedavid* and *vedāntakṛt*. Kṛṣṇa only knows the Vedas, by which presumably the Mantra and Brāhmaṇa portions are meant; but if taken literally he would be the author of Vedānta.[204] Since the Gītā is called an Upaniṣad,[205] the statement about Kṛṣṇa's being the author of Vedānta should perhaps be taken more seriously than hitherto.

We may now revert to the consideration of an earlier verse, XV:7:

mamaivāṃśo jīvaloke
jīvabhūtaḥ sanātanaḥ
manaḥṣaṣṭhānīndriyāṇi
prakṛtisthāni karṣti[206]

A part just of Me in the world of the living
Becomes the individual-soul, the eternal;
The (five) senses, with the thought-organ as sixth
Which rest in material nature, it draws along.[207]

The problem the verse poses is clear: how could an impartite God create a fractional universe out of Himself? Śaṅkara attempts a philosophical solution; Zaehner suggests that the solution may really be religious.[208]

Let us grasp the nettle of XV:16:

dvāv imau puruṣau loke
kṣaraś cākṣara eva ca
kṣaraḥ sarvāṇi bhūtāni
kuṭastho 'kṣara ucyate[209]

Here in the world are two spirits,
The perishable, and the imperishable;
The perishable is all beings;
The imperishable is called the immovable.[210]

What do the two *puruṣas* stand for? This is the central question.

[204] Zaehner, op.cit., p.374.
[205] Radhakrishnan, *The Bhagavadgītā*, op.cit., p.13.
[206] Bolle, op.cit., p.172.
[207] Edgerton, op.cit., Part I, p.143.
[208] Zaehner, op.cit., p.176.
[209] Bolle, op.cit., p.176.
[210] Edgerton, op.cit., Part I, p.145.

Śaṅkara's answer, briefly, is that the perishable *puruṣa* stands for the evanescent *saṁsāra*; that the imperishable *puruṣa* stands for the *māyāśakti* of God. *Saṁsāra itself* is constantly undergoing change, perishing; it is perishable and therefore *kṣara*. But the *śakti* of God, the seed of *saṁsāra* on account of being endless (and beginningless) – *saṁsārabījānantyāt* – is imperishable and therefore *akṣara*. And God stands beyond both.[211]

Śaṅkara's position is cogent, but only within the framework of his own philosophy after it has been superimposed on the Gītā. Hill is probably closer to the spirit of the text when he writes:

> Much unnecessary difficulty has been caused in the interpretation of this passage by the unwillingness of commentators to allow Kṛiṣṇa to call *prakṛiti* '*kṣara puruṣa*'. But the context demands that the two *puruṣas* should be *puruṣa and prakṛiti*; it is on these two that Kṛiṣṇa has been continually harping under various figures and in this Reading he has first spoken of *prakṛiti* as the Fig-tree, and then of individual and universal *puruṣa*, or *jīvabhūta*. Throughout his teaching he has told of the Lord who is one with Brahman and with Kṛiṣṇa and who possesses two 'natures' – the one, 'higher', his own essential nature, *adhyātma*, universal and individual; and the other, 'lower', identified with *prakṛiti*. In relation to *prakṛiti* he is *sādhibhūta*, and *adhibhūta* is *kṣara bhāva* (viii.4). If Kṛiṣṇa may call *puruṣa* and *prakṛiti* the two *prakṛitis* in vii.5, may he not call them the two *puruṣas* here? Poetry rises superior to terminology, and the very confusion of terms helps to suggest that oneness of all which is the ultimate doctrine of the Gītā. S. says that the Imperishable is the *māyaśakti* of the Lord, the germ from which the Perishable being (the whole universe of changing forms) takes its birth, the seat of all the latent impressions of desires, actions, etc., belonging to the numerous mortal creatures. Ānandagiri adds that these two are spoken of as *puruṣas* because they are the *upādhis* of the one *puruṣa*. S. seems unwilling to admit that Kṛiṣṇa, or Brahman, is in any sense, 'higher' than individual Self; the supremacy lies, of course, in the difference between 'free' and 'bound'. R. distinguishes between *kṣara* as 'bound' and *akṣara* as 'free' Spirit. Th. translates *kṣara* 'divisible', and *akṣara* 'indivisible', and considers the first to mean 'individual soul', and the second 'non-individuate universal vitality'. Cf. Svet. Up. i.10: 'What is Perishable is Primary Matter (*pradhāna*); what is immortal and Imperishable is Hara (the "Bearer, the soul"). Over both the Perishable and the Soul the One God (*deva*) rules' (Hume).[212]

[211] *Śrīśāṅkaragranthāvalih*, Sampuṭa 8, p.372.
[212] Hill, op.cit., p.189, n.5. Ś=Śaṅkara. R=Rāmānuja. Th=J.C. Thomson.

Chapter Sixteen again provides a few interesting, if not dramatic, instances of Śaṅkara's departures from what might be taken to be the clear meaning of the text unmediated through any philosophical or other preconceptions. He offers a curious gloss on XVI:7:

pravṛttiṃ ca nivṛttiṃ ca
janā na vidur āsurāḥ
na śaucaṃ nāpi cācāro
na satyaṃ teṣu vidyate[213]

Both activity and its cessation
Demoniac folk know not;
Neither purity nor yet good conduct
Nor truth is found in them.[214]

The words *pravṛtti* and *nivṛtti* are fairly current in Hindu philosophical diction,[215] as Śaṅkara's Introduction to the Gītā itself testifies.[216] They are generally taken to mean activity (*pravṛtti*) and renunciation (*nivṛtti*). But here, without any apparent provocation, Śaṅkara 'surprisingly interprets these words as meaning actions which one should perform for the good of man and those one should abstain from in order to avoid evil'.[217]

Śaṅkara's gloss on a term appearing in XVI:8 is also rather curious. One characteristic of those who are demoniac, as distinguished from divine beings, is said to be that they regard the world as *aparaspara-sambhūtam*. Śaṅkara glosses it to mean that 'its sole origin is the union of the sexes'. But Zaehner notes that this 'seems to be an interpretation of *paraspara-sambhutam* rather than *asparaspara-sambhūtam*, which he takes to mean that 'it has not come to be by mutual causal law'.[218]

Similarly in XVI:11 those with a devilish disposition are described as devoted to limitless care which lasts until *pralaya* (*cintām aparimeyāṃ ca pralayāntām upāśritāḥ*). Without wishing to put too fine a point on it, we observe that *pralaya* is taken in the sense of *maraṇa*[219] by Śaṅkara (and others). But could not *pralaya* here mean cosmic

[213] Bolle, op.cit., p.180.
[214] Edgerton, op.cit., Part I, p.149.
[215] M. Hiriyanna, *Outlines of Indian Philosophy* (London: Allen & Unwin, 1964 [first published 1932]), pp.20-1.
[216] *Śrīśāṅkaragranthāvalih*, Samputa 8, p.1. Also see p.105.
[217] Zaehner, op.cit., p.370. This point is also noted by Hill, op.cit., p.192, n.1.
[218] Zaehner, op.cit., p.371.
[219] Hill, op.cit., p.193, n.1.

dissolution, especially if we realise that the fate of the devilish creatures is indeed contemplated metempsychotically in XVI:20, to which we now turn?

āsurīṃ yonim āpannā
mūḍhā janmani janmani
mām aprāpyaiva kaunteya
tato yānty adhamāṃ gatim[220]

Having come into a demoniac womb,
Deluded in birth after birth,
Not by any means attaining Me, son of Kuntī,
Then they go to the lowest goal.[221]

Several scholars have taken this verse as implying eternal damnation,[222] but not Śaṅkara. He comments: 'That there is no doubt at all about my being accessible so what these condemnable people do not reach is the good path preached by me.'[223] We should note that even Ānandagiri lapses into a modified eternal damnation view when he says that 'when once such men have been reborn in "*āsura* wombs", their case is hopeless; but man as a free agent, while still a man, should try to shake off the *āsura* nature'.[224]

It could be argued that Śaṅkara has offered too optimistic an interpretation of the Gītā here, but only if other parts are overlooked.[225]

The Seventeenth Chapter again provides illustrations both of Śaṅkara's philosophical ideas affecting his exegetical preferences, and also of his apparent deviation from the textual sense without his necessarily being under such influence. The very first verse illustrates the former point. It runs as follows (XVII:1):

ye śāstravidhim utsṛjya
yajante śraddhayānvitāḥ
teṣāṃ niṣṭhā tu kā kṛṣṇa
sattvam āho rajas tamaḥ[226]

[220] Bolle, op.cit., p.182.
[221] Edgerton, op.cit., Part I, p.153.
[222] Zaehner, op.cit., p.373.
[223] *Śrīśāṅkaragranthāvaliḥ*, Sampuṭa 8, p.386.
[224] Hill, op.cit., p.194, n.2.
[225] *Bhagavadgītā* IX:30-4; etc.
[226] Bolle, op.cit., p.186.

Those who, neglecting the law's injunction,
  Perform acts of worship filled with faith, –
What, however, is their basis, Kṛṣṇa?
  Goodness, or passion, or darkness?[227]

The issue turns on the interpretation of the expression *śāstravidhim utsṛjya*. Edgerton's translation here – 'neglecting the law's injunction' – is not the best for our purposes; Hill's – 'who forsake the ordinance of Scripture'[228] – is better. The question is: what degree of latitude is being implied in relation to Scriptures. On a broad interpretation we could say that the abandonment of the *śāstravidhi* involves the abandonment both of the *śāstra* and the *vidhi*. Thus one may forsake both the scriptures and also the injunctions laid down in the scriptures while sacrificing with faith. The other exegetical possibility, on a narrower interpretation, is that one forsakes the *vidhi* but not the *śāstra*, i.e. knowledge of the *śāstra*. (The further possibility, that one may forsake the *śāstra* but not the *vidhi* is obviously self-discrepant, as one would not know the *vidhi* without the *śāstra*.) Now Śaṅkara insists that Arjuna's phrase *śāstra-vidhim utsṛjya* 'can only mean "ignorant of the ordinance of the Scripture"; for, he says, "we cannot suppose that those men are endued with faith who, while knowing the scriptural injunctions about the worship of the gods, & c., set them aside without caring for them" '.[229]

Śaṅkara's bias here in favour of scriptures is quite clear, and consistent with his tendency to uphold the authority of revelation over reason in relation to earlier Advaitins.[230] For, as Hill points out, while Śaṅkara's 'view may be true, that those who deliberately turn aside from Scripture cannot be endued with faith',[231] yet 'there is no reason to suppose that Arjuna may not have thought otherwise; and, indeed, the main desire revealed in Kṛiṣṇa's answer appears to be to correct this idea of his disciple, that faith is compatible with neglect of Scripture. It is hardly probable that after the very definite

[227] Edgerton, op.cit., Part I, p.155.

[228] Hill, op.cit., p.195.

[229] ibid., p.195, n.1.

[230] K. Satchidananda Murty, *Revelation and Reason in Advaita Vedānta* (New York: Columbia University Press, 1959), pp.158-9.

[231] It seems that Hill has inadvertently changed the sense of Śaṅkara's statement here. Śaṅkara did not imply that 'those who turn aside from Scripture cannot be endued with faith', but rather that those who *know* the Scriptural injunctions and *then* set them aside cannot be said to possess faith. The change in sense, however, is minor enough to be overlooked.

teaching given in the last *śloka* of the sixteenth Reading Kṛiṣṇa should then be content to belittle the Scriptures in the realm of duty. There is no reason to suppose that the author of the Gītā would dare, or wish, to be so vitally unorthodox.'[232]

On this view the Gītā is more broadminded' than is apparent from Śaṅkara's gloss.

Saṅkara is somewhat restrictive in his interpretation at two other points in this chapter, though in both cases his lack of exegetical generosity probably has little connection with his philosophical position. In XVII:6 he renders *śarīrastham bhūtagrāmam*,[233] ('the conglomerate of elements within the body', to paraphrase Edgerton),[234] as 'the bodily organs',[235] when the 'phrase probably stands for the whole of that part of the individual which is composed of *prakṛti*'.[236] Similarly, on XVIII:23, which contains the celebrated expression *oṁ tat sat*, he remarks that 'by this means even those acts that are not of the *sāttvika* class and are imperfect turn out to be *sāttvika* and perfect'.[237] This is nowhere stated in the verse, and Śaṅkara's interpretation may even be judged permissive rather than restrictive, as he enables sacrifices which might not be *sāttvika* otherwise to qualify as *sāttvika*. But why try to change the category of sacrifice in this way, restricting it to one when the text does not speak of the classification *here*, though it does so earlier.

We may now examine Śaṅkara's commentary on the last chapter. A point of some interest arises in his gloss on *kāmyānāṃ karmaṇāṃ*[238] ('of acts of desire')[239] in XVIII:2. Zaehner remarks that Śaṅkara 'takes this to include religious sacrifices like the horse-sacrifice. This is quite unwarrantable since in fact Arjuna does perform the horse-sacrifice traditionally offered by all conquerors when a war has been won. In this he has Krishna's full approval.'[240]

The verse needs to be interpreted much more carefully, however. The word *karma* has been used in the Gītā in several senses.[241] Thus it can mean (1) any act, (2) a sacrificial act, (3) *varṇa*-duties, or (4) acts of worship. Śaṅkara has taken it in the second sense. But the possibility of a wider connotation is clear from XVIII:3 wherein *yajña, dāna* and *tapas* are all labelled *karma*. So it could be argued that Śaṅkara has taken the word in a narrower sense than warranted by

[232] Hill, op.cit., p.195, n.1.
[233] Edgerton, op.cit., Part I, p.154. [234] ibid., p.155.
[235] Hill, op.cit., p.196, n.2. [236] ibid. [237] ibid., p.163.
[238] Edgerton, op.cit., Part I, p.162. [239] ibid., p.163.
[240] Zaehner, op.cit., p.385.
[241] M. Hiriyanna, *Outlines of Indian Philosophy*, pp.118-19.

the larger context. This point made, we may now turn to *kāmya karma* as a category of rituals distinguished from *nitya* and *naimittika* actions. The standard position on the distinctions between them may be summarised thus:

> There are both positive and negative commands in the Veda. The positive commands are of various kinds: (1) There are some which prescribe obligatory duties (*nitya karma*). 'Offer twilight prayers every day' is one such command. Another is: 'Perform the *Agnihotra* as long as you live.' Obedience to such commands does not depend upon the option of the indivdual. He who is eligible to perform them ought to perform them unconditionally. (2) The second kind of command relates to occasioned rites (*naimittika-karma*). These are not daily duties, but rituals which should be observed on occasions, as, for instance, the ceremonial bath during the eclipses. These are also obligatory. (3) The third variety of Vedic injunctions consists of those which prescribe optional rites (*kāmya karma*), e.g. 'Let him who desires heaven perform the *Jyotiṣṭoma* sacrifice'. The performance of the *Jyotiṣṭoma* is not obligatory. If a person desires heavenly enjoyment, he has to offer this sacrifice; otherwise not. The injunctions of obligatory and occasioned rites are categorical imperatives; those which are concerned with optional rites are hypothetical imperatives. The performance of the first two varieties of rites does not lead to any merit; but their non-performance will result in demerit. If the optional rites are not performed, there is no demerit; but if they are performed, there accrues merit.[242]

It seems that the contradiction Zaehner refers to[243] arises because Śaṅkara takes the words *kāmya karma* in a technical rather than a general sense. Kṛṣṇa seems to be saying that all actions of any kind, not just sacrificial acts called *kāmya*, should be given up if dictated by desire. Thus the verse has been under-interpreted by Śaṅkara. What Hill says in relation to another commentator on this verse applies here also to Śaṅkara: that he 'seems to take a limited view of the nature of *kāmya karman*: "The two principal kinds of action", he writes, "are religious action, as sacrifice, etc., and duty, or fulfilment of the obligations of the station in which one is born. All other kinds of action can only have some specific interested object in

[242] T.M.P. Mahadevan, *Outlines of Hinduism* (Bombay: Chetana, 1971 [first published 1956), pp.135-6.

[243] It seems more accurate to say that the horse-sacrifice was performed by Yudhiṣṭhira rather than Arjuna, though he participated in it.

view, and are therefore to be renounced." Kṛiṣṇa does not preach the complete reunciation of any kind of work at all; he only demands the conversion of all *kāmya karman* into *niṣkāma*'.[244]

This discussion actually leads into the next point. In his gloss on XVIII:12 Śaṅkara seems to force a distinction between the words *saṃnyāsa* and *tyāga*, a move which is anticipated in his gloss on XVIII:2. Let us review the verse itself (XVIII:12) before proceeding further:

aniṣṭam iṣṭam miśraṃ ca
trividhaṃ karmaṇaḥ phalam
bhavaty atyāgināṃ pretya
na tu saṃnyāsināṃ kvacit[245]

Undesired, desired, and mixed –
Threefold is the fruit of action
That ensues after death for those who are not men of abandonment,
But never for men of renunciation.[246]

Now Śaṅkara 'considers the *atyāgins* to be *karmayogins*, and the *saṃnyāsiṇs* to be those who have renounced all works'.[247] In other words Śaṅkara distinguishes between (1) the renunciation of the fruit of action and (2) the renunciation of action itself. He restricts the use of *tyāga* to (1) and of *saṃnyāsa* to (2). But the Gītā itself does not seem to make any such cut-and-dried distinction. Similarly his gloss on an earlier verse – XVIII:10 – seems to involve a forced distinction. The verse runs:

na dveṣṭy akuśalam karma
kuśale nānuṣajjate
tyāgī sattvasamāviṣṭo
medhāvī chinnasaṃśayaḥ[248]

He loathes not disagreeable action,
Nor does he cling to agreeable (action),
The man of abandonment who is filled with goodness,
Wise, whose doubts are destroyed.[249]

[244] Hill, op.cit., p.202, n.3.
[245] Bolle, op.cit., p.196.
[246] Edgerton, op.cit., Part I, p.165.
[247] Hill, op.cit., p.204, n.2.
[248] Bolle, op.cit., p.196.
[249] Edgerton, op.cit., Part I, p.165.

Śaṅkara explains *akuśala* and *kuśala karma* 'as respectively *kāmya* and *nitya karman*'.[250] It is extremely doubtful that the Gītā has any such distinction in mind. The verse seems to have been over-interpreted.

The next two verses which may be considered now are XVIII:13-14. Some have found the second particularly vexatious. They run as follows:

pancaitāni mahābāho
kāraṇāni nibodha me
sāṃkhye kṛtānte proktāni
siddhaye sarvakarmaṇāṃ

adhiṣṭhānaṃ tathā kartā
karaṇaṃ ca pṛthagvidham
vividhāś ca pṛthakceṣṭā
daivaṃ caivātra pañcamam[251]

O great-armed one, these five
Factors learn from Me,
Which are declared in the reason-method doctrine
For the effective performance of all actions.

The (material) basis, the agent too,
And the instruments of various sorts,
And the various motions of several kinds,
And just Fate as the fifth of them.[252]

The word *kṛtānta* in XVIII:13 may be taken up first. It is translated by Edgerton as 'for the effective performance of all actions';[253] by Hill as 'for the fulfilment of all works';[254] and by Zaehner as 'all works attain fruition'.[255] But Śaṅkara 'interprets *kṛtānta* as "that which puts an end to all action".'[256] He over-interprets, it would appear. The word *sāṅkhya* in the same verse he glosses 'as *vedānta* (possibly meaning the Upaniṣads)'.[257] This is puzzling, to say the least.

Discussion of the next verse is best introduced by the following

[250] Hill, op.cit., p.203, n.3.
[251] Bolle, op.cit., p.196.
[252] Edgerton, op.cit., Part I, p.165. [253] ibid.
[254] Hill, op.cit., p.204.
[255] Zaehner, op.cit., p.386.
[256] Hill, op.cit., p.204, n.3. [257] ibid.

remark of Franklin Edgerton:

> Much needless trouble has been caused by this verse, owing to attempts to make it too philosophical, and particularly to make it fit the theories of the later so-called Sāṃkhya system. It is a quite simple and naive attempt to suggest the factors which are involved in carrying out any action whatever; it is fundamentally wrong to try to identify each 'factor' with bodily parts or 'Sāṃkhya' *tattvas*. Each of the five words is to be taken in the simplest possible sense, and no comment is really needed – except that all existing comments are worthless and misleading.[258]

When he says that it is 'fundamentally wrong to identify each "factor" with bodily parts',[259] Edgerton may have the Hindu commentarial tradition in general in mind, but his remarks apply particularly to Śaṅkara. Śaṅkara glosses *adhiṣṭhāam* as *śarīram*, or the body; *kartā* as *upādhilakṣaṇo bhoktā*, or the doer *qua* enjoyer, conditioned by adjuncts; *karaṇam* as *śrotrādi*, or the ears, etc., i.e. the various senses, etc.,[260] which he counts as twelve (?) in number;[261] *ceṣṭāḥ* as *vāyavīyāḥ prāṇāpānādyāḥ*[262] i.e. the various breaths; and *daivam* as *Āditya*, etc., by whose aid the eyes, etc. perform their functions.[263]

Śaṅkara's anthropocentric interpretation seems to be off the mark here and involves a remarkably forced over-interpretation. This is puzzling, because a straightforward understanding of the verse would hardly undermine Śaṅkara's philosophical position. On the other hand, when words occur relative to action and to the 'doer', the performer of the action, Śaṅkara is keen to safeguard the independence of the pure *ātman* from any identification with the actor or with action. This is important from the point of view of Śaṅkara's position, and therefore his glosses of *kartā* as *upādhilakṣaṇo bhoktā* in XVIII:4 and *karaṇānām vyāpārayitā upādhilakṣaṇaḥ* (the employer of the means, limited by adjuncts) in XVIII:18 are not surprising.

Śaṅkara's gloss on XVIII:45 provides another example of how his philosophical presumptions affect his interpretation. The verse runs as follows:

[258] Edgerton, op.cit., Part I, p.189.

[259] ibid. When he refers to 'Sāmkhya *tattvas*' he has Hill in mind (see Hill, op.cit., p.204, n.3,4).

[260] ibid., p.204, n.4.

[261] *Śrīśāṅkaragranthāvaliḥ*, Sampuṭa 8, p.416.

[262] ibid.

[263] Hill, op.cit., p.204, n.4.

sve sve karmaṇy abhirataḥ
saṃsiddhiṃ labhate naraḥ
svakarmanirataḥ siddhiṃ
yathā vindati tac chṛṇu[264]

Taking delight in his own special kind of action,
A man attains perfection;
Delighting in one's own special action, success
How one reaches, that hear![265]

At issue is the exact significance of the words *saṁsiddhi* and *siddhi*. The word also appears in the next verse. Śaṅkara 'explains *siddhi*, or *saṁsiddhi*, in these *ślokas* as the qualification of the *karmayogin* for *jñānaniṣṭhā*. The words here mean the attainment of complete success in the realm of work, which, being performed with such "abandonment" as Kṛiṣṇa has taught, leads to the higher stage, where "quietude" precedes release'.[266]

The situation in this respect is rather complex, for Śaṅkara seems here to be partly right. The following verses appear to confirm his view that the perfecting of Karmayoga is only a step towards the attainment of full spiritual perfection (XVIII:50-3).

However, the next few verses throw in doubt his claim that *jñānaniṣṭhā* represents the *summum bonum*, for they seem to indicate a passage to devotional theism (XVIII:54-5):

brahmabhūtaḥ prasannātmā
na śocati na kāṅkṣati
samaḥ sarveṣu bhuteṣu
madbhaktiṃ labhate parām

bhaktyā mām abhijānāti
yāvān yaś cāsmi tattvataḥ
tato māṃ tattvato jñātvā
viśate tadanantaram[267]

Here Śaṅkara interprets the apparently theistic verses monistically in a somewhat clever but forced manner.[268]

[264] Bolle, op.cit., p.206.
[265] Edgerton, op.cit., Part I, p.173.
[266] Hill, op.cit., p.209, n.2.
[267] Bolle, op.cit., p.208.
[268] Edgerton, op.cit., Part I, p.175, provides a translation.

Objection: – The statement that, 'by the supreme devotion of knowledge he knows me,' involves a contradiction. – How? – Thus: when the knowledge of a certain object arises in the knower, then and then alone the knower knows that object; no devotion to that knowledge, no repetition of the knowledge, is necessary. Therefore, the statement that 'he knows Me, not by knowledge, but by *devotion* to knowledge, by a repetition of knowledge,' involves a contradiction.

Answer: – This objection does not apply here; for, the word 'devotion (nishṭha)' means that the knowledge aided by all the favourable conditions of its rise and development and freed from obstacles culminates in a firm conviction by one's own experience. When the knowledge of the unity of the individual Self (Kshetrajña) and the supreme Self (Paramatman), generated by the teachings of the Scriptures and the master under conditions favourable to the rise and ripening of that knowledge – viz. purity of mind, humility and other attributes (xiii.7 et seq.) – and accompanied with the reununciation of all works which are associated with the idea of distinction such as the agent and other factors of action, culminates in a firm conviction by one's own experience, then the knowledge is said to have attained supreme consummation. This jnana-nishṭha (Devotion of Knowledge) is referred to as the Supreme or fourth kind of Devotion, Bhakti (vii.17), – supreme as compared with the remaining three kinds of Devotion, with that of the distressed, etc. (vii.16). By this supreme devotion the aspirant knows the Lord as He is, and immediately afterwards all consciousness of difference between the Isvara and the Kshetrajña disappears altogether. Thus there is no contradiction involved in the statement that 'by the Devotion of Knowledge (the aspirant knows) Me.'[269]

Before we bring this discussion to a close, we must consider one more verse of the last chapter. It is a well-known verse which runs as follows (XVIII:66):

sarvadharmān parityajya
mām ekaṃ śaraṇaṃ vraja
ahaṃ tvā sarvapāpebhyo
mokṣayisyāmi mā śucaḥ[270]

Abandoning all (other) duties,
Go to Me as thy sole refuge;

[269] Alladi Mahadeva Sastry (tr.), op.cit., pp.492-3.
[270] Bolle, op.cit., p.210.

From all evils I thee
  Shall rescue: be not grieved![271]

Śaṅkara's gloss on this verse is not without interest. First, he maintains, as has been widely noted, that the word *dharma* in *sarvadharmān* 'includes *adharma*, because all works must be renounced, both good and evil'.[272] Zaehner also remarks that according to Śaṅkara *dharmān* 'refers to both what is lawful and what is unlawful'. But when he proceeds to add that 'the liberated man is emancipated from "the bonds of both law and lawlessness" ' he is really adding a flourish of his own. For Śaṅkara simply says: *dharma-śabdena atra adharmo' pi gṛhyate naiṣkarmyasya vivakṣitvāt.*[273] Moreover, as is also clear from the statements he cites thereafter, he is not talking of the post-, but rather of the pre-liberation, stage.

Śaṅkara's interpretation here seems to be defensible, as the verse speaks of *all* the dharmas – *sarvadharmān* – and this would suggest that, if all are to be included, the good as well as the bad might be caught in the same all-embracing net. It is his next remark, *sarvadharmān parityajya, sarvakarmāṇi ity etat,* which seems to pass beyond the realm of the text into the context of his own philosophy. He here equates *dharma* with *karma* and takes the abandonment of all duties to mean the abandonment of all actions. Such an interpretation presents two problems if we revert to the text: (1) the word *dharma* is a particular kind of action, and so the equation *dharma*=*karma* over-interprets *dharma*; and (2) the Gītā does not teach the abandonment of all action, only the abandonment of the fruits thereof. It is Śaṅkara who teaches the abandonment of all action (and by implication the abandonment of fruits thereof, for there can be no sprout without the seed). He is here reading his own teaching into the teaching of the Gītā or reading his own teaching out of the teaching of the Gītā, however one wishes to put it. As Hill clearly remarks in relation to *parityajya*, the 'word "abandoning" is used in the sense which Kriṣṇa has given it in the earlier *ślokas* of this Reading. Abandonment of *fruit* is taught, not complete renunciation.'[274]

271 Edgerton, op.cit., Part I, p.171.
272 Hill, op.cit., p.212, n.2.
273 *Śrīśaṅkaragranthāvaliḥ*, Sampuṭa 8, p.455.
274 Hill, op.cit., p.212, n.1.

3.

The first section of this chapter introduced the reader, albeit briefly, to the thought of Śaṅkara. The second section dissected critically his commentary on some of the verses of the Gītā. This third section will offer observations of a more general nature on his interpretation of the Gītā as represented by his commentary.

The system of Advaita Vedānta as developed by Śaṅkara contains several key concepts. One is that of *māyā*. The word also occurs in the Gītā. It will therefore be of some interest to examine the extent to which Śaṅkara's interpretation of its usage in the Gītā is affected by his philosophical position.

In developing his view that the ultimate reality is *nirguṇa brahman*, or unqualified consciousness, the question naturally arises: how is such a concept of a sole reality to be reconciled with the multiplicity in the world as experienced by us? The doctrine of *māyā* tries to answer the question by maintaining that this plurality is an appearance which disappears upon the realisation of the ultimate reality, '*like* an object in dream or illusion'. The point may best be explained if we try to understand how illusion occurs in ordinary life, as when we may mistake a rope for a snake.

> If we try to understand the process by which ordinary illusions in life take place, we find that an illusion, say, of snake in a rope, is due to our *ignorance* of what really is there behind the appearance, i.e. ignorance of the substratum or ground (*adhiṣṭhāna*), in this case, the rope. If we could know the rope as the rope, there would be no illusion about it. But mere ignorance of the rope cannot give rise to the illusion. For, otherwise, even a person who has never known what a rope is would always see serpents in things. The ignorance creating an illusion does not simply conceal from our view the real nature of the ground, the rope, but positively distorts it, i.e. makes it appear as something else. Concealment (*āvaraṇa*) of reality and distortion (*vikṣepa*) of it into something else in our mind are then the two functions of an illusion-producing ignorance (*avidyā* or *ajñāna*).[275]

Now if the whole universe is to be treated as such an appearance or a magic-show, who is the magician who displays this cosmic trick? It is God or *saguṇa brahman*:

[275] Satischandra Chatterjee and Dhirendramohan Datta, *An Introduction to Indian Philosophy* (University of Calcutta, 1968), p.370. Italics supplied.

For God, *māyā* is only the will to create the appearance. It does not affect God, does not deceive him. For ignorant people like us, who are deceived by it and see many objects here instead of one brahman or God *māyā* is an illusion-producing ignorance. In this aspect *māyā* is also called, therefore, *ajñāna* or *avidyā* (synonyms for 'ignorance') and is conceived as having the double function of concealing the real nature of Brahman, the ground of the world, and making Him appear as something else, namely, the world. In so far as *māyā positively* produces some illusory appearance it is called positive ignorance (*bhāva-rūpam ajñānam*); and in so far as no beginning can be assigned to the world, *māyā* is also said to be beginningless (*anādi*). But, for those wise few who are not deceived by the world-show, but who perceive in it nothing but God, there is no illusion nor, therefore, illusion-producing *māyā*. God to them is not, therefore, the wielder of *māyā* at all.[276]

In this context Śaṅkara 'constantly draws on the analogy of the magician (*māyāvī*)'. We may note that a magician is not deceived by his own tricks, it is the spectators who are so deceived. Similarly, the 'magician is a juggler only to those who are deceived by his trick and who fancy that they perceive the objects conjured up. But to the discerning few who see through the trick and have no illusion, the juggler fails to be a juggler. Similarly, those who believe in the world-show think of God through this show and call Him its Creator, etc. But for those wise few who know that the world is a mere show, there is neither any real world nor any real Creator.'[277]

Such, in brief, is Śaṅkara's doctrine of *māyā*. We now turn to the Bhagavadgītā. The word *māyā* occurs several times in several contexts.[278] We may now proceed to identify the main features of its use.

The use of the word *māyā* in the Gītā, although dispersed, occurs in a cluster in Chapter Seven. Thus VII:14, 15 run as follows:

daivī hy eṣā guṇamayī mama māyā duratyayā
mām eva ye prapadyante māyām etāṁ taranti te

na māṁ duṣkṛtino mūḍhāḥ prapadyante nar 'ādhamāḥ
māyayā 'pahṛta-jñānā āsuram bhāvam āśritāḥ.[279]

This divine *māyā* of Mine, consisting of the modes is hard to overcome. But those who take refuge in Me alone cross beyond it.

[276] ibid., p.371. [277] ibid., p.389.
[278] See *Bhagavadgītā* IV:6; VII:14,15, 25; XVIII:61, etc.
[279] Transliterated as per R.C. Zaehner, op.cit., p.249.

> The evil doers who are foolish, low in the human scale, whose minds are carried away by illusion and who partake of the nature of demons do not seek refuge in me.[280]

Again the word occurs in a compound in VII:25:

> *n 'āhaṁ prakāśaḥ sarvasya yoga-māyā-samāvṛtaḥ:*
> *mūḍho 'yam n'ābhijānāti loko mām ajam avyayam.*[281]

> Veiled by My creative power (*yogamāyā*) I am not revealed to all. This bewildered world knows Me not, the unborn, the unchanging.[282]

In all these uses of the word *māyā* the power of *veiling* is implied. God is not seen by all because He is veiled by *māyā*; the evil-doer under the influence of its veiling power does not seek God, and those who seek refuge in God go beyond the veil.

Two other occurrences next need to be taken into account. One is from Chapter Four, verse 6:

> *ajo 'pi sann avyay 'ātmā, bhūtānām īśvaro 'pi san,*
> *prakṛtiṁ svām adhiṣṭhāya sambhavāmy ātma-māyayā.*[283]

> Though (I am) unborn, and My self (is) imperishable, though (I am) the lord of all creatures, yet establishing Myself in my own nature, I come into (empiric) being through My power (*māyā*).[284]

The other is from Chapter Eighteen, verse 61:

> *īśvaraḥ sarva-bhūtānāṁ hṛd-deśe, 'rjuna, tiṣṭhati*
> *bhrāmayan sarva-bhūtāni yantr'ārūḍhāni māyayā.*[285]

> The Lord abides in the hearts of all being, O Arjuna, causing them to turn round by His power as if they were mounted on a machine.[286]

[280] See S. Radhakrishnan, *The Bhagavadgītā*, p.218.
[281] Zaehner, op.cit., p.253.
[282] Radhakrishnan, op.cit., p.223.
[283] Zaehner, op.cit., p.183.
[284] Radhakrishnan, op.cit., p.153.
[285] Zaehner, op.cit., p.399.
[286] Radhakrishnan, op.cit., p.374.

In both cases the initiative for the employment of *māyā* comes from God. In the previous section *māyā* was an occurrence; in these verses it is a performance.

The examination of these various uses of the word *māyā* in the Gītā suggests the following conclusions:

(1) that *māyā* is distinguished by being pervaded by the *guṇas* (VII:14a);
(2) that *māyā* belongs to Iśvara (VII:14b; IV;6d etc.);
(3) that *māyā* deludes or veils the wicked especially (VII:15c) but really everyone (VII:25c and XVIII p.61);
(4) that God can perform acts by employing *māyā* (IV:6d and XVIII:61cd);
(5) that those who resort to God alone can go beyond *māya* (VII.14cd).

The first point seems to represent the incorporation of a Sāṅkhyan understanding. Features (3) and (5) fit in neatly with the standard descriptions of *māyā* in Hindu monism as 'an inscrutable power of God that veils the true and projects the untrue. The power of veiling is termed *āvaraṇa*, and of projecting *vikṣepa*.'[287] It may be added, though, that in the Gītā it is the *āvaraṇa* rather than the *vikṣepa* aspect which seems to be prominent. Features (2) and (4) tie in with Hindu theism.

Another verse must also be noted in which the word *māyā* itself does not occur[288] but is introduced by Śaṅkara in the gloss. In glossing the word *kūṭastha* in XII:3 Śaṅkara remarks:

> He is unchangeable (*kūṭastha*) – *kūṭa* means a thing which is good to all appearance but evil within. Accordingly it refers here to that seed of *saṁsāra* – including *avidyā* (nescience) and other things, – which is full of evil within, designated by various terms such as *māyā, avyākrita* (undifferentiated), as in *Svetāśvataropanishad* (iv.10) and in the Gītā (vii.14) *kūṭastha* means He who is seated in *māyā* as Its Witness, as Its Lord – or '*kūṭastha*' may mean 'remaining like a heap'. Hence He is immutable and eternal.[289]

This invites the following strictures from Franklin Edgerton: namely, that here by *kūṭastha* Śaṅkara departs from his previous

[287] Mahadevan, op.cit., p.148.
[288] It also occurs in Śaṅkara's Introduction to his Gītābhāṣya.
[289] Alladi Mahadeva Sastry (tr.), op.cit., p.305. Diacritics supplied.

explanation 'understanding "abiding in trickery", i.e. in *māyā*, the world-illusion of which God is the "overseer". This is worth quoting as an instance of the absurdity and inconsistency of which even the greatest commentators are sometimes guilty. He adds, to be sure, an alternative interpretation, which is substantially that adopted here.'[290] Śaṅkara has nodded, but this instance does not compromise the overall argument.

How then does Śaṅkara handle the occurrence of *māyā*? Remarkably, in none of his glosses on the occurrence of the word does he divest *māyā* of association with God and describe the universe as a mere appearance superimposed on *nirguṇa brahman*. The point is of some importance since, strictly speaking, Advaita Vedānta can dispense with God, for the universe can be seen as directly connected with *nirguṇa brahman* in an illusory way, through *māyā*. But Śaṅkara does *not* perform such a manoeuvre, which seems to testify to two points: that the acceptance of theism in Advaita Vedānta is a genuine philosophical acceptance and not some kind of concession to the religious proletariat – a popularity gimmick – and that Śaṅkara does not, in a general way, try to suppress the theistic character of Gītā or of *māyā* therein. However, inasmuch as in his overall system he uses the word *māyā* to explain the universe as belonging to the order of appearance and the Gītā does not seem to suggest this, his *general* understanding of *māyā* goes beyond that of the Gītā, although he does not seem to betray this in his commentary.

> We have said previously that the world-appearance is due to *māyā*. God regarded as the Creator of the world is, therefore, described as the wielder of *māyā*. Ignorant people like us believe that the world is real and that, therefore, God is really *qualified by māyā*, i.e. possessed of the power of creating the world (*māyāviśiṣṭa*). But really creativity is not an essential character of God, it is only an apparent accidental predicate (*upādhi*) that we illusorily ascribe to God. God is only *apparently associated* with creativity (*māyopahita*). God as immanent (*saguṇa*) and God as transcendent reality (*nirguṇa*) are not two, any more than the man on the stage and that man outside the stage are two. The first is only the apparent aspect of the second. The first is relative to the world, the second is irrelative or absolute.[291]

[290] Edgerton, op.cit., Part I, p.186.

[291] Satischandra Chatterjee and Dhirendramohan Datta, op.cit., pp.391-2. A comparison of Rāmānuja's and Śaṅkara's conceptions of *māyā* may also be helpful in this respect, at this point. 'Rāmānuja, following the *Śvetāśvatara*, speaks also of *māyā*, but he means thereby either God's wonderful power of *real* creation or the *eternal*,

For such a full-blown Advaitic position of Śaṅkara we would be hard put to find support in the Gītā.

Apart from *māyā*, a key doctrine of Śaṅkara's system consists in the view that the *jñāna*, or knowledge, is incompatible with *karma*, or action; that the *jñānī* or one possessed of true knowledge does not really act at all. Or to rephrase: total abandonment of action is possible and in fact required for salvation. This question arises pointedly in the Eighteenth Chapter.

In the final chapter Arjuna initially raises the question: are *sannyāsa* and *tyāga* distinct from each other?[292] In the rest of this section we shall try to find an answer to this question from Śaṅkara's Gītābhāṣya.

Śaṅkara clearly perceives Arjuna's inquiry as centring on the nature of the distinction to be drawn between *sannyāsa* and *tyāga*. As a matter of fact, he even seems a trifle surprised at this, for he remarks: 'Verily, the whole of the doctrine taught in the preceding discourses is to be found in this discourse. Arjuna, however, asks to know only the distinction between *saṃnyāsa* and *tyāga*.'[293]

Moreover, in the connective note with which he introduces the next verse, Śaṅkara again remarks: 'The words *saṃnyāsa* and *tyāga* have been used here and there in the preceding discourse,[294] their

---

unconscious, primal matter which is in Brahman and which is *really* transformed into the world. Śaṅkara also speaks of *māyā* as the power of God, but this creative power, according to him, is not a permanent character of God, as Rāmānuja thinks, but only a free will which can, therefore, be given up at will. The wise who are not deceived by the world-appearance need not conceive God at all as the bearer of this illusion-producing power. Besides, even when conceived as a power, *māyā* is not a distinct entity in Brahman, but inseparable and indistinguishable from it as the burning power is from fire, or will is from the mind that wills. Even when Śaṅkara identifies *māyā* with *prakṛti*, he means nothing more by it than that this creative power is the source or origin (*prakṛti*) of world-appearance, to those who perceive this appearance. The difference between Rāmānuja and Śaṅkara, then, is that while, according to Rāmānuja, the matter of *prakṛti* which is an integral part of God really undergoes modification, Śaṅkara holds that God does not undergo any real change, change is only apparent, not real' (ibid., pp.371-2). Italics supplied.

[292] A. Mahādeva Śāstri, *The Bhagavad-Gītā with the commentary of Śrī Śancarachārya translated from Sanskrit into English* (Madras: V. Ramaswamy Sastrulu & Sons, 1972), p.441ff; Edgerton, op.cit., Part I, p.163.

[293] A. Mahādeva Śāstri, op.cit., p.441. This may be compared with Śrīdhara Swāmi's remark that 'the essence of the whole Gītā is taught clearly in the Eighteenth Chapter *by* distinguishing between renunciation and relinquishment' [Swami Vireshwarananda, *Srimad-Bhagavad-Gītā* (Text, Translation of the Text and of the gloss of Sridhara Swami) (Madras: Sri Ramakrishna Matha, 1948), p.472: italics added].

[294] Śrīdhara Svāmī in his gloss identifies some of these references. For *sannyāsa* he cites V:13, IX:28, and for *tyāga* IV:20 and XII:11 (op.cit., pp.473-4).

connotations, however, not being clearly distinguished. Wherefore, with a view to determining them, the Lord addresses Arjuna ...'[295]

The distinction between *sannyāsa* and *tyāga* is thus the crux of the question.

And what, according to Śaṅkara, is the answer?

It comes in two parts. He seems to say: (1) that the two words are *broadly synonymous*, but then he adds (2) that the two words, though broadly synonymous, are not *exactly* synonymous. He accepts the general synonymity of the words when he remarks that 'the meaning of the words *saṃnyāsa* and *tyāga* is in any way one and the same so far as the general idea is concerned, namely, abandonment';[296] but at the same time he implies that they are not exactly synonymous when he adds that they 'are not quite so distinct in meaning as the words "jar" and "cloth".'[297] The implication is that there is some distinction, though not as radical as that between a pitcher of water (*ghaṭa*) and a piece of cloth (*paṭa*). Ānandagiri paraphrases Śaṅkara as saying that 'the two words convey the same general idea with some distinction'.[298] Thus though they may not be as distinct as 'jar' and 'cloth' there does exist the kind of difference we find between a pot and a jar.[299] Thus, according to Śaṅkara, though there is a general overlap in meaning between the two words *sannyāsa* and *tyāga*, there is not a complete coincidence of meaning.

If we scrutinise the manner in which he glosses these terms in his commentary on the Gītā, we discover that, consistently with the above position, while in some contexts he accepts the two words as synonymous,[300] in others he finds significance in the distinction between the two terms.[301] One place, for instance, in which he clearly accepts synonymity is in his gloss of XVIII:4, where he comments on the occurrence of the word *tyāga* alone: 'The Lord has used this single word here, implying that the meaning of *tyāga* and *saṃnyāsa* is one and the same.' The key section of the gloss runs: *tyāgasannyasāśabdavācyo hi yo' rthaḥ sa eka eveti.*[302]

On the other hand, sometimes Śaṅkara does draw a distinction between the two terms, and in a manner which is quite revealing of his general philosophical position. For instance, in his gloss on

[295] A. Mahādeva Śāstri, op.cit., p.441.

[296] ibid., p.442. [297] ibid. [298] ibid.

[299] 'They convey the same general idea with slight distinction like ghaṭakalaśa' [Śrī Svāmī Sivananda, *Srimad Bhagavad Gita* (Rishikesh: Yoga-Vedanta Forest University, 1949), p.769].

[300] e.g. see glosses on V:13, VI:4, XVIII:7, etc.

[301] e.g. see glosses on XVIII:3, etc.

[302] *Śrīśāṅkaragranthāvaliḥ*, Samputa 7, p.408.

XVIII:9 he remarks that 'the abandonment of works and the abandonment of the desire for the fruits do agree in so far as they alike imply abandonment'.[303] The term used for abandonment of works is *sannyāsa*, for abandonment of the desire for the fruits *tyāga*, and for abandonment in general *tyāga*. Thus for Śaṅkara, though sometimes the words may be used interchangeably, at other times (as in this case) *sannyāsa* and *tyāga* have different meanings. The difference then consists in *sannyāsa* being related to abandonment of action and *tyāga* to the abandonment of the fruits of action; and *tyāga* may subsume *sannyāsa*, but *sannyāsa* does not subsume *tyāga*.

A close look at the way he glosses *sannyāsa* and *tyāga* suggests the conclusion that: (1) in some cases he takes the two words as interchangeable, when the basic meaning of the *fact* of abandonment is involved; but that (2) he does sometimes distinguish between the two on the basis of *what* is abandoned. *Sannyāsa* is taken then to refer to abandonment of works, as distinct from *tyāga*, which then refers to the abandonment of the fruits of action. Furthermore, though he sometimes uses the word *tyāga* to refer also to the abandonment of works (as in his gloss on XVIII:11), he never seems to use the word *sannyāsa* to refer to the abandonment of the fruits of action.

What, if any, is the philosophical significance for Śaṅkara of this distinction between *sannyāsa* and *tyāga*?

It seems to be considerable when viewed in the light of Śaṅkara's overall philosophical orientation. To see this, it is helpful to identify two basic elements of his philosophical system. These are (1) that salvation is possible only through Jñāna; and (2) that Jñāna is characterised by the abandonment of action.[304]

Both these aspects of Śaṅkara's philosophical position find clear articulation in his Gītābhāṣya.[305] It will be noticed that he does not regard Jñāna as characterised by the abandonment of the fruits of action, but of action itself. This is important. While it is true that if action is abandoned its fruit is automatically abandoned – the peas go with the pod – the reverse is not equally true for Śaṅkara.

This then seems to be Śaṅkara's overall position: that salvation is achieved by the 'pre-eminent renunciation of all works'[306] (*mukyaḥ sarvakarmasaṃnyāsaḥ*). As a matter of fact, he holds to this position so firmly that he has to make special efforts to explain – some would say explain away – those verses in the Gītā which run counter to it. But

[303] Mahādeva Śāstri, op.cit., p.450.

[304] For (1) see Sampuṭa 8, op.cit., p.457; for (2) see ibid., p.3; etc.

[305] Śaṅkara cites Anugītā (xlii.26) with approval which states *jñānaṁ sannyāsalakṣaṇam*. It will be noticed that Jñāna is not called *tyāgalakṣaṇam*.

[306] Mahādeva Śāstri, op.cit., p.407.

before we turn to an analysis of such verses it might be useful to clarify Śaṅkara's position, as there appears to be some room for misunderstanding. We may begin by asking two searching questions. (1) *Why* does he say that all action must be abandoned for salvation? (2) *What* does he mean when he says that all Karma must be abandoned?

The first question is more easily answered than the second. According to Śaṅkara, salvation is not possible as long as the slightest trace of the fruits of action remains to be exhausted. As long as action is performed, there will be the fruit of action, which will bar the way to salvation. Therefore, if to achieve salvation we must get rid of fruits of action in its entirety, then in order to get rid of the fruits of action we must get rid of action itself. For 'an action done, whether interested (*kāmya*) or obligatory and disinterested (*nitya*) must produce its effect; – [it cannot of course produce] *mokṣa*, which, being eternal, cannot be produced by an action.'[307]

Now the second question: what does Śaṅkara mean when he says that all Karma is to be abandoned?

The word *karma* has the general meaning of action and the more specific meaning of ritual. Corresponding to these, *sannyāsa* has two meanings: a narrow one and a broad one. The narrower, more specific and technical meaning relates to the *Caturthāśrama*, the fourth stage in the Hindu system of the four Āśramas. As we enter this stage all rituals are given up. This is one sense in which Śaṅkara uses the word *sannyāsa* – the abandonment of ritual action. In this case the abandonment involves the giving up of an outwardly identifiable action – as when someone who, as *gṛhastha*, tended the household fire, as a *sannyāsin* ceases to do so.[308]

But Śaṅkara also connects *sannyāsa* with the more general meaning of the word *karma*: namely, action per se. According to Śaṅkara, 'the Gītāśāstra teaches that he who has acquired a knowledge of the self should resort to renunciation only, not to works'.[309] This raises the obvious question: how can all action be abandoned – for even eating, seeing, hearing, etc., are action, and how can they ever be abandoned except in death? Śaṅkara's answer is routed via verses 8 and 9 of Chapter Five.[310] It is that though a

307 ibid., p.180. 308 ibid., p.182. 309 ibid., p.48.

310 It is as if for Śaṅkara Arjuna's question raised in the first verse of the Eighteenth Chapter, 'What is the *tattva* of *sannyāsa*?' is to be answered on the basis of the clue provided in the eighth and ninth verses of the Fifth Chapter, wherein the *tattvavit* is described as one who 'though seeing, hearing, touching, smelling, eating, going, sleeping, breathing, speaking, letting go, seizing, opening and closing his eyes – remembering that the senses move among sense-objects' and 'steadfast' should think 'I do nothing at all' (A. Mahādeva Śāstri, op.cit., p.164).

Jñānīn may appear to be acting outwardly he 'sees only inaction in actions – in all the movements of the body and the senses – ... he sees the absence of action'.[311]

In other words Śaṅkara uses the word *sannyāsa* in two ways: both to refer to the abandonment of identifiable forms of outward action in some cases, and to refer to the inward abandonment of action in other cases.

Thus Śaṅkara's conception of the abandonment of all *karma* applies at two levels, physical and mental, or to two spheres of action, outward and inward.[312] But however applied the dictum is clear: all action must be abandoned. How, then, does Śaṅkara make his position conform with the Gītā's, which is constantly stirring Arjuna to act?

The way he sets about his work can be seen by a case-study of the verses in the Gītā which are likely to create a 'problem' for his position. Some of these may now be identified: III:4,5,30: V:2; VI:1,2; XI:12; and XVIII:3,7,9,11 and 12.

(1) III:4. This verse clearly states that perfection cannot be attained by *sannyāsa*. How does Śaṅkara handle this? He wholeheartedly agrees. How can perfection, he remarks, be attained by 'mere renunciation *unaccompanied by knowledge*?'[313]

(2) III:5. This verse asserts that no one, even for an instant, ever remains without performing some form of action. This statement is diametrically opposed to Śaṅkara's position that all action must be abandoned. How does Śaṅkara get out of this bind? He remarks that we must distinguish (according to III:3) between the Jñānayogin and the Karmayogin. The verse is meant for Karmayogin, and 'the Karmayogin devotion to action is indeed meant for the ignorant only, not for the wise'.[314] The wise see non-action in all action.

(3) III:30. This verse uses the continuative *sannyasya* with *karmāṇi* as object, which clearly means that action is performed and then cast on Kṛṣṇa.[315] In Śaṅkara's system, *sannyāsa* is the renunciation of action in the sense of its utter non-performance, *not* in the sense of renunciation after performance – for once action is performed results

[311] ibid.

[312] This Śaṅkara states clearly in his introduction to Chapter Five wherein he remarks that 'this samnyasa, which consists of renouncing a few actions only while yet there is an idea of agency, is different from ... the renunciation of all actions – which is resorted to by the man has realised the self' (ibid., p.158).

[313] ibid., p.95; italics added. [314] ibid., p.96.

[315] In his comment on II:21 Śaṅkara uses the argument that elsewhere (V:13) the word *nyāsa* with *saṃ* prefix means 'to renounce' and not 'to deposit'. Grammar wouldn't allow such an option here.

must ensue. How then does Śaṅkara square this verse with his position? He introduces the verse with the note that it tells us how the ignorant (*ajña*) desirous of liberation and fit for Karmayoga should act.[316] Thus, by casting off the verse on the ignorant, he protects his position *vis-à-vis* the Jñānin.

(4) V:2. This verse clearly states that Karmayoga is to be preferred to Karmasannyāsa, which runs counter to his position. He remarks that Karmayoga is being extolled here, and that what is really meant is that the 'Karmayoga is better than *mere* – i.e. unaccompanied with knowledge – Karmasaṃnyāsa'.[317]

(5) VI:1. In this verse one who performs his bounden duty without depending on the fruits of action is called a *sannyāsin*. And what is worse (from Śaṅkara's standpoint) one who is 'without fire' and 'without action' seems to have been denied that description! Thus (a) not only is one who *performs* actions called a *sannyāsin* (an abandoner of action), but (b) one who abandons action is *not* called a *sannyāsin*, or abandoner of action. Let Śaṅkara get out of this one!

His response to the first point is to distinguish between two kinds of *sannyāsa* – primary (*mukhya*) and secondary (*gauṇa*).[318] In these verses, according to Śaṅkara, it is not primary but secondary *sannyāsa* which constitutes the subject of discourse. Primary *sannyāsa* consists of giving up all actions, secondary *sannyāsa* of giving up only the desire for the fruit of action. According to Śaṅkara the abandonment of the desire for the fruits of action is called *sannyāsa* here out of courtesy – out of a desire to praise Karmayoga for which alone Arjuna is eligible.

On the second point Śaṅkara remarks that what is meant is that 'it is not *he alone* who is without fire and without action that is both a *sannyāsin* and a Yogin but also one devoted to action'[319] – in the same vein of praise.

(6) XII:12. This verse glorifies *tyāga* as superior to *dhyāna*, which in turn is described as superior to Jñāna. In Śaṅkara's system pride of place is accorded to Jñāna, a place it has lost in this verse. How does Śaṅkara explain the reversal? He points out that the preceding verses offer various options in descending order from the worship of the Impersonal to the Personal, and that it is only as a last resort that *tyāga* (which in this verse is clearly identified with *sarvakarmaphala-tyāga*) is glorified for the sake of Arjuna for whom Karmayoga has been recommended.[320] This over, the next few verses begin eulogising the Jñānin.

[316] ibid., p.110. [317] ibid., p.160; italics added.
[318] ibid., p.183; also see Samputa 8, p.157.
[319] ibid., p.181. [320] ibid., pp.309-11.

(7) XVIII:3. Śaṅkara is committed to the position that all works are to be abandoned. In this verse, however, two views are recorded: namely, that while according to some all action is to be abandoned as evil, according to others 'sacrifice, gift and austerity'[321] should not be given up. Certain kinds of action thus may not be renounced. How is this to be taken *vis-à-vis* Śaṅkara's position that all action is to be abandoned?

According to Śaṅkara it is not Jñānins but 'the Karmayogins that form the subject of discussion here; and it is with reference to them that these divergent views are held, but not with reference to *jñānaniṣṭhas* (wisdom-devotees) the *saṃnyāsins* who have risen (above all worldly concerns)'. As for the Jñānins, they 'who see the Supreme Reality have only to follow the path of knowledge, accompanied with the renunciation of all works; and they have nothing else to do, and do not therefore form the subject of the alternative views set forth here'.[322]

(8) XVIII:7. This verse categorically states that the renunciation of prescribed action (*niyata karma*) is not proper, and thus takes a position antipodal to Śaṅkara's that all action should be abandoned. For Śaṅkara this verse does not illustrate the case of the Jñānin but the 'case of the ignorant man'. Moreover, he adds, because 'this sort of abandonment is due to ignorance' it is called Tāmasic.[323]

(9) XVIII:9. This verse refers to the best kind of *tyāga* – the Sāttvic type which is described as consisting of the performance of prescribed works with the abandonment of attachment and also the fruit. Hence once more the actual performance of action is recommended, as against Śaṅkara's position that all action should be abandoned. How does he resolve the difference?

He first poses the problem quite pointedly. If *sannyāsa* implies the abandonment of works, and if the previous verses (XVIII:7,8) have also referred to the abandonment of works, how does the question of abandonment of the *fruits* of action crop up here? He then answers his own question by remarking that since the purpose of this verse is to praise abandonment, and since the giving up of fruits is also abandonment, 'the abandonment of the *desire for the fruits* of action is praised as being Sattvic abandonment'.[324]

321 ibid., p.443. 322 ibid., p.445.

323 ibid., p.448. Tamas is associated with ignorance through XIV:8.

324 ibid., p.450. There is also the hint that this is done for Arjuna's benefit who is explicitly addressed in the verse. Arjuna is fit only for Karmayoga which involves the renunciation of the fruit of action rather than action and so 'accordingly, by despising the two sorts of abandonment of *works*, as Rajasic and Tamasic', the abandonment of the fruit of works is praised.

(10) XVIII:11. this verse, like III:5 earlier, points out that the renunciation of all works is an impossibility. Śaṅkara's response is similar. It is to say: 'the meaning is: it is not possible for an *ignorant* man to abandon actions completely.'[325]

(11) XVIII:12. This verse seems to use the words *tyāga* and *sannyāsa* interchangeably. How does Śaṅkara react?

It was pointed out earlier that in some contexts Śaṅkara does use the words interchangeably. This is one of the places where he does so. He glosses *atyāginām* as *aparamārthasannyāsinām* and *sannyāsinām* as *paramārthasannyāsinām.* But the catch lies in the expression *paramārtha.* Śaṅkara, who had earlier distinguished between primary and secondary *sannyāsa*, now distinguishes between real *sannyāsa* and not-so-real *sannyāsa.* And here again the distinction is made not with *tyāga* but with *sannyāsa.* And the Karmayogins are called the practitioners of not-so-real *sannyāsa*, and only the *jñānaniṣṭhas* are called real *sannyāsins.*

Why this subtlety? Because, according to Śaṅkara, unless the action itself is given up, fruit of action will ensue. Giving up the fruit of action is *not enough* for salvation; action itself must be given up.[326] Thus Ānandagiri explains Śaṅkara's distinction between real and not-so-real *sannyāsa* by pointing out that 'those who perform works without desire for their fruits will necessarily reap, after death, the fruits of their respective actions'.[327] And Śaṅkara himself, in his gloss on XVIII:2 clearly states that 'even' ordinary and occasional duties – *nitya* and *naimittika karma* – 'produce their own fruits' and those who are 'not *saṃnyāsins* will have to reap the fruit of ordinary works'.[328]

It is clear, therefore, that Śaṅkara consistently sticks to his basic position throughout his exegetical exercise – namely, that salvation is to be achieved by Jñāna, which involves the complete renunciation of all works.

In his hermeneutical effort to maintain his position through the Gītā as exemplified in the cases cited above, it is quite clear that the distinction between *sannyāsa* and *tyāga* is important for Śaṅkara. This is due to the primacy of the concept of *sannyāsa* as a concomitant of Jñāna through which salvation comes in his system. The key to salvation in Śaṅkara is not *tyāga* but *sannyāsa*,[329] because salvation is

[325] ibid., p.452; italics added.
[326] ibid.,p.453. [327] ibid. [328] ibid., p.443.
[329] Unless the word *tyāga* is used as an exact synonym of *sannyāsa* and is stripped of its other meanings such as the renunciation of the fruit of works.

tied in with the complete renunciation of all works and this meaning shines through more brightly through the term *sannyāsa* than through the term *tyāga*.

The 'problem', if we may use the word, for Śaṅkara, is created by the fact that Arjuna, being an a-Jñānin, is fit only for Karmayoga and so action has to be performed by him. To get him to perform action, Kṛṣṇa has to glorify action, and thus the Gītā at several points seems to swing away from the severity of *sannyāsa* into the tolerance of *tyāga*. Yet there is the realisation too that 'action performed with Bhakti, without concern for immediate reward leads to purity of mind' and the 'man whose mind is pure is competent to tread the path of knowledge, and to him comes knowledge, and thus (indirectly) the Religion of Works forms also means of Supreme Bliss'.[330]

One final question remains to be asked: in his exegetical exercise how faithful has Śaṅkara been to the text of the Gītā?

The question can be answered in two parts: how faithful has he been to the letter of the Gītā, and how faithful has he been to its spirit?

The first is perhaps more easily answered than the second. A semantic differential analysis of the two words *sannyāsa* and *tyāga* with their grammatical variants in the Gītā reveals that in the text, although the two words are often used interchangeably, there is a clear association of the word *sannyāsa* with *karma*, action, and of *tyāga* with *karmaphala*, or fruit of action. As a matter of fact, though the word *sannyāsa* is used in the Gītā for giving up the *desire* for the fruit of action, or attachment to the fruit of action (VI:2,4), or *dependence* on the fruit of action (VI:1), it is not used for giving up the fruit of action itself.

Thus Śaṅkara seems to be on the same semantic wavelength as the Gītā. He is justified in not regarding the two words as completely synonymous, although he recognises the tremendous overlap in their meaning. Moreover, he is also justified in working primarily with the word *sannyāsa*, rather than *tyāga*, consistently with his overall position of Jñānayoga as the Yoga *par excellence*.

But in regarding the Jñānayoga as the Yoga *par excellence* he seems to have somehow gone beyond the Gītā.[331] In fairness to him it must

[330] ibid., p.6.

[331] It is true that at some places the Gītā seems to go all out for Jñāna Yoga, as for instance in IV:36-42. It is also true that the connection with Śaṅkara makes between Jñāna Yoga and *sannyāsa* can be seen as coming directly out of the Gītā (see XVIII:49). It can also be seen as emerging indirectly through the equation of Jñāna with Sāṅkhya and then of Sāṅkhya with Yoga (V:5) and of Yoga with *sannyāsa* (VI:2).

be pointed out that he recognises that the Gītā is meant for Arjuna and espouses Karmayoga[332] in that sense, but in his interpretation of the response of the Gītā to some of the questions raised by Arjuna, for instance in verses 2 to 12 of the Eighteenth Chapter, he seems to use Jñāna rather than Karmayoga as the guiding light.[333] One wonders whether a more direct interpretation of these lines would not be more in keeping with the spirit of the Gītā, at least at that point. Jñānayoga is one of the Yogas mentioned in the Gītā; to interpret the Gītā as if it is *the* Yoga of the Gītā, rather than a Yoga within the Gītā, would not seem to reflect its true spirit.

When we compare Śaṅkara's commentary with the text of the Gītā, therefore, on issues related to *sannyāsa* and *tyāga*, a metaphorical conclusion may not be out of place. Although he seems to be on the same wavelength as the Gītā, the message being thus broadcast seems to be intended for a audience of spiritual aspirants beyond just the seekers on the path of knowledge.

4.

The first section of this chapter took a glance at Śaṅkara's thought; the second analysed some of his glosses on the verses of the Gītā; and the third provided a more general overview of his Gītā-bhāṣya from the vantage point of some philosophical details of his system. In this final section, then, an overall assessment may be offered.

There is a tendency among scholars both Indian and Western to

---

Nevertheless, it would perhaps be truer to say the Gītā espouses a kind of philosophical kathenotheism so far as the Yogas are concerned. It is successively accords primacy to one and/or the other. This is true for the entire work and is most obvious in the latter half of the Eighteenth chapter wherein the emphasis shifts from Karma (XVIII:41-7) to Jñāna (XVIII:49-53) to Bhakti (XVIII:61-9).

[332] Mahādeva Śāstri, op.cit., pp.5-6.

[333] This procedure has elicited a strong adverse comment from W.D.P. Hill [*The Bhagavadgītā* (London: Oxford University Press, 1928), p.257, n.4] who remarks that 'Śaṅkara most perversely twists the doctrine of 2-12 to agree with his preconceived philosophy'. A less extreme position would be to regard Śaṅkara as perhaps unconsciously rather than perversely colouring the text with his interpretation. What K. Satchidananda Murty has to say on Śaṅkara *vis-à-vis* the Veda may then be applied to his interpretation of the Gītā. Dr Murty writes: 'The allegation of some European authors that Śaṅkara has no consistent principles of interpretation is unfounded; what was wrong with him was his notion of what was *important* in the Scripture. Since he started with the presumption that the Veda is meant for teaching Advaita, and that only passages inculcating this are important, he found Advaita in the Veda' [*Revelation and Reason in Advaita Vedānta* (New York: Columbia University Press, 1959), pp.331-2].

assess Śaṅkara's commentary in extreme terms, swerving from the hagiographical at one extreme to the scatological at the other. A more balanced assessment seems to be called for. It should be clear from the preceding discussion that the commentary, judged by the intellectual norms (or should we say fashions) of our age displays both merits and demerits, and in such measure as does not warrant either a standing ovation or a deafening silence from his audience. Normal applause should suffice.[334]

[334] Śaṅkara seems essentially to be interpreting the Gītā from within the framework of his own philosophical system. This does not necessarily mean, however, that as an absolutist he must underplay the Gītā's theism, for theism does have a role to play in Advaita Vedānta. It does mean, though, that he cannot concede ultimacy to it. Nevertheless, while in terms of *his* system theism cannot be ultimate, he does seem to accept the position that the ultimate message of the Gītā is theistic, for he regards verse XI:55 as representing the essence of the Gītā (*sārabhūta*) and it *is* theistic in import and interpreted by him accordingly.

CHAPTER FIVE

Rāmānuja

It was pointed out earlier that the Bhagavadgītā is not a systematic work of philosophy. Any attempt, therefore, to systematise it is bound to produce a twofold effect: (a) to shed more light on those verses which accord with the projected system and clarify them; and (b) to cast into greater darkness those which don't and distort them. The attempt to systematise the Gita could also produce another twofold effect: (a) over-interpretation of those verses which are in accord with one's system, and (b) under-interpretation of those which are not.

Rāmānuja (1017-1137) provides a good illustration of this phenomenon. In the first section of this chapter we will examine specifically some of those verses on which his gloss seems to help us get closer to the intended meaning in the given context. In the second we will instantiate cases in which his interpretation of verses seems to depart, in varying degrees, from the intended meaning of the text. In the third his glosses on Gītā II:20; III:10-11, IX:26-7 and XVII:20-2; III:10; IV:42; and XVIII.1 will be discussed in greater detail to substantiate the general conclusions of the first two sections. Finally, in the fourth section, an overall assessment of his interpretation will be provided.

Before we proceed, however, it may be useful to draw a brief outline of Rāmānuja's system of thought, known as Viśiṣṭādvaita, in a few bold strokes. His system, like other Hindu systems, is concerned with Brahman, or the ultimate reality. The basic question which he faced was the same as Hindu thinkers have faced before and after him: (1) What is the nature of Brahman? Is it ultimately *nirguṇa* or *saguṇa*? (2) How is Brahman related to the world and its creatures? Are they a part of Brahman? and (3) How is Brahman to be realised in order that salvation may be achieved?

From the answers he gave to these questions and the implications they carried emerged the basic formulations of the school of

Viśiṣṭādvaita Vedānta. For Rāmānuja, Brahman was ultimately *saguṇa*; the world was not unreal but more in the nature of the sport (*līlā*) of God. The world and the individual souls were eternal but dependent entities – dependent, that is, on God. And God was to be realised and salvation finally achieved through devotion.[1]

1.

II:12 *na tv evāhaṃ jātu nāsaṃ*
na tvaṃ neme janādhipāḥ
na caiva na bhaviṣyāmaḥ
sarve vayam ataḥ param[2]

But not in any respect was I (ever) not,
Nor thou, nor these kings;
And not at all shall we ever come not to be,
All of us, henceforward.[3]

Rāmānuja interprets the verse to mean that it implies (a) the distinction between God and the souls, *aham* standing for Kṛṣṇa (=God); (b) the existence of a plurality of selves (*ātmans*) not merely empirically but also ultimately. Śaṅkara comments that 'the plural form refers to distinction (*bheda*) of bodies and does not mean that there is a distinction between one self [and another]'.[4]

Scholars are divided on who is right. Zaehner thinks that as there exists a plurality of transmigrating selves the 'obvious sense of the verse would seem to support' Rāmānuja, but Hill believes that Śaṅkara is right in regarding the distinction among the transmigrating souls as 'conventional rather than philosophical'.[5] The verse as it stands clearly implies a plurality of transmigrating selves, but by itself does not warrant either Rāmānuja's suggestion that it implies a distinction between God and the souls or Śaṅkara's that the distinction is merely empirical. The empirical plurality of transmigrating selves is accepted by both Rāmānuja and Śaṅkara. A

[1] See Arvind Sharma, *Viśiṣṭādvaita Vedānta: A Study* (New Delhi: Heritage Publishers, 1978), p.13.

[2] Kees W. Bolle, *The Bhagavadgītā: A New Translation* (Berkeley: University of California Press, 1979), p.56.

[3] Franklin Edgerton, *The Bhagavad Gītā: Translated and Interpreted* Part I (Cambridge, Massachusetts: Harvard University Press, 1944), p.47.

[4] R.C. Zaehner, *The Bhagavad-Gītā* (Oxford: Clarendon Press, 1969), p.125.

[5] W. Douglas P. Hill, *The Bhagavadgītā* (Oxford University Press, 1969), p.65, n.1.

plurality of ultimate selves, on the other hand, is denied by Śaṅkara but accepted by Rāmānuja. The verse *may* by itself be taken as supporting Rāmānuja rather than Śaṅkara.

IV:24 *brahmārpaṇaṃ brahma havir*
brahmāgnau brahmaṇā hutaṃ
brahmaiva tena gantavyaṃ
brahmakarmasamādhinā[6]

The (sacrificial) presentation is Brahman; Brahman is the oblation;
In the (sacrificial) fire of Brahman it is poured by Brahman;
Just to Brahman must he go,
Being concentrated upon the (sacrificial) action that is Brahman.[7]

This is a difficult verse to interpret, but it seems that Rāmānuja gets closer to the intended sense than Śaṅkara, who 'is unusually obscure on this passage. What he seems to be saying is that everything *is* Brahman in so far as it *is*, but in so far as anything shows diversity of any sort it is as non-existent as the silver for which a man may mistake mother-of-pearl. On his realising the mistake the "silver" is simply annihilated. So with the phenomenal world, once one has realised Brahman, the One, it is seen to be simply nothing. All this is very far from the thought of the Gītā.'[8] Moreover, Śaṅkara maintains that 'the knowledge of one who has given up all rites and renounced all action is represented as a sacrifice; to such a man everything connected with his "sacrifice" is Brahman; the idea of Brahman has replaced all idea of accessories'.[9] So according to Śaṅkara the verse 'simply represents *jñāna* as *yajña*'[10] and in the subsequent verses Kṛṣṇa 'enumerates other kinds of sacrifice with a view to extol *jñāna*'.[11]

But Rāmānuja seems to be closer to the original when he develops the following view, for instance: 'The man sinks himself in the idea that all action is instinct with Brahman (*brahmamaya*),' he says, 'because its very essence is Brahman, is the *brahma-karma-samādhi* (mentioned in the text). And because its very essence is Brahman he must go to it because it has become Brahman [for him] and has the essential nature (*svarūpa*) of the self.'[12] Moreover, Rāmānuja

[6] Bolle, op.cit., p.56. [7] Edgerton, op.cit., Part I, p.47.
[8] Zaehner, op.cit., p.192. [9] Hill, op.cit., p.106, n.3.
[10] ibid., p.106, n.3. [11] ibid.
[12] Zaehner, op.cit., p.192.

regards the subsequent verses as describing the various sacrifices which constitute forms of *brahma yoga*,[13] *brahma* being taken in the sense of ritual.[14] This is obviously closer to the text.

V:15 *nādatte kasyacit pāpaṃ*
na caiva sukṛtaṃ vibhuḥ
ajñānenāvṛtaṃ jñānaṃ
tena muhyanti jantavaḥ[15]

He does not receive (the effect of) any one's sin,
Nor yet (of) good deeds, the Lord (soul);
Knowledge is obscured by ignorance;
By that creatures are deluded.[16]

Commentators differ on the referent of the term *vibhuḥ*. Śaṅkara takes it to mean God, who accepts neither the good nor evil acts performed by the devotees.[17] Zaehner is therefore not quite right in saying that Śaṅkara 'switches from the empirical to the absolute (*pāramārthika*) standpoint',[18] as God is not the Absolute; but he is right in saying that Śaṅkara 'attacks devotional religion as being ultimately pointless'.[19] Rāmānuja correctly takes *vibhuḥ* to refer to the individual self and comments: 'He does not receive or reject the good or evil deeds performed by people he respects such as his son simply because they are related to him.' *Vibhu*, meaning 'all-pervading', is indeed quite suitably used of the individual self, since that self has 'become the [very] self of every contingent being' (5.7).[20] Hill concurs, commenting that it is indeed so as 'seems clear from the context'.[21]

X:11 *teṣām evānukampārtham*
aham ajñānajaṃ tamaḥ
nāśayāmy ātmabhāvastho
jñānadīpena bhāsvatā[22]

[13] Hill, op.cit., p.106, n.3.
[14] See M. Hiriyanna, *Outlines of Indian Philosophy* (London: Allen & Unwin, 1964 [first published in 1932]), p.118.
[15] Bolle, op.cit., p.66. [16] Edgerton, op.cit., Part I, p.55.
[17] *Śrīśāṅkaragranthāvaliḥ* – Samputa 8, p.143; see Chapter Three above for details.
[18] Zaehner, op.cit., p.209. [19] ibid.
[20] ibid. [21] Hill, op.cit., p.114, n.3.
[22] Bolle, op.cit., p.114.

To show compassion to those same ones,
Their ignorance-born darkness I
Dispel, (while) remaining in My own true state,
With the shining light of knowledge.[23]

The exegetical point involved here is the correct interpretation of *jñāna*, in the compound *jñāna-dīpa*, the lamp of knowledge. Śaṅkara offers an extended gloss:

> *Out of mere compassion:* out of mercy, anxious as to how they may attain bliss. I dwell in their *antaḥkaraṇa* which is engaged in thinking exclusively of the Self and destroy the darkness of ignorance, – that illusory knowledge which is caused by the absence of discrimination, – by the lamp of wisdom, by the lamp of discriminatory knowledge, fed by the oil of pure Devotion (*bhakti-prasāda*), fanned by the wind of earnest meditation on Me, furnished with the wick of right intuition purified by the cultivation of piety, chastity and other virtues, held in the *antaḥkaraṇa* which is completely detached from all worldly concerns, placed in the wind-sheltered enclosure of the mind which is withdrawn from the sense-objects and untainted by attachment and aversion, and shining with the light of right knowledge generated by incessant practice of concentration and meditation.[24]

Śaṅkara thus interprets *jñāna* very broadly, perhaps too broadly as the context seems to call for a sharper theistic focus. It seems that Rāmānuja is more to the point in suggesting that

> *jñāna* here means knowledge of God. The lamp with which he enlightens the total personality is itself the self: 'As a lamp might stand in a windless place, unflickering – this likeness has been heard of such athletes of the spirit who control their thought and practise integration of the self' (6.19). This revelation of God in the self might be called the 'highest wisdom' corresponding to the 'highest love-and-loyalty' to God mentioned in 18.54.[25]

XV:16 *dvāv imau puruṣau loke*
kṣaraś cākṣara eva ca
kṣaraḥ sarvāṇi bhūtāni
kūṭastho'kṣara ucyate[26]

[23] Edgerton, op.cit., Part I, p.99.
[24] Alladi Mahadeva Sastry, tr., *The Bhagavadgītā with the Commentary of Sri Sankaracharya* (Madras: Samaya Books, 1979), p.265.
[25] Zaehner, op.cit., p.295. [26] Bolle, op.cit., p.176.

Here in the world are two spirits,
  The perishable, and the imperishable;
The perishable is all beings;
  The imperishable is called the immovable.[27]

Again a difficult verse.[28] The problem here is: what does *akṣara* connote? Śaṅkara, and his school, opt for the following explanation:

> that the Imperishable is the *māyāśakti* of the Lord, the germ from which the Perishable being (the whole universe of changing forms) takes its birth, the seat of all the latent impressions of desires, actions, etc., belonging to the numerous mortal creatures. Ānandagiri adds that these two are spoken of as *puruṣas* because they are the *upādhis* of the one *puruṣa*. Ś. seems unwilling to admit that Kṛiṣṇa, or Brahman, is in any sense 'higher' than individual Self: the supremacy lies, of course, in the difference between 'free' and 'bound'.[29]

Rāmānuja distinguishes between *kṣara* and *akṣara* as bound and free spirit respectively:[30]

> In other words, the 'Imperishable Person' is, as Rāmānuja points out, the sum-total of liberated selves, 'each subsisting in its own form and separated from all union with unconscious matter'. Whether or not one wishes to treat Brahman as absolutely One or as the totality of the 'stuff' which is common to all individual selves, is here beside the point: the 'Imperishable' is a timeless mode of existence, it is eternity.[31]

[27] Edgerton, op.cit., Part I, p.145.

[28] Hill (op.cit., p.188, n.7) partly accounts for the difficulty. 'Much unnecessary difficulty has been caused in the interpretation of this passage by the unwillingness of commentators to allow Kṛiṣṇa to call *prakṛiti 'kṣara puruṣa'*, but the context demands that the two *puruṣas* should be *puruṣa* and *prakṛiti*; it is on these two that Kṛiṣṇa has been continually harping under various figures and in this Reading he has first spoken of *prakṛiti* as the Fig-tree, and then of individual and universal *puruṣa* or *jīvabhūta*. Throughout his teaching he has told of the Lord who is one with Brahman and with Kṛiṣṇa and who possesses two "natures" – the one, "higher", his own essential nature, *adhyātma*, universal and individual; and the other, "lower", identified with *prakṛiti*. In relation to *prakṛiti* he is *sādhibhūta*, and *adhibhūta* is *kṣara bhāva* (viii.4). If Kṛiṣṇa may call *puruṣa* and *prakṛiti* in vii.5, may he not call them the two *puruṣas* here? Poetry rises superior to terminology, and the very confusion of terms helps to suggest that oneness of all which is the ultimate doctrine of the Gītā'.

[29] ibid., p.189, Ś=Śaṅkara.

[30] ibid.

[31] Zaehner, op.cit., p.366.

Both Śaṅkara and Rāmānuja have read their own philosophical systems into the verse, but Rāmānuja seems to be closer to the meaning of the text in as much as *akṣara* seems to refer clearly to the *ātman* rather than *māyā*. Śaṅkara does *not* take the word *kūṭastha* in its usual etymological sense of transcendental[32] here, which is puzzling.

XVIII:55 *bhaktyā mām abhijānāti*
yāvān yaś cāsmi tattvataḥ
tato māṃ tattvato jñātvā
viśate tadanantaram[33]

Thru devotion he comes to know Me,
What My measure is, and who I am, in very truth;
Then, knowing Me in very truth,
He enters into (Me) straightway.[34]

The verse needs to be read with the previous one where the spiritual aspirant is described as *brahmabhūtā*, who becomes one with Brahman. This verse speaks of entering into God, and the sequence creates a problem for Śaṅkara, for it reverses the order as found in his system. But this is clearly the sequence described here in the Gītā, and so Rāmānuja 'reasonably points out that this "knowledge" of God is subsequent to the knowledge of self as Brahman'.[35]

2.

We now turn to some of those verses of the Gītā where the interpretation given by Rāmānuja poses problems.

In II:25 the embodied soul is described as *avyakta*, or unmanifest. The word has many senses, but as in that context we are 'dealing with the embodied self which in its essence is unaffected by matter in any form',[36] Śaṅkara seems to be right in glossing it as 'because it is inaccessible to the senses, it cannot be expressed'.[37] Rāmānuja's explanation, that 'it cannot be expressed in terms applicable to objects that can be cut, etc.,'[38] is unduly restrictive. Similarly, in II:45 Arjuna is exhorted to rise above the three *guṇas* (one of which is

[32] Monier Monier-Williams, *A Sanskrit-English Dictionary* (Oxford: Clarendon Press, 1970 [first edition 1899]), p.299.

[33] Bolle, op.cit., p.208.

[34] Edgerton, op.cit., Part I, p.175.

[35] Zaehner, op.cit., p.298.

[36] ibid., p.134.

[37] ibid.

[38] ibid.

sattva) and thereby become *sattvastha*, an expression which Rāmānuja 'interprets: "Let the sattva-guṇa prevail." But Arjuna has just been told to be entirely beyond the three *guṇas*, as later on (XIV:19-27); thus *sattva* must here bear its more general sense of "truth".'[39] Earlier, in II:28 in the context of the discussion of the embodied soul, it is described as rarely known. The context is clearly of the individual soul, but Rāmānuja 'refers the stanza to God rather than the individual self; yet oddly enough in the Gītā it is not so much God who is unknowable as the self'.[40]

Rāmānuja also seems to be off the mark in interpreting III:11.

devān bhāvayatānena
te devā bhāvayantu vaḥ
parasparaṃ bhāvayantaḥ
śreyaḥ param avāpsyatha[41]

With this prosper ye the gods,
And let the gods prosper you;
(Thus) prospering one the other,
Ye shall attain the highest welfare.[42]

The question is: How is *śreyaḥ param* to be understood? Rāmānuja takes it to mean what it seems to mean, namely liberation,[43] but Zaehner notes that Śaṅkara 'is reluctant to admit this and glosses, "by attaining to transcendent wisdom (*jñāna*) gradually" and suggests *svarga*, "heaven", as an alternative. This is more in line with the thinking of the Gītā elsewhere. Worship of the gods does not lead to final liberation. The gods can merely satisfy man's worldly desires (7.20-2), and even sacrifice to Krishna himself will take one no further than Indra's heaven if that is the sacrificer's intention (9.20).'[44]

A much more substantial point is involved in Rāmānuja's interpretation of III:42:

indriyāṇi parāṇy āhur
indriyebhyaḥ paraṃ manaḥ
manasas tu parā buddhir
yo buddheḥ paratas tu saḥ[45]

[39] Hill, op.cit., p.89, n.2. Śaṅkara commits the same error (*Śrīśāṅkaragranthāvaliḥ*, Sampuṭa 8, p.45).
[40] Zaehner, op.cit., p.136. [41] Bolle, op.cit., p.40.
[42] Edgerton, op.cit., Part I, p.35. [43] Zaehner, op.cit., p.165.
[44] ibid. [45] Bolle, op.cit., p.48.

The senses, they say, are high;
Higher than the senses is the thought-organ;
But higher than the thought-organ is the consciousness;
While higher than the consciousness is He (the soul).[46]

Both Hill[47] and Zaehner[48] note that Rāmānuja takes *saḥ* to mean *kāma* but Śaṅkara and

practically all other commentators both ancient and modern take this to mean the *ātman* which occurs in the following stanza (cf. *dehinam*, 'embodied [self]', in verse 40). R. takes it as referring to desire in strict accord with the grammatical context. This seems most unlikely since the whole passage is based on KaU.6.7-8, where we read:

Higher than the senses is the mind
Higher than the mind the soul (*sattva*),
Higher than the soul the self, the great,
Higher than [this] 'great' the Unmanifest.
Higher than [this] Unmanifest the 'Person' (*puruṣa*),
Pervading all, untraceable.[49]

Earlier on in the Third Chapter, Rāmānuja interprets III:23 ['For if I did not continue at all in action, unwearied, My path would follow then altogether, son of Pṛthā'][50] as involving the conformity of Kṛṣṇa's actions to caste-law. 'This seems a rather narrow interpretation of the passage, the gist of which is to persuade Arjuna that he must conform to God not only in his timeless essence but also in his incessant activity within the 'created' order'.[51]

We may now turn to the Fourth Chapter, of which verse eighteen is an exegetical nettle.

karmany akarma yaḥ paśyed
akarmaṇi ca karma yaḥ
sa buddhimān manusyeṣu
sa yuktaḥ kṛtsnakarmakṛt[52]

Who sees inaction in action,
And action in inaction,

[46] Edgerton, op.cit., Part I, p.41.
[47] Hill, op.cit., p.101, n.5.
[48] Zaehner, op.cit., p.177.
[49] ibid. R=Rāmānuja.
[50] Edgerton, op.cit., Part I, p.37.
[51] Zaehner, op.cit., p.170.
[52] Bolle, op.cit., p.54.

He is enlightened among men;
He does all action, disciplined.[53]

Now Śaṅkara, briefly, 'explains that both action and inaction (which is a kind of action) belong to the body, while the deluded believe they belong to the Self; he is wise who understands that action, as being of the body, is inaction of the Self; and that inaction is also a kind of action, and pertains to the body'.[54] It is interesting that Rāmānuja, on the other hand, 'identifies *akarma* with *jñāna* and says that the wise man is he who sees *jñāna* in all true performance of work, and that *jñāna* itself is a kind of action'.[55] Zaehner adds a further explanation from Rāmānuja: 'He who sees actions in their performance as being conformed (*-ākāra*) to wisdom because they inhere in the very essence of the self and who sees wisdom as being conformed to action because it indwells it (*antargata*) ...'[56] and feels that it renders 'admirably the meaning of the verse'.[57]

Now the terms *karma* and *akarma* can be understood on the basis of verses in the Gītā itself. III:6 suggests that, if the senses of action are still (not engaged in action) but the mind is active, this is tantamount to hypocrisy. The next verse suggests that if the senses of action act under mental discipline then one is to be considered detached. Such detachment is equated with inaction later (V:13). All this suggests that seeing 'inaction in action' ties into III:7/V:13 and 'action in inaction' into III:6. Śaṅkara, though not hitting the mark, seems closer to it here than Rāmānuja, if the interpretation I have given to the verse is correct.

In the Sixth Chapter we find the following remarkable verse (30):

yo māṃ paśyati sarvatra
sarvaṃ ca mayi paśyati
tasyāhaṃ na praṇaśyāmi
sa ca me na praṇaśyati[58]

Who sees Me in all,
And sees all in Me,
For him I am not lost,
And he is not lost for Me.[59]

Rāmānuja comments: 'He sees that all self-stuff as it is in itself (*svarūpeṇa*) and after it has shaken off good and evil, is the same in

[53] Edgerton, op.cit., Part I, p.47. [54] Hill, op.cit., p.105, n.4.
[55] ibid. [56] Zaehner, op.cit., p.188. [57] ibid.
[58] Bolle, op.cit., p.76. [59] Edgerton, op.cit., Part I, p.67.

Me, that is, "untrammelled wisdom" (on 6.31)'.[60] This poses a problem, and Zaehner comments on Rāmānuja:

> This seems to me to miss the point: 'all beings' are not obliterated in God, nor is God obliterated in 'the All', hence neither is 'lost' or 'destroyed'. This is what the Gītā says, and it is the great divide between the 'pantheistic' and 'theistic' portions of the poem.[61]

The end of the Sixth Chapter is a good point at which to pause, for according to Rāmānuja, following Yāmuna:

> The first six chapters of the Gītā are devoted to the acquisition of true knowledge of the individual self as being immortal and of the 'stuff' of Brahman, while the next six are devoted to the knowledge of God. In modern terms, then, the subject-matter of the first six chapters would be psychology, that of the second six theology. This is only very roughly true as the attentive reader will have noticed, the first half of Chapter Four, for instance, being devoted almost entirely to Krishna both as incarnate God and as the universal agent.[62]

The opening verse of the Seventh Chapter is also of some interest:

mayy āsaktamanāḥ pārtha
yogaṃ yuñjan madāśrayaḥ
asaṃśayaṃ samagraṃ māṃ
yathā jñāsyasi tac chṛṇu[63]

With mind attached to Me, son of Pṛthā,
Practising discipline with reliance on Me,
Without doubt Me entirely
How thou shalt know, that hear![64]

Hill points out that

> the three adjectives which open this śloka should be noted. They form the conditions of the attainment of knowledge. The aspirant must make his quest in a spirit of devotion to Kṛiṣṇa (*mayy āsaktamanas*),

[60] Zaehner, op.cit., p.235. [61] ibid.

[62] ibid., p.243. Zaehner adds, though: 'Nevertheless from the present chapter until the tremendous theophany in Chapter XI we shall be increasingly concerned with Krishna as God, less with the self's realisation of itself as having its real existence outside space and time'.

[63] Bolle, op.cit., p.84. [64] Edgerton, op.cit., Part I, p.73.

directing to him that attachment which the ignorant direct to the fruit of their works. He must rely wholly on Kriṣṇa (*madāśraya*). He must, moreover, remain ever in the practice of necessary work without desire (*yogaṁ yuñjan*).[65]

Thus Hill seems to have some justification in saying that Rāmānuja 'appears to miss an important point in interpreting *yoga* as *bhaktiyoga*, and making devotion the sole condition of knowledge'.[66]

VII:15 is intrinsically not very important, but it is of some interest because of the rather tangential glosses by Rāmānuja. The word *māyā* occurs here again as in IV:6 and VII:14, and Rāmānuja 'who at 4.6 had equated *māyā* with *jñāna* "wisdom" now glosses it as "tricky arguments"!' 'This is quite unnecessary', as Zaehner notes, 'since in the Gītā māyā is real: it depends on God and is therefore called "divine" but at the same time distracts man's attention from Him'.[67] In the same verse Rāmānuja 'distinguishes four types of evil-doers to correspond to the four types of votaries' to be mentioned in 16. Such a division does not seem to be implied and 'is artificial' as Hill has noted.[68] But it is Rāmānuja's gloss on VII:18 which has drawn much more critical comment and, it would appear, justifiably. The verse runs as follows:

udārāḥ sarva evaite
jñānī tv ātmaiva me matam
āsthitaḥ sa hi yuktātmā
mām evānuttamāṃ gatim[69]

All these are noble;
But the man of knowledge is My very self, so I hold.
For he with disciplined soul has resorted
To Me alone as the highest goal.[70]

Zaehner observes that while Śaṅkara tends to take the expression *jñānī tv ātmaiva me matam* ('But the man of knowledge is My very self, so I hold') much more monistically than the text suggests, Rāmānuja 'goes to the other extreme – "the maintenance of my (God's) very self is dependent on him." God, moreover, according to R. *is* as dependent on the individual self as the latter is on Him. This seems to be totally at variance with the whole tone of the Gītā, for the

[65] Hill, op.cit., p.125, n.1.
[66] ibid.
[67] Zaehner, op.cit., p.249.
[68] Hill, op.cit., p.127.
[69] Bolle, op.cit., p.88.
[70] Edgerton, op.cit., Part I, p.77.

man who has realised his own self in the "Nirvāna that is Brahman too" is thereby free and dependent on nothing, just as God is (3.22), and the love between man and God which Krishna is now beginning to reveal must be a free love – freely given and freely accepted. The phrase "is my very self" probably means no more than "he is the apple of my eye"."[71] Similarly, A.L. Basham observes that it is 'by forcing the sense' that Rāmānuja interpreted ' "the wise man I deem my very self" to imply that just as man cannot live without God, so God cannot live without man'.[72] The importance of Rāmānuja's comment here, in the broader context of his theology, can hardly be exaggerated. As J.B. Carman remarks while dealing with the relationship between God and his exclusive devotee the *jñānī*:

> It is the second side of the relationship between God and the devotee that is somewhat surprising. Rāmānuja understands Lord Krishna to be teaching in the *Gītā* that He is similarly dependent upon His exclusive devotees. There is no question in Rāmānuja's mind of denying the one-sided ontological dependence of the universe on God. Indeed, it is precisely in the *Gītābhāsya* that Rāmānuja makes a distinction between the finite self's relation to its body and God's relation to His cosmic body. In the former case, although the soul is superior to the body, there is some mutual dependence, for the soul also depends on the body to accomplish its purposes. In the case of God, however, there is no such dependence on the cosmos. 'My existence [*sthiti*] is not under their control, which means that they are not helping in any way in My existence ... I am the supporter of all beings; they are no help at all to Me at any time. What I will in My mind itself causes the existence of all beings and also supports and controls them.'[73]

Carman proceeds: 'Rāmānuja puts this mutual dependence between God and his favourite devotees very emphatically in his

[71] Zaehner, op.cit., p.251.

[72] A.L. Basham, *The Wonder That Was India* (New York: Grove Press, 1954), p.332.

[73] John Braisted Carman, *The Theology of Rāmānuja* (New Haven: Yale University Press, 1974), p.192. An interesting parallel surfaces here between the monotheism of Rāmānuja and the polytheism of the Vedas. One of the grounds on which Pratima Bowes distinguishes between 'present-day Hindu polytheism' and 'Vedic polytheism' is that 'while present day Hindu polytheistic worship consists entirely of passive offerings suggesting a one-way dependence of men on gods' in the Vedic case 'gods depend on men in the same way as men depend on gods (not, of course, to the same extent), in so far as the gods are conceived to subsist by virtue of ritual offering' (*The Hindu Religious Tradition: A Philosophical Approach* [London: Routledge & Kegan Paul, 1977], p.102).

comment on Gītā 7.18'[74] – the verse under review. Carman also notes that in 'two passages in the ninth chapter, Rāmānuja goes even further in describing God's reversal of the ordinary metaphysical relationship between Himself and His creatures'.[75]

It is clear that Rāmānuja has over-interpreted the verse under review – and not accidentally either. In this chapter of the Gītā he again over-interprets the expression in VII:19: *Vāsudevaḥ sarvamiti* ('Vāsudeva (Kṛṣṇa) is all')[76] as 'Vāsudeva is *my* all'.[77] In commenting on the last verse of the chapter he 'attempts to assign various kinds and degrees of knowledge to the various types of votary; but the division is artificial and the Sanskrit text cannot bear the strain'.[78]

The Eighth Chapter contains a verse which has tested the exegetical skill of commentators (VIII:4):

adhibhūtaṃ kṣaro bhāvaḥ
puruṣaś cādhidaivatam
adhiyajño'ham evātra
dehe dehabhṛtāṃ vara[79]

Essential Being is perishable existence;
Essential Deity is the person;
Essential Sacrifice am I, here in
the body, O best of men embodied.[80]

Both Rāmānuja and Śaṅkara, as well as modern scholars, agree that the expression *adhiyajño* applies to Kṛṣṇa as the text itself says. The difference arises over the interpretation of the word *dehe*, Śaṅkara taking it to mean the body of the officiant – 'because sacrifice has to be performed by the body, it is inherent in the body'.[81] Rāmānuja takes it to refer to the bodies of gods towards whom the sacrifice is directed: 'because I am really present in Indra and the other Gods who form my body and because sacrifice is [really] dedicated to Me'. According to Zaehner:

[74] Carman, op.cit., p.192. Carman quotes Rāmānuja here to the following effect. 'I consider that the *jñānīs* are My very soul. This means that the support for My existence is under their control. Why is this so? Because the *jñānī* does not have even the possibility of sustaining his soul without Me. He takes Me alone as his incomparable goal. Therefore without him, I cannot sustain My soul. Therefore he is My soul'.

[75] ibid. [76] Edgerton, op.cit., Part I, p.77. [77] Hill, op.cit., p.127, n.4.

[78] ibid. [79] Bolle, op.cit., p.92.

[80] Hill, op.cit., p.133.

[81] Zaehner, op.cit., p.261.

> This is probably what the Gītā means. Sacrifice is always offered up to some personal entity – even the Christian sacrifice is offered up to the 'Father', a 'Person' if ever there was one. Moreover, Krishna is personally present in the body of every living thing – man, ghost, or god – and it is there that He is either loved or hated (cf.16.18: 'envying and hating Me who dwell in their bodies as I dwell in all').[82]

It seems more reasonable to take *deha* as referring to the physical body – either of the officiant or of Kṛṣṇa – rather than of the deities. Hill points out that Rāmānuja's explanation – that Kṛṣṇa is 'present in Indra and other *devas* as the true object of worship –' neglects the reference to incarnation, and is more suitable for the word *adhidaiva*.[83] A reference by Kṛṣṇa to himself seems the most likely explanation, for in the Gītā, although Kṛṣṇa says that sacrifices made to others are in effect made to him, he does not say that he is present in the body of other deities but does *say* and *show* that other deities are present in his body (XI:6-7), and Arjuna sees them as such (XI:15). In Chapter Eight Rāmānuja again over-interprets verse 15, or as Zaehner puts it, 'lets himself go'.[84] 'Thus: "Their wisdom conformed to Me as I really am, out of the excess of the love they bear Me, they are unable to sustain the existence of their very selves without Me; their minds attached to Me, putting their trust in Me and worshipping Me, they win through to Me who am their highest prize".'[85]

The verse is really quite simple and straightforward in its purport.

Earlier on he seems to miss the cue in VIII:3: *akṣaram brahma paramaṁ svabhāvo' dhyatmam ucyate*[86] ('Brahman is the Imperishable, the Supreme; Its Being is called Essential Self').[87] He is 'misled'[88] by the use of the term *svabhāva* and 'interprets *brahma* as the pure self divorced from *prakṛti* (*prakṛtivinirmuktātmasvarūpa*) and *adhyātma* as *prakṛti* apart from Self. The former, he says, must be sought, and latter avoided; therefore both should be known'.[89] The verse admittedly is not an easy one to explain, but even so Rāmānuja's gloss seems to be off the mark. Actually the verse could be made to square fairly neatly with his system if a different tack were adopted.

[82] ibid. It is interesting that not only Zaehner's but B.L.D. Barnett's idea should be 'particularly interesting in relation to the Christian sacrifice' (Hill, op.cit., p.133, n.5).
[83] Hill, op.cit., p.133, n.5. [84] Zaehner, op.cit., p.266.
[85] ibid. [86] Bolle, op.cit., p.92. [87] Hill, op.cit., p.132.
[88] ibid., p.132, n.2. [89] ibid.

In the Ninth Chapter some of the glosses by Rāmānuja are rather teasing. In IX:1, for instance, the words *jñāna* and *vijñāna* are mentioned in such a way as to imply a distinction between the two. Rāmānuja glosses *jñāna* as *bhakti* and *vijñāna* as worship.[90] It is true that the determination of the exact connotation of the terms is not without its problems, but even so Rāmānuja's interpretation appears far-fetched. Another set of related expressions in the Ninth Chapter seem to involve Rāmānuja in exegetical difficulties. In IX:19 Kṛṣṇa claims that he is both *sat* and *asat*. Rāmānuja explains *sat* as present existence and *asat* as past and future existence (and one thought Śaṅkara was a crypto-Buddhist!). Scholars are again divided on the correct interpretation of *sat* and *asat*,[91] but Rāmānuja's suggestion is not very convincing.

In the course of glossing on the Tenth Chapter Rāmānuja again makes some rather puzzling remarks. In X:2 Rāmānuja 'interprets *prabhava* as *prabhāva*, greatness. But the context demands the meaning "origins". They do not know Kṛṣṇa's origin because he has no origin'.[92] Zaehner concurs: 'in the context "origin" fits very much better and is always used in the sense elsewhere in the Gītā'.[93] The verse translates as follows:

The throngs of gods know not My
  Origin, nor yet the great seers.
For I am the starting-point of the gods,
  And of the great seers, altogether.[94]

Rāmānuja glosses the word *-pāpaiḥ* in X:3 in such a way as to display his animus against monism. He 'quite arbitrarily, takes *-papaiḥ* to mean monistic conceptions which identify god with anything and everything'.[95] All that *pāda* of the verse means is: 'Is freed from all evils'.[96] His gloss of *mad-yoga* in XII:11 has raised eyebrows. The verse runs:

athaitad apy aśakto'si
  kartuṃ madyogam āśritaḥ
sarvakarmaphalatyāgaṃ
  tataḥ kuru yatātmavān[97]

[90] Zaehner, op.cit., p.274.
[91] See ibid., p.281; Hill, op.cit., p.143, n.1.
[92] Hill, op.cit., p.147, n.2. [93] Zaehner, op.cit., p.292.
[94] Edgerton, op.cit., Part I, p.97.
[95] Zaehner, op.cit., p.292. [96] Edgerton, op.cit., Part I, p.97.
[97] Bolle, op.cit., p.148.

But if even this thou art unable
  To do, resorting to My discipline,
Abandonment of the fruit of all actions
  Do thou then effect, controlling thyself.[98]

Hill indicates what is meant: 'Turn to the method of work without desire which I have taught you, even on the lower level where active devotion is less prominent',[99] and notes that Rāmānuja 'takes these words with the first words of the *śloka* and *madyoga* as meaning *bhakti yoga*'.[100] Zaehner is even more critical and comments that Rāmānuja, 'for no apparent reason, takes it to mean that one should concentrate on the "imperishable" nature of the individual self which automatically gives rise to the highest loving devotion'.[101] Rāmānuja has over-interpreted the verse no doubt, but he is not as much off base as these comments might make it appear, since the entire context of the chapter is primarily devotional. In the traditional description of the chapters too it is referred to as the chapter on Bhaktiyoga.[102]

The Thirteenth Chapter provides instances of serendipity and ingenuity in relation to Rāmānuja's exegetical skills. An important verse of the chapter is the following (XIII:2):

kṣetrajñaṃ cāpi māṃ viddhi
  sarvakṣetreṣu bhārata
kṣetrakṣetrajñayor jñānaṃ
  yat taj jñānaṃ mataṃ mama[103]

Know also that I am the Field-knower
  In all Fields, son of Bharata.
Knowledge of the Field and Field-knower,
  This I hold to be (true) knowledge.[104]

Rāmānuja takes the key expression *kṣetrajña* to mean, Zaehner notes,

> that God knows all 'fields' and 'knowers of the field', all bodies and individual selves which together constitute his favourite concept of the 'body of the Lord'. In this I think he is right not because he interprets

[98] Edgerton, op.cit., Part I, p.123.
[99] Hill, op.cit., p.169, n.3.
[100] ibid.
[101] Zaehner, op.cit., p.328.
[102] Edgerton, op.cit., Part I, pp.124, 125.
[103] Bolle, op.cit., p.152.
[104] Edgerton, op.cit., Part I, p.127.

the passage in accordance with his own philosophy, but because we must assume that the author of the Gītā was familiar with the passage from the *Chāndogya* Upanishad which we have just quoted; the 'field' includes the 'hidden hoard of gold' just as the body includes the 'self within the heart'. Thus the Gītā does not contradict the Upanishads but merely asserts again that there is One who, as the Śvetāśvatara puts it, is 'Lord of primeval Nature, [Lord of all] knowers of the field'. 'Knowledge' or 'wisdom' means to be able to distinguish God as 'knower of every field' from both individual selves and from material Nature.[105]

In XIII:6 we encounter the word *saṅghāta*, 'not easy to explain'.[106] Hill notes that Rāmānuja 'perceiving the difficulty' posed by the verse 'brings the modifications to an end with "pain" and proceeds thus: *saṅghātaś cetanādhṛitiḥ*, i.e. "This is the body, the basis (*ādhṛitiḥ*=*ādhāraḥ*) of the principle of intelligence" '[107] instead of taking *saṅghāta, cetanā* and *dhṛti* separately. Hill observes that 'this is ingenious but not convincing'.[108] In glossing XIII:33, however, Rāmānuja succumbs to his philosophical preconceptions when he takes the work *kṣetrī*, 'owner of the field', to refer to the self and not God. 'God not only *knows* the whole universe composed of his two Natures, they are also his very own (4.6:6.5-6)'.[109] The verse is also reproduced below for ready reference.

yathā prakāśayaty ekaḥ
kṛtsnaṃ lokam imaṃ raviḥ
kṣetraṃ kṣetrī tathā kṛtsnaṃ
prakāśayati bhārata

As alone illumines
This whole world the sun,
So the Field-owner the whole Field
Illumines, son of Bharata.[109a]

Rāmānuja's exegetical ingenuity was referred to earlier, but sometimes it falls short of the mark, as for instance with XIV:20, which runs as follows:

[105] Zaehner, op.cit., p.335. [106] Hill, op.cit., p.174, n.7.
[107] ibid. [108] ibid. [109] Zaehner, op.cit., p.350.
[109a] Edgerton, op.cit., Part I, pp.132, 133.

guṇān etān atītya trīn
dehī dehasamudbhavān
janmamṛtyujarāduḥkhair
vimukto 'mṛtam aśnute[110]

Transcending these three Strands,
That spring from the body, the embodied (soul),
From birth, death, old age, and sorrow
Freed, attains deathlessness.[111]

Now 'most commentators and translators have found the compound *dehasamudbhavān* difficult, because it seems to imply that the *guṇas* are caused by the body, whereas the body is rather caused by the *guṇas*'.[112] To solve this difficulty Rāmānuja 'takes *deha* as equivalent to *prakṛiti*, but the close proximity of *dehī* renders this improbable'.[113]

In the Fifteenth Chapter (XV:15) Kṛṣṇa declares himself to be *vedāntakṛt* or 'the author of the Upaniṣads'[114] but Rāmānuja glosses it to mean the producer of the 'fruit of the Vedas'.[115] Quite obviously Rāmānuja bypasses the ordinary meaning of the expression probably under the influence of the view that the Vedas, inclusive of the Vedānta, are *apauruṣeya*. This does seem to have been the common Vedantic position,[116] so one would expect that Śaṅkara would have to work his way around it too. Such indeed turns out to be the case. But while there is some justification for the exegetical bypass mentioned above there seems too little for glossing *loke* in XV:18 as *smṛti* – as Rāmānuja does by taking the word *loka* not in its usual sense as the world, but in the sense of *avalokana*, i.e. viewing, considering. *Smṛti* then is so called because it takes the meaning of the Vedas into account – *vedārthāvalokanāt*.[117] This is surely far-fetched.

Rāmānuja also seems to over-interpret XVIII:4, though not outrageously. The verse runs as follows:

niścayaṃ śṛṇu me tatra
tyāge bharatasattama
tyāgo hi puruṣavyāghra
trividhaḥ samprakīrtitaḥ[118]

[110] Bolle, op.cit., p.166.
[111] Edgerton, op.cit., Part I, p.139.
[112] Hill, op.cit., p.182, n.1.
[113] ibid.
[114] Edgerton, op.cit., Part I, p.145.
[115] Hill, op.cit., p.188, n.6.
[116] Hiriyanna, op.cit., p.169.
[117] Hill, op.cit., p.189, n.1.
[118] Bolle, op.cit., p.194.

Hear my decision in this matter
  Of abandonment, best of Bharatas;
For abandonment, O man-tiger,
  Is reputed to be threefold.[119]

This threefold dimension of *tyāga* obviously refers to its characterisation as *tāmasa, rājasa* and *sāttvika* in verses 7-9 that follow. Here, however, Rāmānuja offers his *own* threefold classification. He 'divides abandonment into (1) abandonment of fruit, (2) abandonment of the idea that Self is agent, and thus of attachment, and (3) abandonment of all idea of authorship, with the realisation that the Lord is the author of all action'.[120] The classification is interesting, but it is Rāmānuja's own. XVIII:16 also provides an illustration of over-interpretation by Rāmānuja. It runs as follows:

tatraivaṃ sati kartāram
  ātmānaṃ kevalaṃ tu yaḥ
paśyaty akṛtabuddhitvān
  na sa paśyati durmatiḥ[121]

This being so, as agents herein
  Whoso however the self alone
Regards, because his intelligence is imperfect,
  He does not see (truly), the fool.[122]

It is clear from the context that the doership belongs to the five agencies mentioned in XVIII:14, among whom God is *not* one, the word *daiva* therein standing for Fate,[123] and not God. Yet Rāmānuja thinks the verse implies that 'the action of the *jīvātman* depends on *paramātman*'.[124] Rāmānuja also offers a somewhat idiosyncratic interpretation of the word *dharma* in XVIII:47. This is an important verse, which reproduces a line from another verse (III:35) and runs as follows:

śreyān svadharmo viguṇaḥ
  paradharmāt svanuṣṭhitāt

[119] Edgerton, op.cit., Part I, p.163.
[120] Hill, op.cit., p.203, n.2.
[121] Bolle, op.cit., p.198.
[122] Edgerton, op.cit., Part I, p.165.
[123] ibid.
[124] Hill, op.cit., p.205.

svabhāvaniyataṃ karma
kurvan nā 'pnoti kilbiṣam[125]

Better one's own duty, (even) imperfect,
Than another's duty well performed.
Action pertaining to his own estate
Performing, he incurs no guilt.[126]

How Rāmānuja can take *svadharma* to mean *karmayoga* here and *paradharma* to mean *jñānayoga* is hard to fathom. If anything, it makes etymologically and perhaps even philosophically at least equal if not more sense to take *svadharma* as *jñānayoga* (*ātman=brahman*) and *paradharma* as *bhaktiyoga* (*para*=Īśvara).

3.

In his gloss on II:20 Rāmānuja states: *nāyam bhūtva bhavitā vā na bhūyaḥ ayam kalpādau bhutvā bhūyaḥ kalpānte ca na bhavitā iti na.*[127] It is probably in reference to this comment that Edgerton writes:

> The objection commonly raised aginst R's interpretation is that the soul should not be spoken of as having 'come to be', since it has existed from everlasting. But this is a slight and superficial inconsistency, really only verbal in character, much more serious ones are very common in the Gītā.[128]

It is not entirely clear whether Edgerton regards the inconsistency as belongong to Rāmānuja, to the Gītā, or to Rāmānuja's interpretation of the Gītā.

It may now be pointed out that, as far as Rāmānuja's cosmology is concerned, the inconsistency is quite superficial, largely because of the theory of creation found in Rāmānuja. It is thus spelled out in his gloss on Vedānta Sūtra I.1.13.

> That which is denoted as 'Being', i.e. the highest Brahman which is the cause of all, free from all shadow of imperfection, etc., resolved 'to

[125] Bolle, op.cit., p.46. [126] Edgerton, op.cit., Part I, p.172, 173.

[127] Mahāvana Śāstrī (ed.), *Śrīmadbhagavadgītā Śrīmadrāmānujācāryakṛtabhāṣyasametā* (Bombay: Lakṣmīvenkaṭeśvara Press, 1959), p.19. It is the statement concerning the soul coming into being at the beginning of the *kapla* (*kalpādau*) which is the subject of debate here.

[128] Edgerton, op.cit., p.92, n.5. R=Rāmānuja.

> be many'; is thereupon sent forth the entire world, consisting of fire, water, etc.; introduced, in this world so sent forth, the whole mass of individual souls into different bodies divine, human, etc., corresponding to the desert of each soul – the souls thus constituting the Self of the bodies; and finally, itself entering according to its wish into these souls – so as to constitute their inner Self – evolved in all these aggregates, names and forms, i.e. rendered each aggregate something substantial (vastu) and capable of being denoted by a word.[129]

In a special sense then, in Rāmānuja's system, the soul 'comes to be' even though everlasting and his gloss seems to be designed to forestall the erroneous impression that because in this sense it has come to be in some sense it shall cease to be. Thus on Rāmānuja's own terms the gloss seems to be quite justified.

Now follows a discussion of the eleemosynary theology of Rāmānuja in the Gītābhāṣya. At least on three occasions in the Gītā, the giving of gifts becomes a point of discourse by Kṛṣṇa to Arjuna.[130] The first of these occasions appears in III:10-11, the second in IX:26-7 and the third in XVII:20-2.

The discussion of *dāna* in Chapter Seventeen is fairly straightforward:

> Alms given with thought, 'Alms must be given', to one, who cannot make return, at the right place and time, and to the right recipient, is called the alms of Purity.
>
> But that which is given for the sake of a gift in return, or with an eye on fruit hereafter, or grudgingly, is called the alms of Energy.
>
> Alms given at the wrong place and time, and to the wrong recipients, unceremoniously and with contempt, is called the alms of Darkness.[131]

This discussion does not present any problem to Rāmānuja, as they are regarded by him as 'Acts which are established by the Śāstras'.[132] In the system of Rāmānuja, 'Even after acquiring *jñāna* and *bhakti*, one has to perform *karma* till the very end – not only the rites enjoined in the Vedas but also prayer and worship';[133] hence

[129] George Thibaut (tr.) *The Vedānta-sūtras with the commentary of Rāmānuja*, Part III (Oxford: Clarendon Press, 1904), p.226.

[130] A possible reference in Bhagavadgītā I:42 is overlooked as irrelevant.

[131] Hill, op.cit., p.198.

[132] J.A.B. van Buitenen, *Rāmānuja on the Bhagavadgītā* (Ś-Gravenhage: H.L. Smits), p.161.

[133] Mahadevan, op.cit., p.154.

Rāmānuja's easy acceptance of these verses is understandable. We should recall here that *bhakti* in the Viśiṣṭādvaitic tradition has not yet acquired the dimensions of *prapatti*.[134] Nor can it be argued that because *karma* is an ancillary yoga it should not be treated towards the end of the Gītā because, according to the tripartite division of the Gītā by Yāmuna, which Rāmānuja follows, the last six chapters are recapitulatory in nature.[135]

The discussion of sacrifice and sacrificial gifts[136] in III:10-11 seems to call forth more comment from Rāmānuja,[137] but will be discussed later.[138]

The third case of gifts, this time offered in *pūjā*, is presented by IX:26-7.

> If any earnest soul make offering to me with devotion, of leaf or flower or fruit or water, that offering of devotion I enjoy.
>
> Whatever work thou doest, whatever thou dost eat, whatever dost thou sacrifice or give, whatever be thine austere practices, do all, O son of Kuntī, as an offering to me.[139]

The latter verse does not offer much difficulty, as God is recognised as the Master, the *śeṣīn* in Viśiṣṭādvaitic theology. It is Rāmānuja's gloss on the first verse which constitutes a theological curiosity, if not a conundrum. The problem arises because here we are dealing not with ritual acts or with acts directed towards gods but with an act directed towards God, and God is the receptacle of a whole pleroma of qualities and virtues already spoken of in the Introduction to the Gītābhāṣya. Does he need the offering of a flower? Of course not – he is perfect. Moreover, he is Lord of the world, so the flower is his too. But so is the devotee making the offering! Rāmānuja finds his way round the difficulty by saying that just as gods can be distinguished

> The worshippers of God are distinguished too. There are votaries who lovingly offer God a leaf, a flower, a fruit or water, things which are available to anyone. If someone offers God such a leaf etc. with pious intention, this offering being his sole object because his uncommon love of God urges him on to make this offering, then God will even

[134] van Buitenen, op.cit., p.24.
[135] ibid., pp.11, 179. [136] Hill, op.cit., p.96.
[137] van Buitenen, op.cit., p.69, n.127.
[138] ibid.
[139] Hill, op.cit., p.144.

accept this leaf etc. and partake of them because He will hold them dear, although he can never have experience of anything but himself and although this leaf etc. are foreign to his desire.[140]

It appears that the theological import of the comment has been lost in the above translation of the last line quoted above. The key clause runs: *manorathapathadūravarti priyam prāpya evāśnāmi.*[141] As S. Radhakrishnan points out:

> Commenting on the passage of the Gītā that 'I enjoy whatever is offered with devotion be it a leaf or a flower', Rāmānuja observes: 'Even though I remain in the enjoyment of my own natural unbounded and inestimable bliss, I enjoy these as if I obtained a beloved object which lies far beyond the path of my desire'.

It is not metaphysical frigidity but devotional serendipity which seems to hold the key to the meaning of the verse.

The discussion of the question of gifts in the Gītā is intimately tied in the Gita-bhāṣya of Rāmānuja with his own theology. This point clearly surfaces in Rāmānuja's discussion of III:10 which refers to the fact of cosmic creation.[142]

> After creating creatures along with (rites of worship)
> Prajāpati (the Creator) said of old:
> By this ye shall procreate yourselves –
> Let this be your Cow-of-wishes.[143]

It will now be shown how Rāmānuja provides a Viśiṣṭādvaitic orientation also to this verse, which ostensibly deals with *prajāpati* and *yajña* rather than with Viṣṇu and *bhakti*, his favourite themes.

The first point to note is that for Rāmānuja the word *prajāpati* in the verse does not mean *brahmā* as one would be inclined to believe,[144] but rather Nārāyaṇa, the *viśvasṛṣṭā*.[145] Thus Rāmānuja

[140] van Buitenen, op.cit., pp.118-19. [141] Mahāvana Śāstri (ed.), op.cit., p.152.

[142] More precisely it refers to the creation of 'creatures' rather than the universe per se. In the terminology of Rāmānuja the verse really refers to the creation of *cit* and not *acit*, for the word used is *prajāḥ*.

[143] Franklin Edgerton, *The Bhagavad Gītā* (New York: Harper & Row, 1944), p.19.

[144] Edward J. Thomas, *Bhagavadgītā* (London: John Murray, 1959), p.42.

[145] See Mahāvana Śāstri (ed.), op.cit., p.48. As J.A.B. van Buitenen points out 'when unspecified (*nirupādhika-*) the word *prajāpati* – refers to Nārāyaṇa' according to Rāmānuja who also quotes Mahāna Up.11, 3 (op.cit., p.69, n.127). It is interesting to note that in this context Śaṅkara identifies Viṣṇu *not* with *prajāpati* but with the *yajña*, quoting the *śruti*: '*yajño vai viṣṇuḥ*' (*Śrīśāṅkaragranthāvaliḥ* Sampuṭa 8, p.76).

begins by giving the verse a clearly Vaiṣṇavite orientation.

The next point to note is that Rāmānuja has to relate the creation of *cit* to Nārāyaṇa. It is here that his gloss on III:10 has to be more specific on this point than his gloss on Brahmasūtra 1.1.13 cited earlier, wherein he deals with the question of God causing the creation of the universe *in general*.[146]

The order of creation suggested in that passage is one of the creation of the universe followed by the creation of the souls. But why the creation of the souls? It is to this question that Rāmānuja's gloss on III:10 seems to be at least in part directed:

> When creating the world God observed that the creatures were incapacitated by their natural conjunction with beginningless acit, that their distinctions by name-and-form were lost, that they were submerged in himself and that, for these reasons, they were incapable of attaining one of man's major ends and therefore only qualified for things non-spiritual; in order to resuscitate them He compassionately created them together with sacrifices and said: 'By means of this sacrifice are you to cultivate your ātmans; this sacrifice will fulfil your aspirations of release and all other desires which are relevant to these aspirations.'[147]

Thus an apparently sacrifice-oriented passage dealing with *prajāpati* is exegetically transformed by Rāmānuja into one dealing with the *tattvatraya* of Viśiṣṭādvaita philosophy.

We may now turn to another verse on the Third Chapter, III:42:

> *indiryāni parāny āhuḥ indriyebhyaḥ paraṁ manaḥ*
> *manasas'tu parā buddhir yo buddheḥ paratas tu saḥ*

> The senses, they say, are great, greater than the senses is the mind, greater than the mind is the intelligence but greater than the intelligence is he.[148]

The verse constitutes a part of the answer given by Kṛṣṇa to Arjuna's question, 'By what or whom impelled does man commit sin, even though not wanting to, O Kṛṣṇa, as if forcibly constrained'.[149] Lord Kṛṣṇa replies by saying, 'It is *kāma*, it is *krodha*'[150] which thus impels a man to act, and then proceeds to describe how they could be overcome.[151] In doing so he summarises the chief elements of the

[146] Thibaut (tr.), op.cit., p.226.
[147] van Buitenen, op.cit., p.59.
[148] Transliteration and translation as per S. Radhakrishnan, *The Bhagavadgītā* (London: Allen & Unwin, 1958), p.149.
[149] III:36. [150] III:37. [151] III:37-43.

yogic psycho-spiritual concept of the human personality as consisting of the senses, beyond them of the mind, beyond the mind of *buddhi* and beyond the *buddhi*[152] of –? Herein the text says *yo buddeḥ paratas tu saḥ* – what is beyond the *buddhi* is that.[153]

Now what is this that?

In the opinion of most ancient commentators and modern scholars the singular masculine pronoun here refers to the *ātman.*[154] Somewhat surprisingly, however, Rāmānuja glosses *saḥ* with the remark: *kāma ity artaḥ*[155] – that by *saḥ, kāma* is meant. And if we ask what is meant by *kāma* he says *icchāparyāyaḥ kāmaḥ.*[156] The oddity of Rāmānuja's gloss was noticed earlier. It is examined in detail here in the context of the plausibility of these two differing interpretations.

Rāmānuja's interpretation, on the face of it, appears highly improbable, notwithstanding Vedāntadeśikan's efforts to justify it.[157] Several reasons are adduced to demonstrate why *saḥ* should be interpreted as *ātman.*

(1) From a Sāṇkhyan point of view, the picture of the human personality presented in the verses of which this verse forms a part can be looked upon as an abridged version of the Sāṇkhyan *tattvas.*[158] Nataraja Guru relies on the Sāṇkhyan connection to take He (*saḥ*) to mean (the Absolute):[159] He comments on the verse thus:

> The word *āhuh* (they say) evidently refers to the immemorial undercurrent of tradition which is the basis of the Kapila system proper, to which the unitive treatment of *purusha* (spirit) and *prakriti* (nature) in terms of the Absolute is not altogether strange. *Saḥ* (He), which corresponds to the *purusha* (spirit) of Samkhya, brings the subject of contemplation as near as possible to the Absolute Self implicit in the next verse, where even the *purusha* (spirit) of this verse may be said to be, in principle, transcended.

[152] III:43. [153] ibid.

[154] See Wāsudeva Laxmaṇa Śāstri Pansīkar (ed.), *The Bhagavadgītā* (Bombay: Nirṇayasāgara Press, 1912), p.179, passim; also see R.C. Zaehner, *The Bhagavadgītā* (Oxford: Clarendon Press, 1969), p.177.

[155] See A.V. Narasinhācārya and T.C. Narasinhācārya (eds.), *Śrīmadbhagavadgītā* Vol.I (Madras: Ananda Press, 1910), p.257.

[156] ibid., p.256.

[157] ibid. Even Abhinavagupta, who seems to take *kāma* in a positive sense glosses the *saḥ* in III:42 as *ātmā* (Wāsudevada Laxmaṇa Śāstri Pansīkar (ed.), op.cit., p.179).

[158] See T.M.P. Mahadevan, *Outlines of Hinduism* (Bombay: Chetana, 1960), pp.120-1; but also see Zaehner, op.cit., p.178.

[159] Nataraja Guru, *The Bhagavadgītā* (London: Asia Publishing House 1961), p.209.

The duality between *purusha* (spirit) and *prakriti* (nature) implied in the Samkhya system of Kapila is here glided over, and a steady and progressive gradation maintained between the various factors, giving no room to the process of *samkara* (evolution) and *pratisamkara* (involution) which should have been implied if Samkhya duality had been accepted by the Gītā. *Purusha* (spirit) is no more a lame man depending on the help of a blind man with proper limbs, which is the usual metaphor of the Samkhya philosophers to describe the relation between spirit and nature (see Ishvara Krishna's *Samkhya Karika*, 21, 'For the spirit's contemplation of nature and for its final separation the union of both takes place, as of the lame man, and the blind man. By that union a creation is formed'). *Purusha* (spirit) is now the unitive representative of the Absolute. Herein lies the revaluation of the Gītā.[160]

(2) This passage of the Gītā is closely paralleled by one in the Kaṭha Upaniṣad. Thus W.D.P. Hill remarks that Rāmānuja 'refers to *saḥ* as kāma' and J.C. Thomson 'follows him':

But the parallel passage in Kaṭh. Up.iii.10 makes it quite clear that *saḥ* is *ātman*: 'For higher than the senses are the objects of sense, and higher than the objects of sense is the mind, and higher than the mind is the reason: higher than the reason is the Great Self'. Cf. also Kaṭh. Up.vi.7.[161]

(3) F. Otto Schrader, after noting that Abhinavagupta 'does *not* understand *saḥ* as referring to *kāmaḥ* but to *ātmā*, as do Śaṅkara and others',[162] adds by way of a footnote:

Which, by the way, is (*pace* Rāmānuja) the only correct view, not merely because of the parallelism with *Kāṭhaka Upaniṣad* (III:10), but also because according to *Bhag. Gītā* III:40 the Evil One can penetrate into man only as far as his *buddhi* and, consequently, 'he' who is 'beyond *buddhi*' must be the one and only stronghold from which, according to III:43, *kāma* can be successfully combated, i.e. the *ātman*.[163]

[160] ibid., p.210.

[161] Hill, op.cit., p.101, n.5. Also see K.T. Telang, *The Bhagavadgītā with the Sanatsujātīya and the Anugītā* (Delhi: Motilal Banarsidass, 1975 [first published 1882]), p.57, n.6; Radhakrishnan, op.cit., p.149; Zaehner, op.cit., p.177, etc.

[162] F. Otto Schrader, 'Ancient Gita Commentaries', *The Indian Historical Review*, Vol.X, No.2 (June 1934), p.353.

[163] ibid., n.14.

Thus on these grounds it is widely admitted that *saḥ* refers to the *ātman*.[164]

But is there any way in which Rāmānuja's gloss could be justified – and even rendered plausible?

It seems possible to argue that Rāmānuja's gloss could be defended from four points of view at least – grammatically, psychologically, cosmogenically and devotionally.

Rāmānuja takes *saḥ* as referring 'to desire in strict accord with the grammatical context'.[165] The whole set of verses is bracketed, as it were, by *kāma* if we take *saḥ* in that sense – starting with verse 39 and ending with verse 43. But of course the more important question is: does it make sense to do so?

In a purely psychological way the interpretation makes sense if we regard desire as preceding action, and as constituting its basis. Then it could be said that from desire proceed thoughts in the higher mind (*buddhi*), which filter to the lower mind (*manas*) and activate the senses (*indriyas*). Thus a psychological rather than a metaphysical interpretation is not totally lacking in cogency.

It could also be argued that even if *saḥ* is equated with *kāma* the dictum *kāmamaya evāyaṁ puruṣaḥ*[166] would yield the same sense arrived at by other scholars through a somewhat circuitous route.

Finally, it could be argued that in the devotional poetry of the Āḷvārs, the love of God, the desire of God, is the supreme end, the supreme *puruṣārtha*. Taken in this sense, the entire complexion of the situation changes, and love of God can be viewed as something that is higher than *buddhi*.

What is striking is, of course, the fact that Rāmānuja, who could have used the last two approaches, does not use them. His later glosses in the chapter show that he continues to regard *kāma* in negative terms,[167] which throws us back on the psychological argument.[168] But given the background of the verse, the metaphysical interpretation seems to be closer to the mark than the psychological. We may now revert to our discussion of *tyāga*.

The first verse of the last chapter of the Gītā pursues the nuance of abandonment and raises the question: are *saṃnyāsa* and *tyāga*

[164] See Franklin Edgerton, *The Bhagavad Gītā* (New York: Harper & Row, 1944), p.22 etc.

[165] Zaehner, op.cit., p.177.

[166] Quoted by Radhakrishnan, op.cit., p.150, n.1.

[167] Mahāvana Śāstrī (ed.), op.cit., p.64.

[168] It seems somewhat puzzling that Rāmānuja does not even gloss the verse (VII:11) in which the word *kāma* is used in a positive sense, so much so that Lord Kṛṣṇa identifies himself with it.

identical or different? We may here compare the answer we get to this question through Rāmānuja's Gītābhāṣya with the answer we get from the text of the Gītā[169] itself.

Rāmānuja's response to the issue of the identity of or difference between *saṃnyāsa* and *tyāga* is first to formulate the issue pointedly. Rāmānuja paraphrases Arjuna's question in such a manner as to spell out the points at issue quite perspicaciously and perspicuously:

> The intention here is this. Do the two words *sannyāsa* and *tyāga* have different meanings or are they of the same meaning. In case they have different meanings, then I wish to know their true nature as being separate (from each other), If, indeed, they are of the same meaning, its true nature should be explained.[170]

Rāmānuja then proceeds to formulate his answer. His answer is that the two words are synonymous. He clearly remarks that 'the nature of these two is one only'[171] and also about 'the oneness of the meaning of these two'.[172] Rāmānuja can be read as adducing the following main arguments in support of his conclusion that the two words mean one and the same thing.[173]

[169] To avoid cumbersomeness, as may have been noted, the Bhagavadgītā is often referred to simply as the Gītā in this book.

[170] M.R. Sampatkumaran, *The Gitabhasya of Rāmānuja* (Eng. tr.), (Madras: Prof. M. Rangacharya Memorial Trust, 1969), p.474. Also see A. Govindacharya, *Srī Bhagavad-Gītā with Srī Rāmānujāchārya's Viṣiṣthadvaita – Commentary* (Madras: Vaijayanti Press, 1898), p.521. J.A.B. van Buitenen summarises: 'Now what do both words exactly signify? If they are synonymous, what exactly is their difference?' (op.cit., p.162).

[171] Sampatkumaran, op.cit., p.474; Govindacharya, op.cit., p.521.

[172] Sampatkumaran, op.cit., p.476; Govindacharya, op.cit., p.522.

[173] A certain section in A. Govindacharya's translation of Rāmānuja's commentary seems somewhat to dilute the full acceptance of the synonymity of the two words by Rāmānuja. The relevant passage is spotlighted parenthetically in what follows from A. Govindacharya's translation of Rāmānuja on XVIII:2. 'The contention here is whether the tone of the Sastras (Authoritative Works) is for the abandonment of Kamya works alone or whether it is for the resignation of the fruits of *all* kinds of works (*nitya* etc.). [In the former sense, the term *sannyāsa* is used and in the latter *tyāga*. In both cases what is common is renunciation (of something or other). In this sense] both *tyāga* and *sannyāsa* are identical' (op.cit., p.522). It appears to me that this translation is somewhat misleading on the following counts. (1) The first sentence of the parenthesised part of the quotation seems to suggest that Rāmānuja accepts the idea that *saṃnyāsa* refers to *only* the abandonment of action and *tyāga* to the fruits thereof. But Rāmānuja's actual position seems to be that in this verse *tyāga* and *saṃnyāsa* are used interchangeably without any such distinction, that they are synonymous. The issue for Rāmānuja is not *terminological*, namely, that abandonment of works intended for satisfaction of worldly desires=*saṃnyāsa* and the abandonment of fruits of action=*tyāga*. The issue is *substantive*, i.e., whether by abandonment

(1) Rāmānuja observes in his commentary on XVIII:2 that 'here' 'he (Sri Krishṇa) has used in one place the word *sannyāsa*, and elsewhere the word *tyāga*. From this it is learnt that the synonymity of the words *tyāga* and *sannyāsa* has been accepted (by Him)'.[174]

(2) Rāmānuja next quotes XVIII:4 in his commentary on XVIII:2 and argues, it would appear, that though the question is about *saṃnyāsa and tyāga* the 'decisive statement is about the word *tyāga* alone in the declaration'[175] and this shows that they are synonymous, one doing duty for the other.

(3) Rāmānuja quotes XVIII:7 in his commentary on XVIII:2 as showing that the *saṃnyāsa* and *tyāga* 'are synonymous with each other'. The verse refers to 'the renunciation (*sannyāsa*) of works ... their abandonment (*tyāga*) though delusion',[176] obviously using the words interchangeably.

(4) Rāmānuja also quotes XVIII:12 in his commentary as using the words Atyāgins=those who have not renounced, interchangeably with Saṃnyāsins=those who have renounced.[177]

Then he concludes: 'It is conclusively established (by the Lord) that the oneness of the meaning of these two (words) necessarily follows from these'.[178]

It was noted earlier how Rāmānuja remarks that the decisive statement made by Kṛṣṇa is about *tyāga* (and not *saṃnyāsa*) in the present context. And for Rāmānuja this is important – for him, of the two, exegetically *tyāga* is the primary category, although he regards the two as synonymous. Thus in his commentary on XVIII:4 Rāmānuja offers his own threefold classification of *tyāga* in apposition if not opposition to the Gītā's own (XVIII:7,8,9). He divides *tyāga* into '(1) abandonment of fruit, (2) abandonment of the idea that self is agent, and thus of attachment, and (3) abandonment of all idea of authorship, with the realisation that the Lord is the author of all action'.[179] This threefold distinction assumes further significance in

---

(whether we call it *tyāga* or *saṃnyāsa*) we mean the abandonment of desire-prompted works or the abandonment of fruits of action. (2) The second sentence of the parenthesised part of the quotation does not seem to have a corresponding statement in the Sanskrit text as per Mahāvana Śāstrī (ed.), op.cit.

[174] Sampatkumaran, op.cit., p.475.

[175] ibid., p.476. [176] ibid. [177] ibid.

[178] ibid. A. Govindacharya, in his translation on Rāmānuja's commentary (op.cit., p.522) has slightly rearranged the material so as to read: 'That they are used synonymously and to signify the same sense is evident from such passages also ...'. Then he cites XVIII:4, XVIII:7, and XVIII:12, thereby putting the end-statement at the top.

[179] Hill, op.cit., p.203, n.2.

Rāmānuja's commentary on XVIII:12. In this verse, as noted earlier, the two words occur in the same line, and Rāmānuja uses the opportunity further to nail his position that *saṃnyāsa*=*tyāga* (*saṃnyāsaḥ sa eva ca tyāga*). He glosses *saṃnyāsa* as *kartṛtvādiparityāgaḥ*[180] and *saṃnyāsinām* as *kartṛtvādiparityāginam*, thus applying this threefold division of *tyāga* to *saṃnyāsa*.[181] Futhermore in XVIII:55, the *śloka* which is 'called the *carama sloka* (the final verse) and is reverenced in the school of Rāmānuja as containing a summary of the whole Gītā doctrine',[182] the gerund *parityajya* is from the root *tyaj* and not *as*.[183] In his commentary on this famous *śloka* Rāmānuja again invokes his threefold classification of *tyāga* referred to earlier, wherein he glosses the word *dharma* 'as *karmayoga, jñānayoga*, and *bhaktiyoga*, these, he says, must be practised with the abandonment of fruit and agency and authorship (the threefold *tyāga*)'.[184]

It is clear therefore from the foregoing analysis that for Rāmānuja (1) '*tyāga* and *saṃnyāsa* are synonymous'[185] and (2) although they are synonymous, he operates exegetically primarily with the concept of *tyāga* rather than *saṃnyāsa*.

We may move now from the commentary to the text. Do the two conclusions drawn on the basis of Rāmānuja's commentary coincide with the conclusions we might draw from an analysis of the text above?

The first conclusion based on Rāmānuja was that the words *saṃnyāsa* and *tyāga* are synonymous. Can this position be sustained on the basis of a semantic differential analysis of the two terms in the Gītā?

An analysis of the uses of the nouns *tyāga* and *saṃnyāsa* and of other forms from the verbal roots underlying the two words reveals the following:[186]

[180] Mahāvana Śāstrī (ed.), op.cit., p.277.

[181] 'Therefore, *saṃnyāsa* is the renunciation of one's interest in, and of the results of and one's agency of, one's acts and so is synonymous with *tyāga*' (J.A.B. van Buitenen, op.cit., p.165).

[182] Hill, p.269, n.1.

[183] The verbal root in the word *saṃnyāsa* seems to be *as*, and not *nyas* as has been suggested by some scholars, especially from Poona; see Prahlad C. Divanji and S.M. Katre, *Critical Word-Index of the Bhagavadgītā* (Bombay: New Book Co., 1946), p.149; V.S. Apte, *The Practical Sanskrit-English Dictionary*, Vol.II (Poona: Prasad Prakashan, 1957), p.1625. The correct analysis of the word *saṃnyāsa* would then be *sam* prefix, plus *ni* prefix, plus root *as* with noun-making suffix (see Taranath Tarkavachaspati, compiler, *Vācaspatya*, Vols.21-2 [Calcutta: Saraswati Press, 1883], p.5219). The Dhātupāṭha does not enumerate *nyas* as a root (see Pandit Jibananda Vidyasagar (ed.), *Dhaturupadarsha* [Calcutta: Sucharu Press, 1875] passim).

[184] Hill, op.cit., p.212, n.2.

[185] van Buitenen, op.cit., p.162.

[186] G.A. Jacob, *A Concordance of the Upanishads and the Bhagavadgītā*, (Bombay: Government Central Book Depot, 1891) was used for this purpose (pp.410-11, 968).

(1) The word *tyāga* is used in the Bhagavadgītā in various senses of abandonment[187] – including

(i) the abandonment of action[188]
(ii) the abandonment of fruits of action[189]

(2) The word *saṃnyāsa* is used in the Bhagavadgītā in the sense of

(i) the abandonment of action[190]
(ii) the abandonment of desires[191]
(iii) the casting of actions *on* something[192]

On comparing the two uses we find that the word *saṃnyāsa* is not used in the sense of abandoning the fruits of action. *Saṃnyāsa* is used in the sense of giving up action, of giving up desires, of casting off actions, of giving up *dependence* on the fruit of action,[193] and possibly in the sense of giving up the *desire* of the fruit of action or *attachment* to the fruit of action;[194] but the word *saṃnyāsa* is not used in the sense of abandoning the fruit of action itself.

Similarly, although the word *tyāga* is used in the sense of giving up *karma, dharma,* resolve, attachment, etc., it is not used in the sense of casting of actions on God (*nikṣhepārtha*).[195]

The words *tyāga* and *saṃnyāsa*, therefore, are not exactly synonymous. As a matter of fact, Rāmānuja has used the word *saṃnyāsa*, and *tyāga*, to carry a meaning it does not carry in the Gītā by making them synonymous. He has used them to include meanings they do not have in the Gītā.

The second conclusion drawn from an analysis of Rāmānuja's commentary was that, although he regards *tyāga* and *saṃnyāsa* as synonyms, he works primarily with the word *tyāga*. Can this position be sustained on the basis of an examination of the text?

One would think so. It has been noted how the notion of *saṃnyāsa* is associated with the giving up of action. But this is precisely what Kṛṣṇa does *not* want Arjuna to do.[196] Moreover, it is repeatedly pointed out that action is an ineluctable condition of existence itself.[197] Thus action cannot be given up: no *saṃnyāsa* is possible in

[187] I:33; II:3,48; IV:9; VIII:6; etc. [188] XVIII:3, etc.
[189] V:12; XVIII:9; etc.
[190] XVIII:7. [191] VI:4. [192] III:30; V:13; XII:6; XVIII:57; etc.
[193] VI:1. [194] These are possible interpretations of VI:2,4.
[195] The famous verse – XVIII:66 – does not call for the casting off of all *dharmas* on God; it calls for the casting off of all *dharmas* to be followed by seeking God's succour.
[196] II:47. [197] III:5, XVIII:11.

its gross sense. Nor is the abandonment of certain kinds of works desirable.[198] What should Arjuna do then? Either he should give up personal motivation behind action, or he should give up the fruits of action.[199] He should give up the underlying cause of action – desire (which is genuine *saṃnyāsa*[200]) or he should give up the effect of action – fruits (which is *tyāga* in one sense, not included in *saṃnyāsa*). Now, whereas the word *saṃnyāsa* covers only the first option, the word *tyāga* covers both the options. Of the two, therefore, *tyāga* is more fully representative of the Gītā.

To sum up: both *tyāga* and *saṃnyāsa* and their grammatical variations are used frequently in the Gītā. But so far as the text of the Gītā goes, whereas *tyāga* is used to cover the sense of abandonment in all its senses – including that of abandonment of action and that of the abandonment of fruits of action, *saṃnyāsa* is never used in this last sense – that of abandonment of the fruits of action. Rāmānuja therefore does not quite conform to the Bhagavadgītā when he treats the words as exactly synonymous. Of the two, however, he works with *tyāga* rather than with *saṃnyāsa*, which is more in keeping with the tenor and texture of the Gītā than if he were to use *saṃnyāsa* because of the semantic limitation of the word pointed out above.

The conclusion we are led to on the basis of a comparison of the discussion of the distinction between *tyāga* and *saṃnyāsa* in Rāmānuja's commentary on the Gītā and the discussion on the basis of the Gītā itself is that whereas in his discussion Rāmānuja seems to overstep the 'letter' of the Gītā he seems to quite abide by its 'spirit'.[201]

4.

This is not always true, however, as will now be demonstrated by an examination of two key concepts – of *kṣetrajña* and the *jīvanmukta*.

We may begin by picking up a thread relinquished earlier that there seems to be a trend in recent studies to indicate that Rāmānuja is closer to getting at the true meaning and significance of the Gītā than any other commentator, especially Śaṅkara. Thus Zaehner remarks that 'the Gītā was probably composed in the third or fourth century B.C. and it is thus our first literary source of *bhakti*, as

[198] XVIII:5-6,7. [199] XVIII:11. [200] VI:4.

[201] This conclusion, that Rāmānuja abides by the spirit of the Gītā, applies only to Rāmānuja's position on the *saṃnyāsa* – *tyāga* issue from the point of view of this essay. It is *not* a general comment on his Gītābhāṣya.

devotional religion is called in India'.[202] Later he remarks that 'the full significance of this aspect of the Gītā was first brought into relief by Rāmānuja, the great theistic philosopher of the eleventh century who did so much to make *bhakti* philosophically respectable'.[203] As a matter of fact, Rāmānuja evolved a whole system of philosophy known as Viśiṣṭādvaita in which 'God is the Supreme Soul and all creation forms his "body" – both the souls in eternity and the world in time'.[204]

Thus in Rāmānuja's system there is a plurality of souls. The question then arises: what evidence does Rāmānuja find for such a doctrine in the Gītā?

One of the words used by Rāmānuja for souls is *kṣetrajña*. He clearly remarks in his gloss on Bhagavadgītā II:12 that *kṣetrajñāḥ ātmano' pi nityā eva*;[205] that is to say, the souls are eternal. Note that both *plurality* and eternality has been posited on the basis of this text. Or to explain the gloss in some detail:

> God declares, 'I, the Lord, have always existed and will always exist, and likewise the individual *ātmans*, Arjuna and all others who are subject to My lordship, have always existed and will always exist. No doubt can be entertained that I who am the Lord, the Supreme *Ātman*, am immortal; likewise Arjuna and all others, though being mere *kṣetrajñas* – nothing but *ātmans* – should be considered immortal.'
>
> This means that on the strength of the authority of God himself who is teaching Arjuna the truth we have to admit
>
> 1. that there is difference between God and the individual *ātmans*;
> 2. that there is difference between the individual *ātmans* themselves;
> 3. that this difference is absolutely real.[206]

The question then naturally arises – does the Bhagavadgītā speak of a plurality of metaphysical as distinguished from empirical souls? One such word for the soul would be *kṣetrajña*. If this word occurs in the plural, and not in a context denying this plurality, a *prima facie* case in favour of a plurality of souls will emerge on the basis of the Gītā and thus confirm Rāmānuja's interpretation.

The word *kṣetrajña* occurs several times in the Gītā. All the verses in which it occurs are reproduced below. They are in the Thirteenth Chapter of the Gītā.

[202] R.C. Zaehner, *Hinduism* (Oxford University Press, 1966), p.93.
[203] ibid., p.98. [204] ibid., p.99.
[205] Mahāvana Śāstrī (ed.), op.cit., p.13.
[206] van Buitenen, op.cit., p.50.

1 *śrībhagavān uvaca*
idaṁ śarīraṁ kaunteya
kṣetram ity abhidhīyate
etad yo vetti taṁ prāhuḥ
kṣetrajña iti tadvidaḥ

The Blessed Lord said:
This body, O Son of Kuntī (Arjuna), is called the field and him who knows this, those who know thereof call the knower of the field

2 *kṣetrajñaṁ cā 'pi māṁ viddhi*
sarvakṣetreṣu bhārata
kṣetrakṣetrajñayor jñānaṁ
yat taj jñānam mataṁ mama

Know Me as the Knower of the field in all fields, O Bhārata (Arjuna). The knowledge of the field and its knower, do I regard as true knowledge.

26 *yāvat saṁjāyate kiṁcit*
sattvaṁ sthāvarajaṅgamam
kṣetrakṣetrajñasaṁyogāt
tad viddhi bharatarṣabha

Whatever being is born, moving or unmoving, know thou, O Best of the Bharatas (Arjuna), that it is (sprung) through the union of the field and the knower of the field.

34 *kṣetrakṣetrajñayor evam*
antaraṁ jñānacakṣuṣā
bhūtaprakṛtimokṣaṁ ca
ye vidur yānti te param

Those who perceive thus by their eye of wisdom the distinction between the field and the knower of the field, and the deliverance of beings from nature (*prakṛti*), they attain to the Supreme.[207]

It is clear that in none of these occurrences is the word used in the plural. Obviously, in this case, Rāmānuja, it seems, has

[207] Bhagavadgītā XIII:1,2,26,34. Transliteration and translation as per S. Radhakrishnan, *The Bhagavadgītā* (London: Allen and Unwin, 1958), pp.300, 302, 310 and 313.

over-interpreted the Bhagavadgītā, and has done so not arbitrarily but systemically.

Kṣetrajña occurs in the Gītā, but not *jīvanmukta*. However, though the word does not occur, it will soon become obvious that the concept does. But while the concept of living liberation or *jīvanmukti* occurs in the Gītā it does *not* occur in the system of philosophy known as Viśiṣṭādvaita Vedānta associated with Rāmānuja. The point obviously calls for further exegetical investigation, for several verses describe the achievement of salvation in the Gītā. Some do not specify whether salvation is achieved here or in the hereafter (e.g. IV:31,38; VI:15,27, etc.) or leave one in doubt on the question (e.g. XVIII:45-55). Yet others specify the achievement of salvation in future births (e.g. VI:45) or at the moment of death (e.g. VIII:5-7, 13). But there are at least four verses which clearly seem to imply *jīvanmukti* or living liberation, a view to which Rāmānuja is opposed.[208] How then does Rāmānuja tackle these verses?

The last verse of the Second Chapter runs as follows:

eṣā brāhmī sthitiḥ pārtha
nai 'nāṃ prāpya vimuhyati
sthitvā 'syām antakāle 'pi
brahmanirvāṇam ṛcchati

This is the fixation that is Brahmanic, son of Pṛthā; Having attained it he is not (again) confused. Abiding in it even at the time of death, He goes to Brahman-nirvāṇa.[209]

It is generally admitted to imply *jīvanmukti*.[210] However, this is not admitted by Rāmānuja.[211] His argument may be summarised thus:

This position is disinterested activity, which presupposes knowledge of the eternal *ātman*, marks the *sthitaprajña*. This position will lead one to *brahman* and deliver one from perplexity, that is from *saṃsāra*. If one persists in this position until one's dying-hour, one will attain the *ātman* which comprises nothing but beatitude.

[208] See Anima Sen Gupta, *A Critical Study of the Philosophy of Rāmānuja* (Varanasi: Chowkhamba Sanskrit Series Office, 1967), p.133; Mahadevan, op.cit., p.155.

[209] Edgerton, op.cit., Part I, p.30, 31. [210] See Hill, op.cit., p.94, n.1.

[211] Mahāvana Śāstrī (ed.), op.cit., p.41.

Relation *Karmayoga-jñānayoga*

> Knowledge of the *ātman* combined with *karmayoga* leads to *jñānayoga*; through *jñānayoga* one arrives at the true contemplation of the realising *ātman*. This contemplation, again, is propaedeutic to *bhaktiyoga*; through *bhakti* alone one is capable of attaining God.[212]

The important point to realise is that by reading Rāmānuja's gloss on II:72 above we might be led to believe that salvation is achieved here and now because Rāmānuja uses the statement 'one does not again attain to *saṁsāra*' to gloss *na vimuhyati*.[213] but closer study reveals that this is only said of the *sthitaprajña* en route to salvation. He does, after all, belong to the topmost category of the *jñāna-niṣṭha*, but only a *bhakta* can be liberated.

There are four degress of *jñānaniṣṭhā*:

1. when one focuses the mind on nothing but the *ātman* and, being content with that, expels all other desires;
2. when one is a *muni*, who is not grieved whenever there is reason, who has no desire for pleasing objects and who is exempt from wishful thought, fear and anger;
3. when one is indifferent to pleasing objects and exempt from joy and hatred;
4. when one focuses the mind on the *ātman* and withdraws the senses from the objects.[214]

The next verse that seems to refer explicitly to *jīvanmukti* runs as follows(V:19):

ihai 'va tair jitaḥ sargo
yeṣāṃ sāmye sthitaṃ manaḥ
nirdoṣaṃ hi samaṃ brahma
tasmād brahmaṇi te sthitāḥ

> Right in this world they have overcome birth, Whose mind is fixed in indifference; for Brahman is flawless and indifferent; Therefore, they are fixed in Brahman.[215]

Here it is the expression *ihaiva* which emphasises the here-and-now quality of salvation. How does Rāmānuja get around this one? He glosses it as *sādhanānuṣṭhāna-daśāyām*:[216] even in the state of

[212] van Buitenen, op.cit., pp.65-6.
[213] Mahavāna Śāstrī (ed.), op.cit., p.41.
[214] van Buitenen, op.cit., pp.63-4.
[215] Edgerton, op.cit., Part I, pp.56-7.
[216] Mahāvana Śāstrī (ed.), op.cit., p.90.

observing the several practices (which lead to *mokṣa*).[217] Thus the force of the expression is made anticipatory of later realisation rather than confirmatory of it here and now.

V:23 also proses a problem for Rāmānuja and for the same reason – its use of the emphatic *ihaiva* – and Rāmānuja uses the same exegetical device to get round it.[218]

The last verse which may be cited as referring directly to living liberation also belongs to the same chapter (V:28). It runs as follows:

yatendriyamanobuddhir
munir mokṣaparāyaṇaḥ
vigatecchābhayakrodho
yaḥ sadā mukta eva saḥ

Controlling the senses, thought-organ, and intelligence, The sage bent on final release, whose desire, fear, and wrath are departed – Who is ever thus, is already released.[219]

Herein the crucial expression is *sadā mukta eva*. Rāmānuja glosses: *sādhyadaśāyām iva sādhanadaśāyām api mukta sa ity arthaḥ*:[220] 'The meaning is, that he is verily liberated even in his state of preparation as in his state of perfection.'[221]

Thus it seems that Rāmānuja employs a fundamental exegetical procedure to neutralise those verses of the Gītā which seem to suggest *jīvanmukti* – this is to claim that such statements anticipate in the stage of preparation the results which follow on its culmination. Whether such a procedure does justice to the verses of the Gītā is for the reader to judge.

How then does Rāmānuja fare as an interpreter of the Gītā?

If it be accepted that the Gītā, though speaking with many voices, is primarily theistic in its orientation, and if it be further acknowledged, as indeed it is almost universally, that Rāmānuja's own system of thought is theistic in its orientation rather than absolutistic, then it can be argued that room for an ideological affinity between the text and its interpreter created thereby would enable him to respond better to the spirit of the text. And this may well be so. But the problem is that the theism of Rāmānuja is not a

[217] Īśvaradatta Vidyālaṇkāra, *Rāmānuja's Commentary on the Bhagavadgītā* (Muzaffarpur, Bihar: Prof. Īśvaradatta, G.B.B. College, 1930), p.103.

[218] Mahavāna Śāstrī (ed.), op.cit., p.92; Īśvaradatta Vidyālaṇkāra, op.cit., p.105.

[219] Edgerton, op.cit., pp.58-9.

[220] Mahavāna Śastrī (ed.), op.cit., p.93.

[221] Iśvaradatta Vidyālaṅkāra, op.cit., p.107.

simple pietistic theism; it is a philosophically formulated theism, and when he tries to read this system back into the Gītā he runs into the same difficulties which others faced and tries to overcome them by employing similar procrustean procedures. This is not to deny that subject to this overall limitation Rāmānuja, like Śaṅkara before him, extends and enlarges the understanding of the Gītā within the Hindu religious tradition. But even the point that the parallelism of theism in the Gītā and in Rāmānuja's system would predispose him to a sounder interpretation of the Gītā should not be accepted uncritically. Rāmānuja's theism is not the only one known to Hinduism. Not only is there the theism of Madhva, of Nimbārka, of Vallabha to mention only a few, but even the absolutism of Advaita Vedānta does not so much deny theism as transcend it. The moment a scholastically specific theism is sought in the Gītā rather than theism *per se* in general, that particular interpretation seems to run into the type of difficulties which any crystallised structure of thought does when confronted with at times the ambiguity, at other times the plasticity, and at yet other times the clarity, of the text of the Gītā.[222] Further scholarly studies, however, could well alter this estimate.[223]

[222] From this point of view, the reputed Advaitin S. Radhakrishnan offers a much more positive assessment of Rāmānuja's commentary then even he might have realised when he wrote (*The Bhagavadgītā* [New Delhi: Blackie & Son (India) Ltd., 1974 (first published 1948)] pp.18-19; emphasis added): 'Rāmānuja develops in his commentary on the Gītā a type of personal mysticism. In the secret places of the human soul, God dwells but He is unrecognised by it so long as the soul does not acquire the redeeming knowledge. We acquire this knowledge by serving God with our whole heart and soul. Perfect trust is possible only for those who are elected by divine grace. Rāmānuja admits that the paths of knowledge, devotion and action are all mentioned in the *Gītā*, but he holds that its main emphasis is on devotion. The wretchedness of sin, the deep longing for the Divine, the intense feeling of trust and faith in God's all-conquering love, the experience of being divinely elected are stressed by him. The Supreme is Viṣṇu, for Rāmānuja. He is the only true God who will not share his divine honours with others. Liberation is service of and fellowship with God in Vaikuṇṭha or heaven.'

[223] For the tenets of Viśiṣṭādvaita Vedānta, in addition to the books already mentioned, see also Krishna Datta Bharadwaj, *The Philosophy of Rāmānuja* (New Delhi: Sir Shankar Lall Charitable Trust Society, 1958); P.N. Srinivasachari, *The Philosophy of Viśiṣṭādvaita* (Madras; Adyar Library, 1943); M. Yamunacharya, *Rāmānuja's Teachings in His Own Words* (Bombay: Bharitya Vidya Bhavan, 1963); etc. For other books covering Rāmānuja's commentary on the Gītā, see G.S. Sadhale (ed.), *The Bhagavadgītā with Eleven Commentaries* (Bombay: 'Gujarati' Printing Press, 1935); with M.R. Śankara and V.G. Āpṭe (eds.), *Śrīmadbhagavadgītā Vedāntācārya – Śrī – Venkaṭanāthakṛta – Tātparya Candrikākhya – Ṭīkāsaṃvalita – Śrīmad – Rāmānujācārya – Viracita Bhāṣyasahitā* (Bombay: Ānandāśrama Press, 1923); etc.

CHAPTER SIX

Madhva

1.

Madhva or Madhvācārya (1199-1278) is the third of the classical exegetes, along with Śaṅkara and Rāmānuja, whose names are taken together. Just as Śaṅkara is the main representative of Advaita Vedānta and Rāmānuja of Viśiṣṭādvaita Vedānta, so Madhva is the representative, par excellence, of Dvaita Vedānta. Let us first briefly distinguish these systems, since the differences between them ultimately influence the interpretation of the Gītā which these scholiasts opt for.

According to the Advaita system of Vedānta, as we have seen, the ultimate reality, or Brahman, is ultimately without any distinctions whatsoever, internal or external, and the distinctions we see in empirical existence are ultimately unreal, there being in reality only one homogeneous principle. According to Viśiṣṭādvaita Vedānta, the ultimate reality, or Brahman, ultimately possesses internal distinctions, but there is nothing external to it. The universe and the creatures possess a distinct, but not separate, reality and are contained within Brahman. According to Dvaita Vedānta, the ultimate reality, or Brahman, ultimately possesses both internal and external distinctions. The universe and the creatures are distinct as well as separate from it; this external world is not contained in, but is under the control of, God, who is Himself endowed, as also in Viśiṣṭādvaita, with numerous glorious attributes. It can be seen how their basic outlook generates the main features of the various systems. Thus if there is only one distinctionless reality as in Advaita, salvation comes from the realisation of the identity of the true self of the spiritual aspirant with Brahman. In Viśiṣṭādvaita Vedānta Brahman possesses internal distinctions, and therefore realisation results from the knowledge of one's inseparability or proximity to God in loving devotion. In Dvaita Vedānta Brahman possesses both internal and external distinctions, and realisation therefore comes from a proper understanding of these distinctions in the context of God's transcendent majesty. For God must now cease to be both the efficient and the material cause of the universe and the creatures; he is only the efficient cause, the only true independent reality by whose grace alone salvation is achieved in a post-mortem state. A popular verse summarises Madhva's system thus:

> In Śrī Madhva's system, Hari is the supreme being, the world is real, difference is true, the host of *jīvas* are dependent on Hari, there are grades of superiority and inferiority among them, *mokṣa* consists in the soul's enjoyment of its innate bliss, faultless *bhakti* is the means thereto, perception, inference and verbal testimony are the three ways of knowing (*pramāṇas*), and Hari is knowable only through the Vedas.[1]

Before we begin to examine Madhva's interpretation of the Gītā it would be useful, as in previous chapters, to indicate in advance how his system relates to his commentary. The relation, as expressed in his two works on the Gītā, the *Gītābhāṣya* and the *Gītātātparya*, is not unexpected.

> He attempts to derive from the *Gītā* tenets of dualistic (*dvaita*) philosophy. It is self-contradictory, he contends, to look upon the soul as identical with the Supreme in one sense and different from Him in another. The two must be regarded as eternally different from each other and any unity between them, partial or entire, is untenable. He interprets the passage 'that art thou' as meaning that we must give up the distinction between mine and thine and hold that everything is subject to the control of God. Madhva contends that devotion is the method emphasised in the *Gītā*.[2]

In this chapter Madhva's Gītābhāṣya, along with the sub-commentary of Jayatīrtha has been utilised.[3] The procedure adopted is as follows. In this section we have given a general introduction. In the second we shall provide examples of those glosses by Madhva on

[1] T.M.P. Mahadevan, *Outlines of Hinduism* (Bombay: Chetana, 1971), p.156.

[2] S. Radhakrishnan, *The Bhagavadgītā* (New Delhi: Blackie 1974 [first published 1948]), p.19.

[3] V. Srīpāda et al. (eds.), *Gītabhāshya of Sri Madhwacharya with Prameyadeepika of Sri Jayatirtha – A Commentary of Bhagavadgītā* (Poornaprajnanagar, Bangalore: Poornaprajana Vidyapeetha, 1981).

the verses of the Gītā whereby our understanding of these verses seems to be enriched, and in the third examples of those glosses which do not seem felicitous. Finally, in the fourth section, an assessment will be offered.

2.

Madhva's gloss on some of the verses of the Bhagavadgītā helps to enhance our understanding of them. Thus, for instance, early in the Second Chapter he introduces an interesting idea in his gloss on the thirteenth verse, which runs as follows:

dehino 'smin yathā dehe
kaumāraṃ yauvanaṃ jarā
tathā dehāntaraprāptir
dhīras tatra na muhyati

As to the embodied (soul) in this body
Come childhood, youth, old age,
So the coming to another body;
The wise man is not confused herein.[4]

Now the idea of the *ātman* being the *sākṣī* or 'witness' is, of course, patent in Śaṅkara's Advaita,[5] but Madhva introduces the concept here with a measure of philosophical finesse. For he argues that it is the *ātman* as witness which is common to the bodily modifications characterised by childhood, etc., and that it continues to be the witness in another incarnation. For, he argues, the next body is incapable of experiencing the states of childhood, etc. It is only with the prior conscious realisation 'I am a man' that the experiencing of the various states is possible. Even in sleep, for instance, such awareness is lacking.

Again, in his interpretation of Bhagavadgītā II:14 he succeeds in subtilising the exegesis. The verse runs:

[4] Franklin Edgerton, *The Bhagavad Gītā* Part I (Cambridge, Mass.: Harvard University Press, 1944), pp.16, 17. In this chapter the transliteration and translation of the text of the Gītā is as per this book, unless indicated otherwise.

[5] Eliot Deutsch and J.A.B. van Buitenen, *A Source Book of Advaita Vedānta* (Honolulu: University of Hawaii Press, 1971), p.310.

mātrāsparśās tu kaunteya
śītoṣṇasukhaduḥkhadāḥ
āgamāpāyino 'nityās
tāṃs titikṣasva bhārata

But contacts with matter, son of Kuntī,
Cause cold and heat, pleasure and pain;
They come and go, and are impermanent;
Put up with them, son of Bharata![6]

It is the description of the 'contacts with matter' as things that 'come and go, and are impermanent' which is the subject of commentarial focus. Madhva comments that these contacts do not possess *even* dynamic continuity, and it is in this sense that they are called *anitya* or impermanent. The point is elaborated by Jayatīrtha. He points out that continuity can be of two kinds, constant and periodic. The *flow* of the Ganges is constant, though each drop of water is not. This flow is an illustration of constant continuity. By contrast, flowers blossom in season year after year and this is an illustration of periodic continuity. Madhva says that when it is said of 'contacts' that they are impermanent, it should not be mistaken as a statement to the effect that they possess dynamic continuity of the constant kind and that it is only transcendental permanence (such as that of a rock as compared to a river)[7] which is denied of them. The reason for denying dynamic continuity is physiological – such contacts do not persist during sleep, etc.

Madhva's philosophy emphasises distinctions, and perhaps this accounts for his tendency, and one may even say his skill, in drawing fine distinctions. He does this in his gloss on II:21:

veda 'vināśinaṃ nityaṃ
ya enam ajam avyayam
kathaṃ sa puruṣaḥ pārtha
kaṃ ghātayati hanti kam

Who knows as indestructible and eternal
This unborn, imperishable one,
That man, son of Pṛthā, how
Can he slay or cause to slay – whom?

[6] Edgerton, op.cit., Part I, pp.16, 17.
[7] For a distinction between *kūtastha-nityatā* and *pravāha-nityatā*, see K. Satchidananda Murty, *Revelation and Reason in Advaita Vedānta* (New York: Columbia University Press, 1959), p.40.

Among the various expressions used to characterise the *ātman* in this verse are *avināśī* and *nitya*. On the face of it the two expressions are tautological. Rāmānuja merely says that it is eternal (*nitya*), because it cannot be destroyed, and connects the two syntactically through the instrumental case.[8] Śaṅkara makes some effort to distinguish between the two, taking *avināśī* to indicate that the *ātman* can never be destroyed (*antyābhāva*) and *nitya* to mean that it does not undergo modification (*vipariṇāma*). Madhva, however, glosses *avināśinam* as *naimittikanāśarahitam*, and *nityam* as *svābhāvika-nāśar-ahitam*, thereby virtually reflecting Śaṅkara's interpretation. But that is not of as much interest as the distinction drawn between two kinds of destruction. This seems to be more in keeping with the tenor of the verse itself, as its verbs speak of 'slay or cause to slay'. Thus Madhva takes *avināśī* to indicate the indestructibility of the *ātman* through extraneous factors, e.g. killing, and *nitya* to refer to the indestructibility of the soul through internal factors, e.g. dying of natural causes. Madhva also offers the exegetical option of connecting the *ātman* as *nitya* here with the *mātrāsparśās* as *anitya* in II:14 according to Jayatīrtha. Although Madhva himself does not make so direct a connection, it seems a reasonable elaboration of his gloss that *avināśī* could also mean free from defects, for the *ātman* is to be everywhere taken as always existing (when, by contrast, the 'contacts' come and go). This optional interpretation, however, seems to us to lack the penetration of the original interpretation.

In II:24 the epithet *sthāṇu* is used for the *ātman*. The word means 'standing firmly, stationary, firm fixed, immovable, motionless' as well as 'a stump, stem, trunk, stake, post, pile, pillar (also as a symbol of motionlessness)'.[9] Śaṅkara is content to gloss it as firm (*sthira*),[10] and Rāmānuja takes the string of epithets of which it is a part as all indicating the unshakable and firm nature of the *ātman* (*sthirasvabhāvaḥ aprakampyaḥ*).[11] Madhva again draws a distinction between the epithets indicating eternality and the epithet *sthāṇu* indicating its firm and stationary nature. The latter, Madhva suggests, is employed to foreclose the exegetical possibility that, though the *ātman* is eternal, i.e. uniform, it is still capable of being adventitiously affected. Madhva also introduces an element

[8] H. Goyandakā, *Śrīmadbhagavadgītā Śrīrāmānujabhāṣya Hindi Anuvāda Sahita* (Gorakhpur: Gita Press, Saṁvat 2025), p.46.

[9] Monier Monier-Williams, *A Sanskrit-English Dictionary* (Oxford: Clarendon Press, 1970), p.1262.

[10] Śaṅkara, *Gītābhāṣya* (*Śrīśāṅkaragranthāvaliḥ* Sampuṭa 8 – Śrīraṅgam: Śrīvāṇīvilā-samudrāyantrālayaḥ, no date), p.34.

[11] Goyandakā, op.cit., p.48.

characteristic of his philosophy in this gloss, namely, that the *ātman* possesses all these features on account of having the same form as God's (*īśvara-sarūpatvāt*). This does not materially affect the point made above. But it leads to another. If the *ātman* is motionless, how can it be the witness of the transmigrating self? It is interesting how Jayatīrtha rejects the Advaitic position in this respect. He points out that according to the *māyāvādins* – that is, the upholders of the doctrine of *māyā* – the Advaitins, of the two aspects – motion or activity and motionlessness or inactivity – one is illusory: namely, motion or activity. It is inaction which is absolutely true and there is no real contradiction between its being so and apparent activity, just as the sky is without form (and colour) but appears to be blue without being so, so that the contradiction is only apparent. This position is rejected by Jayatīrtha. If we now turn to Madhva's own gloss, we find that he establishes the reconcilability of the motionlessness as well as the constant witnessing on the part of *ātman* on the basis of its comparability to God about whom both kinds of statements are found (*ubhayavidha-vākyāt*). And this is possible not because of *māyā* but because of God's (and therefore *ātman*'s) incomprehensible power (*acintyaśakti*).[12] Madhva is to be credited for perceiving the problem here even if the solution offered is particular to his school.

Another verse from the Second Chapter may now be considered. It is a difficult verse to interpret and runs as follows (II:29):

āścaryavat paśyati kaścid enam
āścaryavad vadati tathai 'va cā 'nyaḥ
āścaryavac cai 'nam anyaḥ śṛṇoti
śrutvā 'py enaṃ veda na cai 'va kaścit

By a rare chance one may see him,
And by a rare chance likewise may another declare him,
And by a rare chance may another hear (of) him;
(But) even having heard (of) him, no one whatsoever knows him.

It is easily recognised that both Śaṅkara and Rāmānuja take *āścaryavat* to mean 'very rarely'. Although Minor says that Telang 'followed Madhva' to take it to mean wonder,[13] Madhva himself says *durlabhatvena ity arthaḥ* and so takes it in the same sense as the

[12] Śrīpāda, op.cit., pp.51, 55.
[13] Robert N. Minor, *Bhagavad-Gītā: An Exegetical Commentary* (New Delhi: Heritage Publishers, 1982), p.51.

rest. One point of interest here is Jayatīrtha's prefatory comment on Madhva's gloss, to the effect that the verse does not seem to fit the context, a feeling which perhaps other readers also tend to share but which has generally gone unremarked. The other point of interest is provided by Madhva's gloss itself, which is brief and becomes significant in view of the fact that Rāmānuja

> refers the stanza to God rather than the individual self; yet oddly enough in the Gītā it is not so much God who is unknowable as the self. Thus the possibility of knowing God is mentioned in 7.3 and 7.30, but it is a remote one. In 9.13 it is *bhakti*, love and devotion, that enables man to know God as the eternal source of all things, and in 15.19 it is by love that a man comes to know God as the 'Person (All-) Sublime' who is 'more exalted than the Imperishable (Brahman) itself'. Similarly in his final message in 18.55 Krishna says: 'By love-and-loyalty (a man) comes to know Me as I really am, how great I am and who; and once he knows Me as I am, he enters (Me) forthwith.' Knowledge of God, then, would appear to be dependent on love and not vice versa. The self, on the other hand, whether you think of it as your own eternal, timeless essence or as the eternal substrate of all things, cannot be loved because it is 'indeterminate', 'for difficult (indeed) is it for embodied men to reach-and-tread the unmanifested way' (12.5).[14]

The passage has been cited in full because it contains several interesting observations, and we can see how, in one stroke, they lose their divergent character if the cue is taken from Madhva, that *God* and the *ātman* have the same form, so that the verse can be interpreted either way or as applying to both on account of *sarūpatvāt*, though Madhva himself takes it to refer to the *ātman*.

The next verse in the Second Chapter which merits attention is the one containing the words *sāṅkhya* and *yoga* (II:39). It is worth remarking that, although by the time the classical commentaries on the Gītā become available from about the ninth century A.D., both Sāṅkhya and Yoga were well-established schools of Hindu thought, yet none of the three great classical commentators – Śaṅkara,[15] Rāmānuja[16] and Madhva[17] – fall into the trap of identifying these words with those schools. Madhva glosses *sāṅkhyam* as *jñānam* and *yogaḥ* as *upāyaḥ*, and even cites appropriate verses in support.

[14] R.C. Zaehner, *The Bhagavadgītā* (London: Oxford University Press, 1969), p.136.
[15] Śaṅkara, op.cit., p.42. [16] Goyandakā, op.cit., p.61.
[17] Śrīpāda, op.cit., p.69.

We may now consider the well-known verse of the Second Chapter (47):

karmany evā 'dhikāras te
mā phaleṣu kadācana
mā karmaphalahetur bhūr
ma te sango 'stv akarmaṇi

On action alone be thy interest,
Never on its fruits;
Let not the fruits of action be thy motive,
Nor be thy attachment to inaction.

Madhva makes several interesting points in this connection. Some of them have an element of over-interpretation, as when he glosses to imply that there should be no desire for the fruit in Arjuna who is a *jñānin*, how much *less* so in anyone else. That is to say, neither Arjuna nor anyone else should perform actions directed to the attainment of desires. Here Madhva presents in seminal form an idea which comes to vigorous life in the following exegesis by M. Hiriyanna:

> The significance of this principle is to elevate the moral quality of actions above their content. What really matters is the motive inspiring their doing – how actions are done and not what they are. 'God cares,' some one has stated, 'more for the adverb than for the verb.' Thus the work in which Arjuna engages himself as a result of Śrī Krishna's teaching is stupendous in its magnitude, being nothing less than setting right the world which is running off the rails. The actions, which ordinary people like ourselves have to perform, bear no comparison to it. While the one, for instance, would in a historical estimate count for a great deal, the other would be nowhere. Yet in point of their moral worth, the two do not differ in the least. Such a detached carrying out of one's duties, whatever they may be, is called *karma-yoga.*[18]

Madhva makes an interesting point in relating two verses of the Second Chapter (II:59-60):

[18] M. Hiriyanna, *The Essentials of Indian Philosophy* (London: Allen & Unwin, 1948), p.55.

viṣayā vinivartante
nirāhārasya dehinaḥ
rasavarjaṃ raso 'py asya
paraṃ dṛṣṭvā nivartate

yatato hy api kaunteya
puruṣasya vipaścitaḥ
indriyāṇi pramāthīni
haranti prasabhaṃ manaḥ

The objects of sense turn away
From the embodied one that abstains from food,
Except flavour; flavour also from him
Turns away when he has seen the highest.

For even of one who strives, son of Kuntī,
Of the man of discernment,
The impetuous senses
Carry away the mind by violence.

He points out that the kind of stabilised mentality of the *sthitaprajña* referred to in the earlier verses is not attained *without effort*. If we deny our senses the objects of the senses, then by their 'fasting' there arises the inability to enjoy the sense-objects. Or the desire for the sense-objects also ceases. Madhva distinguishes here between the desire for the object and the desire for the relish of the object (*viśayākāṅkṣā* from *rasākāṅkṣā*). That only goes away after direct realisation (*aparokṣajñānam*).[19] Madhva then glosses the next verse as stating that the mind distracts the senses of a person who is a *jñānin* but is lacking in immediate realisation and is putting in *only ordinary effort*. Thus Madhva takes *yatato* as implying effort as all commentators do, but adds his own touch that it implies an ordinary measure of effort, with the obvious implication that an even higher measure of effort would not imply failure. That this line of interpretation is in keeping with the spirit of the Gītā is clear from such verses as III:43.

The sixty-ninth verse of the Second Chapter of the Gītā is a difficult one, as it involves a reversal of our diurnal and nocturnal associations:

[19] Śrīpāda, op.cit., p.80ff.

yā niśā sarvabhūtānāṃ
  tasyāṃ jāgarti saṃyamī
yasyāṃ jāgrati bhūtāni
  sā niśā paśyato muneḥ

What is night for all beings,
  Therein the man of restraint is awake;
Wherein (other) beings are awake,
  That is night for the sage of vision.

Madhva seems to offer a particularly lucid exposition. The 'night' of all creatures is characterised by the knowledge of the divinity of God. They know nothing of it, asleep as it were in it. But the man of knowledge, possessed of self-restraint, is awake therein. That is to say he directly sees God – this is meant. And the night of sense-enjoyments in which the creatures are awake, therein he is asleep, knows nothing of it.[20] He moves about as if at a loss in the world of sense-enjoyment; a somnambulist in the night of sense-enjoyments – to draw Madhva further out. The Islamic reversal of daily routine during *ramaḍān* comes inadvertently to mind and suggests a symbolic actualisation of this verse.

Madhva also links this verse with II:55 and by implication with II:54 wherein Arjuna asks:

  arjuna uvāca
sthitaprajñasya kā bhāṣā
  samādhisthasya keśava
sthitadhīḥ kiṃ prabhāṣeta
  kim āsīta vrajeta kim

  Arjuna said:
What is the description of the man of stabilised mentality,
  That is fixed in concentration, Keśava?
How might the man of stabilised mentality speak,
  How might he sit, how walk?

It should be noted that Arjuna's question is fairly concrete: how does the *sthitaprajña* walk and talk? The next verse does not answer his question, it is too general (II:55).

[20] ibid.

śrībhagavān uvāca
prajahāti yadā kāmān
sarvān pārtha manogatān
ātmany evā 'tmanā tuṣṭaḥ
sthitaprajñas tado 'cyate

The Blessed One said:
When he abandons desires,
All that are in the mind, son of Pṛthā,
Finding contentment by himself in the self alone,
Then he is called of stabilised mentality.

In his gloss on that verse it is Madhva who tries to do what Kṛṣṇa should have done – he attempts to answer the question concretely by saying that the activity of locomotion, etc. of the realised being is not particularly directed towards the attainment of an end. It is like the action of an intoxicated person as shown by the verse *yā niśā*, etc.

Similarly, Madhva's explanation of the other figurative verse in Chapter Two is to be commended for its lucidity. The verse in question is II:70:

āpūryamāṇam acalapratiṣṭhaṃ
samudram āpaḥ praviśanti yadvat
tadvat kāmā yaṃ praviśanti sarve
sa śāntim āpnoti na kāmakāmī

It is ever being filled, and (yet) its foundation remains unmoved –
The sea: just as waters enter it,
Whom all desires enter in that same way
He attains peace; not the man who lusts after desires.

To paraphrase Madhva: one whose restraint remains unshaken even when flooded by sense-experiences, who does not become puffed up, who does not try (to seek pleasures) nor pines away in their absence, such a person is spoken of. For the ocean does not attain to much increase or diminution with the merging of the rivers in it or otherwise, nor is it concerned in the matter. Such a one has attained salvation – this is meant.

The third verse of the Third Chapter next claims attention. Madhva does two things with it which most commentators do not: he introduces the concept of *adhikāra* in a comprehensive way, and he introduces the idea of God's will, which will subsequently become an important element in the Gītā. The verse runs as follows:

loke 'smin dvividhā niṣṭhā
purā proktā mayā 'nagha
jñānayogena sāṃkhyānāṃ
karmayogena yoginām

In this world a two-fold basis (of religion)
Has been declared by Me of old, blameless one:
By the discipline of knowledge of the followers of reason-method,
And by the discipline of action of the followers of discipline-method.

Madhva's gloss may be paraphrased thus: God spoke with the intended purport that, although *buddhi-yoga* is superior,[21] yet, on account of your (Arjuna's) eligibility (for *karmayoga*), you (Arjuna) are fit for *karma* and to be constrained therein. People are of two kinds. Some are established in *jñāna* by renouncing the duties of a householder, etc. like Sanaka, etc. And others are established in *jñāna* while remaining householders, like Janaka, etc. They are also following my *dharma*; this is meant. By *sāṃkhyānām* is meant (the path) of the *jñānīs* such as Sanaka, etc. By *yoginām* is meant the followers of the path of works (*yoga*), such as Janaka, etc. Even those who are established in *jñāna* are eligible for performing work because such eligibility arises out of the will of the Lord or out of compassion for the people; they too (who perform works) are Yogins. *Niṣṭhā* means situation. You, like Janaka, etc. are eligible for *jñāna* along with *karma*; not like Sanaka, etc. for its abandonment; this is meant.[22]

Madhva's gloss on the next verse has a few peculiar features, especially the way he interprets the word *puruṣa*, but he makes two good points. The verse runs as follows (III:4):

na karmaṇām anārambhān
naiṣkarmyaṃ puruṣo 'śnute
na ca saṃnyasanād eva
siddhiṃ samadhigacchati

Not by not starting actions
Does a man attain actionlessness,
And not by renunciation alone
Does he go to perfection.

[21] II:49-50.
[22] See Madhva's gloss on II:39.

First, the expression *karmaṇām anārambhāt*, 'by not starting action', has been taken by most commentators in a general sense[23] and when taken in a special sense is identified with sacrifices, etc., as by Śaṅkara[24] (*yajñādīnām*), or with actions enjoined in the scriptures, as by Rāmānuja[25] (*śāstrīyānām karmaṇām*). Although it is true that there 'seems to be no reason ... to restrict the meaning of the word',[26] the gloss by Madhva seems to be contextually the most appropriate. He glosses *karmaṇām* as *yuddhādīnām* – battle, etc. Secondly, Madhva makes a fine philosophical point in his gloss about the beginninglessness of *saṁsāra*. Why *saṁsāra* is *anādi* in Hindu thought is a matter of some interest, and some explanations have been offered. At one point M. Hiryanna suggests an answer in terms of the beginninglessness of *karma*:

> Here, no doubt, a question will be asked as to when the responsibility for what one does was *first* incurred. But such a question is really inadmissible, for it takes for granted that there was a time when the self was without any disposition whatsoever. Such a view of the self is an abstraction as meaningless as that of mere disposition which characterises no one. The self, as ordinarily known to us, always means a self with a certain stock of disposition; and this fact is indicated in Indian exposition by describing karma as beginningless (*anādi*). It means that no matter how far back we trace the history of an individual, we shall never arrive at a stage when he was devoid of all character. Thus at all stages, it is self-determination; and the karma doctrine does in no sense imply the imposition of any constraint from outside. So deep is the conviction of some of the adequacy of *karma* to account for the vicissitudes of life and the diversity of human conditions that they see no need, as we shall point out later, to acknowledge the existence even of God, conceived as the creator of the world and as its controlling judge.[27]

Madhva draws out the implication of the *saṁsāra* being *anādi* in the context of the Gītā thus. He argues that, because the universe is *anādi*, there is beginningless *karma*, which can never be worked out. Had the universe been *sādi*, or with a beginning, the path of non-action might have worked by bringing action to an end. But as it is *anādi*, it

[23] W.D. Hill, *The Bhagavadgītā* (Oxford: Oxford University Press, 1969), p.95; Zaehner, op.cit., pp.162-3.
[24] Hill, op.cit., p.72. [25] Goyandakā, op.cit., p.95.
[26] Zaehner, op.cit., p.163.
[27] Hiriyanna, op.cit., pp.47-8.

is only through desirelessness, not renunciation of outward action, that salvation can be attained.[28]

Madhva's glosses on III:5-8 deserve serious consideration as they involve a reconsideration of the significance of these verses, which run as follows:

na hi kaścit kṣaṇam api
jātu tiṣṭhaty akarmakṛt
kāryate hy avaśaḥ karma
sarvaḥ prakṛtijair guṇaiḥ

karmendriyāṇi saṃyamya
ya āste manasā smaran
indriyārthān vimūḍhātmā
mithyācāraḥ sa ucyate

yas tv indriyāṇi manasā
niyamyā 'rabhate 'rjuna
karmendriyaiḥ karmayogam
asaktaḥ sa viśiṣyate

niyataṃ kuru karma tvaṃ
karma jyāyo hy akarmaṇaḥ
śarīrayātrā 'pi ca te
na prasidhyed akarmaṇaḥ

For no one even for a moment
Remains at all without performing actions;
For he is made to perform action willy-nilly,
Every one is, by the Strands that spring from material nature.

Restraining the action-senses
Who sits pondering with this thought-organ
On the subjects of sense, with deluded soul,
He is called a hypocrite.

But whoso the senses with the thought-organ
Controlling, O Arjuna, undertakes
Discipline of action with the action-senses,
Unattached (to the fruits of action), he is superior.

[28] Śrīpāda, op.cit., p.143.

Perform thou action that is (religiously) required;
For action is better than inaction.
And even the maintenance of the body for thee
Can not succeed without action.

The point to note here is the remarkable convergence between a modern analysis of the Gītā in general terms offered by M. Hiriyanna and the comment in specific terms made by Madhva. We may let Hiriyanna go first, according to whom the Gītā has

> as its essential basis the principle that activity is natural to man and that no view of life which overlooks that feature or minimises its importance can be right. More than once is it stated in the course of the work that no man can abjure activity altogether; but this natural activity needs to be properly directed, for otherwise it is apt to be utilised for selfish or material ends and thus become the means of obscuring from man the higher end for which he exists.
>
> What is the direction in which the activity should be exercised? In answer to this question, the Gita enjoins on all the performance of their respective duties. 'One should never abandon one's specific work, whether it be high or low.' It attaches little or no value to the intrinsic worth of the deed that is done by any person, so long as it is his own *dharma* (*svadharma*). The word *sva-dharma* may bear a wide significance but, as required by the particular context and as specified more than once in the course of the book, it means chiefly, though not solely, the duties incumbent upon the main classes into which society is divided.[29]

It is clear from the nature of the verses that the context here is comparable to the passage cited above. It is therefore a point of considerable interest that Madhva glosses *karma-yogam* as *svavarṇā-śramocitam* in III:7 and that he glosses the initial word of III:8 which is *niyatam* as *svavarṇāśramocitam*. The importance of his gloss becomes clear when compared with that of Śaṅkara and Rāmānuja, who do not gloss *karmayogam* in III:7 at all.[30] Both of them, however, gloss *niyatam* in III:8 but differently. Śaṅkara 'explains: "the obligatory (*nitya*) act, which one is bound to perform, and which is not prescribed as a means to a specific end" '.[31] Rāmānuja 'interprets

[29] M. Hiriyanna, *Outlines of Indian Philosophy* (London: Allen & Unwin, 1964 [first published 1932], pp.123-4.

[30] Śaṅkara, op.cit., p.75; Goyandakā, op.cit., p.97.

[31] Hill, op.cit., p.96, n.1.

nityam as *vyāptam* – "pervading", so "natural"'.[32] It seems that Śaṅkara's interpretation is too narrow and Rāmānuja's too broad and that Madhva may have assessed the significance here more accurately. But while appreciating Madhva's insight here, attention must be drawn to the limitations in which it is embedded. First, Madhva makes a special point of indicating that the *āśramas* include *sannyāsa*, which seems to be a peculiar concern of his. Secondly, he speaks both of *varṇa* and *āśrama* with equal emphasis in the context of the Gītā while it is known that there 'is not much reference in the work to the *āśrama-dharma*, the twin comparison of *varṇa-dharma*',[33] and finally, the Gītā itself goes on to speak not of *varṇa* or *āśrama* duties but of work performed in the spirit of *yajña* from III:9 onwards.

Madhva's gloss on III:9 comes as a slight surprise. A Vaiṣṇava scholiast like him passes up the opportunity of equating *yajña* with Viṣṇu in the verse, which runs:

yajñārthāt karmaṇo 'nyatra
loko 'yam karmabandhanaḥ
tadartham karma kaunteya
muktasaṅgaḥ samācara

Except action for the purpose of worship,
This world is bound by actions;
Action for that purpose, son of Kuntī,
Perform thou, free from attachment (to its fruits).

It adds to our surprise that it is the absolutist Śaṅkara who 'quotes, "Verily the sacrifice is Viṣṇu", and says that work done for sacrifice is "work done for *īśvara*" '.[34] This sense can be obtained from Madhva's gloss, but only indirectly.[35] According to Hill 'this passage (9-16) refers primarily to literal sacrifice; the idea of sacrifice is extended and spiritualised' in the next chapter of the Gītā. Rāmānuja also takes the passages ritualistically, but Madhva introduces the Mīmāṁsā concept of *arthavāda* and treats III:10-13 as such:

sahayajñāḥ prajāḥ sṛṣṭvā
puro 'vāca prajāpatiḥ
anena prasaviṣyadhvam
eṣa vo 'stv iṣṭakāmadhuk

[32] ibid.
[33] M. Hiryanna, *Outlines*, p.119, n.2.
[34] Hill, op.cit., p.96, n.2.
[35] Śrīpāda, op.cit., p.150.

devān bhāvayatā 'nena
te devā bhāvayantu vaḥ
parasparaṃ bhāvayantaḥ
śreyaḥ param avāpsyatha

iṣṭān bhogān hi vo devā
dāsyante yajñabhāvitāḥ
tair dattān apradāyai 'bhyo
yo bhuṅkte stena eva saḥ

yajñaśiṣṭāśinaḥ santo
mucyante sarvakilbiṣaiḥ
bhuñjate te tv aghaṃ pāpā
ye pacanty ātmakāraṇāt

After creating creatures along with (rites of) worship,
Prajāpati (the Creator) said of old:
By this ye shall procreate yourselves –
Let this be your Cow-of-Wishes.

With this prosper ye the gods,
And let the gods prosper you;
(Thus) prospering one the other,
Ye shall attain the highest welfare.

For desired enjoyments to you the gods
Will give, prospered by worship;
Without giving to them, their gifts
Whoso enjoys, is nothing but a thief.

Good men who eat the remnants of (food offered in) worship
Are freed from all sins;
But those wicked men eat evil
Who cook for their own selfish sakes.

Madhva simply says that these statements are *arthavāda*. Jayatīrtha elaborates that these verses do not seem to fit the context and refers to one classification of *arthavāda* as fourfold – as consisting of (1) *stuti* (praise), (2) *nindā* (censure), (3) *parakṛtiḥ* (precedent) and (4) *purākalpa* (historical anecdote). It seems that, according to Madhva, the verses concerned glorify *yajña*.

Madhva's gloss on Bhagavadgītā III:20 is of considerable interest from two points of view. First, despite the clear statement in the verse that Janaka and others achieved *saṁsiddhi* (salvation?) through *karma*, Madhva insists that salvation is not possible without *jñāna*. His arguments on this point will be considered elsewhere. Here it is another point which excites interest. While glossing on this verse, Madhva remarks on the factors which determine salvation at the moment of death, and considers the question of whether death at a holy place secures liberation. He quotes verses which claim that liberation results either from knowledge of Brahman *or* from dying at Prayāga *or* from bathing in rivers, etc., but concludes that liberation results only from transcendental knowledge. Cases where salvation is claimed otherwise are cases of eulogy (*stutiparatā*), or else the word liberation means liberation from sins (*pāpān muktiḥ*). Statements glorifying pilgrimage centres cannot annul the general rule that liberation is a consequence of knowledge. At best it is a case of glorification of means in terms of ends, as when it is said of a clever servant 'He indeed is the king!'[36] There is a tendency sometimes to associate devotion with superstition and blind faith. This charge certainly cannot be laid at the door of Madhva here.

Madhva's glosses on III:33-4 are brief but highly suggestive. Let us first consider the verses themselves:

sadṛśaṃ ceṣṭate svasyāḥ
prakṛter jñānavān api
prakṛtiṃ yānti bhūtāni
nigrahaḥ kiṃ kariṣyati

indriyasye 'ndriyasyā 'rthe
rāgadveṣau vyavasthitau
tayor na vaśam āgacchet
tau hy asya paripanthinau[37]

One acts in conformity with his own
Material nature, – even the wise man;
Beings follow (their own) nature;
What will restraint accomplish?

Of (every) sense, upon the objects of (that) sense
Longing and loathing are fixed;
One must not come under control of those two,
For they are his two enemies.

[36] ibid., p.168.
[37] Kees Bolle, *The Bhagavadgītā: A New Translation* (Berkeley: University of California Press, 1979), p.46.

Madhva begins by connecting these verses with the previous ones before he connects them one with the other. In III:31-2 Kṛṣṇa refers to those who do not heed his teachings. III:33, following upon 31 and 32, appears abrupt until we note Madhva's remark that III:33 seeks to explain why people do not follow Kṛṣṇa's teaching. Madhva also glosses the word *prakṛti* in the verse as *pūrvasaṁskārah*, or karmic impressions, and is caught in the middle of a controversy. The expression *prakṛtim yānti bhūtāni* is translated by some as 'All creatures follow nature' and by others as 'All creatures follow their own nature'. According to Zaehner:

> The first version seems preferable since in 3.27-9 all action of any kind has been attributed to the constituents of Nature. This point is again made very clearly indeed in 18.59: (But if,) relying on your ego, you should think, 'I will not fight', vain is your resolve, (for) Nature will constrain you.[38]

But he also notes that verse 34 contradicts verse 33:

> This stanza seems to contradict the last in that it allows a certain amount of free will to man, and Ś. seems conscious of this. Passion and hate (attraction and repulsion) are natural in man, he says, but they must be used to restrain each other, and this can only be done within the frame of one's own caste and the laws that govern it.[39]

Now, if free-will is allowed to man, it makes *more* sense that it be related to the operation of his personal nature than to cosmic nature. In this sense Zaehner contradicts himself, while both Śaṅkara and Madhva appear to be more consistent. Indeed Madhva goes on to say, despite III:33d *nigrahaḥ kim kariṣyati* (what will restraint accomplish) that 'even so restraint should be practised per force' (*tathāpi śaktito nigrahaḥ kāryaḥ*). Madhva comes out strongly on the side of free-will by citing a verse which translates: 'Mental impressions (*saṁskāra*) are indeed powerful, and even Brahmā and others are under its sway. Nevertheless, it can be done away with by mighty effort.'[40] In this sequence of verses Madhva seems to perceive the interconnections lucidly.

Similarly, Madhva makes an interesting point in glossing III:37. The point concerns the relationship between *kāma* and *krodha*, a point overlooked by many commentators. It has gone unnoticed that,

[38] Zaehner, op.cit., p.174. [39] ibid., p.175.
[40] Śrīpāda, op.cit., p.177.

although *kāma* and *krodha* are mentioned separately, they are referred to as the foe in the singular. This means, if we follow the grammatical form consistently, either that only one of the two is the foe or that the two are really one. Some commentators of the Kāśmīra Śaiva school try to put all the emphasis on *krodha* and save *kāma* from the onslaught. Madhva seems to choose the more reasonable route of emphasising the affinity if not the identity of *kāma* and *krodha*. He puts the emphasis on *kāma* and brackets *krodha* with it because *krodha* is born of *kāma*; he cites II:62 in support. Madhva insists that there can be no *krodha* without *kāma*, appearances to the contrary notwithstanding. He cites an interesting example wherein anger does *not* seem to result from thwarted desire, as when one gets enraged on hearing the denunciation of one's master. But Madhva argues that this anger results from the desire born out of devotion to the guru of not wanting to hear him criticised. 'Those who say otherwise lack subtlety on account of being mixed up.'[41]

Madhva's gloss on III:39 contains some interesting though unorthodox elements. The verse runs:

āvṛtam jñānam etena
jñānino nityavairiṇā
kāmarūpeṇa kaunteya
duṣpūreṇā 'nalena ca

By this is obscured the knowledge
Of the knowing one, by this his eternal foe,
That has the form of desire, son of Kuntī,
And is an insatiable fire.

Madhva glosses *jñāna* as knowledge acquired through the scriptures (*śāstrato jñānam*); *jñāninaḥ* as one who does not know much although a *jñānī* (*jñānino … alpajñāninaḥ*). This helps to get good sense from the first line – that the knowledge acquired by the *jñānī*, who possesses only limited knowledge, is obscured by *kāma*. In glossing the second line Madhva offers some spectacularly imaginative etymologies of the words *duṣpūra* and *anala* as applied to *kāma*. They are fanciful and unscientific but pack a lot of punch in what he has to say, though they are homiletic rather than scholarly in nature. Madhva interprets *duṣpūra* as applying to *kāma*, to indicate that desires are hard to fulfil (*duḥkhena hi kāmaḥ pūryate*), and adds that the position of the Indra, the chief of the gods, is not easily obtained. He

[41] ibid., p.180.

glosses *anala*, which normally means fire, in the same spirit, applying as it does to the insatiability of fire. The expression *duspūreṇa analena* refers to the insatiability of desire. Madhva argues that after attaining the status of Indra one wants to attain the status of Brahmā, and desire is called *anala* because one never says enough (*alaṁbuddhiḥ nāstity analaḥ*).[42] Madhva here is conforming to the habit of most traditional commentators of providing imaginative etymologies as proof of exegetical skill.[43]

The Fourth Chapter of the Bhagavadgītā contains the famous *avatāra* verses and Madhva's comments on these are of considerable interest. The verses run as follows (IV:6-9):

ajo 'pi sann avyayātmā
bhūtānām īśvaro 'pi san
prakṛtiṃ svām adhiṣṭhāya
saṃbhavāmy ātmamāyayā

yadā-yadā hi dharmasya
glānir bhavati bhārata
abhyutthānam adharmasya
tadā 'tmānaṃ sṛjāmy aham

paritrāṇāya sādhūnāṃ
vināśāya ca duṣkṛtām
dharmasaṃsthāpanārthāya
saṃbhavāmi yuge-yuge

janma karma ca me divyam
evaṃ yo vetti tattvataḥ
tyaktvā dehaṃ punarjanma
nai 'ti mām eti so 'rjuna

Tho unborn, tho My self is eternal,
Tho Lord of Beings,
Resorting to My own material nature
I come into being by My own mysterious power.

For whenever of the right
A languishing appears, son of Bharata,

[42] ibid., p.182.
[43] See Arvind Sharma, 'The role of etymology in Hindu hermeneutics: an analysis', *Our Heritage* 26(2) (1978), pp.39-48.

A rising up of unright,
  Then I send Myself forth.

For protection of the good,
  And for destruction of evil-doers,
To make a firm footing for the right,
  I come into being in age after age.

My wondrous birth and actions
  Whoso knows thus as they truly are,
On leaving the body, to rebirth
  He goes not; to Me he goes, Arjuna!

Madhva makes the following interesting points in relation to these verses. He connects the *avatāra* verse with a subsequent verse of the Gita (XI:11) which, along with the preceding verse, runs as follows:

anekavaktranayanam
  anekādbhutadarśanam
anekadivyābharaṇaṃ
  divyānekodyatāyudham

divyamālyāmbaradharaṃ
  divyagandhānulepanam
sarvāścaryamayaṃ devam
  anantaṃ viśvatomukham

Of many mouths and eyes,
  Of many wondrous aspects,
Of many marvellous ornaments,
  Of marvellous and many uplifted weapons;

Wearing marvellous garlands and garments,
  With marvellous perfumes and ointments,
Made up of all wonders, the god,
  Infinite, with faces in all directions.

The implication seems to be that the true form of the Lord is cosmic, one displayed in the theophany. That is the special form of the Lord (*rūpaviśeṣaṇam*).[44] This form is suppressed by the Lord in his incarnation, in which he appears as if in a human form. This is

[44] Śrīpāda, op.cit., p.188.

assumed by Kṛṣṇa according to Bhagavadgītā IV:6 by *ātmamāyā* translated variously as 'by my own mysterious power',[45] 'by my delusive power',[46] 'by my creative energy',[47] etc. Madhva glosses *ātmamāyayā* by *ātmajñānena*, and thus in a sense renders a word connotative of ignorance by one of knowledge. This, however, is not as puzzling as might appear at first sight, once we realise that when God is sometimes represented as a 'magician' 'the point of comparison with a magician is that he is in no way deluded by that spectacle as others are'. So, in relation to God, Māyā is a positive quality, as is clear from the use of expressions such as *ātmamāyā*. But in relation to others that very *māyā* conceals God, thus VII:25 for instance:

na 'haṃ prakāśah sarvasya
yogamāyāsamāvṛtaḥ
mūḍho 'yaṃ nā 'bhijānāti
loko mām ajam avyayam

I am not revealed to every one,
Being veiled by My magic trick-of-illusion;
'Tis deluded and does not recognise
Me the unborn, imperishable, – this world.

If attention is confined to God in relation to Māyā, the glosses of Śaṅkara and Rāmānuja are worth reviewing here. Another point which Madhva raises is whether incarnation is the only way in which God protects the good. Madhva emphatically says that this need not be done by assumption of birth alone (*na janmanaiva*),[48] but that God so chooses to out of his own free will. Jayatīrtha adds the note that this *līlā*, or sport, is not engaged in out of a desire to avoid (the boredom of) laziness either.[49]

Madhva's glosses on the verses cited above deserve three special comments. The first is that Madhva connects the form of God with *viśvatomukham* in IX:15. That verse runs as follows:

jñānayajñena cā 'py anye
yajanto mām upāsate
ekatvena pṛthaktvena
bahudhā viśvatomukham

[45] Edgerton, op.cit., Part I, p.43.
[46] Hill, op.cit., p.104. [47] Zaehner, op.cit., p.182.
[48] Śrīpāda, op.cit., p.192. [49] ibid., p.193.

With knowledge-worship also others
  Worshipping wait upon Me,
In My unique and manifold forms,
  (Me as) variously (manifested), facing in all directions.

By making connection with Kṛṣṇa's universal form in a cosmic rather than a doxological or liturgical sense, Madhva makes its interpretation *relatively* more sectarian.

The second point to be noted is that according to the generally accepted belief the concept of incarnation is post-Vedic. But Madhva quotes passages from the Ṛg-Veda (Khila section) in glossing IV:8. The third emerges from Madhva's gloss on the word *tattvataḥ* in IV:9. Madhva argues that the knowledge of Kṛṣṇa's divine birth and deeds is not restricted to one incarnation but extends to all his divine births and deeds.

Another set of three verses in the Fourth Chapter glossed on by Madhva deserves to be noticed. They run as follows (IV:11-13):

ye yathā māṃ prapadyante
  tāṃs tathai 'va bhajāmy aham
mama vartmā 'nuvartante
  manusyāḥ pārtha sarvaśaḥ

kāṅkṣantaḥ karmaṇāṃ siddhiṃ
  yajanta iha devatāḥ
kṣipraṃ hi mānuṣe loke
  siddhir bhavati karmajā

cāturvarnyaṃ mayā sṛṣṭaṃ
  guṇakarmavibhāgaśaḥ
tasya kartāram api māṃ
  viddhy akartāram avyayam

In whatsoever way any come to Me,
  In that same way I grant them favour.
My path follow
  Men altogether, son of Pṛthā.

Desiring the success of (ritual) acts,
  They worship the (Vedic) deities in this world;
For quickly in the world of men
  Comes the success that springs from (ritual) acts.

The four-caste system was created by Me
With distinction of Strands and actions (appropriate to each);
Altho I am the doer of this,
Know Me as one that eternally does not act.

In his remarks on these verses[50] several aspects of Madhva's commentary on the Gītā are illustrated: his Kṛṣṇology, his skill in connecting verses together meaningfully, and his lucidity of exposition. In his gloss on IV:11 Madhva clearly states that all those who worship other gods are responded to by Kṛṣṇa. Liberation is *not* achieved by worshipping Kṛṣṇa in the form of other gods, however; and although Kṛṣṇa rewards the worship of other gods, no subordination on his part to these gods is involved. Madhva also makes a connection with the more liberal verses of the Gītā. For instance, he cites part of VII:20 which carries essentially the same message as his gloss on IV:11.

The relationship between IV:11 and IV:12 is not very direct, and it is here that Madhva seems to supply the cue by beginning his gloss in IV:12 with the question: Why do they follow my path?[51] The verse then provides the answer – because success is swift, as a result of worshipping the gods through whom he is in reality being worshipped.

In his gloss of IV:13 Madhva goes to work on the *pāda: guṇakarma-vibhāgaśaḥ* like most commentators. Almost all commentators and translators refer to XVIII:42-4 for the division of *karma*, but the Gītā nowhere offers a clear-cut division of *guṇas* among the *varṇas*. In his division Madhva differs from Śaṅkara in associating only *tamas* with *śūdras*,[52] while Śaṅkara describes *śūdras* as possessing *tamas* tinged by *rajas*. Jayatīrtha, however, moves Madhva's classification closer to Śaṅkara.

The thirty-second verse of the Fourth Chapter has led to a difference of opinion among scholars on the meaning of *vitatā brahmaṇo mukhe*. The verse runs as follows:

evaṃ bahuvidhā yajñā
vitatā brahmaṇo mukhe
karmajān viddhi tān sarvān
evaṃ jñātvā vimokṣyase

[50] ibid., p.196ff.
[51] ibid., p.197. [52] ibid.

Thus many kinds of sacrifice
  Are spread out in the face of Brahman.
Know that they all spring from action!
  Knowing this thou shalt be freed.

On the controversial expression *vitatā brahmaṇo mukhe*, W.D.P. Hill identifies three possible explanations: (1) 'are known from the vedas'; (2) 'are expounded as means of attaining the true nature of *ātman*'; (3) 'are offered in the presence of Brahman'. The first explanation is suggested by Śaṅkara, the second by Rāmānuja. Hill remarks:

> The interpretation of Brahman as the Veda may be definitely rejected; as also R.'s explanation. The third interpretation is very possible; but I would suggest that the phrase carries on the idea in the previous *śloka* of 'going to Brahman', and that all these various forms of sacrifice, provided that they are performed by 'knowers of sacrifice', are represented as 'spread out at the gate to Brahman', that each one may adopt for performance the sacrifice he prefers, and none the less enter through the door to Brahman.[53]

Madhva's gloss clearly anticipates Hill:

> (Spread out) in the mouth of Brahman, that is, God (*paramātman*). 'For I of all acts of worship am both the recipient and the lord.'[54] (The Lord) will say thus. All these (sacrifices) are products of mental, verbal or physical acts. Knowing thus and having performed them you will be liberated. What you will undertake for the purpose of gaining liberation after giving up fighting also involves action. Therefore what has been laid down should not be abandoned – this is meant.

The way Madhva connects the verse with the general argument of the Gītā is adroit without being forced.

Two verses in the Fifth Chapter of the Gītā have caused difficulties for scholars by the use of the words *prabhu* and *vibhu*, which are usually applied to God, in the context of the individual soul. (V:14-15):

na kartṛtvaṃ na karmāṇi
  lokasya sṛjati prbhuḥ
na karmaphalasaṃyogaṃ
  svabhāvas tu pravartate

[53] Hill, op.cit., p.110. [54] IX:24.

nā 'datte kasyacit pāpaṃ
na cai 'va sukṛtaṃ vibhuḥ
ajñānenā 'vṛtaṃ jñānaṃ
tena muhyanti jantavaḥ

Neither agency nor actions
Of the (people of the) world does the Lord (soul) instigate,
Nor the conjunction of actions with their fruits;
But inherent nature operates (in all this).

He does not receive (the effect of) any one's sin,
Nor yet (of) good deeds, the Lord (soul);
Knowledge is obscured by ignorance;
By that creatures are deluded.

Rāmānuja takes both to refer to the individual soul, Śaṅkara takes *prabhu* to refer to the individual soul and *vibhu* to God.[55] Both Zaehner and Hill[56] side with Rāmānuja. Madhva says: 'The *prabhu* is the *jīva* disregarding (the *jīva*'s) material nature'.[57] Jayatīrtha equates the explanation of *prabhu* with *vibhu*, recognising the problem. Madhva seems to be on the right track here.

The twenty-seventh verse of the Fifth Chapter has tested the patience of scholars. As a matter of fact, the whole idea of *prāṇa vāyu* is rather obscure.[58] It occurs in the verse concerned:

sparśān kṛtvā bahir bāhyāṃś
cakṣuś cai 'vā 'ntare bhruvoḥ
prāṇāpānau samau kṛtvā
nāsābhyantaracāriṇau

Putting out outside contacts,
And fixing the sight between the eye-brows,
Making even the upper and nether breaths,
As they pass thru the nose;

Madhva is of help here in three ways. First, the expression *samau kṛtvā* in *prāṇāpānau samau kṛtvā nāsābhyantaracāriṇau*, is 'left unexplained by Śaṅkara, Śrīdhara explains it as "having suspended the movement of *prāṇa* and *apāna*" '.[59] This is confirmed by Madhva, who also

[55] Zaehner, op.cit., pp.208-9.
[56] Hill, op.cit., p.14, n.3.
[57] Śrīpāda, op.cit., p.229.
[58] Surendranath Dasgupta, *A History of Indian Philosophy* Vol.II (Delhi: Motilal Banarsidass, 1975 [first edition, Cambridge 1922]), p.449.
[59] ibid., n.2.

refers to *kumbhaka*. Secondly, the idea of fixing the eyes between the eyebrows is puzzling, for elsewhere the Gītā recommends gazing on the tip of the nose (VI:13), whose exact meaning is also debated. Jayatīrtha notes this contradiction and sees an attempt on the part of Madhva to resolve it by quoting a line which suggests the tip of the nose (*nasāgra*) and the middle of the eyebrows (*bhruvor madhye*) as optional points of concentration. Thirdly, the word for eye is used in the singular, and similar use elsewhere (XI:8) suggests that vision is meant rather than the eyes. This is also recognised by Madhva.

In the course of his glosses on the Sixth Chapter Madhva offers some interesting insights. The third verse of that chapter has virtually been passed over without comment by most modern scholars[60] with the exception of Radhakrishnan.[61] It runs as follows (VI:3):

ārurukṣor muner yogaṃ
karma kāraṇam ucyate
yogārūḍhasya tasyai 'va
śamaḥ kāraṇam ucyate

For the sage that desires to mount to discipline
Action is called the means;
For the same man when he has mounted to discipline
Quiescence is called the means.

Madhva begins by raising the pertinent question: how long is one to act if *karma* is said to be the means?[62] The answer implied is: till one becomes *yogārūḍha*, or firmly fixed in *yoga*: that is, when the end has been accomplished: that is, when transcendental knowledge has been achieved. Madhva also clarifies the point regarding *śama* being the cause. The cause of what? Of supreme bliss which results from transcendental knowledge. Here Madhva makes the interesting observation that, despite Śaṅkara, even the *jñānin* has a result indicated for him in the form of *samādhi*, etc. He further distinguishes between *asamprajñāta samādhi*,[63] the final stage of yogic absorption, and the normal mental sates in which one discourses of God.

Madhva has interpreted the term *yoga* here along the lines of Patañjali's Yoga, and this may be thought surprising; but his

[60] Hill, op.cit., p.116; Zaehner, op.cit., p.220.
[61] Radhakrishnan, op.cit., p.188.
[62] Śrīpāda, op.cit., p.243.
[63] Hiriyanna, *Outlines*, p.296.

inclusion of *karma* and *kāraṇa* fully into the interpretation of the verse is refreshing.

VI:6 is on the face of it a fairly simple verse, but the use of the same word *ātman* in different senses, while imparting a poetic quality to the verse, also creates exegetical problems. The 'riddle of Ātmans leaves room for a variety of interpretations', and we shall see how Madhva interprets it. The verse has been cited earlier. The first appearance of the word *ātman* Madhva equates with the mind (*ātmā manaḥ*); the second with the embodied soul (*ātmano jīvasya*); the third again with the mind (*ātmā manaḥ*); and the fourth with *buddhi*, or soul (*atmanā buddhyā jīvena eva vā*).[64] Thus we obtain the following sense: one whose mind has been subdued by the *buddhi*, for such a soul the mind is a friend. We also obtain the following optional sense: that mind is a friend of the soul which has been subdued by the soul. Madhva cites verses in support of both interpretations. The second line of the verse Madhva explains in the following manner. In the case of one who has not subdued his mind (*anātmanaḥ ajitamanaskasya*) the mind[65] is like an enemy acting inimically. A mind not under control is called *anātman*, just as a servant who does not behave like one cannot be called a servant.

Madhva's gloss on VI:9 is important, as he proves the equanimous equation of the verse not monistically but theistically. The verse runs as follows:

suhṛnmitrāryudāsīna-
madhyasthadveṣyabandhuṣu
sādhuṣv api ca pāpeṣu
samabuddhir viśiṣyate

To friend, ally, foe, remote neutral,
Holder of middle ground, object of enmity, and kinsman,
To good and evil men alike,
Who has the same mental attitude, is superior.

Madhva argues that all are to be considered the same, because the beings by themselves are of the nature of consciousness (*cidrūpāḥ eva hi jīvāḥ*) and all the differences are attributable to God (*sarveṣāṃ sādhutvādikam sarvam īśvarakṛtam eva*). Madhva quotes from the Brahma (Brahmapurāṇa?) to support his point along the following lines:

[64] Śrīpāda, op.cit., p.246.
[65] ibid., n.1.

All Jīvas by themselves have the form of consciousness and are free from all defects. Whatever defects belong to them are to be regarded as adventitious. All that is theirs proceeds from God; nothing at all from themselves. In this way are all to be equated; dissimilarities are born of delusion.

Now the question arises: up to what point is this egalitarianism to be pushed? In Advaita Vedānta, at this stage, the two levels of truth are typically invoked. Madhva proceeds along practical rather than metaphysical lines and points out that equality in outlook does not mean parity in extending worship to all alike – here virtue counts. He also differentiates between pairs of terms, such as (1) *suhṛd* and *mitra*, (2) *ari* and *dveṣya*, and (3) *udāsīna* and *madhyastha*; for, as Jayatīrtha remarks, there seems to be no difference in meaning between them. Madhva distinguishes between them in the following manner. The two synonymous words for 'friends' are differentiated thus: a *suhṛd* is one who does a favour without concern that it should be returned; a *mitra* is one who protects one in adversity. The synonyms for 'enemy' are distinguished as follows: an *ari* causes physical injury; a *dveṣya* is someone who does not offer shelter. The synonyms for 'indifferent' are distinguished as follows: an *udāsīna* neither returns good for good nor evil for evil; a *madhyastha* is one who acts thus.[66]

Madhva's gloss on VI:30 also deserves comment, for the connections he makes which are not immediately obvious. The verse runs as follows:

yo māṃ paśyati sarvatra
sarvaṃ ca mayi paśyati
tasyā 'haṃ na praṇaśyāmi
sa ca me na praṇaśyati

Who sees Me in all,
And sees all in Me,
For him I am not lost,
And he is not lost for Me.

Madhva connects this verse with IX:22:

ananyāś cintayanto māṃ
ye janāḥ paryupāsate
teṣāṃ nityābhiyuktānāṃ
yogakṣemaṃ vahāmy aham

[66] ibid., p.254.

Thinking on Me, with no other thought,
What folk wait upon Me,
To them, when they are constant in perseverance,
I bring acquisition and peaceful possession (of their aim).

The way Madhva connects the two verses is interesting as he does it both internally and externally. He glosses *na praṇaśyāmi* or 'I am not lost to him', or 'For him I am not lost', as *sarvadā yogakṣemavahaḥ syām ity arthaḥ*. That is to say, 'I in effect ever take care of them.' That 'he is not lost to me' Madhva explains as 'He is always devoted to me' (*sarvadā madbhakto bhavati*). The external evidence in support of this connection is offered by Madhva from the Garuḍa Purāṇa. The verse runs:

sarvadā sarvabhūteṣu
samaṃ māṃ yaḥ prapaśyati
acalā tasya bhaktiḥ syāt
yogakṣemam vahāmy aham

The convergence is not sensationally spectacular between *yo māṃ paśyati sarvatra* and *samaṃ māṃ yaḥ prapaśyati*, but clearly suggestive.

Madhva's gloss on VI:37 raises an interesting point. The verse runs:

ayatiḥ śraddayo 'peto
yogāc calitamānasaḥ
aprāpya yogasaṃsiddhiṃ
kāṃ gatiṃ kṛṣṇa gacchati

An unsuccessful striver who is endowed with faith,
Whose mind falls away from discipline
Without attaining perfection of discipline,
To what goal does he go, Kṛṣṇa?

We are concerned with the word *ayatiḥ* here. It is generally translated 'unsuccessful striver',[67] 'one whose passions are not curbed',[68] 'one who cannot control himself',[69] or 'one who strives in vain'.[70] All of these versions carry the twin implications of (1) effort undertaken, (2) without success. Madhva glosses the word as *apryatnaḥ*; that is, to refer to one who is making no effort at all.

[67] ibid. [68] Hill, op.cit., p.254.
[69] Radhakrishnan, op.cit., p.207. [70] Zaehner, op.cit., p.239.

Madhva's interpretation opens up the whole issue of works and faith, especially if we consider a parallel situation in XVII:1, where again Arjuna puts a similar question: how far does faith carry those who worship disregarding scriptural injunctions?[71] Does Arjuna herein want to know how far faith alone can carry a non-striver? Madhva's gloss at least raises this interesting possibility.

His gloss on another verse is also helpful in understanding its full significance. The verse runs as follows (VI:44):

pūrvābhyāsena tenai 'va
hriyate hy avaśo 'pi saḥ
jijñāsur api yogasya
śabdabrahmā 'tivartate

For by that same former practice
He is carried on even without his wish.
Even one who (merely) wishes to know discipline
Transcends the word-Brahman (the Vedic religion).

Scholars puzzle over the meaning of *śabdabrahma*. First, there is the question of what is *śabdabrahma*. Then there is the question of what is implied by going beyond it. *Śabdabrahma* can be taken to stand for (1) Vedic ritual,[72] (2) the sound *om*,[73] or (3) *prakṛti*.[74] Going beyond *śabdabrahma* could mean liberation, or advancing beyond Vedic ritual. Madhva's gloss here is deceptive, because on the face of it it seems to square with the generally accepted position; for he remarks: *śabdabrahmātivartate. paraṃ brahma prāpnotīty arthaḥ*. This is what the Maitri Upaniṣad (VI:22) and the Viṣṇu Purāṇa (VI:5) state, as S. Radhakrishnan points out – quoting Maitri that 'when a person has become well-versed in Śabdabrahma, he reaches the Brahman which is beyond it'.[75]

But there are problems. In Maitri VI:22 *śabdabrahma* is not expounded as Vedic ritual, but as *om*. Besides, the verse seems to be contrastive – it says that even one desirous of knowing *yoga* transcends *śabdabrahma*. Moreover, the very next verse refers to the need of several *more* lives to attain salvation. Jayatīrtha therefore explains that it is not the superiority of the *yogī* over the ritualist which is asserted here,[76] but rather that it is stated that it is the

[71] For a thorough discussion of the point, see Bhagavadgītā XVII and K.L. Seshagiri Rao, *The Concept of Śraddhā* (Patiala: Roy Publishers, 1971), passim.
[72] Radhakrishnan, op.cit., p.209.
[73] Hill, op.cit., p.123, n.2. [74] ibid.
[75] Radhakrishnan, op.cit., p.209. [76] Śrīpāda, op.cit., p.269.

realised, not merely the neophyte, *yogī* who goes beyond Vedic duties and prohibitions.

Madhva's gloss on VI:46 is significant because the verse is of a kind which recurs in the Gītā and causes difficulties by reversing or re-ordering priorities that one is getting used to, as happens, for instance, in XII:12. Madhva's technique of handling the problem is interesting. But first the verse:

tapasvibhyo 'dhiko yogī
jñānibhyo 'pi mato 'dhikaḥ
karmibhyaś cā 'dhiko yogī
tasmād yogī bhavā 'rjuna

The man of discipline is higher than men of austerities,
Also than men of knowledge he is held to be higher;
And the man of discipline is higher than men of ritual action;
Therefore be a man of discipline, Arjuna.

In the verse the *yogī* is proclaimed superior to (1) *tapasvins*, (2) *jñānins*, and (3) *karmins*, after virtually all of them have been glorified – *tapasvins* in IV:28; *jñānins* in IV:34-5 and *karmins* in III:20, etc. Madhva's basic procedure is to maintain that these words have special connotations here. Thus *tapasvin* does not mean *any* ascetic, but one subjecting himself to unnecessarily difficult penances. XVII:5-6 could be adduced in support. Similarly *jñānin* here is not taken to mean a man of knowledge in general – not a *jñānayogī* but a *yogajñānī*, to use Madhva's own expression; that is to say, one who has (mere) knowledge of *yoga*. It is difficult to construe it otherwise, for, as Jayatīrtha explains, *jñāna* is the fruit of *yoga* (*nanu jñānam yogasya phalam*). *Karmin* is not explained, but it is easy to see how it could mean a mere ritualist. Jayatīrtha also makes the interesting point regarding *jñānin* and *tapasvin*: that both *jñāna* and *tapas* are mentioned together in IV:10 (*jñānatapasā pūtā*) but must be distinguished here.

The Seventh Chapter may now be examined in the light of Madhva's commentary. Here the eighth verse is of interest, for Jayatīrtha remarks, in his commentary on Madhva's commentary, that it signals a change of context, although no concluding expressions such as *iti*, etc. have been used to indicate the end of the preceding topic. The commencement of a new topic suffices to indicate the conclusion of the previous one.[77]

Gītā VII:8 runs as follows:

[77] ibid., p.280.

raso 'ham apsu kaunteya
prabhā 'smi śaśisūryayoḥ
praṇavaḥ sarvavedeṣu
śabdaḥ khe pauruṣaṃ nṛṣu

I am taste in water, son of Kuntī,
I am light in the moon and sun,
The sacred syllable (*om*) in all the Vedas,
Sound in ether, manliness in men.

Madhva raises a point of some interest here. As Jayatīrtha notes, Kṛṣṇa has just claimed that he is the alpha and the omega of everything (VII:6) and now, in apparent contradiction at least, proceeds to identify himself with selected aspects of creation after having identified himself with the whole of it. Thus Madhva clarifies that 'I am *rasa*' is the initial insight. It is also the case with water, etc.; namely, that Kṛṣṇa is them too. But because savour represents the nature and essence of water, therefore it is especially definitive (*viśeṣato niyāmakaḥ*) of it. Kṛṣṇa's identification with *rasa* among waters should not be understood as restrictive in the sense that there is water, it has flavour and Kṛṣṇa is only to be identified with that flavour: rather that he may be specially and gloriously and not exclusively identified with it.[78]

An interesting grammatical and theological point arises in connection with VII:13-14 which run as follows:

tribhir guṇamayair bhāvair
ebhiḥ sarvam idaṃ jagat
mohitaṃ nā 'bhijānāti
mām ebhyaḥ param avyayam

daivī hy eṣā guṇamayī
mama māyā duratyayā
mām eva ye prapadyante
māyām etāṃ taranti te

By the three states (of being), composed of the Strands,
These (just named), all this world,
Deluded, does not recognise
Me that am higher than they and eternal.

[78] ibid., p.279.

For this is My divine strand-composed
Trick-of-illusion, hard to get past;
Those who resort to Me alone
Penetrate beyond this trick-of-illusion.

The use of *mayaṭ* in *guṇamaya*, and the subsequent description of *māyā* as *guṇamayī*, raises the question: in what sense is the affix employed? Three possibilities exist – that it denotes (1) identity, or (2) modification, or (3) abundance. The *guṇas* are equated with *māyā*, and *māyā* with God's *śakti*.

In VII:15 the word *asura* appears. Madhva's gloss on the word is of considerable interest from a linguistic point of view, as the etymology of the word *asura* is a matter of some controversy. The traditional derivation of the word *asura* from *sura* with *nañ* prefix is no longer accepted by critical scholarship, and the preferred explanation is *asu* + *ra*, where *asu* means breath or strength. M. Hiriyanna, while recognising this historical critical contribution to Vedic etymology, pointed out that in certain contexts even Sāyaṇa moved in that direction. In this light Madhva's explanation of *asura* as *asuṣu ratāḥ asurāḥ*[79] is full of interest, as he also cites the Nāradīya (-*Nārada Purāṇa*) in support: *jñānapradhānā devās tu asurās tu ratā asau*. Jayatīrtha, his commentator, has difficulties with this citation, because *asu*, in the singular, stands for *indriyas* or senses which are many, and because of the absence of *sandhi* between the two *padas*. Jayatīrtha irons out the difficulties thus. '*Asu* is used in the singular as a generic noun and there is no defect on account of lack of *sandhi* because *sandhi* between *padas* is optional (*asav iti jātāu ekavacanam padasandher vivakṣādhīnatvād asandhir na doṣaḥ*)'.[80]

A theological rather than an etymological point emerges in Madhva's gloss on VII:27. The verse is often passed over without comment by scholars[81] and Madhva's gloss on it is brief, but its brevity seems to belie its significance. It runs as follows:

icchādveṣasamutthena
dvandvamohena bhārata
sarvabhūtāni saṃmohaṃ
sarge yānti paraṃtapa

[79] ibid., p.290.
[80] ibid., p.291.
[81] Zaehner, op.cit., p.254; Hill, op.cit., p.130; Radhakrishnan, op.cit., p.224; etc.

It arises from desire and loathing,
  The delusion of the pairs (of opposites), son of Bharata;
Because of it all beings to confusion
  Are subject at their birth, scorcher of the foe.

In his gloss Madhva raises the following interesting issue: according to the verse in question all creatures, deluded by the pair of desire and aversion, are bewildered at the time of periodic creation (*sarga*); however, desires, etc. are consequent on the appearance of the body; before the bodies appear there is only nescience. How do the bodies appear out of nescience? Madhva's answer is that nescience is under the control of God. Thus Madhva distinguishes two steps in the chain leading to the emergence of the universe in which the *jīvas* wander around bewildered. The verse mentions the polarities of desire and aversion – but this is only an immediate cause. There is an intermediate cause (*avāntara kāraṇa*) which is connected with God's *māyā*, which accounts for the persistence of nescience and God's control over it during the period of dissolution.

In turning to the eleventh verse of the Eighth Chapter we turn from cosmological to soteriological considerations. It is another verse with which modern scholars seem to have little difficulty.[82] Most recognise that in this verse *padam* can denote both 'word' or 'place/state' and that it could well have a dual connotation here (VIII:11):

yad akṣaraṃ vedavido vadanti
  viśanti yad yatayo vītarāgāḥ
yad icchanto brahmacaryaṃ caranti
  tat te padaṃ saṃgraheṇa pravaksye

Which Veda-knowers call the imperishable,
  Which ascetics free from passion enter,
Seeking which men live the life of chastity,
  That place I shall declare to thee in brief.

Madhva's commentary is brief, but within its brief span he identifies the word *padam* as that abode which is attained by those desirous of liberation. He nails this down scripturally with a citation (from Kaṭha Upaniṣad 3.9 and Maitri 6.26), *tad viṣṇoh paramaṃ padam*, and grammatically by citing from the Dhātupāṭha, *pada gatau*. Thus for Madhva *padam* is a place not a word. The reason is

[82] Radhakrishnan, op.cit., p.231; Zaehner, op.cit., p.264; Hill, op.cit., p.134.

explained by Jayatīrtha, who also includes a consideration of the other meaning of the word *pada* as word – especially a special 'word', the *praṇava*. Jayatīrtha, in explaining Madhva's gloss, makes two interesting points: (1) that it is intended to dispel the mistaken impression that meditation on *om* only leads to gradual liberation and not to immediate post-mortem liberation, and (2) that at the moment of death it is hardly possible to *utter* the 'sound of *om* or the name of Viṣṇu'.

From soteriology we move back to cosmology in considering Madhva's gloss on VIII:17-20.

sahasrayugaparyantam
ahar yad brahmaṇo viduḥ
rātriṃ yugasahasrāntāṃ
te 'horātravido janāḥ

avyaktād vyaktayaḥ sarvāḥ
prabhavanty aharāgame
rātryāgame pralīyante
tatrai 'vā 'vyaktasaṃjñake

bhūtagrāmaḥ sa evā 'yaṃ
bhūtvā-bhūtvā pralīyate
rātryāgame 'vaśaḥ pārtha
prabhavaty aharāgame

paras tasmāt tu bhāvo 'nyo
'vyakto 'vyaktāt sanātanaḥ
yaḥ sa sarveṣu bhuteṣu
naśyatsu na vinaśyati

As compassing a thousand world-ages
When they know the day of Brahman,
And the night (of Brahman) as compassing a thousand ages,
Those folk know what day and night are.

From the unmanifest all manifestations
Come forth at the coming of (Brahman's) day,
And dissolve at the coming of night,
In that same one, known as the unmanifest.

This very same host of beings,
Coming into existence over and over, is dissolved

At the approach of night, willy-nilly, son of Pṛthā,
And comes forth at the approach of day.

But higher than that is another state of being,
Unmanifest, (higher) than (that) unmanifest, eternal
Which when all beings
Perish, perishes not.

Madhva's gloss on these verses provides a slightly different angle from the usual one. He introduces his comments by saying that Kṛṣṇa, having said that there is no rebirth on attaining to him, now wishes to establish this point and, in order to demonstrate his power over what is called *avyakta*, speaks of universal dissolution, etc. Madhva makes two special points here: (1) that the word thousand stands for many (*sahasraśabdo anekavācī*), and (2) that *brahmaṇo* is the genitive, not of *brahmā*, but of the supreme *brahman* (*brahma param*). For the first point he finds support in the Kūrmapurāṇa (?), and for the latter in the last verse cited above, which declares it as the ultimate survivor.

Madhva begins his gloss on the Ninth Chapter by stating that here what has already been said in the Seventh Chapter is clarified. In the interest of brevity we shall take him at his word and pass on to Chapter Ten.

In the sixteenth verse of the Tenth Chapter Arjuna requests Kṛṣṇa to speak of his divine powers. The word he uses for these powers is *vibhūti*. Śaṅkara glosses it as *māhātmyavistaraḥ*[83] – the extent of your greatness, which is rather straightforward. Madhva glosses *vibhūtayaḥ* as *vividhabhūtayaḥ*, which in turn is explained by Jayatīrtha as *nānābhūtāni rūpāṇi*.[84] This interpretation seems to be a better earnest of the shape of things to come, though Śaṅkara of course is not in any sense wrong. Madhva's gloss on the word Vāsudeva in X:37 is of far more importance. In order to realise its significance let it be noted that Śaṅkara does not care to elaborate[85] and Rāmānuja glosses the word by saying that Kṛṣṇa's glory consists in his being the son of Vasudeva as no other sense is possible (*arthāntarābhāvād*).[86] Madhva shows clearly that another sense is in fact possible and may even be preferable. To gauge the significance of his remarks it should be realised that the word *vāsudeva* has been etymologised in two different ways in the Mahābhārata. Hemachandra Raychaudhuri says:

[83] Śaṅkara, op.cit., p.237.
[84] Śrīpāda, op.cit., p.366.
[85] Śaṅkara, op.cit., p.249.
[86] Goyandkā, op.cit., p.345.

The Mahābhārata, the great storehouse of Hindu tradition, usually takes Vāsudeva to mean 'the son of Vasudeva' (c. Mbh., iii, 14.8). But in certain passages a different etymology is given.

Vasanāt Sarvabhūtānām Vasutvāddevayonitaḥ
Vāsudevastato vedyo brihattvād Vishṇuruchyate. Mbh., v, 70.3

'He is called Vāsudeva in consequence of his enveloping all creatures with the screen of illusion, or of his glorious splendour, or of his being the support and resting place of the gods.'

Chhādayāmi jagad viśvam bhūtvā sūrya ivāmśubhiḥ
Sarvabhūtādhivāsaścha Vāsudevastatohyaham. Mbh., xii. 341.41

'Assuming the form of the Sun I cover the universe with my rays. And because I am the home of all creatures, therefore, am I called by the name of Vāsudeva.'[87]

It is remarkable that Madhva quotes the second verse cited by Raychaudhuri and states that Vāsudeva is so called because he 'covers, abides in all and causes them to abide everywhere' (*āchādayati sarvam vāsayati vasati ca sarvatreti*). It must be added, though, that if in this case he comes out with flying colours, his etymologies of other names, such as Rāma, Kapila, etc., are rather fanciful and forced.[88]

Madhva draws a useful distinction in glossing another verse of the Tenth Chapter (X:41):

yad-yad vibhūtimat sattvaṃ
śrīmad ūrjitam eva vā
tat-tad evā 'vagaccha tvaṃ
mama tejoṃśasaṃbhavam

Whatever being shows supernal-manifestations,
Or majesty or vigour,
Be thou assured that that in every case
Is sprung from a fraction of My glory.

[87] Hemachandra Raychaudhuri, *Materials for the Study of the Early History of the Vaishnava Sect* (New Delhi: Oriental Books Reprint Corporation, 1975 [first published 1920]), p.20.
[88] Śrīpāda, op.cit., pp.370-1.

He comments that we must distinguish in this verse between (1) those manifestations of Viṣṇu which are his own form (*vaisnavādīni tatsvarūpāny eva*), and (2) those manifestations which possess his brilliance but are not identical with him (*tejoyuktāni*). To the former class belong Rudra, Indra, Rāma, etc., and to the latter the sons of Manu, etc.[89]

Madhva's remarks on the last verse of the Tenth Chapter may also be savoured as we leave that chapter. The verse runs (X:42):

athavā bahunai 'tena
kiṃ jñātena tavā 'rjuna
viṣṭabhyā 'ham idaṃ kṛtsnam
ekāṃśena sthito jagat

After all, this extensive
Instruction – what boots it thee, Arjuna?
I support this entire
World with a single fraction (of Myself), and remain so.

Madhva makes several brief but significant comments. He points out that the remark 'What need is there …' is not meant to imply that what has been said is of no use (*nisphalatvajñāpanāya*) but that what has already been said covers the main ground (*vaksyamāṇaprādhānya-jñāpanārtham*).[90] He points out further that when it is said to Arjuna 'What need is there for such detailed knowledge by *you*?' Arjuna is being complimented and the implication is that he is earmarked for greater things (*tvam tu bahuphalaprāptiyogya iti*).[91] But it is by a third comment made on the use of the interrogative pronoun *kim* that Madhva heightens the impact of the verse in an interesting way. He says that the use of *kim* is well-known for eulogising opposites, as in the example: 'If desire and aversion are present of what use are austerities; and if desire and aversion are absent, of what use are austerities?' (As there is no need for austerities if such be the case.) Thus the singling out of *vibhūtis* really makes no difference either way if we see God everywhere. This last position is interesting from the exponent of a school which emphasises distinctions.

Madhva's glosses on the Eleventh Chapter follow the pattern of the earlier ones. For instance, the close connection of grammar and theology persists as in the gloss on XI:11.

[89] ibid., p.374.
[90] ibid., p.376. [91] ibid.

divyamālyāmbaradharaṃ
divyagandhānulepanam
sarvāścaryamayaṃ devam
anantaṃ viśvatomukham

Wearing marvellous garlands and garments,
With marvellous perfumes and ointments,
Made up of all wonders, the god,
Infinite, with faces in all directions.

Madhva glosses *sarvāścaryamayam* as *sarvāścaryātmakam*. Jayatīrtha explains the significance of this comment by indicating the 'correct' sense in which the suffix *mayaṭ* is to be understood (which echoes an earlier and more detailed discussion by Madhva himself in his gloss on VII:13). He dismisses the view that *mayaṭ* is used here in the sense of abundance (*prācuryārthe*) as erroneous because of the use of *sarva* (all) in *sarvāścaryamayam*, and therefore takes *mayaṭ* as representing identity (*tādātmya*). In other words, God was marvellous through and through, not merely spectacular in some aspects.[92]

The gloss on XI:16 is full of interest, as Madhva treats the verse of the Gītā as symbolic of the great glory of God. The verse runs:

anekabāhūdaravaktranetraṃ
paśyāmi tvāṃ sarvato 'nantarūpam
nā 'ntaṃ na madhyaṃ na punas tavā 'diṃ
paśyāmi viśveśvara viśvarūpa

With many arms, bellies, mouths, and eyes,
I see Thee, infinite in form on all sides;
No end nor middle nor yet beginning of Thee
Do I see, O All-God, All-formed!

His remarks on this verse are best presented in two parts. First of all, Madhva takes this verse as referring not merely to the *manifold* but to the *infinite* glory of God. He seems to take the cue from *anantarūpam* or 'infinite in form', an expression which appears in the verse itself. He also cites verses from other sources as well as from the Bhagavadgītā itself (XII:13; XIII:12) to make the point that words expressive of 'many' as they appear in the verse should be taken to mean 'infinite'. Thus he says that the word *aneka*, or many, in

[92] ibid., p.380.

anekabāhu- is *anantavācī*, i.e. denotes infinity, so that what is meant is not 'many arms' but 'an infinity of arms' (*anantabāhum iti vaksyati*). There is the fine distinction to be drawn here between 'numerous' and 'innumerable', or infinite. The word *viśva*, as it occurs in the verse in the expressions *viśveśvara* and *viśvarūpa*, is also taken by him in the same sense (*viśvaśabdaś ca anantavācī*).[93]

This raises the philosophical issue of how the one could be the many. God is one and infinite and yet he appears in infinitely different forms. Madhva cites a line from the Yajur Veda: *yad ekam avyaktam anantarūpam* – the one unmanifest with infinite forms. The problem is specified in a line from the Ādityapurāṇa: *anantasya na tasyāntaḥ saṅkhyānam cāpi vidyate*: there is no end of him the endless, but enumeration is also possible. Madhva's comments on both of these citations indicate the direction in which the solution is likely to be sought. On the quote from the Yajur Veda he remarks: 'It is the infinite itself which establishes the unlimited (nature of the manifestation).' On the quote from the Ādityapurāṇa he remarks: 'All those individual forms become collectively unlimited (*tāni caikaikāni rūpāṇi anantānīti caikatra bhavati*).'[94]

This apparent contradiction between qualitative infinity and numerical infinity does not seem improper to Madhva (*na caitad ayuktam*), because the power of God is incomprehensible (*acintyasáktitvād īśvarasya*). Madhva then quotes verses both from the Smṛti (Viṣṇupurāṇa) and the Śruti (Kaṭha 2.9) on the limitation of logical reasoning in this respect.

Madhva is particularly sensitive in relation to the attributes pertaining to God throughout his glosses on Chapter Eleven. He is ever on the alert if he senses them being compromised through a misunderstanding in any way. A straightforward illustration of this is provided by his gloss on XI:17:

kirīṭinaṃ gadinaṃ cakriṇaṃ ca
tejorāśiṃ sarvato dīptimantam
paśyāmi tvām durnirīksyaṃ samantād
dīptānalārkadyutim aprameyam

With diadem, club, and disc,
A mass of radiance, glowing on all sides,
I see Thee, hard to look at, on every side
With the glory of flaming fire and sun, immeasurable.

[93] ibid., pp.382-3.
[94] ibid., p.384.

Madhva notes that the verse ends by describing God as *aprameya*, as 'incomparable',[95] or 'incomprehensible',[96] or, better still, as one of whom nothing can be predicated, lest the immediately preceding comparisons of his flaming form with fire and the sun generate the doubt that his form is limited in some way (*mitatvaśaṅkā*).

Madhva's comment on another verse of the same chapter is full of theological interest. The verse runs as follows (XI:20):

dyāvāpṛthivyor idam antaraṃ hi
vyāptaṃ tvayai 'kena diśaś ca sarvāḥ
dṛṣṭvā 'dbhutaṃ rūpam ugraṃ tave 'daṃ
lokatrayaṃ pravyathitaṃ mahātman

For this region between heaven and earth
Is pervaded by Thee alone, and all the directions;
Seeing this Thy wondrous, terrible form,
The triple world trembles, O exalted one!

Madhva's gloss is direct to the point of being obscure, and we have to turn to Jayatīrtha's explanation to grasp its full significance. When it is said 'This region between heaven and earth is pervaded by thee' it suffices to establish God's oneness. Why then should the word 'thee *alone*' (*ekena*) be added? This is to avoid the following possible misunderstanding, that because God is one and the same in various forms all the various directions are also his *different* forms. Such an interpretation is not correct, as the *viśvarūpa*, or universal form, is referred to in the singular in XI:3 when Arjuna says: 'I desire to see thy form' (*dṛṣṭum icchāmi te rūpam*) and not *forms*.[97]

The point seems to be correct, but the argument is weak *here*, for when Kṛṣṇa responds to Arjuna's request he displays numerous forms (XI:5-6). Thus it is God who is one, not his forms.

It is, however, Madhva's gloss on the second half of the verse which cannot fail to interest the historian of religion. The reaction of the onlooker to Kṛṣṇa's theophany has often been cited as an expression of the numinous experience. It is here that Madhva's remark on the 'tremendous mystery' of the encounter becomes fascinating, for he does not see 'awe' as an invariable feature of the numinous experience, *pace* Otto. He writes:

[95] Radhakrishnan, op.cit., p.275. [96] Hill, op.cit., p.160.
[97] Śrīpāda, op.cit., p.393.

It is not a general rule that his form should be terrifying. For it is not so in the case of Nārada. To some God reveals himself thus.[98]

Two more verses of the Eleventh Chapter are worth noting in view of Madhva's gloss on them. The first of these is XI:31:

ākhyāhi me ko bhavān ugrarūpo
namo 'stu te devavara prasīda
vijñātum icchāmi bhavantam ādyam
na hi prajānāmi tava pravṛttim

Tell me, who art Thou, of awful form?
Homage be to Thee: Best of Gods, be merciful!
I desire to understand Thee, the primal one;
For I do not comprehend what Thou hast set out to do.

Madhva remarks: 'It is in order to know more about the essential nature (*dharma*) (of Kṛṣṇa) that he asks: "Who are you?" as with those other names.' This last comment, according to Jayatīrtha, refers to Arjuna identifying Kṛṣṇa with Rudra or Yama, etc. when he sees Kṛṣṇa's terrific form. So, to resume Madhva's gloss, 'although knowing (Kṛṣṇa) he asks (him) "Who are you?" in order to know his order of being (*jātijñānārtham*). Had he (Arjuna) not known Kṛṣṇa, then the exclamation "Viṣṇu" was not possible. Moreover, the verse beginning "You are imperishable"[99] (implies that Arjuna knew who Kṛṣṇa was).'[100]

Madhva's gloss is important for two opposite reasons: because Arjuna is shown as knowing that Kṛṣṇa is Viṣṇu, and because Arjuna truly does not know who Kṛṣṇa is. He may know who he is nominally, but he does not know who God is ontologically. The recognition by Madhva of the identity of Viṣṇu and Kṛṣṇa is of some scholarly significance. 'A distinguished Hindu scholar, the late Sir R.G. Bhandarkar, thought that Kṛṣṇa was not yet identified with Viṣṇu in the Gītā, tho' he was soon afterwards. See his *Vaiṣṇavism, Śaivism and Minor Religious Systems*, page 13. But Kṛṣṇa is directly addressed as Viṣṇu in XI:24 and 30; and I do not believe that Viṣṇu can here mean "the sun".'[100a]

The next verse worth noting is the following (XI:34):

[98] ibid., p.392.
[99] XI:18. [100] Śrīpāda, op.cit., p.394.
[100a] Edgerton, op.cit., Part II, p.31, n.2.

droṇaṃ ca bhīṣmaṃ ca jayadrathaṃ ca
karṇaṃ tathā 'nyān api yodhavīrān
mayā hatāṃs tvaṃ jahi mā vyathiṣṭhā
yudhyasva jetāsi raṇe sapatnān

Droṇa and Bhīṣma and Jayadratha,
Karṇa too, and the other warrior-heroes as well,
Do thou slay, (since) they are already slain by Me; do not hesitate!
Fight! Thou shalt conquer thy rivals in battle.

The verse is important because it is a confident prediction of Arjuna's success in battle about the outcome of which Arjuna had his doubts (II:6). These doubts sprang in part from the redoubtable nature of his adversaries, four of whom are mentioned here by name as they were the most formidable. Madhva himself explains the inclusion of only two of them: of Jayadratha and Karṇa. Jayadratha was a formidable foe because of a boon from his father that whosoever caused his head to fall on the earth would have his own head split to pieces, Karṇa because he possessed a special missile called *vāsavī*. Jayatīrtha supplements Madhva's remarks by adding reasons for the mention of Droṇa and Bhīṣma by name: Droṇa was Arjuna's preceptor, and Bhīṣma could only die at his own will.

Jayatīrtha also adds the interesting comment that *even* when the outcome of the battle was in doubt it was meet for Arjuna to engage in battle, for in the case of either victory or defeat the result was beneficial (II:37): victory conferred kingdom and death in battle a place in heaven. Now, says Jayatīrtha, even that lingering doubt of defeat has been removed (*parājayaśaṅkāpi nāsti*).[101]

The twelfth verse of the Twelfth Chapter has been something of a puzzle, and it will be interesting to see what Madhva does with it. It runs as follows (XII:12):

śreyo hi jñānam abhyāsāj
jñānad dhyānaṃ viśiṣyate
dhyānāt karmaphalatyāgas
tyāgāc chāntir anantaram

For knowledge is better than practice,
And meditation is superior to knowledge,
And abandonment of the fruit of actions is better than meditation;
From abandonment (comes) peace immediately.

[101] Śrīpāda, op.cit., p.398

The problem is apparent. A hierarchy is set up in the verse in which *jñāna* is stated to be superior to *abhyāsa*, *dhyāna* to *jñāna* and *tyāga* to *dhyāna*, which seems to reverse if not challenge the priorities found elsewhere in the Gītā. Madhva's resolution of the difficulty may not be acceptable to all, but he shows considerable imagination in tackling it. He does so by redefining the connotations of the words thus:

abhyāsa	=	*(ajñānapūrva) abhyāsa*
jñāna	=	*jñānamātra*
dhyāna	=	*sajñāna-dhyāna*
tyāga	=	*dhyānayuktatyāga*

If we now read the Gītā verse with the terms so redefined, *jñāna* is said to be superior to mere ignorant practice (*abhyāsa*), meditation accompanied by knowledge (*dhyāna*) to mere knowledge, and renunciation accompanied by *dhyāna* to *dhyāna* alone.[101a]

Madhva's comments on verses 14-19 of the Twelfth Chapter are of interest, as this is one of the flatter sections of the Gītā and often elicits little comment.[102] The verses run as follows:

saṃtuṣṭaḥ satataṃ yogī
yatātmā dṛḍhaniścayaḥ
mayy arpitamanobuddhir
yo madbhaktaḥ sa me priyaḥ

yasmān no 'dvijate loko
lokān no 'dvijate ca yaḥ
harṣāmarṣabhayodvegair
mukto yaḥ sa ca me priyaḥ

anapekṣaḥ śucir dakṣa
udāsīno gatavyathaḥ
sarvārambhaparityāgī
yo madbhaktaḥ sa me priyaḥ

yo na hṛṣyati na dveṣṭi
na śocati na kāṅkṣati
śubhāśubhaparityāgī
bhaktimān yaḥ sa me priyaḥ

[101a] ibid., pp.424-5. [102] Zaehner, op.cit., pp.329-30; etc.

samaḥ śatrau ca mitre ca
tathā mānāpamānayoḥ
śītoṣṇasukhaduḥkheṣu
samaḥ saṅgavivarjitaḥ

tulyanindāstutir maunī
saṃtuṣṭo yena kenacit
aniketaḥ sthiramatir
bhaktimān me priyo naraḥ

The disciplined man who is always content,
Whose self is controlled, of firm resolve,
Whose thought and consciousness are fixed on Me,
Who is devoted to Me, he is dear to Me.

He before whom people do not tremble,
And who does not tremble before people,
From joy, impatience, fear, and agitation
Who is free, he too is dear to Me.

Unconcerned, pure, capable,
Disinterested, free from perturbation,
Abandoning all undertakings,
Who is devoted to Me, is dear to Me.

Who neither delights nor loathes,
Neither grieves nor craves,
Renouncing good and evil (objects),
Who is full of devotion, he is dear to Me.

Alike to foe and friend,
Also to honour and disgrace,
To cold and heat, joy and sorrow
Alike, freed from attachment,

To whom blame and praise are equal, restrained in speech,
Content with anything that comes,
Having no home, of steadfast mind,
Full of devotion, that man is dear to Me.

Madhva makes even these seemingly descriptive verses interesting by providing them with analytical content. He does this in three ways. First, he suggests that *santuṣṭaḥ satatam yogī* of XII:14(a) ('the disciplined man who is always content') be read with XII:19(b): *santuṣṭo yena kenacit* ('content with anything that comes'). When this is done a connection can be seen: XII:14(a) states what is to be accomplished (*vyākhyeya*). Secondly, he suggests that XII:15(c): *harṣāmarṣabhayodvegair mukto* ('from joy, impatience, fear and agitation who is free ...') should be read with XII:17(a): *yo na hṛṣyati* ... ('who neither delights ...') The doubt can arise regarding XII:15(c): does the disciplined man rejoice in having overcome joy, impatience, etc.? This is removed by XII:17(a): he does not. Finally, he suggests that XII:16(c), *sarvārambha-parityāgī* ('abandoning all undertakings'), be read with XII:17(c): *śubhāśubhaparityāgī* ('renouncing good and evil'). When this is done a connection emerges between the otherwise disparate statements – the first statement is a general one (*sāmānya*) and the second a special instance (*viśeṣa*) thereof.

As he moves into the Thirteenth Chapter, Madhva continues to identify finer nuances of the words as they appear in the text. Thus, for instance, in commenting on XIII:7 he defines *dambha* or hypocrisy as displaying importance or a virtue knowing that one possesses only a little of it.[103] In his gloss on XIII:9 he distinguishes between *sakti* and *abhiṣvaṅga*, or between attachment and cleaving, the latter being an extreme form (*atipakva*) of the former.[104] In his gloss on XIII:19 both *vikāras* and *guṇas* are mentioned as born of *prakṛti*. The fact that *vikāras* and *guṇas* are mentioned in apposition has gone virtually unnoticed by modern scholars.[105] Ancient commentators seem to have their own views in the matter. Śaṅkara takes *vikāras* to mean *buddhi*, etc. as evolutes of *prakṛti*, and strangely enough abandons this Sāṅkhyan background when glossing the next word *guṇān*, which he connects with joys, sorrows, etc.[106] Rāmānuja travels even further in the same direction and refers to desires, aversion, etc. in relation to *vikāras* and *amānitva*, etc. of XIII:7 in relation to *guṇas*.[107]

It is therefore striking that Madhva takes *guṇas* to mean what they seem to mean here[108] – the *guṇas* of Sāṅkhya (*guṇā sattvādayaḥ*).[109] Jayatīrtha specifically rejects the interpretation of *guṇas* as either *sukha, duḥkha, māna*, etc. or as cause and effect (*kāryakāraṇa-lakṣaṇa*) in his gloss on Madhva.[110] But the question still remains: how are the

[103] Śrīpāda, op.cit., p.433. [104] ibid., p.434.
[105] Zaehner, op.cit., p.344; Radhakrishnan, op.cit., p.308; Hill, op.cit., p.177; etc.
[106] Śaṅkara, op.cit., p.326. [107] Goyandakā, op.cit., pp.445-6.
[108] Zaehner, op.cit., p.345; Hill, op.cit., p.177; etc.
[109] Śrīpāda, op.cit., p.437. [110] ibid., p.438.

vikāras to be understood?

Madhva makes a few substantial points of theological interest in his gloss on XIII:12.

jñeyaṃ yat tat pravakṣyāmi
yaj jñātvā 'mṛtam aśnute
anādi matparaṃ brahma
na sat tan nā 'sad ucyate

What is the object of knowledge, that I shall declare,
Knowing which one attains freedom from death:
(It is) the beginningless Brahman, ruled by Me;
Neither existent nor non-existent it is called.

The problem, as is well known, centres on *anādimatparaṃ brahma*. Madhva leaves various loose ends in his gloss. These are tied together neatly by Jayatīrtha, who explains the issues and the suggested resolution thus:

> If it be thus explained that that which is not *ādimat* is *anādimat* (without beginning) then by resorting to the *bahubrīhī* (compound analysis) as that of which no beginning exists is *anādi* suffices to explain the meaning and the suffix *matup* (*mat* in *anādimat*) becomes redundant. Perceiving such a flaw some separate the clauses *anādi* and *matparam* and explain: I am that to whom belongs the *parā śakti*, called Vāsudeva. This is wrong. For such a meaning is not possible. There is no difference such as this is '*brahma*' and this is Vāsudeva. It has been said: 'There is no distinction of former and latter among the incarnations'. With this in mind one should explain in such a way that the *matup* suffix does not appear redundant. (Hence Madhva comments with the clause beginning *ādimat.*) Those that have a beginning are *ādimanti*. That which does not possess such beginnings is *anādimat*. What is meant is that body, senses, qualities, actions, etc. are his (God's) because of his supernal potency (and not by birth). Or else the compound may be explained as earlier. In no way is *matup* redundant.

Madhva's gloss on another verse of the Thirteenth Chapter is of exegetical interest. The concerned verse is XIII:24:

dhyānenā 'tmani paśyanti
kecid ātmānam ātmanā
anye sāṃkhyena yogena
karmayogena cā 'pare

By meditation, in the self see
Some the self by the self;
Others by discipline of reason,
And others by discipline of action.

The issue is the interpretation of *sāṅkhyayoga*. Śaṅkara identifies Sāṅkhya here with the basic elements of the sytem known by that name,[111] while Rāmānuja 'identifies *dhyāna* with *bhakti* and *sāṁkhyayoga* with *jñāna*'.[112] Madhva comments: *sāṅkhyena vedokta-bhagavatsvarūpa-jñānena*. According to him *sāṅkhya* means the knowledge of God as expounded in the Vedas. Thus Madhva identifies Sāṅkhya neither with *śeśvara* or *nirīśvara sāṅkhya*, as traditionally understood, nor with pure *jñānayoga*. Jayatīrtha, in explaining Madhva, clearly dismisses the association of the *sāṅkhya* here with the system of Kapila as erroneous.

A few verses of the Fourteenth Chapter may be considered before we move on to the Fifteenth. One of them runs as follows (XIV:7):

rajo rāgātmakaṃ viddhi
tṛṣṇāsaṅgasamudbhavam
tan nibadhnāti kaunteya
karmasaṅgena dehinam

Know that passion is of the nature of desire,
Springing from thirst and attachment;
It, son of Kuntī, binds
The embodied (soul) by attachment to actions.

The verse is simple but presents a slight logical difficulty. Therein *rajas* is described as *tṛṣṇāsaṅgasamudbhavam* (springing from thirst and attachment') whereas it would seem more logical to regard thirst and attachment as springing from *rajas*. This is exactly what Madhva does and adjusts grammar to logic by commenting: *tṛṣṇāsaṅgayoḥ samudbhavaṃ, tayoḥ kāraṇam*. As Jayatīrtha explains: *samudbhavati asmād iti samudbhavaṃ kāraṇam anyathā 'prakṛtisambhavaḥ' ityukta-virodhāt*. To elaborate: in XIV:5 *rajoguṇa* has been described as springing from *prakṛti*. There is therefore an obvious contradiction if in XIV:7 *rajoguṇa* is stated to spring from thirst and attachment. Therefore the compound *tṛṣṇāsaṅga-samudbhavam* must be analysed in such a way that thirst and attachment can be read as springing from *rajas*, rather than vice versa.

[111] Śaṅkara, op.cit., p.334. [112] Hill, op.cit., p.178, n.1.

It is the last verse of the Fourteenth Chapter, however, which should prove of greater interest. It runs as follows (XIV:27):

brahmaṇo hi pratiṣṭhā 'ham
amṛtasyā 'vyayasya ca
śāśvatasya ca dharmasya
sukhasyai 'kāntikasya ca

For I am the foundation of Brahman,
The immortal and imperishable,
And of the eternal right,
And of absolute bliss.

Interest in this verse derives from the fact that in it Kṛṣṇa claims to be the 'foundation' of Brahman (*brahmaṇo hi pratiṣṭhā' ham*). This is quite obviously a statement of great importance as herein the superiority of theism over monism seems to be asserted. Yet curiously enough the Hindu theistic commentators, by contrast with Western theists, do not seem to show any particular enthusiasm for the statement. Thus 'Rāmānuja, who identifies God as the highest Brahman in his theology, realises that Brahman here is subordinate, and therefore interprets it as the individual *ātman*'.[113] Madhva glosses: *brahmaṇo māyāyāḥ*! So that Kṛṣṇa ends up as the foundation not of Brahman but *māyā*. But this is so because, according to Madhva, Brahman = Kṛṣṇa and if taken literally the verse would make Kṛṣṇa his own foundation. Jayatīrtha comments:

> By 'for (I am the foundation) of Brahman' (*brahmaṇo hi*) thus the supreme *brahman* (*parabrahmaṇo hi*) is spoken of: It is so explained. This is false. On account of the statement that 'I am the foundation'.

The Fifteenth Chapter is a short one, as chapters of the Gītā go, but is exegetically one of the more intricate. Madhva's comments on some of the verses are of considerable interest, and his concluding remarks to the chapter of great interest.

To begin at the beginning, Madhva adds an interesting exegetical flourish in explaining the famous metaphor of the inverted fig-tree found in the first verse of the chapter:

[113] Hill, op.cit., pp.414-15.

ūrdhvamūlam adhaḥśākham
aśvatthaṃ prāhur avyayam
chandāṃsi yasya parṇāni
yas taṃ veda sa vedavit

With roots aloft and branches below,
The eternal peepal-tree, they say –
Whose leaves are the (Vedic) hymns,
Who knows it, he knows the Veda.

Madhva explains *chandāṃsi yasya parṇāni* as follows:[114] *phalakāraṇatvāt chandasāṃ parṇatvam. na hi kadācid apy ajāte parṇe phalotpattiḥ.* That is to say: the Vedas has been described as the leaves of the cosmic tree because the Vedas produce 'fruits' and nowhere is the appearance of fruits heard of without foliage. As to what fruits the Vedas produce, the answer is provided by Jayatīrtha – Mokṣa, etc. (*tatra phalaṃ mokṣādikam*).[115]

A verse of the Fifteenth Chapter about the meaning of parts of which the scholars are uncertain is XV:15:

sarvasya cā 'haṃ hṛdi saṃniviṣṭo
mattaḥ smṛtir jñānam apohanaṃ ca
vedaiś ca sarvair aham eva vedyo
vedāntakṛd vedavid eva cā 'ham

I am entered into the heart of every one;
From Me come memory, knowledge, and disputation;
I alone am that which is to be known by all the Vedas;
And I am the author of the Upaniṣads and the Vedas' knower.

At issue is the meaning of the word Vedānta, and the claim that Kṛṣṇa is Vedāntakṛt, or the maker of Vedānta. According to Madhva, investigations concerning the determination of the meaning of the Vedas are called *vedānta* (*vedanirṇayātmikā mīmāṁsā vedāntaḥ*). Madhva also quotes from the Sāma Veda to the following effect: *sa vedāntakṛt sa kālaka iti sa hy eva yuktisūtrakṛt sālakaḥ.*

Jayatīrtha's explanation of Madhva's gloss is helpful here:

> Lest the expression *vedāntakṛt* (be taken to mean) that he is the author of the Upaniṣads it is said to dispel the mistaken notion. By Veda is

[114] Śrīpāda, op.cit., p.463.
[115] ibid., p.464.

meant the meaning of the Veda. By its end is meant conclusion. Such is its nature. From that meaning that word is to be understood. The investigation pertains to *brahman*. He is the author of that, this is left unsaid (by Madhva). How is this conclusion reached. In this respect the verse from the Sāmaveda is quoted. *Yuktisūtrakṛt*: by this is meant that he is the author of the statements which logically explain the definitive conclusions regarding the meaning of the Vedas. He (God) is called *kālaka* by the second form of the root *kala* which has the recognised meaning of knowledge, the rest has been explained before.[115a]

Verses 16-18 of the Fifteenth Chapter deal with the doctrine of the two (*kṣara, akṣara*) or three (plus *uttama*) *puruṣas*. Scholars are divided about the proper understanding of this doctrine. The verses run as follows:

dvāv imau puruṣau loke
kṣaraś cā 'kṣara eva ca
kṣaraḥ sarvāṇi bhūtāni
kūṭastho 'kṣara ucyate

uttamaḥ purusaṣ tv anyaḥ
paramātme 'ty udāhṛtaḥ
yo lokatrayam āviśya
bibharty avyaya īśvaraḥ

yasmnāt kṣaram atīto 'ham
akṣarād api co 'ttamaḥ
ato 'smi loke vede ca
prathitaḥ puruṣottamaḥ

Here in the world are two spirits,
The perishable, and the imperishable;
The perishable is all beings;
The imperishable is called the immovable.

But there is a highest spirit, other (than this),
Called the Supreme Soul;
Which, entering into the three worlds,
Supports them, the undying Lord.

[115a] See XI:32.

Since I transcend the perishable,
And am higher than the imperishable too,
Therefore in the world and the Veda I am
Proclaimed as the highest spirit.

Madhva's remarks on this issue are helpful, but their relevance becomes more apparent after we have considered Hill's remarks on the controversy surrounding the verses. Hill wants to identify *prakṛti* with *kṣara puruṣa*, and *puruṣa* with *akṣara puruṣa*, and Kṛṣṇa or God with *uttama puruṣa*, to obtain a situation paralleled in Śvetāśvatara I:10:

> What is perishable is primary matter (*pradhāna*); what is immortal and imperishable is Hara (the bearer, the soul). Over both the perishable and the soul the one God (*deva*) rules.[116]

Madhva virtually reverses the identifications, for he remarks: *kṣarabhūtāni brahmādīni. kūṭasthā prakṛtiḥ*. That is to say: creatures such as Brahmā, etc. are *kṣara; prakṛti* is transcendental. It seems that the level at which Hill and Madhva are pegging their systems is different – with Hill it includes the world; with Madhva one seems to move at the cosmic level, just above the mundane world. Jayatīrtha offers an interesting insight here. He begins by saying that *kṣara* and *akṣara* should *not* be identified with *jaḍa* and *jīva* respectively, for the word which occurs in XV:16 is *bhūtāni* and the word *bhūta* is used conventionally for inanimate objects as well as embodied souls (*na hi jaḍamātre bhūtaśabdaḥ rūḍaḥ. kiṃ tu jīveṣv api*). The use of the word *puruṣa* per se, according to Jayatīrtha, also supports this view. He glosses *prakṛti*, identified by Madhva with *akṣara*, as *cetanā*, and states that *jīvas* are not *kūṭastha*, or transcendental (presumably like *prakṛti*), because they are liable to modifications – represented by emotions such as those of happiness.

In the glosses on the verses of the Sixteenth Chapter Madhva displays his semantic skills in identifying the finer shades of meaning of the various words which might otherwise appear to be mechanically catalogued. Thus he explains *piśuna* in XVI:2 as 'stating someone's shortcomings to the king, etc. to cause him trouble', which takes the sense of the word beyond tattling or backbiting. Similarly, he explains *kṣamā* in XVI:3 more fully as not reacting with anger at the perpetrator out of absence of anger. The expression *aparaspara-saṃbhūtam* occurs in XVI:8:

[116] Cited by Hill, op.cit., p.189, n.7.

asatyam apratiṣṭham te
jagad āhur anīśvaram
aparasparasaṃbhūtaṃ
kim anyat kāmahaitukam

Without truth, without religious basis, they
Say is the world, without a God,
Not originating in regular mutual causation;
In short, motivated by desire alone.

The expression *aparasparasaṃbhūtam* has occasioned some discussion, and Jayatīrtha makes his own contribution to it in commenting on Madhva. Madhva has also something of his own to say of a more general nature. He sees in this expression a denial of III:14-15:

annād bhavanti bhūtāni
parjanyād annasaṃbhavaḥ
yajñād bhavati parjanyo
yajñaḥ karmasamudbhavaḥ

karma brahmodbhavaṃ viddhi
brahmā 'kṣarasamudbhavam
tasmāt sarvagataṃ brahma
nityaṃ yajñe pratiṣṭhitam

Beings originate from food;
From the rain-god food arises;
From worship comes the rain (-god);
Worship originates in action.

Action arises from Brahman, know;
And Brahman springs from the Imperishable;
Therefore the universal Brahman
Is eternally based on worship.

The mutual relationship as visualised here is seen as *parasparasaṃbhava* by Madhva. The same could probably be said of III:10-12:

sahayajñāḥ prajāḥ sṛṣṭvā
puro 'vāca prajāpatiḥ
anena prasaviṣyadhvam
eṣa vo 'stv iṣṭakāmadhuk

devān bhāvayatā 'nena
  te devā bhāvayantu vaḥ
parasparaṃ bhāvayantaḥ
  śreyaḥ param avāpsyatha

iṣṭān bhogān hi vo deva
  dāsyante yajñabhāvitāḥ
tair dattān apradāyai 'bhyo
  yo bhuṅkte stena eva saḥ

After creating creatures along with (rites of) worship,
  Prajāpati (the Creator) said of old:
By this ye shall procreate yourselves –
  Let this be your Cow-of-Wishes.

With this prosper ye the gods,
  And let the gods prosper you;
(Thus) prospering one the other,
  Ye shall attain the highest welfare.

For desired enjoyments to you the gods
  Will give, prospered by worship;
Without giving to them, their gifts
  Whoso enjoys, is nothing but a thief.

Jayatīrtha explains that one should not take *aparasparasaṃbhūtam* to mean that it is born of something *else* (*parasmāt saṃbhūtam*). All that is meant is that it is not a case of mutual generation.

Madhva continues to draw fine word-distinctions in his glosses on the verses of the Seventeenth Chapter. Thus on XVII:8, wherein the qualities of *sāttvika* food are described by such expressions as *prīti*, *hṛdya* and *sthira*, he distinguishes among their semantic flavour. *Prīti* is that dietetic item which is pleasant in the immediate present; *hṛdya* is that which causes pleasant sensations even subsequently; *sthira* are those which are nourishing in the long run.[117] Similarly, in commenting on the word *maunam* in XVII:16, Madhva takes it in the spiritually richer sense of reflectiveness (*mananaśīlatvam*). It is usually taken simply as silence.

The last chapter of the Bhagavadgītā is also the longest, and being the last it is also counted among the most significant. The chapter begins with a consideration of the difference between *tyāga* and *sannyāsa*, a distinction expounded in XVIII:2 thus:

[117] Śrīpāda, op.cit., p.491.

kāmyānāṃ karmaṇāṃ nyāsaṃ
saṃnyāsaṃ kavayo viduḥ
sarvakarmaphalatyāgaṃ
prāhus tyāgaṃ vicakṣaṇāḥ

The renouncing of acts of desire
Sages call renunciation.
The abandonment of all action-fruits
The wise call abandonment.

Madhva's gloss on the verse is direct.[118] He states that *sannyāsa* means the renunciation of all optional karmas (*kāmyakarma*), either by not desiring their result or by not doing them at all. And by *tyāga* is meant the abandonment of the fruit. The point is elaborated by Jayatīrtha thus:

> Some interpret the verse *kāmyānām karmaṇām* to mean that *sannyāsa* means the (actual) abandonment of optional actions (*kāmya karma*) in the form of the horse-sacrifice, etc. And that *tyāga* means the giving up of the result of all actions of an obligatory nature (*nitya* and *naimittika*) (without their physical abandonment). But this is not true. With this in mind [Madhva glosses the verse beginning with *phala*]: *Tyāga* is indeed the giving up of the fruit of optional actions (*kāmya karma*), for their performance or non-performance is not spoken of [in the verse] – this is meant. And why so [this is explained by Madhva in his gloss beginning with *tathā hīti*]. By non-performance the actual performance of optional duties was not given up by seekers of liberation such as Janaka and Aśvapati, only the instituted results of horse-sacrifice, etc. It is not proper to give up the obligatory duties from any point of view because they have the result of purifying the mind.

Madhva's gloss on the word *dānam* in XVIII:5 is remarkable for its apparent modernity, for he writes: *dane tv abhayadānam antarbhavati* – the gift of fearlessness is included in the term *dāna*. The following remark by a student of Indian culture who was also a political leader will not be without interest in this context in which Nehru describes the impact of the entry of Gandhi in the political arena in the 1920s:

[118] ibid., p.498.

Political freedom took new shape then and acquired a new content. Much that he said we only partially accepted or sometimes did not accept at all. But all this was secondary. The essence of his teaching was fearlessness and truth and action allied to these, always keeping the welfare of the masses in view. The greatest gift for an individual or a nation, so we had been told in our ancient books, was *abhaya,* fearlessness, not merely bodily courage but the absence of fear from the mind. Chanakya and Yagnavalka had said, at the dawn of our history, that it was the function of the leaders of a people to make them fearless. But the dominant impulse in India under British rule was that of fear, pervasive, oppressing, strangling fear; fear of the army, the police, the widespread secret service; fear of the official class; fear of laws meant to suppress, and of prison; fear of the landlord's agent; fear of the moneylender; fear of unemployment and starvation, which were always on the threshold. It was against this all-pervading fear that Gandhi's quiet and determined voice was raised: Be not afraid.[119]

The forty-ninth verse of the Eighteenth Chapter is important because a key word from the point of view of Advaitic philosophy occurs there in the form of *naiṣkarmya.* It runs as follows:

asaktabuddhiḥ sarvatra
jitātmā vigataspṛhaḥ
naiṣkarmyasiddhiṃ paramāṃ
saṃnyāsenā 'dhigacchati

His mentality unattached to any object,
Self-conquered, free from longings,
To the supreme perfection of actionlessness
He comes thru renunciation.

Madhva glosses *naiṣkarmyasiddhim* as *naiṣkarmyaphala-yoga-siddhim,* and the full significance of this remark lies in the explicit denial by Jayatīrtha that *naiṣkarmyasiddhi* means *mokṣa* here. He is right in pointing out that such a claim would contradict a later verse – XVIII:55:

bhaktyā mām abhijānāti
yāvān yaś cā 'smi tattvataḥ
tato māṃ tattvato jñātvā
viśate tadanantaram

[119] Jawaharlal Nehru, *The Discovery of India* (Calcutta: Signet Press, 1946), p.311, italics added.

Thru devotion he comes to know Me,
  What My measure is, and who I am, in very truth;
Then, knowing Me in very truth,
  He enters into (Me) straightway.

Jayatīrtha's comment on verses 61, 62 is also helpful from the point of view of clarifying a possible ambiguity. To identify the ambiguity it is best to cite the verses first:

īśvaraḥ sarvabhūtānāṃ
  hṛddeśe 'rjuna tiṣṭhati
bhrāmayan sarvabhūtāni
  yantrārūḍhāni māyayā

tam eva śaraṇaṃ gaccha
  sarvabhāvena bhārata
tatprasādāt parāṃ śāntiṃ
  sthānaṃ prāpsyasi śāśvatam

Of all beings, the Lord
  In the heart abides, Arjuna,
Causing all beings to turn around
  (As if) fixed in a machine, by his magic power.

To Him alone go for refuge
  With thy whole being, son of Bharata;
By His grace, supreme peace
  And the eternal station shalt thou attain.

It will be noticed that in these verses Īśvara is mentioned by Kṛṣṇa as someone distinct from him, as it were. This is noted by Jayatīrtha who remarks that on account of the indirect nature of the statements it seems as if Kṛṣṇa is not *īśvara* (*parokṣavacanāt kṛṣṇasya anīśvaratvam pratīyate*). In the verses that follow, Jayatīrtha comments, Kṛṣṇa resorts to the first person to remove this doubt (XVIII:63-5):

iti te jñānam ākhyātaṃ
  guhyād guhyataraṃ mayā
vimṛśyai 'tad aśeṣeṇa
  yathe 'cchasi tathā kuru

sarvaguhyatamaṃ bhūyaḥ
śṛṇu me paramaṃ vacaḥ
iṣṭo 'si me dṛḍham iti
tato vaksyāmi te hitam

manmanā bhava madbhakto
madyājī māṃ namaskuru
mām evai 'syasi satyaṃ te
pratijāne priyo 'si me

sarvadharmān parityajya
mām ekaṃ śaraṇaṃ vraja
ahaṃ tvā sarvapāpebhyo
moikṣayisyāmi mā śucaḥ

Thus to thee has been expounded the knowledge
That is more secret than the secret, by Me;
After pondering on it fully,
Act as thou thinkest best.

Further, the highest secret of all,
My supreme message, hear.
Because thou art greatly loved of Me,
Therefore I shall tell thee what is good for thee.

Be Me-minded, devoted to Me;
Worshipping Me, revere Me;
And to Me alone shalt thou go; truly to thee
I promise it – (because) thou art dear to Me.

Abandoning all (other) duties,
Go to Me as thy sole refuge;
From all evils I thee
Shall rescue: be not grieved!

Madhva's remarks on what is regarded as the *carama śloka*, or the final pronouncement of the Gītā, are interesting and make eminent sense logically. He equates the giving up of Dharmas (*sarvadharmān parityajya*) or *dharma-tyāgaḥ* with *phalatyāgaḥ*, the giving up the fruits of (righteous action, when *dharma* = *karma*?); for, he asks, 'How else is one to engage in war' if one gives up all *dharmas* literally? In support he quotes the second line of XVIII:11. We might as well cite the entire verse:

na hi dehabhṛtā śakyaṃ
tyaktuṃ karmāṇy aśeṣataḥ
yas tu karmaphalatyāgī
sa tyāgī 'ty abhidhīyate

For a body-bearing (soul) can not
Abandon actions without remainder;
But he who abandons the fruit of action
Is called the man of (true) abandonment.

3.

We must now turn to the performance of a less complimentary duty – that of identifying some of Madhva's glosses in which he seems to miss the import of the verses (in question), or in which he imports his own interpretation into the understanding of them under the influence of his philosophical presuppositions.

In commenting on II:13 Madhva cites scriptural authority as proof of the existence of the embodied soul. The verse concerned has been cited earlier.

In commenting on the last *pāda* – *dhīras tatra na muhyati* – Madhva remarks that the steady person is not confused by specious arguments because he knows the truth on the basis of *śruti*. And why is the *śruti* authoritative? Because it is eternal (*anādikālaparigrahasiddhatvāt*). Now this line of argument seems out of place here for several reasons. For one, the Gītā is not particularly supportive of scriptural authority in general. For another, even though it does support scriptural tradition either indirectly (III:10-16) or directly (XVI:24) at certain points, it does not seem to do so in the present context. Not only is Vedic authority not invoked but aspersions are cast on it towards the end of this discourse (II:52-3):

yadā te mohakalilaṃ
buddhir vyatitariṣyati
tadā gantāsi nirvedaṃ
śrotavyasya śrutasya ca

śrutivipratipannā te
yadā sthāsyati niścalā
samādhāv acalā buddhis
tadā yogam avāpsyasi

When the jungle of delusion
  Thy mentality shall get across,
Then thou shalt come to aversion
  Towards what is to be heard and has been heard (in the Veda).

Averse to traditional lore ('heard' in the Veda)
  When shall stand motionless
Thy mentality, immovable in concentration,
  Then thou shalt attain discipline.

Madhva seems philosophically to overinterpret another key verse (II:16):

nā 'sato vidyate bhāvo
  nā 'bhavo vidyate sataḥ
ubhayor api dṛṣṭo 'ntas tv
  anayos tattvadarśibhiḥ

Of what is not, no coming to be occurs;
  No coming not to be occurs of what is;
But the dividing-line of both is seen,
  Of these two, by those who see the truth.

Madhva glosses it thus: 'The Ātman was spoken of as eternal. Is the Ātman alone eternal or something else besides? Something else as well. What is that? Thus is said the verse beginning *nāsato.* There is the absence neither of *asat* or cause or of *sat* or *brahman.*' Jayatīrtha explains that by *asat* Madhva means *prakṛti.* This is confirmed by what Madhva says next. He cites a line from the Viṣṇu Purāṇa establishing the eternal existence of *prakṛti, puruṣa* and *kāla.* He also cites verses from Purāṇic and Vedic sources to justify taking *asat* in the sense of 'cause' (the *avyakta*); he could even have cited IX:19.

In the process of obtaining this meaning, however, considerable violence has been done to the text and the context. The line which, in both the critical and vulgate text, reads as *nāsato vidyate bhāvo* ... has been read as *nāsto vidyate 'bhāvo.*[120] Next, the word *asat* itself has been interpreted rather unusually. To base an exegesis on the esoteric interpretation of the word in the context of a possibly corrupt reading seems to be a highly dubious hermeneutical procedure.

[120] S.K. Belvalkar (ed.), *The Bhagavadgītā* (Poona: Bhandarkar Oriental Research Institute, 1945), p.8.

In the same chapter Madhva seems to overinterpret the next verse also (II:17):

avināśi tu tad viddhi
yena sarvam idaṃ tatam
vināśam avyayasyā 'sya
na kaścit kartum arhati

But know that that is indestructible,
By which this all is pervaded;
Destruction of this imperishable one
No one can cause.

Madhva comments that the all-pervasive cannot be 'destroyed by curse, etc.'[121] Jayatīrtha explains the point further by adding that earlier on natural destruction was precluded (*pūrvam svābhāviko nāśo niṣiddhaḥ*) and now, by saying that it cannot be destroyed by someone else, an external agency, destruction on account of adventitious factors is also precluded. When it is naturally indestructible as such, how much more so in the face of curses, etc?[122] The introduction of the idea of someone trying to wreak destruction through curses, etc. seems gratuitous, though the distinction between destruction through natural (*svābhāvika*) and adventitious (*naimittika*) factors is not without interest.

In the following verse Madhva again introduces an interpretative angle peculiar to his own philosophical bent. The verse runs (II:18):

antavanta ime dehā
nityasyo 'ktāḥ śrīriṇaḥ
anāśino 'prameyasya
tasmād yudhyasva bhārata

These bodies come to an end,
It is declared, of the eternal embodied (soul),
Which is indestructible and unfathomable.
Therefore fight, son of Bharata!

Madhva uses this verse to relate the soul to God, though this consideration seems to be beyond the scope of the verse as we read it. He comments that the soul has been referred to as *śarīrin*, or embodied so as to exclude God (*īśvaravyāvṛttaye*). But it is called

[121] Śrīpāda, op.cit., p.42. [122] ibid., p.43.

aprameya, that is, incomprehensible or incomparable, because it has the same form as God (*aprameyeśvarasarūpatvāt*). Now it is true that both God (XI:42) and soul are called *aprameya* in the Gītā, but to extend this common locution into a philosophy of one being in the image of the other, as Madhva seems to, appears to stretch the point a little.[123]

Another part of the Second Chapter in interpreting which Madhva reveals his own views on the Vedas and his understanding of their message is constituted by verses 41-4:

vyavasāyātmikā buddhir
eke 'ha kurunandana
bahuśākhā anantāś ca
buddhayo 'vyavasāyinām

yām imāṃ puṣpitāṃ vācaṃ
pravadanty avipaścitaḥ
vedavādaratāḥ pārtha
nā 'nyad astī 'ti vādinaḥ

kāmātmānaḥ svargaparā
janmakarmaphalapradām
kriyāviśeṣabahulāṃ
bhogaiśvaryagatiṃ prati

bhogaiśvaryaprasaktānāṃ
tayā 'pahṛtacetasām
vyavasāyātmikā buddhiḥ
samādhau na vidhīyate

The mental attitude whose nature is resolution
Is but one in this world, son of Kuru;
For many-branched and endless
Are the mental attitudes of the irresolute.

This flowery speech which
Undiscerning men utter,
Who take delight in the words of the Veda, son of Pṛthā,
Saying that there is nothing else,

[123] ibid., pp.43-4.

Whose nature is desire, who are intent on heaven,
(The speech) which yields rebirth as the fruit of actions,
Which is replete with various (ritual) acts
Aiming at the goal of enjoyment and power, –

Of men devoted to enjoyment and power,
Who are robbed of insight by that (speech),
A mental attitude resolute in nature
Is not established in concentration.

Madhva's own views influence his understanding of these verses in several ways. He remarks that it is only non-Vedic views which are characterised by irresolution, not the Vedic (*syur avaidikāni matāny avyavasāyātmakāni, na tu vaidikāni*).[124] The text does not say so, and although it could be taken to imply this if viewed as a Hindu response to Buddhism, at this point even that construction appears highly speculative. Turning next to the point of Vedic exegesis, Madhva is in line with much scholarly opinion in holding that *vedavādaratāḥ* refers to people who are caught up in the mere words of the Vedas, but shows his hand in interpreting *nānyad astíti vādinaḥ*: those who say 'There is naught else'. 'What else is not' is not elaborated on by modern commentators,[125] and Śaṅkara and Rāmānuja seem to take it to mean that there is naught else apart from the result of sacrificial ritual in the form of heaven, etc.[126] This seems to be more in harmony with the context, but Madhva suggests that denial of God is involved. It must be pointed out again that this interpretation takes on a certain reasonableness in the light of some later passages in the Gītā (XVI:8.17), but whether Madhva's position can be sustained here is a moot point.

The next two verses of the Second Chapter have caused difficulties for strict upholders of Vedic authority, for they seem to draw attention to the limitation of the Vedas (II:45-6):

traigunyaviśayā vedā
nistraigunyo bhavā 'rjuna
nirdvandvo nityasattvastho
niryogakṣema ātmavān

[124] ibid., p.73.
[125] Hill, op.cit., p.89; Zaehner, op.cit., p.143; Radhakrishnan, op.cit., p.117; etc.
[126] Śaṅkara, op.cit., p.44; Rāmānuja, op.cit., p.65.

yāvān artha udapāne
sarvataḥ samplutodake
tāvān sarveṣu vedeṣu
brāhmaṇasya vijānataḥ

The Vedas have the three Strands (of matter) as their scope;
Be thou free from the three Strands, Arjuna,
Free from the pairs (of opposites), eternally fixed in goodness,
Free from acquisition and possession, self-possessed.

As much profit as there is in a water-tank,
When on all sides there is a flood of water,
No more is there in all the Vedas
For a brahman who (truly) understands.

Madhva is a strong believer in Vedic authority. In his system, according to a verse attributed to Vyāsatīrtha which sums up its tenets, 'Hari is knowable only through the Vedas'.[127] It is true that he is more inclined to use reason in support of revelation than Rāmānuja and that God remains 'unknowable in the sense that he cannot be exhaustively known even with the aid of revelation'.[127a] Nevertheless, subject to these qualifications, Vedic authority is primary.

Madhva's glosses on both these verses interpret them so as to align them with the polar star of Vedic authority. The statement that the Vedas have the three *guṇas* as their province is said to be only apparently so (*pratīto 'rthaḥ*) when they are understood in the context of heaven, etc.[128] Madhva warns against being deluded by the apparent meaning, and quotes a battery of passages to establish that the Vedas are not negated.[129]

Nor does the next verse (II:46) go down too well with the assertion of Vedic authority, as it seems to imply its redundancy in the face of actual Brahman-experience. But Madhva interprets it in a very different light. Basically, he argues that the ritual sections of the Vedas produce their own result, and so do the knowledge sections, but the results of the latter are far superior to the former. Indeed, to the *jñānī*, the results of the former also accrue, and it is this point which underlies the comparison of water as confined to a well and as spreading all over in a flood. The point is that the well is submerged in the flood, as the results of *karma* are in *jñāna* (*sarveṣu vedeṣu yat*

[127] Mahadevan, op.cit., p.153.
[127a] Hiriyanna, *Essentials*, p.191.
[128] Śrīpāda, op.cit., p.75. [129] ibid., pp.75-6.

phalam tat vijānato'pi jñānino brāhmaṇasya phale 'ntarbhavati).[130]

The word *brāhmaṇa* in the verse is to be understood in the sense, not of the *brāhmaṇa varṇa*, but of the knower of *brahman* (*aparokṣ-ajñānī*),[131] a point further clarified by Jayatīrtha that, by the word *brāhmaṇa*, *kṣatriyas*, etc. are not excluded (*na kṣatriyādivyāvṛttiḥ*).[132] This last point is generally accepted, but Madhva's interpretation of the subsumption of the fruits of *karma* in *jñāna* as the key to unlocking the obscurity of the verse must remain open to debate.

In the next verse (II:47) Madhva again turns the meaning round in a way which takes the average reader by surprise. The verse has been cited earlier. Madhva gets an astonishing amount of mileage out of the simple pronominal form *te* (*tava*), i.e. 'thy'. According to Madhva, it is used by way of synecdochc (*upalakṣaṇārtham*): Arjuna stands for all *jñānins*. This claim, that Arjuna is a *jnānī*, is in itself open to question. But not only does Madhva say so, he proceeds to draw conclusions on the basis of this important assumption. In effect, according to Madhva, what Kṛṣṇa is telling Arjuna is this: even though you are a *jñānī* and therefore possess a special status which protects you from being karmically bound should you desire the fruit of actions, even you should abandon them; then how much more so one who is not a *jñānī*![133] This interpretation is as forced as it is fascinating.

It was shown earlier how some verses of the Gītā cannot be used to uphold the unqualified assertion of Vedic authority. One such is II:52:

yadā te mohakalilaṃ
buddhir vyatitarisyati
tadā gantāsi nirvedam
śrotavyasa śrutasya ca

When the jungle of delusion
Thy mentality shall get across,
Then thou shalt come to aversion
Towards what is to be heard and has been heard (in the Veda).

The word *nirveda* in this verse is drastically reinterpreted by Madhva to save Vedic authority from being impugned, or literally passed over. As Jayatīrtha clearly states, in order to put aside the other sense of *nirveda* as *vairāgya* or detachment,[134] the word is

130 ibid., p.77.
131 ibid.
132 ibid., p.78.
133 ibid.
134 ibid., p.100.

explained as copious gain (*nirvedaṃ nitarāṃ lābham*). Thus while the second line is usually translated, 'Then shalt thou feel disgust for what thou shalt hear and hast heard',[135] namely, *śruti* or the Vedas, if we follow Madhva the meaning is transformed as follows: 'Then shalt thou derive the full benefit[136] from what thou shalt hear and hast heard'. As Hill remarks, such interpretations are 'merely attempts to save the Veda from criticism'.[137]

At this point an earlier verse may be cited, the violent exegesis of which, as carried out by Madhva, is supported by him on the basis of scriptural authority. The verse in question is II:50:

buddhiyukto jahātī 'ha
ubhe sukṛtaduṣkṛte
tasmād yogāya yujyasva
yogaḥ karmasu kauśalam

The disciplined in mental attitude leaves behind in this world
Both good and evil deeds.
Therefore discipline thyself unto discipline;
Discipline in actions is weal.

Madhva insists that, appearances notwithstanding, the verse does not proclaim the abandonment of all good and bad actions (and consequent results thereof), but rather states the fruit of knowledge (*jñānaphalam*). According to Madhva, the *jñānī* gives up the fruits of works as they relate to the world of mortals; even though good, they are given up as undesirable. What the *jñānī* does not give up is the great fruit which will accrue to him (in a post-mortem state) as a result of worship (*na bṛhatphalam upāsanādijanitam ... jahāti*). In support of this eschatology Madhva quotes several passages, and also refutes the Advaitic soteriological assumption of the *ātman* being one with *brahman* (*na caikībhūta eva brahmaṇā saha*).[138] So far as the divergence from the Advaitic position is concerned, no special comment is required, as the Gītā can be read to support different eschatologies, but Madhva's interpretation of this particular verse to squeeze his own sense out of it seems particularly forced.

Madhva's glosses on three other verses of the Second Chapter may be noticed before we move on. The first is a curious comment on II:54. The verse has been cited earlier.

[135] Hill, op.cit., p.91.
[136] ibid., p.91, n.6. [137] ibid.
[138] ibid., p.89.

Madhva seems to imply that Arjuna already knows the answer to the question he has just asked (*na cārjuno na jānāti*) and then, as if to answer the natural query, 'Why does he raise the issue?', he cites a verse which translates:

> The ancient kings know and the divine sages likewise. Even so they question about *dharma* for the sake of discussing the secret import. Those secrets do not appear manifest in the Purāṇas to those with limited intelligence.[139]

What Madhva seems to be suggesting is that Arjuna is perpetrating a pedagogical set-up, of course with the best of intentions. Earlier on, he identified Arjuna as a *jñānī*. Madhva seems to have his own understanding of who Arjuna really is.

Madhva's comments on the concluding verse of the Second Chapter possess considerable, if predictable, significance. The verse runs as follows (II:72):

eṣā brāhmī sthitiḥ pārtha
nai 'naṃ prāpya vimuhyati
sthitvā 'syām antakāle 'pi
brahmanirvāṇam ṛcchati

This is the fixation that is Brahmanic, son of Pṛthā;
Having attained it he is not (again) confused.
Abiding in it even at the time of death,
He goes to Brahman-nirvāṇa.

The verse as such clearly seems to indicate the possibility of ante-mortem liberation – even if it occurs at the moment of death. But Madhva, with his doctrinal commitment to post-mortem salvation, shifts the weight to the other foot. He writes:

> Being present in that (state) even at the moment of death he goes to *brahma*. Or else obtains another birth. For it will be said 'whichever ... (*yaṃ yaṃ vāpi*: VIII:6).' In case *prārabdha karma* persists another birth even in the case of *jñānīs* is acceptable ... Karmas can produce results covering many embodiments.[140]

Madhva seems to be over-interpreting the text here.

[139] ibid., p.106.
[140] ibid., p.127.

The first half of the Third Chapter, apart from a discussion of action in general, also deals in some detail with the sacrificial cycle and ritual action in that context.[141] A verse which seems to mark this change of context is III:8:

niyataṃ kuru karma tvaṃ
karma jyāyo hy akarmaṇah
śarīrayātrā 'pi ca te
na prasidhyed akarmaṇaḥ

Perform thou action that is (religiously) required;
For action is better than inaction.
And even the maintenance of the body for thee
Can not succeed without action.

At issue is the understanding of the word *niyata*. It is usually translated in English as prescribed or required (action). Madhva, in the course of his brief comment on the verse, glosses *niyatam* as *svavarṇāśramocitam* (*karma*).[142] The question is: has he over-interpreted the expression? A similar doubt arises in relation to his comment on the previous verse, which runs (III:7):

yas tv indriyāṇi manasā
niyamyā 'rabhate 'rjuna
karmendriyaiḥ karmayogam
asaktaḥ sa viśiṣyate

But whoso the senses with the thought-organ
Controlling, O Arjuna, undertakes
Discipline of action with the action-senses,
Unattached (to the fruits of action), he is superior.

In this case Madhva glosses *karmayogam* as *svavarṇāśramocitam*. He adds further: It is not just that the rule applies to the householder stage. For Sannyāsa, etc. have also been laid down (*na tu gṛhasthakarmaniyamaḥ. sannyasādividhānāt*).[142a]

The identification of *karmayoga* and *niyatakarma* with *varṇāśramadharma* raises some problems. It is true that *karmayoga* may be

[141] III:10-16.
[142] G.S. Sadhale (ed.), *The Bhagavad-Gītā with Eleven Commentaries* (Bombay: 'Gujarati' Printing Press, 1935), p.284.
[142a] Śrīpāda, op.cit., p.148.

identified here with the order of *varṇas*, although Kṛṣṇa talks about this arrangement explicitly only later (IV:13; XVIII:41-5). But the Bhagavadgītā in general does not have much to say about the *āśramas*; indeed 'there is not much reference in the work to Āśrama-Dharma, the twin companion of Varṇa-Dharma'.[143] This then is the first criticism against Madhva's identification: the inclusion of *āśrama* with *varṇa* as identified in *varṇāśrama*. The second relates to the identification of the same *varṇāśrama* with *niyata karma*. For when the text of the Gītā discusses the nature of *niyata karma*, it does not involve the *varṇas* in the discussion. 'The full content of the phrase *niyata karma* becomes clearer at the close of Kṛṣṇa's instruction',[144] in XVIII:7-9. These verses run as follows:

niyatasya tu saṃnyāsaḥ
karmaṇo no 'papadyate
mohāt tasya parityāgas
tāmasaḥ parikīrtitaḥ

duḥkham ity eva yat karma
kāyakleśabhayāt tyajet
sa kṛtvā rājasaṃ tyāgaṃ
nai 'va tyāgaphalaṃ labhet

kāryam ity eva yat karma
niyataṃ kriyate 'rjuna
saṅgaṃ tyaktvā phalaṃ cai 'va
sa tyāgaḥ sāttviko mataḥ

But abandonment of a (religiously) required
Action is not seemly;
Abandonment thereof owing to delusion
Is reputed to be of the nature of darkness.

Just because it is troublesome, what action
One abandons through fear of bodily affliction,
Such a man performs an abandonment that is of the nature of passion;
By no means shall he get any fruit of (this) abandonment.

Simply because it ought to be done, when action
That is (religiously) required is performed, Arjuna,
Abandoning attachment and fruit,
That abandonment is held to be of goodness.

[143] Hirayanna, *Outlines*, p.119, n.2.
[144] Hill, op.cit., p.96, n.1.

Hence it is best to regard *niyata karma* as belonging to a different order of classification of *karma* than the one represented by the *varṇas*. In some of his glosses on other verses of the Third Chapter Madhva seems to view them from a frame of reference exterior to them. This frame is provided by the distinction between two kinds of *samādhi* drawn in Patañjali's Yoga – the *saṁprajñāta* and the *asaṁprajñāta*. The distinction is explained as follows:

> *ekāgra* or the state of concentration, when permanently established, is called *saṁprajñātayoga* or the trance of mediation, in which there is a clear and distinct consciousness of the object of contemplation. It is known also as *samāpatti* or *samprajñāta samādhi* inasmuch as *citta*, or the mind, is, in this state, entirely put into the object and assumes the form of the object itself. So also the state of *niruddha* is called *asaṁprajñāta yoga* or *asaṁprajñāta samādhi*, because all mental modifications being stopped in this state, nothing is known or thought of by the mind. This is the trance of absorption in which all psychoses and appearances of objects are stopped and there are no ripples in the placid surface of *citta*, or the mind. Both these kinds of *samādhi* are known by the common name of *samādhi-yoga* or the cessation of mental modifications, since both conduce to self-realisation.[145]

The point may be illustrated by examining Madhva's glosses on two verses of the Third Chapter. Let III:17 be examined first:

yas tv ātmaratir eva syād
ātmatṛptaś ca mānavaḥ
atmany eva ca saṃtuṣṭas
tasya kāryaṃ na vidyate

But who takes delight in the self alone,
The man who finds contentment in the self,
And satisfaction only in the self,
For him there is found (in effect) no action to perform.

Madhva says that the verse implies the attainment of *asaṁprajñāta-samādhi*. He takes his cue from the word *ātmarati* and states that nothing is to be done by him who is placed in *asaṁprajñātasamādhi*; otherwise, if one is not solely absorbed in the

[145] Satischandra Chatterjee and Dhirendramohan Datta, *An Introduction to Indian Philosophy* (University of Calcutta, 1969) pp.299-300. Sanskrit terms italicised.

self, there is some other attachment in the case of everyone (*anyadā'nyaratir apīṣat sarvasya bhavati*).[146] Madhva even presses the appearance of the word *mānava* in the verse in support of his view by claiming that by its use the *asaṁprajñātasamādhi* of the *jñānī* is indicated, as the root of the word *mānava* stands for knowledge (*mānava iti jñānina evāsaṁprajñātasamādhir bhavatīti darśayati 'manu avabodhane' iti dhātoḥ*).[147]

It is difficult to avoid the impression that all this transpersonal psychological sophistication has been forced upon the verse. The same may be said of Madhva's gloss on III:19:

tasmād asaktaḥ satataṃ
kāryaṃ karma samācara
asakto hy ācaran karma
param āpnoti pūruṣah

Therefore unattached ever
Perform action that must be done;
For performing action without attachment
Man attains the highest.

Madhva remarks that, because it is only one positioned in *asaṁprajñātasamādhi* who does not act (and you are not in that state), therefore perform action.[148] The discussion of *samādhi* here seems to be quite extraneous.

We next come to a key verse of the Gītā, Madhva's gloss on which clearly reveals his own philosophical preoccupation. The verse is III:20:

karmaṇai 'va hi saṃsiddhim
āsthitā janakādayaḥ
lokasaṃgraham evā 'pi
sampaśyan kartum arhasi

For only thru action, perfection
Attained Janaka and others.
Also for the mere control of the world
Having regard, thou shouldst act.

Madhva insists that, despite what the verse seems to say, salvation cannot be attained by *karma* alone:

[146] Śrīpāda, op.cit., p.163. [147] ibid.
[148] ibid., p.167.

With action, that is performing action indeed, this is meant. Having indeed performed action, or else then obtaining knowledge. Not without knowledge. For the fact of their (i.e. of Janaka, etc.) being a *jñānī* is celebrated in the Mahābhārata, etc.[149]

Madhva concludes his extended gloss on the same note: Therefore *mokṣa* results from transcendental knowledge. Action is only a means to it (*ato 'parokṣajñānad eva mokṣaḥ. karma tu tatsādhanam eva*).[150]

He may be right, but the text here does not say so. Whether the Gītā as a whole allows for liberation directly through *karma* without routing it through *bhakti* or *jñāna* is also an interesting issue.

The concluding verses of the Third Chapter held Madhva's attention long enough for him to provide a gloss on them, and for that reason they hold our attention now. The verses are as follows (III:41-3):

tasmāt tvam indriyāny ādau
niyamya bharatarṣabha
pāpmānam prajahi hy enaṃ
jñānavijñānanāśanam

indriyāṇi parāny āhur
indriyebhyaḥ paraṃ manaḥ
manasas tu parā buddhir
yo buddheḥ paratus tu saḥ

evaṃ buddheḥ paraṃ buddhvā
saṃstabhyā 'tmānam ātmanā
jahi śatruṃ mahābāho
kāmarūpaṃ durāsadam

Thou therefore, the senses first
Controlling O bull of Bharatas,
Smite down this evil one,
That destroys theoretical and practical knowledge.

The senses, they say, are high;
Higher than the senses is the thought-organ;
But higher than the thought-organ is the consciousness;
While higher than the consciousness is He (the soul).

[149] ibid., p.168. [150] ibid., p.169.

Thus being conscious of that which is higher than consciousness,
Steadying the self by the self,
Smite the enemy, great-armed one,
That has the form of desire, and is hard to get at.

Although our intention in this section is to animadvert on Madhva's glosses in relation to the text, we are compelled to begin the critique with a compliment. Madhva makes a neat comment in moving from verse 41 to 42. Verse 41 calls upon Arjuna to slay *kāma* but does not specify any weapon. And Madhva connects the two verses by saying that now the knowledge which is like a weapon for destroying the enemy (*kāma*) is made known. But in specifying the various steps of this knowledge he seems to trip at one point. The point is provided by the pronoun *saḥ* at the end of verse 42. What does it stand for? Jayatīrtha identifies two views: (1) according to the Māyāvādins (= Advaitins) *saḥ* stands for *jīva* (although *ātman* would be more accurate); and (2) according to Bhāskara *saḥ* stands for *kāma*. According to Madhva it stands for *paramātman*. Madhva offers some justification, but modern scholarly opinion is pretty well settled in favour of regarding *saḥ* as referring to the *ātman*.[151]

Madhva's comments on the Fourth Chapter call for a brief response. He introduces the chapter with remarks which result from a misunderstanding of *saḥ* in III:42 as indicated earlier. Having identified *saḥ* with *paramātmā*, he begins his gloss on the Fourth Chapter by saying that here, among other things, that which is beyond *buddhi* is glorified (*buddeḥ parasya māhātmyam*),[152] and Jayatīrtha makes the supplementary remark that Viṣṇu is glorified (*viṣṇor māhātmyam ucyate*).[153] That may be so, but the comments are based on an erroneous understanding, as pointed out earlier. The misunderstanding also seems to colour Madhva's gloss on IV:4-5. For he comments: 'It was said that (cast) all on me (III:30). (Arjuna) wishing to know of (God's) glory (on whom he was asked to cast all actions) right from the beginning asks the question'[154] beginning with *aparam* (IV:4):

arjuna uvāca
aparaṃ bhavato janma
paraṃ janma vivasvataḥ
katham etad vijānīyāṃ
tvam ādau proktavān iti

[151] Zaehner, op.cit., p.177.
[152] Śrīpāda, op.cit., p.187. [153] ibid. [154] ibid., p.188.

Arjuna said:
Later Thy birth,
Earlier the birth of Vivasvant:
How may I understand this,
That Thou didst proclaim it in the beginning, as Thou sayest?

Madhva's gloss on IV:16-17 next claims attention. The verses run as follows:

kim karma kim akarme 'ti
kavayo 'py atra mohitāḥ
tat te karma pravakṣyāmi
yaj jñātvā mokṣyase 'śubhāt

karmaṇo hy api boddhavyaṃ
boddhavyaṃ ca vikarmaṇaḥ
akarmaṇaś ca boddhavyaṃ
gahanā karmaṇo gatiḥ

What is action, what inaction?
About this even sages are bewildered.
So I shall explain action to thee,
Knowing which, thou shalt be freed from evil.

For one must understand the nature of action, on the one hand,
And must understand the nature of mis-action,
And must understand the nature of inaction:
Hard to penetrate is the course of action.

The verses contain a mention of three terms connected with *karma*: (1) *karma*, (2) *vikarma* and (3) *akarma*. But before we turn to this classification we must note Madhva's introductory comments on IV:17. It should be remembered that the last *pāda* of the previous verse says *yaj jñātvā mokṣyase 'śubhāt* (knowing which, thou shalt be freed from evil). Madhva begins his gloss on the succeeding verse: 'You will not be liberated merely by knowing that.'[155] Such contradiction seems a bit out of place, even if the verse is meant to elaborate a threefold (*karma, akarma, vikarma*) distinction as opposed to the twofold one of the previous verse (*karma, akarma*). According to Madhva *karma* seems to mean proper action, *akarma* non-performance of action and *vikarma* forbidden action.

[155] ibid., p.201.

Madhva's gloss on IV:25 offers some interesting insights into the attitudes he brings to bear on his approach to the Bhagavadgītā. The verse runs as follows:

daivam evā 'pare yajñaṃ
yoginaḥ paryupāsate
brahmāgnāv apare yajñaṃ
yajñenai 'vo 'pajuhvati

To naught but sacrifice to the deities some
Disciplined men devote themselves.
In the (sacrificial) fire of Brahman, others the sacrifice
Offer up by the sacrifice itself.

Several points deserve attention here. First, Madhva takes *daivam* to mean, not sacrificial deities, but God (*bhagavān*).[156] Jayatīrtha makes the supplementary remark that it is incorrect to take *daivam* as pertaining to the *devas* (*daivam devaviśayam*), because *dravyayajñas* are mentioned in IV:28 implying the worship of deities; hence taking it in that sense here involves tautology.[157] Secondly, he maintains that the worship of God in this sense (which is usually called *pūjā* and distinguished from *yajña*) is *yajña*.[158] And, finally, he maintains that people in the last stage of life – *yatyāśrama* (*sannyāsa*) – thus also perform *yajña* in this form.[159]

Madhva seems to be reading far more into the verse than is intended. He wants to find room in the Gītā for his favourite beliefs: (1) that worship of Viṣṇu is *yajña*, and (2) that ritual action is to be performed in all stages of life.

Some of Madhva's glosses on verses of the Fifth Chapter seem a trifle gratuitous. For instance, he says in relation to the following verse (V:22) that 'enjoyment of desires is being disparaged for the sake of renunciation' (*sannyāsārthaṃ kāma-bhogaṃ nindayati*).[160]

ye hi saṃsparśajā bhogā
duḥkhayonaya eva te
ādyantavantaḥ kaunteya
na teṣu ramate budhaḥ

[156] ibid., p.208. [157] ibid., p.209.
[158] ibid., p.208. [159] ibid.
[160] ibid., p.233.

For the enjoyments that spring from (outside) contacts
Are nothing but sources of misery;
They have beginning and end, son of Kuntī;
The wise man takes no delight in them.

One has to be careful with using the word *sannyāsa* too freely in the context of the Gītā because of its emphasis on *karmayoga*, and because it is such a multivalent word.

Similarly, in relation to V:23 Madhva remarks that the 'access of passion and anger can only be forborne in the human body and not elsewhere – this is the idea. For the world of Brahmā is only for those who have overcome desires'.[161] Is all this really implied in the verse itself?

śaknotī 'hai 'va yaḥ soḍhuṃ
prāk śarīravimokṣaṇāt
kāmakrodhobhavaṃ vegaṃ
sa yuktaḥ sa sukhī naraḥ

Who can control right in this life,
Before being freed from the body,
The excitement that springs from desire and wrath,
He is disciplined, he the happy man.[162]

Madhva's glosses on the Sixth Chapter abound in instances where his philosophical predispositions govern his exegesis. The very first verse is a case in point.

śrībhagavan uvāca
anāśritaḥ karmaphalaṃ
kāryaṃ karma karoti yaḥ
sa saṃnyāsī ca yogī ca
na niragnir na cā 'kriyaḥ

The Blessed One said:
Not interested in the fruit of action,
Who does action that is required (by religion),
He is the possessor of both renunciation and discipline (of action);
Not he who builds no sacred fires and does no (ritual) acts.

[161] ibid.

[162] 'In this world' is probably to be preferred as a translation of *iha* than 'in this life'.

The clear implication is that the non-tending of fire and the non-performance of ritual is associated with *sannyāsa* and *yoga*. Madhva, however, succeeds in reversing the sense, and argues that because fire is not tended and ritual is not performed one in such a situation cannot be called a *sannyāsī* and a *yogī*. He refers to IV:25 and takes as firmly established what he really so tenuously urges – that even in the fourth stage rituals, etc. are to be maintained (*caturthāśramiṇo 'py agniḥ kriyā coktā daivam evety ādau … yasmān niragnir akriyaḥ sannyāsī yogī ca na bhavaty eva*).[163] Similarly, in his gloss on VI:15 he goes out of his way to deny *jīvanmukti*. The verse runs as follows:

yuñjann evam sadā 'tmānaṃ
yogī niyatamanāsaḥ
śāntiṃ nirvāṇaparamāṃ
matsaṃsthām adhigacchati

Thus ever disciplining himself,
The man of discipline, with controlled mind,
To peace that culminates in nirvāṇa,
And rests in Me, attains.

Madhva glosses *nirvāṇaparamām* as *śarīratyāgottarakālīnām* without any apparent provocation.

Similarly he imparts to verses 18-22 a typically particularistic flavour:

yadā viniyataṃ cittam
ātmany evā 'vatiṣṭhate
niḥspṛhaḥ sarvakamebhyo
yukta ity ucyate tadā

yathā dīpo nivātastho
ne 'ṅgate so 'pamā smṛtā
yogino yatacittasya
yuñjato yogam ātmanaḥ

yatro 'paramate cittaṃ
niruddhaṃ yogasevayā
yatra cai 'vā 'tmanā 'tmānaṃ
paśyann ātmani tuṣyati

[163] Śrīpāda, op.cit., p.241. The reference is to IV:25.

sukham ātyantikaṃ yat tad
buddhigrāhyam atīndriyam
vetti yatra na cai 'vā 'yaṃ
sthitaś calati tattvataḥ

yaṃ labdhvā cā 'paraṃ lābhaṃ
manyate nā' dhikaṃ tataḥ
yasmin sthito na duḥkhena
guruṇā 'pi vicālyate

When the thought, controlled,
Settles on the self alone,
The man free from longing for all desires
Is then called disciplined.

As a lamp stationed in a windless place
Flickers not, this image is recorded
Of the disciplined man controlled in thought,
Practising discipline of the self.

When the thought comes to rest,
Checked by the practice of discipline,
And when, the self by the self
Contemplating, he finds satisfaction in the self;

That supernal bliss which
Is to be grasped by the consciousness and is beyond the senses,
When he knows this, and not in the least
Swerves from the truth, abiding fixed (in it);

And which having gained, other gain
He counts none higher than it;
In which established, by no misery;
However grievous, is he moved;

In these verses he glosses *ātmani* in VI:18 as *bhagavati*, equating soul and God.[164] In VI:18 he converts the yoga of the *ātman* (*yogam atmanaḥ*) to yoga pertaining to God (*bhagavad-viṣayaṃ yogam*).[165] In VI:20 he substitutes the word *ātman* with three different terms in the last line, *ātmanā manasā, ātmani dehe ... ātmānam bhagavantam paśyan*, so that what in the original reads 'and when, the self by the self,

[164] ibid., p.257. [165] ibid.

contemplating, he finds satisfaction in the self' comes out through the pen of Madhva as 'and when the mind, contemplating God, finds satisfaction in the body'. In VI:21 he glosses *tattvataḥ* (from the truth) as *bhagavadrūpāt* (from the form of god).[166]

The trend is maintained as the net is cast wider and more verses are taken into account – VI:29-31:

sarvabhūtastham ātmānaṃ
sarvabhūtāni ca 'tmani
īkṣate yogayuktātmā
sarvatra samadarśanaḥ

yo māṃ paśyati sarvatra
sarvaṃ ca mayi paśyati
tasyā 'haṃ na praṇaśyāmi
sa ca me na praṇaśyati

sarvabhūtasthitaṃ yo māṃ
bhajaty ekatvam āsthitaḥ
sarvathā vartamāno 'pi
sa yogī mayi vartate

ātmaupamyena sarvatra
samaṃ paśyati yo 'rjuna
sukhaṃ vā yadi vā duḥkhaṃ
sa yogī paramo mataḥ

Himself as in all beings,
And all beings in himself,
Sees he whose self is disciplined in discipline,
Who sees the same in all things.

Who sees Me in all,
And sees all in Me,
For him I am not lost,
And he is not lost for Me.

Me as abiding in all beings whoso
Reveres, adopting (the belief in) one-ness,
Tho abiding in any possible condition,
That disciplined man abides in Me.

[166] ibid., p.258.

By comparison with himself, in all (beings)
  Whoso sees the same, Arjuna,
Whether it be pleasure or pain,
  He is deemed the supreme disciplined man.

As the reader can see, the verses move back and forth between cosmic monism and monotheism, but for Madhva the movement is in only one direction. In VI:29 he predictably glosses *ātmānam* as *parameśvaram* and *ātmani* as *parameśvare*, thereby taking references to *ātman* as references to God.[167] If he does not do so in the case of VI:32 it is because he regards it as just another way of saying the same thing.[168]

Madhva's gloss on VI:36 represents an even more severe case of bias. The verse simply deals with problems of mind control:

For one not self-controlled, discipline
  Is hard to reach, I believe;
But by the self-controlled man who strives
  It may be attained thru the proper method.

Madhva seems to imply in his gloss that this difficulty is particularly hard on *nāstikas* among others, which is commonsensical enough but hardly traceable in the text.[169]

The fourth verse of the Seventh Chapter has presented problems to both traditional and modern commentators, because the elements mentioned therein are difficult to square with the standard Sāṇkhyan list of 24 *tattvas*. But first the verse (VII:4):

bhūmir āpo 'nalo vāyuḥ
  khaṃ mano buddhir eva ca
ahaṃkāra itī 'yaṃ me
  bhinnā prakṛtir aṣṭadhā

Earth, water, fire, wind,
  Ether, thought-organ, and consciousness,
And I-faculty: thus My
  Nature is divided eight-fold.

Madhva makes two points of some interest here but of doubtful validity. He begins by saying that the verse deals with knowledge,

[167] ibid., p.262. [168] ibid., p.265.
[169] ibid., p.266.

which has already been declared (*pratijñātam jñānam āha*).[170] As Jayatīrtha points out, he has VII:8 (*raso 'ham apsu*) in mind.[171] It comes later. The similarity, moreover, is misleading and the contexts are quite different. Secondly, he suggests that the *mahat* missing from the listing is to be subsumed under *ahaṅkāra*.[172] But another name for *mahat* is *buddhi*: '*Mahat* is the seed of the world. In its psychical aspect, it is called *buddhi* in intellect.'[173] And *buddhi is* mentioned.

There are other curiosities also in Madhva's glosses on the Seventh Chapter. For one, the pregnant utterance in VII:19: *vāsudevaḥ sarvam iti* ('Vāsudeva [kṛṣṇa] is all') is *not* glossed, and VII:21-2 is glossed in a rather sectarian manner. The verses run as follows:

yo-yo yāṃ-yāṃ tanuṃ bhaktaḥ
  śraddhayā 'rcitum icchati
tasya-tasyā 'calāṃ śraddhāṃ
  tām eva vidadhāmy aham

sa tasyā śraddhayā yuktas
  tasyā 'rādhanam īhate
labhate ca tataḥ kāmān
  mayai 'va vihitān hi tān

Whatsoever (divine) form any devotee
  With faith seeks to worship,
For every such (devotee), faith unswerving
  I ordain that same to be.

He, disciplined with that faith,
  Seeks to propitiate that (divine being),
And obtains therefrom his desires,
  Because I myself ordain them.

It is maintained that, while the forms (*tanu*) of Brahmā, etc. when worshipped produce only limited results, this does not apply to the incarnatory forms of Viṣṇu, such as Rāma or Kṛṣṇa.[174] Madhva's glosses on the last two verses of the Seventh Chapter also seem to be somewhat unsatisfactory. The following verses conclude the chapter (VII:29-30):

[170] ibid., p.274. [171] ibid.
[172] ibid. [173] Mahadevan, op.cit., p.121.
[174] Śrīpāda, op.cit., p.294.

jarāmaraṇamokṣāya
mām āśritya yatanti ye
te brahma tad viduḥ kṛtsnam
adhyātmaṃ karma cā 'khilam

sādhibhūtādhidaivaṃ māṃ
sādhiyajñaṃ ca ye viduḥ
prayāṇakāle 'pi ca māṃ
te vidur yuktacetasaḥ

Unto freedom from old age and death
Those who strive, relying on Me,
They know that Brahman entire,
And the over-soul, and action altogether.

Me together with the over-being and the over-divinity,
And with the over-worship, whoso know,
And (who know) Me even at the hour of death,
They (truly) know (Me), with disciplined hearts.

The second line of the first verse could be taken to imply, when read with the first, that human effort could play a role in the achievement of *mokṣa*. But in Madhva's system *mokṣa* is only possible through God's grace, and in this gloss Madhva identifies God with Nārāyaṇa.[175] The only difficulty with this is that the word Nārāyaṇa does not occur in the Gītā at all. On the question of grace Madhva cites the famous verse of Kaṭha Upaniṣad (I.2.23).[176] The emphasis on grace leads Madhva to deny that the first verse could represent a *vidhi*. This seems to suggest a rather closed mind on the point, and one sold on the Augustinian as opposed to the Pelagian notion of grace.

The Eighth Chapter may now be analysed. The opening verses are heavy on metaphysics and run as follows (VIII:1-4):

arjuna uvāca
kiṃ tad brahma kim adhyātmaṃ
kiṃ karma puruṣottama
adhibhūtaṃ ca kiṃ proktam
adhidaivaṃ kim ucyate

[175] ibid., p.299.

[176] S. Radhakrishnan (ed.), *The Principal Upaniṣads* (London: Allen & Unwin, 1953), p.619.

adhiyajñaḥ kathaṃ ko 'tra
dehe 'smin madhusūdana
prayāṇakāle ca kathaṃ
jñeyo 'si niyatātmabhiḥ

śribhagavān uvāca
akṣaraṃ brahma paramaṃ
svabhāvo 'dhyātmam ucyate
bhūtabhāvodbhavakaro
visargaḥ karmasaṃjñitaḥ

adhibhūtaṃ kṣaro bhāvaḥ
puruṣaś cā 'dhidaivatam
adhiyajño 'ham evā 'tra
dehe dehabhṛtāṃ vara

Arjuna said:

1. What is That Brahman? What, Essential Self? What, Work, O Person Supreme? And what is said to be Essential Being? What is called Essential Deity?

2. How and who here in this body is Essential Sacrifice, O Madhusūdana? And how at the time of going hence art thou to be known by men of governed spirit?

The Blessed Lord said:

3. Brahman is the Imperishable, the Supreme; Its Being is called Essential Self; the creative force that causes beings to spring into existence is called Work;

4. Essential Being is perishable existence; Essential Deity is the person; Essential Sacrifice am I, here in the body, O best of men embodied.[177]

Madhva's gloss seems a bit out of joint at places. He begins by stating that what is to be done at the time of death is taught in this chapter. This is true – but that is only a part of what is taught.[178] Nevertheless, this might seem like a quibble compared to what

[177] Hill, op.cit., pp.132-3.
[178] Śrīpāda, op.cit., p.302.

follows. According to Jayatīrtha, *akṣara* does not stand for *brahma* but *prakṛti*, and *paramam* does not qualify *brahma* but *akṣaram*.[179] Thus the answers to the questions are given from a penultimate level.[180] This also serves to protect the Vedas (*akṣara brahma*) from catechetical involvement here.[181] Just as the Vedas are to be protected from implication in VIII:3(a), so God has to be safeguarded from implication with the *jīvas* in VIII:3(b); the word *sva* in *svabhāva* is seen to ensure that. Re VIII:3(c) it is stated that in the expression *bhūtabhāvodbhava, bhūta* and *bhāva* are to be separated, the former referring to animate and the latter to inanimate objects.[182] The question is – can the verse carry this load? Similarly, the word *atra dehe* is carefully understood as avoiding a reference to God's own body.

Madhva in his gloss on VIII:8 plays around with the etymology of *divyam*. The verse runs as follows:

abhyāsayogayuktena
cetasā nā 'nyagāminā
paramaṃ puruṣaṃ divyaṃ
yāti pārthā 'nucintayan

If disciplined in the discipline of practice
Be one's mind, straying to no other object,
To the supreme divine Spirit
He goes, son of Pṛthā, meditating thereon.

It is clear that by *divya* 'divine' is meant, but Madhva takes it to mean that in his own way. He uses the root *divu*, to sport (*divu krīḍāyām*), to explain the word – the sport being God's creative activity (*divyam sṛṣṭyādikrīḍāyuktam*).[183]

The gloss on the eleventh verse of the Ninth Chapter is important, as it states his views on the nature of *avatāras*. The verse runs as follows along with the succeeding one (IX:11-12):

avajānanti māṃ mūḍhā
manuṣīm tanum āśritam
paraṃ bhāvam ajānanto
mama bhūtamaheśvaram

[179] ibid., p.303.
[180] ibid., p.302. [181] ibid.
[182] ibid.
[183] ibid., p.313.

moghāśā moghakarmāṇo
moghajñānā vicetasaḥ
rākṣasīm āsurīṃ cai 'va
prakṛtiṃ mohinīṃ śritāḥ

Fools despise Me
That have assumed human form,
Not knowing the higher state
Of Me, which is the great lord of being.

They are of vain aspirations, of vain actions,
Of vain knowledge, bereft of insight;
In ogrish and demoniac
Nature, which is delusive, they abide.

Madhva maintains throughout his extensive gloss on IX:11 that there is no difference between God as such and his incarnated forms. Although God possesses a body like a human being (*mānuṣavat pratītām tanum*), it is not actually human (*na tu manusyarūpām*).[184] This seems to be in keeping with the text. It is when he discusses the result accruing to those who disregard God as merely human that some difficulties arise, as he seems to over-extend the verse interpretatively. The consequences for those who disregard God are described in IX:12 in negative terms; they are of 'vain aspirations, of vain actions, of vain knowledge, bereft of insight'. But, in an extended comment, he proceeds to show how even those who hate God achieve the fruit of devotion (*kadācit śāpabalāt dveṣiṇo' pi bhaktiphalam bhagavān dadātīti*).[185] It is not the charity of his interpretation which is in question here but its accuracy. It also conflicts with the statement elsewhere in the Gītā (XVI:19-20):

tān ahaṃ dviṣataḥ krūrān
saṃsāreṣu narādhamān
kṣipāmy ajasram aśubhān
āsurīṣv eva yoniṣu

āsurīṃ yonim āpannā
mūḍhā janmani-janmani
mām aprāpyai 'va kaunteya
tato yānty adhamāṃ gatim

[184] ibid., p.338. [185] ibid., p.339.

These cruel and hateful
  Base men, in the ceaseless round of existences,
These wicked ones, I constantly hurl
  Into demoniac wombs alone.

Having come into a demoniac womb,
  Deluded in birth after birth,
Not by any means attaining Me, son of Kuntī,
  Then they go to the lowest goal.

The point, however, needs to be understood carefully, for a somewhat muted criticism of Madhva is being offered here. He does not claim that those who hate God are nevertheless saved by God.[186] What he claims is that those who were former devotees but turned away from God may be saved, as in the case of Śiśupāla, or that even those who hate God may be saved by the intercession of devotees, as in the case of Hiraṇyakaśipu and Prahlāda.[187] Our criticism is that these considerations are out of context. By contrast, while he over-glosses this verse, Madhva does not gloss the key expression *avidhipūrvakam* in IX:23 at all! And while he thus gives no interpretation whatever to a key expression, he seems to over-interpret certain expressions in the same chapter and to under-interpret others.

A case of over-interpretation is supplied by IX:29:

samo 'haṃ sarvabhūteṣu
  na me dveṣyo 'sti na priyaḥ
ye bhajanti tu māṃ bhaktyā
  mayi te teṣu ca 'py aham

I am the same to all beings,
  No one is hateful or dear to Me;
But those who revere Me with devotion,
  They are in Me and I too am in them.

The purport of Madhva's gloss is elucidated by Jayatīrtha thus: 'In the case of both devotees and detractors on account of affection and enmity you dispense accordingly: a large measure of happiness to someone of limited devotion. Contrariwise, in the case of someone who is inimical to you even a little, you dispense sorrow in a large

[186] ibid., p.340. [187] ibid.

measure'.[188] These remarks seem to go against the spirit of the whole verse.

The next few verses suggest under-interpretation. They run as follows (IX:30-4) and conclude the chapter:

api cet sudurācāro
bhajate mām ananyabhāk
sādhur eva sa mantavyaḥ
samyag vyavasito hi saḥ

kṣipraṃ bhavati dharmātmā
śaśvacchāntiṃ nigacchati
kaunteya pratijānīhi
na me bhaktaḥ praṇaśyati

māṃ hi pārtha vyapāśritya
ye 'pi syuḥ pāpayonayaḥ
strivo vaiśyas tathā śūdrās
te 'pi yānti parāṃ gatim

kiṃ punar brāhmaṇāḥ puṇyā
bhaktā rājarṣayas tathā
anityam asukhaṃ lokam
imaṃ prāpya bhajasva mām

manmanā bhava madbhakto
madyājī māṃ namaskuru
mām evai 'syasi yuktvai 'vam
ātmānaṃ matparāyaṇaḥ

Even if a very evil doer
Reveres Me with single devotion,
He must be regarded as righteous in spite of all;
For he has the right resolution.

Quickly his soul becomes righteous,
And he goes to eternal peace.
Son of Kuntī, make sure of this:
No devotee of Mine is lost.

[188] ibid., p.352.

For if they take refuge in Me, son of Pṛthā,
Even those who may be of base origin,
Women, men of the artisan caste, and serfs too,
Even they go to the highest goal.

How much more virtuous brahmans,
And devout royal seers, too!
A fleeting and joyless world
This; having attained it, devote thyself to Me.

Be Me-minded, devoted to Me;
Worshipping Me, pay homage to Me;
Just to Me shalt thou go, having thus disciplined
Thyself, fully intent on Me.

In IX:30 Kṛṣṇa seems to offer open-hearted acceptance to all sinners, but Madhva contracts the scope of the all-encompassing embrace by remarking that generally a devotee of God is not an evil-doer (*na bhavaty eva prāyas tadbhaktaḥ sudurācāraḥ*).[189] The trend is retained in the gloss on IX:31, where it is said that the devotee is to be regarded as good because he soon becomes righteous. But Madhva adds: 'This happens only in the case of gods and those possessing elements of divinity' (*deva-devāṁśādiṣv eva ca tad bhavati*).[190] What is even more interesting is that, while the Gītā seems to disregard moral turpitude in relation to devotion, Madhva reverses the trend in his gloss by quoting the Upaniṣads on the moral qualifications required for the spiritual path. He cites Kaṭha I.2.24: as *nāvirato duścaritān nāśānto nāsamāhitaḥ*[191] (not he who has ceased from bad conduct, not he who is not tranquil, not he who is not composed...).[192] Significantly, Madhva has *nābhakto* for *nāśānto*![193]

Those aforementioned verses are very significant because they seem to open up the possibility of salvation to all. And they are particularly important for Madhva, for if left unqualified, they militate against his doctrine of eternal damnation which he explicitly develops in his subsequent gloss on XVI:20.

The first two verses of the Tenth Chapter call for comment on both textual and contextual grounds. They run as follows (X:1-2):

[189] ibid. [190] ibid., p.353.
[191] Radhakrishnan, *Principal Upaniṣads*, p.620.
[192] Robert Ernest Hume, *The Thirteen Principal Upaniṣads* (Oxford: Oxford University Press, 1968) p.350.
[193] Śrīpāda, op.cit., p.353.

bhūya eva mahābāho
śṛṇu me paramaṃ vacaḥ
yat te 'haṃ prīyamāṇāya
vakṣyāmi hitakāmyayā

na me viduḥ suragaṇāḥ
prabhavaṃ na maharṣayaḥ
aham ādir hi devānāṃ
maharṣīṇāṃ ca sarvaśaḥ

Yet further, great-armed one,
Hear My highest message,
Which to thee, that delightest in it, I
Shall declare, in that I wish thee well.

The throngs of gods know not My
Origin, nor yet the great seers.
For I am the starting-point of the gods,
And of the great seers, altogether.

Madhva takes the form *prīyamāṇa*[194] in the sense of one taking delight. Thus Arjuna is shown as delighted, and this according to Jayatīrtha raises the question of reconciling Arjuna's present pleasant mood with his earlier depression (I:47 – *śokasaṁvigna-mānasaḥ*).[195] It is explained that the grief was caused by attachment to relatives, but now Arjuna is gratified by the divine discourse. The remarks, though not out of court, seem out of place. In the next verse it is the interpretation of the word *prabhavam* that calls for comment. Jayatīrtha identifies the issue: some have interpreted the word *prabhava* as referring to God's power (*sāmarthya*) and others to his origin (*utpatti*). Madhva wants to accept both the senses and say something more.[196] He comments: *prabhavam prabhāvam. madīyām jagadutpattiṁ vā. tad vaśatvāt tasyety ucyate.*[197] The meaning is progressively expanded. *Prabhava* means glory which the gods, etc. do not know in full – nor know its manifestation in God's divine origin, or in the origination of the universe, which orignates from Him. Is all this necessary? But the other points made in this context need not invite criticism. When it is said that the gods, etc. do not know Kṛṣṇa's origin, the point is that he has none; otherwise in their omniscience they would have known it. The explanation of *ahamādir*

[194] ibid., p.357.
[195] ibid.
[196] ibid., p.358.
[197] ibid.

hi is not without merit: how can he have an origin who controls creation itself![198] Our criticism applies only to the early part of the gloss, but it does extend to Madhva's explanation of the word *anādi* in the succeeding verse (X:3), as *anaḥ ceṣṭayitā ādiś ca sarvasya*[199] – he is *anādi* because he is the instigator and the origin of all. Neat but forced.

This exercise carries one through to the Thirteenth Chapter, which provides several instances of what would appear to be cases of sectarian bias. Consider, for instance, XIII:30:

yadā bhūtapṛthagbhāvam
ekastham anupaśyati
tata eva ca vistāram
brahma sampadyate tadā

When the various states of beings
He perceives as abiding in One,
And from that alone their expansion,
Then he attains Brahman.

Madhva takes *ekastham* to mean established in Viṣṇu: *ekastham ekasmin viṣṇau sthitam. tata eva ca viṣṇoḥ vistāram.*[200] This seems to involve a monotheistic over-interpretation of the verse. Bhagavadgītā XIV:4 provides an instance of a feminine theological over-interpretation of an even greater degree, wherein *mahat* is first identified with *prakṛti*, which is triply distinguished within itself as *śrī, bhū* and *durgā*, and these are distinguished from *umā, sarasvatī*, etc.[201] Such an elaboration seems highly contrived when the verse is read:

sarvayoniṣu kaunteya
mūrtayaḥ sambhavanti yāḥ
tāsām brahma mahad yonir
aham bījapradaḥ pitā

In all wombs, son of Kuntī,
Whatsoever forms originate,
Of them great Brahman is the womb,
I am the father that furnishes the seed.

[198] ibid. [199] ibid., p.359.
[200] ibid., p.449. [201] ibid., p.453.

Further examples of the importation of Dvaitic theology into the exegesis of the Gītā are provided by the Fifteenth Chapter, the early verses of which run as follows (XV:1-2):

śrībhagavān uvāca
ūrdhvamūlam adhaḥśākham
aśvattham prāhur avyayam
chandāṃsi yasya parṇāni
yas taṃ veda sa vedavit

adhaś co 'rdhvaṃ prasṛtās tasya śākhā
guṇapravṛddhā viṣayapravālāḥ
adhaś ca mūlāny anusaṃtatāni
karmānubandhīni manusyaloke

The Blessed One said:

With roots aloft and branches below,
The eternal peepal-tree, they say –
Whose leaves are the (Vedic) hymns,
Who knows it, he knows the Veda.

Below and upward extend its branches,
Nourished by the Strands, with the objects of sense as sprouts;
Below also are stretched forth its roots,
Resulting in actions, in the world of men.

Madhva identifies *ūrdhva* in the verse with Viṣṇu, and Jayatīrtha explains transitionally that Viṣṇu is to be identified with the sun.[202] The exegesis is imaginative, and would perhaps have pleased Max Müller, but it seems to bear little direct relation to the text. Similarly, the roots (*mūlāni*) are identified by Madhva with *bhagavadrūpāṇi*, or forms of God, because it is God who dispenses the fruits of karma (*bhagavānapi karmānubandhena hi phalaṃ dadāti*).[203]

A much more striking example of how Madhva's theological orientation influences his interpretation of the Gītā is provided by XV:8:

śarīraṃ yad avāpnoti
yac cā 'py utkrāmatī 'śvaraḥ
gṛhītvai 'tāni saṃyāti
vāyur gandhān ivā 'śayāt

[202] ibid., p.463. [203] ibid., p.465.

When he acquires a body,
And also when he departs (from it), the Lord
Moves taking them along,
As the wind odours from their home.

Most scholars are agreed that the word *īśvara* here does *not* mean God but the embodied soul. But Madhva argues otherwise. The preceding verse says that the individual soul *karṣati*, or draws along the senses and the mind. According to Madhva, this creates the impression that the *jīva* is an independent actor, while in his system God alone acts (*ekaḥ sarvottamaḥ jñeyaḥ eka eva karoti yat*).[204] Thus Madhva, consistently with his philosophical outlook, takes *īśvara* in its primary sense as God, and says that verse eight is designed to remove the mistaken impression which may have been generated by the previous verse that the soul can act on its own. 'Whenever the Jīva obtains a body or leaves it, then it is God who takes hold of these (senses) and goes (to another body).'[205] He then quotes several verses in support of his position. His position may have considerable support elsewhere, but seems forced on the Gītā here, though the appearance of the word Īśvara does impart to it some degree of verisimilitude.

A similar situation arises in the case of Madhva's gloss on XVI:5, where his argument seems to be grammatically ingenious but contextually forced. The verse runs as follows:

daivī sampad vimokṣāya
nibandhāyā 'surī matā
mā śucaḥ sampadaṃ daivīm
abhijāto 'si pāṇḍava

The divine lot leads to release,
The demoniac lot is considered to lead to bondage.
Be not grieved: to the divine lot
Thou art born, son of Pāṇḍu.

He glosses *abhijātaḥ* as *pratijātaḥ*[206] in effect saying that Arjuna is not 'born to the divine lot' but rather 'reborn to the divine lot'. The grammatical point turns on the use of the accusative in *daivīm* and is

[204] Mahadevan, op.cit., p.156, n.21.
[205] Śrīpāda, op.cit., p.470. The parenthetical insertions are based on Jayatīrtha, op.cit., p.471.
[206] ibid., p.480.

dealt with in detail by Jayatīrtha. Although ingenious, it does not seem sufficiently convincing to alter the generally accepted sense. The gloss on XVI:20 presents a similar situation:

āsurīṃ yonim āpannā
mūḍhā janmani-janmani
mām aprāpyai 'va kaunteya
tato yānty adhamāṃ gatim

Having come into a demoniac womb,
Deluded in birth after birth,
Not by any means attaining Me, son of Kuntī,
Then they go to the lowest goal.

It is apparently in accord with the Gītā. As Jayatīrtha says and Madhva implies, eternal damnation (*nityanarakam*)[207] is in store for those who are born in demoniac wombs. Many Western scholars seem to accept or at least lean towards such an interpretation. Thus R.C. Zaehner:

> It is often asserted that the Hindus (except Madhva and his school) do not believe in eternal damnation. If, however, by damnation we mean eternal separation from God, then the Gītā, in these verses, seems to accept precisely this. These 'vilest among men' have no excuse, not even that of ignorance, for they hate the God 'who dwells in their bodies'; and God, being thus deliberately rejected, so far from helping them, 'hurls them' ever again 'into devilish wombs' so that in the end they 'tread the lowest way'. If, then, the blessed find in the 'highest way' their final release from phenomenal existence, does it not follow that those who 'tread the lowest way' are similarly 'released' into a timeless inferno of self-destruction? The lowest forms of incarnate life, according to Manu (12.42), are inanimate objects, insects, fish, snakes, and so on. Once one has reached this level, it is difficult to see what hope there is – so, according to the Gītā, there is no alternative but to 'tread the lowest way': the gates of hell are now wide open to receive him.[208]

What, then, is the difficulty with Madhva's interpretation? The difficulties are twofold. First, Madhva believes in eternal damnation, and so it is easy to see why he would have little hesitation in

[207] ibid.
[208] Zaehner, op.cit., p.373.

accepting such a position here. But this leads to the second and more vital point: does the Gītā contain a doctrine of eternal damnation?

It is true some scholars have hinted that the universalism of the Gītā may be subject to this very serious limitation – eternal damnation. Thus it has been suggested, on the basis of III:32[209] and XVI:19-21,[210] that the possibility of the Gītā teaching such a doctrine cannot be ruled out. A reading of the Gītā as a whole, however, especially when verses such as IV:36, IX:29-34 are kept in mind and the parallel between the *pāpayoni* of IX:32 and *āsurayoni* of XVI:19 is recognised, makes it unlikely that the Gītā subscribes to such a doctrine, though we can see how the fierceness of the condemnation of persistent perversity at some points would tempt one to raise the possibility. It should be noted that the *caramaśloka* of XVIII:66 offers release from all (*sarva*) sins.

The case is a close one, and perhaps not a closed one as yet. But in the next example Madhva can be seen as forcing the meaning much more clearly. This example is provided by his gloss on XVII:26:

sadbhāve sādhubhāve ca
sad ity etat prayujyate
praśaste karmaṇi tathā
sacchabdaḥ pārtha yujyate

In the meaning of 'real' and in the meaning of 'good'
The word *Sat* is employed;
Likewise of a laudable action
The word *Sat* is used, son of Pṛthā.

Madhva maintains that *sadbhāvaśabdena prajananam sūcitam*: the use of the word *sadbhāva* indicates origination.[211] *Sat* indicates existence not creation. Jayatīrtha pleads the case on behalf of Madhva thus: 'Creation involves imparting existence to what is formerly non-existent. Although the word *sadbhāva* denotes only being, even so here as in this case one wishes to speak of Brahman as the creator of the universe it is taken as leading to the generation of a special being (i.e. becoming)'.[212] It is not at all clear why Brahman must be regarded as the creator in this context.

The last chapter also provides a few instances in which Madhva's

[209] A.L. Herman, *The Bhagavadgītā* (Springfield, Ill.: Thomas, 1973), p.126.
[210] Minor, op.cit., pp.350-1.
[211] Śrīpāda, op.cit., p.496. [212] ibid., pp.496-7.

interpretation of the text seems somewhat erratic. XVIII:14-15 is a case in point:

adhiṣṭhānaṃ tathā kartā
karaṇaṃ ca pṛthagvidham
vividhāś ca pṛthakceṣṭā
daivaṃ cai 'vā 'tra pañcamam

śarīravāṅmanobhir yat
karma prārabhate naraḥ
nyāyyaṃ vā viparītaṃ vā
pañcai 'te tasya hetavaḥ

The (material) basis, the agent too,
And the instruments of various sorts,
And the various motions of several kinds,
And just Fate as the fifth of them.

With body, speech, or mind, whatever
Action a man undertakes,
Whether it be lawful or the reverse,
These are its five factors.

This verse has generated many controversial interpretations, perhaps artificially. But apart from the contentious nature, or otherwise, of the verse, Madhva straightaway identifies *kartā* with *viṣṇuḥ: kartā viṣṇuḥ, sa hi sarvakartā ity uktam. jīvasya cākartṛtve pramāṇam uktam* (Viṣṇu is the doer, he indeed is the all-doer, it is said. And evidence has been adduced to indicate the non-doership of the *jīva*).[213] It is clear from the context, however, that the individual agent is meant.

Madhva's gloss on XVIII:17 raises an interesting issue. The verse runs as follows:

yasya nā 'haṃkṛto bhāvo
buddhir yasya na lipyate
hatvā 'pi sa imāṃl lokān
na hanti na nibadhyate

Whose state (of mind) is not egoised,
Whose intelligence is not stained,

[213] ibid., p.504.

He, even tho he slays these folk,
  Does not slay, and is not bound (by his actions).

Zaehner thinks that the Gītā teaches a dangerous doctrine here:

Killing only takes place on the phenomenal plane, not on that of the Absolute. This disturbing doctrine had already been proclaimed in 2.18-19 ... as it had been in the Upanishads: here it is reaffirmed with a vengeance. As the dialogue draws to its end Krishna's thoughts become ever more concentrated on the immediate matter in hand – the successful prosecution of the war.[214]

These remarks serve to provide a focus for Madhva's gloss. For Madhva says that 'he who gets bound slightly is one who has a trace of egoism remaining in him (*yas tvīṣad badhyate sa īṣad ahaṅkārī ca*)'.[215] Thus according to Madhva it is possible to get bound to the extent that the trace of ego remains. The point is developed by Jayatīrtha, who cites the slaying of Vṛtra by Indra, and comments: 'Indeed even in the case of one free from egoism such as Indra, etc. slight (*īṣat*) bondage is seen as by the killing of Vṛtra.'[216] Thus Madhva is more circumspect than others in interpreting the verse as a *carte blanche* for violence by drawing attention to the fact that even the presence of a trace of the ego causes Karmic complications.

It may be best to conclude this section with a glaring example of what happens when Madhva's theological presuppositions get the better of his otherwise sensitive and acute mind. The example is provided by XVIII:20:

sarvabhūteṣu yenai 'kaṃ
  bhāvam avyayam īkṣate
avibhaktaṃ vibhakteṣu
  taj jñānaṃ viddhi sāttvikam

Whereby in all beings one
  Unchanging condition men perceive,
Unmanifold in the manifold,
  Know that that knowledge is of goodness.

For no reason based on the text, but obvious in the light of his Vaiṣṇava background, Madhva glosses *ekaṃ bhāvam* as *viṣṇum*.[217]

[214] Zaehner, op.cit., p.388. [215] Śrīpāda, op.cit., p.506.
[216] ibid., p.506. In *īṣat* see Pāṇini III.3.126.
[217] Śrīpāda, op.cit., p.511.

4.

Madhva seems to share the fate of the other classical exegetes of the Gītā, such as Śaṅkara and Rāmānuja. All of them operate from within a given philosophical system, while commenting on a work which may not possess a system at all, or possess a system all its own. All of them enhance our understanding of some of the verses and open up new exegetical possibilities. On the other hand, out of enthusiasm for their own views, they also read these views back into the Gītā. This is a wider phenomenon of which the commentaries provide only one example. It may be best to conclude this last chapter with some observations on this general phenomenon by S.C. Roy:

> It is, however, not rarely that an Indian textbook of the oldest period, which was conceived and composed in a purely non-sectarian and universalistic spirit, is taken by later commentators to be a sectarian product and interpreted accordingly. We have already quoted as an example of this Mádhva's commentary on the Bṛhadáraṇyaka Upaniṣad ... Similarly, the Vedánta Sûtras are interpreted by Rámânûja in a way as if the author of the Sûtras were a staunch Vaiṣṇava, and what is more, Puranic names of gods and goddesses like Śrî or Lakṣmî and Viṣṇu which have long been associated with sectarian modes of worship are freely employed as substitutes for Brahma and Prakṛti.[218] The explanation of such mode of interpretation is to be found in the fact that when a particular sect of religion or school of philosophy becomes popular and tends to gain ascendency, there is natural inclination on the part of its adherents to connect it with older ways of thought and more authoritative texts of a remoter period, and thereby to establish their own favourite system on ancient traditions and scriptures. This leads to the twisting and turning of these ancient texts, and far-fetched sectarian and scholastic interpretations being put on their words in the light of later and more

[218] Sometimes the translators end up being misled by the commentators. Thus G. Thibaut, who translated Rāmānuja's commentary into English (and Śaṅkara's as well), 'stresses the influence on the Brahma-sūtra of Bhāgavata thought which begins with the *Bhagavad-Gītā*, but this is due to the fact that he is affected by Rāmānuja's commentary, for the *Brahma-sūtra* actually criticises and rejects the Bhāgavata doctrines' (Hajime Nakamura, *A History of Early Vedānta Philosophy* Part I [Delhi: Motilal Banarsidass, 1983], p.496, n.5).

developed thought. This has happened in the case of Śaṅkara, Rámánûja, Mádhva and other eminent scholars with regard to their treatment of the Upaniṣads, the Gîtá and Brahmasûtras.[219]

[219] S.C. Roy, *The Bhagavad-Gītā and Modern Scholarship* (London: Luzac, 1941), pp.235-6. It may be added that the universalistic spirit of the Gītā has been questioned (see Robert N. Minor, 'The Gītā's way as the only way', *Philosophy East and West* XXX(3) (1980), pp.339-54), despite forewarnings by S.C. Roy (op.cit., p.235) against succumbing, as Tilak did, to this temptation (ibid., pp.234-5). The diacritical marks in the quotation from Roy may appear quaint to the modern reader but conform to his text.

Conclusion

1.

In the previous chapters several ancient and classical interpretations of the Gītā were examined. We are now ready to ask, if perhaps not to answer, the question: which one of them, if any, is true or correct?

In order for us to say that there is a correct interpretation of the Gītā we must rest secure in the belief that there is, or can be, a true or correct interpretation. There seem to be several possible responses to this issue.

Let us first consider a modern text-critical response. This would argue that, as the Gītā is a given text revealed at a point in time, its correct interpretation is provided by what the author intended it to mean at that point in time. Even if this hermeneutical stance is uncritically accepted, we face a host of problems. First, can we be certain of the age of the Gītā? This is a thorny issue in itself, though there seems to be a growing tendency to assign it to the second century B.C. Even if this is accepted we must possess a clear picture of the history, culture and society of that period, not to mention philological accuracy. The pitfalls of the approach can be dramatised by a simple consideration. The Mauryan Dynasty was replaced by the Śuṅga in about 187 B.C.[1] Now, was the Gītā, if composed in the second century B.C., composed before, during, or after this critical dynastic transition? If the text is to be understood in the light of its times, this is a vital item of information, about which we have no clue.

Secondly, is the Gītā a single or a composite text? This is another thorny problem with which students of the Gītā are familiar. If it is a

[1] R.C. Majumdar (ed.), *The Age of Imperial Unity* (Bombay: Bharatiya Vidya Bhavan, 1960), p.90.

composite text and we succeed in dissecting it, the dating of each component will be the next step, which will serve to multiply the problem indicated above many times over. It could be argued that the Gītā as such may be taken to have come into being from the time of the emergence of the composite text. This helps reduce the dimension of the problem, though it does not remove it; but it raises another. If the Gītā is a composite text, would it not be more likely to be susceptible to multiple understandings right from its birth?

Thus, even if there is a correct interpretation from a text-critical point of view, it may remain inaccessible. To be sure, advances can be made along the line, as in biblical studies, and perhaps we may have to travel hopefully forever; but this does not make the journey any less worthwhile. All that is being suggested is that we may not jump to destinations; I obviously mean conclusions.

The text-critical approach involves a crucial assumption – that the text did possess a single or singular message in the context of its own times. We should not put too fine a point on this: after all it could be an identifiable message that there are many identifiable messages. But once this possibility is conceded, the danger is that for a religious tradition the medium can *become* the message, instead of *having* a message – which indeed it may have had originally. And this may well have been the case with the Gītā. But I am getting ahead of myself. For we must here revert to the question raised in the Introduction: are Hindu scriptures meant to be univalent or multivalent?

There seem to be two clearly identifiable responses to this question from within the Hindu religious tradition. The first, which seems to be the majority view, is that the texts are univalent. The various schools of Vedānta, for instance, have engaged in prolonged polemics over the centuries on the issue of the correct interpretation of scriptural passages. In fact the very word for debate in Sanskrit – *śāstrārtha* – seems to imply a debate conducted to determine the (correct) purport of scripture or scriptural text. The great debate among the philosophical schools has not been on the question of whether the scriptures have one or many correct interpretations, but rather on what is the one correct scriptural interpretation. Thus, at the risk of his popularity among modern Hindus, K. Satchidananda Murty has pointed out that, according to the 'view of Jaimini and Kumārila (acceptable to all authorities such as Śankara and Rāmānuja)', 'the Vedic faith is exclusive', which 'shows that Hinduism is as exclusive as the Semitic faiths and brooks no rivals. So modern exponents of Hinduism should make it explicit that such statements as "All religions are true" are made only on their own authority and do not represent the orthodox Hindu tradition,'[2] in the sense that the orthodox Hindu tradition often takes the view that only one scriptural interpretation, and that too of its own scripture, is true.

The second reponse has been to allow for multiple interpretations. The passage cited below from S. Radhakrishnan concludes with an interesting expression – *anekārthatā* (manifoldness of meaning) from the text Nyāyasudhā – an expression which quite clearly allows for multiple interpretations. 'The Vedas bring together the different ways in which the religious-minded of that age experienced reality and describe the general principles of religious knowledge and growth. As the experiences themselves are of a varied character, so their records are many-sided (*viśvatomukham*) or "suggestive of many interpretations" (*anekārthatām*).'[3]

The force of this position is strengthened by the fact that one of the oldest interpreters of the Vedas, Yāska (*c*.500 B.C.) actually does see the Vedas as suggestive of many interpretations, for he 'mentions several kinds of interpreters: etymologists, ritualists, polytheists, *ātmavādins* (those who sought spiritual truths), and lastly those who said that the Veda is nonsense useful in magic (the school of Kautsa). Yāska himself admits that there are all kinds of "*mantra*-seeings" in the Veda, some expressing "high" ideas and some "low", and he thus implies that different interpreters may take anyone of these ideas as the "engrossing theme of the Veda", and then interpret the whole of the Veda in that light. He, for instance, mentions various views regarding the Vedic gods – whether there are many or one, whether thay have any shape or not – and states his own view that they are all aspects or manifestations of the one Ātman.'[4]

There is some evidence to suggest that, not only was this multivalency of scripture recognised within the Hindu tradition, but it also led to some soul-searching, or at least induced introspection, among the transmitters of the tradition. One of the more frequently quoted verses of the Mahābhārata contains a clear recognition of such multivalency, not only in the revealed, and hence primary, texts of the tradition (*śruti*), but also in its secondary literature (*smṛti*). It runs:

[2] K. Satchidananda Murty, *Revelation and Reason in Advaita Vedānta* (New York: Columbia University Press, 1959), p.219; see also pp.51-2 and 271-2.

[3] S. Radhakrishnan, *The Hindu View of Life* (London: Unwin Books, 1974 [first published 1927]), p.15.

[4] Satchidananda Murty, op.cit., p.311.

śrutayo vibhinnāḥ smṛtayo vibhinnāḥ
naiko munir yasya vacaḥ pramāṇam
dharmasya tattvaṃ nihitaṃ guhāyāṃ
mahājano yena gataḥ sa panthāḥ[5]

The (texts of the) *śruti* differ; the (texts of the) *smṛti* differ; there is no one sage whose word (alone) is authoritative. The essence of *dharma* is hidden in a cave. That which is traversed by the virtuous (lit. great) is the path (to follow).

The question which must now be asked is this: Which of these two approaches has the Hindu religious tradition itself adopted towards the Gītā?

The question is difficult to answer. On the one hand we could argue that the Gītā, as one of the three basic texts of Vedānta (*prasthānatrya*),[6] became naturally drawn into the polemics among the Vedantic schools, as is widely known, and as has been documented in this book. Such polemics assume that scriptural texts possess one correct meaning. But while this seems to hold overall, we discover that the scholiasts sometimes indicate several possible meanings for the same verse, suggesting thereby that at least *individual* passages could be multivalent, if not the whole text. One example from Śaṅkara must suffice. It is drawn from his gloss on XVIII:41:

brāhmaṇakṣatriyaviśāṃ
  śūdrāṇāṃ ca paraṃtapa
karmāṇi pravibhaktāni
  svabhāvaprabhavair guṇaiḥ

Of brahmans, warriors, and artisans,
  And of serfs, scorcher of the foe,
The actions are distinguished
  According to the Strands that spring from their innate nature.[7]

The expression in question is *svabhāvaprabhavair guṇaiḥ* (according to the strands that spring from their inner nature). Śaṅkara asks,

[5] See K.B. Panda, *Sanātan Dharma and Law* (Cuttack: Naitika Punaruthān Samiti, no date), p.82 with first word of quote corrected.

[6] Hajime Ṇakamura, *A History of Early Vedānta Philosophy* Part I (Delhi: Motilal Banarsidass, 1983), p.300.

[7] Franklin Edgerton, *The Bhagavad Gītā* Part I (Cambridge, Massachusetts: Harvard University Press, 1944), pp.170, 171.

after stating that the castes are divided: by what standard are they divided? And he goes on to say:

> According to the qualities (*guṇas*) born of nature. Nature (*svabhava*) is the Iśvara's *prakṛiti*, the Maya made up of the three *guṇas*. It is in accordance with the *guṇas* of the *prakṛiti* that duties – such as serenity and the like – are assigned to the Brahmaṇas, etc. respectively.
>
> Or to explain in another way: The source of the Brahmaṇa's nature (*svabhava*) is the *guṇa* of Sattva; the source of the Kshatriya's nature is Rajas and Sattva, the latter being subordinate to the former; the source of the Vaiśya's nature is Rajas and Tamas, the latter being subordinate to the former; the source of the Sudra's nature is Tamas and Rajas, the latter being subordinate to the former. For, as we see, the characteristic features of their nature are serenity, lordliness, activity, and dullness respectively.
>
> Or to interpret yet in another way: – Nature (*svabhava*) is the tendency (*saṁskara, vasana*) in living beings acquired by them in the past births, and manifesting itself in the present birth by way of being ready to yield its effects: and this nature is the source of the *guṇas*, it being impossible for the *guṇas* to manifest themselves without a cause. The assertion that nature (*saṁskara, vasana*) is the cause (of the *guṇas*) means that it is a kind of specific cause. The duties, such as serenity, are assigned to the four classes in accordance with the *guṇas* of Sattva, Rajas and Tamas, which are brought into manifestation by their respective natural tendencies, and which lead to those duties as their natural effects.[8]

It is clear that three possible interpretations have been provided. It is also clear that they are not contradictory, though they are different.

The idea of the divisions of society into *varṇas*, or classes, is suggestive of another line of thought which has little to do with the passage cited above but is not without relevance to the issue under examination. For could not the reason why a scripture is differently interpreted by different social groups be that society consists of different classes – whether they be two, as in Marx, or three as in Dumézil, or four as in the Hindu *varṇas*, or many more like the numerous ethnic nodes in American or Soviet society, for instance.

[8] A. Mahādeva Śāstri, *The Bhagavad-Gītā with the commentary of Śri Śankarachārya* (sic) (Madras: V. Ramaswamy Sastrulu & Sons, 1972), pp.472-3, italics added. Śaṅkara is not alone in offering optional interpretations; Rāmānuja does so as well. See Edgerton, op.cit., Part I, p.184.

In this way the multivalency of scripture could be related to the sociology of knowledge. These comments, of course, are offered not as gospel truth but as potentially fruitful suggestions. For not only the structure of society, but the structure of consciousness, could be related to this multivalency. For instance, it is usual to consider a religious scripture as 'inspired' by those who comment on it within a tradition. But it often turns out that the commentators, while admitting in principle that the entire text is inspired, in practice treat some parts of it as more inspired than others. The tradition of *mahāvākyas* in Vedānta clearly testifies to this.[9] In relation to the Gītā it is revealing that many exegetes select some verse, or set of verses, as representing its core or essence. Śaṅkara acts thus;[10] so does the Śrīvaiṣṇava tradition associated with Rāmānuja.[11] Among modern Hindus, Gandhi[12] acts in this way; and even some modern Western scholars also.[13] Thus the psychology of knowledge becomes as important as the sociology of knowledge. Nor should history be neglected in this context, for the Hindu texts themselves suggest that the *same* statement could possess a *different* message for the recipients of the message, depending on their level. A somewhat poetic, but nevertheless relevant, illustration is provided by the Bṛhadāraṇyaka Upaniṣad (V:2):

> The threefold offspring of *prajā-pati*, gods, men and demons, lived with their father *prajā-pati* as students of sacred knowledge. Having completed their studentship the gods said, 'Please tell (instruct) us, sir.' To them then, he uttered the syllable *da* (and asked) 'Have you understood?' They (said): 'We have understood, you said to us "*dāmyata*", "control yourselves".' He said, 'Yes, you have understood.'
>
> Then the men said to him, 'Please tell (instruct) us, sir.' To them he uttered the same syllable *da* (and asked) 'Have you understood?' They said 'We have understood. You said to us "give".' He said, 'Yes, you have understood.'
>
> Then the demons said to him, 'Please tell (instruct) us, sir.' To them he uttered the same syllable *da* and asked, 'Have you

[9] Satchidananda Murty, op.cit., pp.69-98.

[10] W.D.P. Hill, *The Bhagavadgītā* (Oxford University Press, 1969), p.167, n.1.

[11] John Braisted Carman, *The Theology of Rāmānuja* (New Haven: Yale University Press, 1974), p.215. It is interesting in view of the present discussion that Rāmānuja offers *two* explanations of Bhagavadgītā XVIII:66 (ibid., pp.215-16).

[12] Arvind Sharma, 'The Gandhian hermeneutical approach to the Gita: a case-study of ahimsa', *Indian Cultures Quarterly* 30(4):1-11.

[13] R.C. Zaehner, *The Bhagavad-Gītā* (Oxford: Clarendon Press, 1969), p.185.

> understood?' They said, 'We have understood, you said to us, "*dayadhvam*", "be compassionate". He said, 'Yes, you have understood.' This very thing the heavenly voice of thunder repeats *da, da, da*, that is, control yourselves, give, be compassionate. One should practise this same triad, self-control, giving and compassion.[14]

On either view – that the scriptures are univalent or multivalent – the apparent ambiguity of the text is not in question. On the univalent view such ambiguity is only temporary, until the one correct interpretation is established. On the multivalent view it is creative. But both approaches seem to concede – one implicitly and the other explicitly – the existence of such ambiguity. Now the Gītā has been approached from both points of view: each of the scholiasts claims to offer the correct interpretation. Saṅkara, the first major scholiast, for instance, clearly sets out to establish the precise meaning of the Gītā.[15] But the Bhagavadgītā has not always been allied with a single philosophical school by Hindu scholiasts. In fact, when the view is developed that the six orthodox schools of Hindu thought do not represent rival, but rather complementary, pictures of reality, the Gītā is pressed into service by Vijñānabhikṣu (*c.*1550 A.D.) who, 'while fully recognising the difference between the six systems of philosophy, tried to discover a common truth behind them all, and to point out how they can be studied together, or rather in succession, and how all of them are meant to lead honest students into the way of truth.'[16] While developing this position, he quotes from the Gītā when accommodating the Nyāya and Vaiśeṣika schools in his general scheme thus:

> If therefore we read the following verse from the Bhagavad-gītā III:29:– 'Those who are deceived by the constituent *guṇas* of *prakriti*, cling to the workings of the *guṇas* (*sattva, rajas*, and *tamas*). Let therefore those who know the whole truth take care not to distract

[14] The first *da* = *dāmyata*, the second *datta* and the third *dayadhvam*. See S. Radhakrishnan (ed.), *The Principal Upaniṣads* (London: Allen & Unwin, 1963), pp.289-90. The principle of different levels of understanding and competence is applied further at the level of human beings themselves in the concept of *adhikāra-bheda*, or criterion of eligibility (see T.M.P. Mahadevan, *Outlines of Hinduism* [Bombay: Chetana, 1971], p.21; Troy Wilson Organ, *Hinduism: Its Historical Development* [Woodbury, New York: Barron's Educational Series, 1974], pp.57, 157, 161, 204, 214).

[15] A. Mahādeva Śāstri, op.cit., p.4.

[16] F. Max Müller, *The Six Systems of Indian Philosophy* (London: Longmans, 1899), pp.590-1.

> men of moderate understanding who do not as yet know the whole truth;' – we see that here the followers of the Nyāya and Vaiseshika systems, though they hold to the false belief that the Self can be an agent, are not treated as totally in error, but only as not knowing the whole truth, if compared with the *sāmkhyas*, who know the whole truth. Even such knowledge as they possess leads step by step by means of the lower impassiveness (*apara-vairāgya*) to liberation; while the knowledge of the *sāmkhyas* only, as compared with the lower knowledge, is absolute knowledge, and leads by means of higher impassiveness (*paravairāgya*) straight to liberation. For it follows from the words quoted from the Bhagavad-gītā that he only who knows that the Self is never an agent, can arrive at the whole truth.[17]

The example could illustrate two points: the *extension* of the principle of *samanvaya*, or harmonisation, in Brahmasūtra I.1.4 beyond the Upaniṣadic statements to all the statements of Hindu orthodox schools. In that case it would strengthen the view that there is one correct and coherent explanation, though scholars might dispute which the correct one is. If, however, the same texts are seen as supporting different philosophical systems with equal validity, the case for a multivalent understanding of the Gītā is strengthened. It ultimately boils down to how we view contradictions: as proof of error, or 'as alternate ways of attaining the supreme end'. Hence the importance attached to its discussion in the Introduction.

Once we move through the ancient and medieval to the modern period, two distinct views on the question are clearly identifiable.

The view that the Gītā is univalent is clearly expressed by B.G. Tilak. The passage in which he states this conclusion indicates also how he arrived at it.

> In my boyhood I was also told that *Bhagavad Gītā* was universally acknowledged to be a book containing all the principles and philosophy of the Hindu religion, and I thought if this be so I should find an answer in this book to my query; and thus began my study of the *Bhagavad Gītā*. I approached the book with a mind prepossessed by no previous ideas about any philosophy, and had no theory of my own for which I sought any support in the *Gītā*. A person whose mind is prepossessed by certain ideas reads the book with a prejudiced mind. For instance, when a Christian reads it he does not want to know what the *Gītā* says but wants to find out if there are any principles in the *Gītā* which he has already met with in the Bible, and if so the

[17] ibid., pp.592-3.

> conclusion he rushes to is that the *Gītā* was copied from the Bible. I have dealt with this topic in my book *Gītā Rahasya* and I need hardly say much about it here, but what I want to emphasise is this, that when you want to read and understand a book, especially a great work like the *Gītā* – you must approach it with an unprejudiced and unprepossessed mind. To do this, I know is one of the most difficult things. Those who profess to do it may have a lurking thought or prejudice in their minds which vitiates the reading of the book to some extent. However, I am describing to you the frame of mind one must get into if one wants to get at the truth and, however difficult it be, it has to be done. The next thing one has to do is to take into consideration the time and the circumstances in which the book was written and the purpose for which the book was written. In short the book must not be read devoid of its context. This is especially true about a book like *Bhagavad Gītā*. Various commentators have put as many interpretations on the bok, and surely the writer or composer could not have written or composed the book for so many interpretations being put on it. He must have but one meaning and one purpose running through the book, and that I have tried to find out. I believe I have succeeded in it, because having no theory of mine for which I sought any support from the book so universally respected, I had no reason to twist the text to suit my theory. There has not been a commentator of the *Gītā* who did not advocate a pet theory of his own and has not tried to support the same by showing that the *Bhagavad Gītā* lent him support.[18]

The other view, that the Gītā is multivalent, is advocated by S. Radhakrishnan. After a survey of the chief commentators, he concludes:

> The differences of interpretation are generally held to be differences determined by the viewpoint adopted. The Hindu tradition believes that the different views are complementary. Even the systems of Indian philosophy are so many points of view, or *darśanas*, which are mutually complementary and not contradictory. The *Bhāgavata* says that the sages have described in various ways the essential truths. A popular verse declares: 'From the viewpoint of the body, I am Thy servant, from the viewpoint of the ego, I am a portion of Thee; from the viewpoint of the self I am Thyself. This is my conviction.' God is

[18] Ainslie T. Embree (ed.), *The Hindu Tradition* (New York: Random House, 1972), pp.310-11.

experienced as Thou or I according to the plane in which consciousness centres.[19]

This brings us to the decisive question: how does the Gītā view itself, as univalent or as multivalent, from the point of view of being a *mokṣa-śāstra*, or a manual for salvation, as the ancient Hindu exegetical tradition took it to be?

In so far as it is possible to be objective in these matters, there is little doubt that the Gītā offers several optional paths to salvation. As a single instance consider XIII:24-5:

dhyānenā 'tmani paśyanti
kecid ātmānam ātmanā
anye sāṃkhyena yogena
karmayogena cā 'pare

anye tv evam ajānantaḥ
śrutvā 'nyebhya upāsate
te 'pi cā 'titaranty eva
mṛtyuṃ śrutiparāyaṇāḥ

By meditation, in the self see
Some the self by the self;
Others by discipline of reason,
And others by discipline of action.

But others, not having this knowledge,
Hearing it from others, revere it;
Even they also, nevertheless, cross over
Death, devoted to the holy revelation which they hear.[20]

R.C. Zaehner makes the interesting observation on these verses that 'this and the following stanza bear no relation whatever either to what precedes or to what follows'.[21] Thus, being free-standing, they cannot be said to have been lifted out of context. They offer salvation in a variety of ways, apart from *jñāna-yoga* and *karma-yoga*.

[19] S. Radhakrishnan, *The Bhagavadgītā* (New Delhi: Blackie 1974 [first published 1946]), p.20.
[20] Edgerton, op.cit., Part I, pp.130, 131.
[21] Zaehner, op.cit., p.346.

Bhakti is not mentioned explicitly, though perhaps implied in earlier and subsequent verses.[22]

It is clear, therefore, that the Gītā shares in the ambiguity of the tradition on the question of the univalency and/or multivalency of scriptural texts. It might be helpful at this stage to identify four aspects

[22] Read XII:27-8 with XIII:2 for instance. This instance is typical of the Gītā. Verses from Chapter Nine (14-15) were cited in the Introduction and verses 23-5, though they introduce some qualifications are also often cited, as also IV:11 in such a context. It is also a matter of some interest that this multivalency is recognised by the classical exegetes themselves. The battle among them is the battle for ultimacy – which Yoga – that of Jñāna or Bhakti, and in the latter case which brand of *bhakti-yoga* – Rāmānuja's or Madhva's – leads to ultimate salvation, or if you wish, ultimately leads to salvation. The ancillary role of other Yogas is not denied. This is in keeping with the Gītā. Consider, for instance, the numerous options that are held out in Chapter XII:8-12, which are cited here in Edgerton's translation:

Fix thy thought-organ on Me alone;
Make thy consciousness enter into Me;
And thou shalt come to dwell even in Me
Hereafter; there is no doubt of this.

But if to fix thy thought
Steadfastly on Me thou art not able,
With the discipline of practice then
Seek to win Me, Dhanamjaya

If thou hast no ability even for practice,
Be wholly devoted to work for Me;
For My sake also actions
Performing, thou shalt win perfection.

But if even this thou art unable
To do, resorting to My discipline,
Abandonment of the fruit of all actions
Do thou then effect, controlling thyself.

For knowledge is better than practice,
And meditation is superior to knowledge,
And abandonment of the fruit of actions is better than meditation;
From abandonment (comes) peace immediately.

Edgerton's note on the last verse is also very helpful. He remarks: 'Here three different ways of salvation are briefly mentioned, in climactic order: (1) the Sāṃkhya way of knowledge, (2) the kind of Yoga often mentioned in the Mokṣadharma section (see e.g. Mbh. 12.294.5-25), and (3) the Gītā's favourite way, which it also calls Yoga, acting unselfishly with no interest in results. Characteristically, the way of devotion to God is, in the latter part of the chapter, emphatically exalted above all other ways (though they may be combined with it). The colophon, in fact, entitles the chapter "discipline of devotion" (*bhakti-yoga*)' (Franklin Edgerton, *The Beginnings of Indian Philosophy* [Cambridge, Massachusetts: Harvard University Press, 1965], p.237).

of the issue: (1) theory, (2) the practice of the theory, (3) practice, and (4) the theory of the practice. In theory the texts may be held to be either univalent or multivalent. In the practice of the theory they turn out to be multivalent because scholiasts who insist that the scriptures have only one correct interpretation come up with several such 'one correct interpretations'. In practice the text has been, and is, understood variously by the people in general. The fact that, despite what the scholiasts might say, people do interpret the text according to their own understanding in practice is recognised (though not condoned) by Śaṅkara himself, who remarks in the introduction to his commentary:

> The famous Gītā-Śāstra is an epitome of the essentials of the whole Vedic teaching; and its meaning is very difficult to understand. Though, to afford a clear view of its teaching, it has been explained word by word and sentence by sentence, and its import critically examined by several commentators, *still I have found that to the laity it appears to teach diverse and quite contradictory doctrines.* I propose, therefore, to write a brief commentary with a view to determine its precise meaning.[23]

Not only did people then, as now, take the Gītā to be multivalent, they must have also contributed to this multivalency by having their own different interpretations of parts of it or even the whole of it.

In the theory of the practice it is clearly acknowledged that people will differ in their understanding of the scriptural texts. At this point the following 'pragmatic explanation' offered by Indian thinkers to explain the multiplicity of philosophical schools needs to be considered:

> They believed that all persons were not fit for all things and that in religious, philosophical and social matters we should take into consideration these differences and recognise consequent distinctions of natural aptitudes (*adhikārabheda*). The different philosophical disciplines, as already pointed out, were taken in India as the different ways of shaping practical lives. Consequently, it was all the more necessary to discriminate the fitness of their followers. The many systems of philosophy beginning from the materialism of the Cārvāka school and ending with the Vedānta of Śaṅkara were thus conceived to offer different paths for philosophical thinking and living to persons

[23] A. Mahādeva Śāstri, op.cit., p.4; italics added and diacritics supplied.

of differing qualifications and temepraments.[24]

We might wonder whether such an apporach was adopted in relation to the Gītā. It was.[25] According to Śaṅkara, Arjuna was not qualifed for the path of knowledge and therefore was taught the path of works by Kṛṣṇa. It would appear that according to Śaṅkara Arjuna was not of superior (*uttama*), but rather only of average (*madhyama*) calibre. On the other hand, Rāmānuja and Madhva have no such reservations regarding Arjuna.

2.

It is clear that notwithstanding doctrinal differences on scriptural univalency or multivalency in theory, the student of the Gītā must in practice deal with the reality of different interpretations of the text. And given such multivalency as is found in fact, if not always in theory, it should not be surprising that when the English-speaking world discovered the Bhagavadgītā in 1785, the 'Hindu Gītā' lost little time in becoming the 'universal Gītā'. As Kṛṣṇa had proclaimed: 'wherever they may be, men follow in my footsteps' (IV:11).[26]

[24] Satischandra Chatterjee and Dhirendramohan Datta, *An Introduction to India Philosophy* (University of Calcutta, 1968), pp.11-12.

[25] A. Mahādeva Śāstri, op.cit., pp.5-6. It is an interesting point to consider whether followers of the path of knowledge are more prone to emphasise differences in eligibility than followers of the path of devotion or works.

[26] Zaehner, op.cit., p.185.

Bibliography

Aksharajna — *Sri Ramana*. Tiruvannamalai: Niranjanananda Swami, 1948.

Apte, V.S. — *The Practical Sanskrit-English Dictionary*. Two volumes, Poona: Prasad Prakashan, 1957.

Aurobindo, Sri — *Essays on the Gita*. Pondicherry: Sri Ashram, 1959.

Bandhu, Vishva — *The Vedas and Sastras*. Hoshiarpur: Vishveshvarananda Institute, 1966.

Barnett, L.D. — *Bhagavadgītā*. Boston: Beacon Press, 1951.

Basham, A.L. — *The Wonder that was India*. New York: Grove Press, 1954.

Belvalkar, Shripad Krishna (ed.) — *The Bhīṣmaparvan*. Poona: Bhandarkar Oriental Research Institute, 1947. (Sometimes cited with V.S. Sukthankar as co-editor, both the names being associated with the critical edition of the Mahābhārata.)

Bhandarkar, Sir Ramakrishna Gopal — *Vaiṣṇavism, Śaivism and Minor Religious Systems*. Strassburg: K.J. Trubner, 1913.

Bharadwaj, Krishna Datta — *The Philosophy of Rāmānuja*. New Delhi: Sir Shankar Lall Charitable Trust Society, 1958.

Bhattacharyya, Haridas (ed.) — *The Cultural Heritage of India*. Volume II. Calcutta: Ramakrishna Mission Institute of Culture, 1962.

Bolle, Kees W. — *The Bhagavadgītā: A New Translation*. Berkeley: University of California Press, 1979.

Bowes, Pratima — *The Hindu Religious Tradition: A Philosophical Approach*. London: Routledge & Kegan Paul, 1977.

Brown, D. Mackenzie — 'The philosophy of Bal Gangadhar Tilak', in *Journal of Asian Studies* XVIII:2.

Brunton, Paul — *A Search in Secret India*. London: Rider, 1954.

Caleb, C.C. — *The Song Divine*. London: Luzac, 1911.

Campbell, Joseph (ed.) *Philosophies of India* by Heinrich Zimmer. New York: Meridian Books, 1964

Carman, John Braisted *The Theology of Rāmānuja*. New Haven: Yale University Press, 1974.

Chatterjee, Satischandra & Datta, Dhirendramohana *An Introduction to Indian Philosophy*. University of Calcutta, 1968 [first edition 1939].

Coppleston, F. *Religion and the One: Philosophies East and West*. New York: Crossroad, 1982.

Dasgupta, Surendranath *A History of Indian Philosophy*. Five volumes. Cambridge University Press, 1922-1955. (The name Surendranath is initialised as S.N.)

Deussen, Paul *The Philosophy of the Upaniṣads*. New York: Dover Publications, 1966. [Earlier edition: Edinburgh: T. & T. Clark, 1906]

Deutsch, Eliot and van Buitenen, J.A.B. *A Source Book of Advaita Vedānta*. Honolulu: University Press of Hawaii, 1971.

Dhavamony, Mariasusai *Love of God According to Śaiva Siddhānta* Oxford: Clarendon Press, 1971.

Edgerton, Franklin *The Bhagavad Gītā: Translated and Interpreted*. Parts I and II. Cambridge, Massachusetts: Harvard University Press, 1944.

The Beginnings of Indian Philosophy. Cambridge, Massachusetts: Harvard University Press, 1965.

Eliade, Mircea *Yoga, Immortality and Freedom*. New York: Pantheon Books, 1954.

Embree, Ainslie T. (ed.) *The Hindu Tradition*. New York: Random House, 1972.

Farquhar, J.N. *An Outline of the Religious Literature of India*. Delhi: Motilal Banarsidass, 1967. [Also: Oxford University Press, 1920].

Gandhi, M.K. *Discourses on the Gita*. (tr. Mahadev Desai). Ahmedabad: Navajivan Publishing House, 1948.

Gita – My Mother. Bombay: Bharatiya Vidya Bhavan, 1965.

Ashram Observances in Action. Ahmedabad: Navajivan Publishing House, 1955.

Garbe, Richard *India and Christendom*. La Salle, Ill.: Open Court, 1959.

Gibb, H.A.R. *Islam: A Historical Survey*. Oxford: Oxford University Press, 1978.

Gibb, H.A.R. & Kramers, J.H. (eds.) *Shorter Encyclopedia of Islam*. Leiden: E.J. Brill, 1974.

Govindacharya, A. *Srī Bhagavad-Gītā with Srī Rāmānujachārya's Viṣiṣthadvaita – Commentary*. Madras: Vaijayanti Press, 1898.

Goyandakā, H. *Śrīmadbhagavadgītā Śrīrāmānujabhāṣya Hindi Anuvāda Sahita.* Gorakhpur: Gita Press, Saṁvat 2025.

Gupta, Anima Sen *A Critical Study of the Philosophy of Rāmānuja.* Varanasi: Chowkhamba Sanskrit Series Office, 1967.

Guru, Nataraj *The Bhagavad Gītā.* New York: Asia Publishing House, 1961.

Hardon, John A. *Religions of the World.* Maryland: New Man Press, 1963.

Hazra, R.C. *Studies in the Purāṇic Records of Hindu Rites and Customs.* Delhi: Motilal Banarsidass, 1975. [Also: Calcutta, Univ. of Dacca, 1940].

Herman, A.L. *The Bhagavadgītā.* Springfield, Ill.: Charles A. Thomas, 1973.

Hill, W. Douglas P. *The Bhagavadgītā.* London: Humphrey Milford, 1928. Abridged edition: Oxford University Press, 1969.

Hiriyanna, M. *The Essentials of Indian Philosophy.* London: Allen & Unwin, 1978 [first published 1948].

Outlines of Indian Philosophy. London: Allen & Unwin, 1964 [first published 1932].

Honda, Jan *Die Religionen Indiens.* Two volumes. Stuttgart: Kohlhammer, 1960.

Hopkins, Thomas J. *The Hindu Religious Tradition.* Belmont, California: Dickenson, 1971.

Hume, R.E. *The World's Living Religions.* New York: Scribner, 1959.

The Thirteen Principal Upaniṣads. Oxford: Oxford University Press, 1968 [first published 1921].

Ingalls, Daniel H.H. 'Bhāskara the Vedāntin' in *Philosophy East and West* XVII.

Jacob, G.A. *A Concordance of the Upanishads and the Bhagavadgītā.* Bombay: Government Central Book Depot, 1891.

Johnston, E.H. *Early Sāṁkhya.* London: Royal Asiatic Society, 1937.

Kale, M.R. (ed.) *The Abhijñānaśākuntalam of Kālidāsa.* Delhi: Motilal Banarsidass, 1980.

Karmarkar, D.P. *Bal Gangadhar Tilak: A Study.* Bombay, 1956.

Katre, S.M. *Critical Word-Index of the Bhagavadgītā.* Bombay: New Book Co., 1946.

Macnicol, Nicol *Indian Theism.* Oxford: Oxford University Press, 1915.

Mahadevan, T.M.P. *Outlines of Hinduism.* Bombay: Chetana, 1971.

Maharishi, Sri Raman — *The Song Celestial*. Tiruvannamalai: Sri Niranjanananda Swami, 1951.

Majumdar, R.C. (ed.) — *The Vedic Age*. Bombay: Bharatiya Vidya Bhavan, 1965.

The Age of Imperial Unity. Bombay: Bharatiya Vidya Bhavan, 1953.

The Classical Age. Bombay: Bharatiya Vidya Bhavan, 1962.

Martin, E.O. — *The Gods of India*. London: Dent, 1914.

Mathai, P.S. — *A Christian Approach to the Bhagavad Gītā*. Calcutta: YMCA, 1956.

Mayeda, Sengaku — 'The authenticity of the Bhagavadgītābhāṣya ascribed to Śaṅkara' in *Wiener Zeitschrift für die Kunde Süd- und Ostasiens und Archiv für Indische Philosophie* Band IX.

Minor, Robert — *Bhagavadgītā: An Exegetical Commentary*. Delhi: Heritage, 1982.

'The Gita's way as the only way' in *Philosophy East and West* XXX(3).

Monier-Williams, Monier — *A Sanskrit-English Dictionary*. Oxford: Clarendon Press, 1970.

Müller, F. Max — *The Six Systems of Indian Philosophy*. London: Longmans, Green, 1899.

Murty, K. Satchidananda — *Revelation and Reason in Advaita Vedānta*. New York: Columbia University Press, 1959.

Nakamura, Hajime — *A History of Early Vedānta Philosophy*. Part I. Delhi: Motilal Banarsidass, 1983.

Narasiṁhācārya, A.V. & T.A. (eds.) — *Śrīmadbhagavadgītā*. Madras: Ananda Press, 1910.

Nehru, Jawaharlal — *The Discovery of India*. Calcutta: Signet Press, 1946.

Nikhilananda, Swami — *The Bhagavadgītā*. New York: Ramakrishna Vivekananda Centre, 1944.

— (tr.) — *The Gospel of Sri Ramakrishna*. New York: Ramakrishna Vivekananda Centre, 1942.

Otto, Rudolph — *The Original Gītā*. London: Allen & Unwin, 1939.

Pansīkar, Wāsudeva Laxmaṇa Śāstri (ed.) — *The Bhagavadgītā*. Bombay: Nirṇayasāgara Press, 1912.

Payne, Robert — *The Life and Death of Mahatma Gandhi*. New York: Dutton, 1969.

Prabhavananda, Swami and Isherwood, C. — *The Bhagavad Gītā*. Hollywood: Marcel Rodd, 1945.

Radhakrishnan, S. — *The Brahma Sūtra: The Philosophy of Spiritual Life*. London: Allen & Unwin, 1971.

Indian Philosophy. Two volumes. New York: Macmillan, 1962.

— and Moore, C.A. (eds.) *A Source Book of Indian Philosophy.* Princeton University Press, 1957.

The Bhagavadgītā. London: Allen & Unwin, 1948. Later edition: New Delhi: Blackie, 1974.

— (ed.) *The Principal Upaniṣads* London: Allen & Unwin, 1953.

The Hindu View of Life. London: Unwin Books, 1974 [first published 1927].

Raghavan, V. 'Bhāskara's Gītābhāṣya' in *Wiener Zeitschrift für die Kunde Süd- und Ostasiens und Archiv für Indische Philosophie* Band XII-XIII.

Ranade, R.D. *The Bhagavadgītā.* Nagpur: M.S. Modak, 1959.

Rao, K.L. Seshagiri *The Concept of Śraddhā.* Patiala: Roy Publishers, 1971.

Raychaudhuri, Hemachandra *Materials for the Study of the Early History of the Vaishnava Sect.* New Delhi: Oriental Books Reprint Corporation, 1975. [Earlier edition: University of Calcutta, 1920].

Roy, S.C. *The Bhagavadgītā and Modern Scholarship.* London: Luzac, 1941.

Sadhale, G.S. (ed) *The Bhagavad-Gītā with Eleven Commentaries.* Bombay: 'Gujarati' Printing Press, 1935.

Sampatkumaran, M.R. *The Gitabhasya of Rāmānuja* (Eng.tr.). Madras: Prof. M. Rangacarya Memorial Trust, 1969.

Śaṅkara *Gītābhāṣyam.* Also cited as *Śrīśāṅkaragranthāvaliḥ* Sampuṭa 8; Śrīraṅgam: Śrīvāṇīvilāsamudrāyantrālayaḥ, no date.

Śaṅkara, M.R. and Āpṭe, V.G. (eds.) *Śrīmadbhagavadgītā Vedāntācārya – Śrī – Venkaṭanāthakṛta – Tātparyacandrikākhyaṭīkāsaṃvalita – Śrimad – Rāmānujācārya – Viracita – Bhāsyasahitā* Bombay: Ānandāśrama Press, 1923.

Sarma, B.N. Krishnamurti 'Bhāskara – a forgotten commentator on the Gītā' in *Indian Historical Quarterly* IX.

Sarma, D.S. *Lectures on the Bhagavad Gītā.* Rajamundry: N. Subbarau Pantulu, 1937.

Sarma, Sreekrishna *Gītā Samīkṣā.* Tirupati: Sri Venkateswara University, 1971.

Śāstri, A. Mahādeva *The Bhagavadgītā with the Commentary of Śrī Śankarachāryā. Translated from Sanskrit into English.* Madras: V. Ramaswamy Sastrulu, 1961. Same as Sastry, below.

Śastrī, Śrī Māhāvena (ed.) *Śrīmadbhagavadgītā Śrīmadrāmānujācāryakṛtābhāṣyasametā.* Bombay: Lakṣmīvenkaṭeśvara Press, 1959.

Sastry, Alladi Mahadeva (tr.) *The Bhagavad Gītā with the Commentary of Sri Sankaracharya.* Madras: Samata Books, 1979.

Schilapp, Paul Arthur — *The Philosophy of Sarvepalli Radhakrishnan*. New York: Tudor Publishing Company, 1952.

Schrader, F. Otto — 'Ancient Gītā commentaries' in *The Indian Historical Quarterly* X:2.

Sharma, Arvind — *Abhinavagupta Gītārthasaṅgraha*. Leiden: E.J. Brill, 1983

Viśiṣṭādvaita Vedānta: A Study. New Delhi: Heritage Publishers, 1978.

'The role of etymology in Hindu hermeneutics: an analysis', *Our Heritage* 26(2).

Sharma, Chandradhar — *Indian Philosophy*. New York: Barnes & Noble, 1962.

Singer, Milton (ed.) — *Krishna: Myths, Rites, Attitudes*. Honolulu: East-West Center Press, 1966.

Sivananda, Śrī Svāmī — *Srimad Bhagavad Gītā*. Rishikesh: Yoga-Vedanta Forest University, 1949.

Smith, Huston — *The Religions of Man*. New York: Harper & Row, 1958.

Srinivasachari, P.N. — *The Philosophy of Viśiṣṭādvaita*. Madras: Adyar Library, 1943.

Śrīpāda, V. et al (eds.) — *Gītābhāshya of Sri Madhwacharya with Prameyadeepika of Sri Jayatirtha – a Commentary of Bhagavadgita*. Poornaprajnanagar, Bangalore: Poornaprajana Vidyapeetha, 1981.

Sukthankar, V.S. and Belvalkar, S.K. (eds.) — *The Āśvamedhikaparvan*. Poona: Bhandarkar Oriental Research Institute, 1960.

Swami, A.C. Bhaktivedanta — *The Bhagavadgītā As It Is*. London: Collier Macmillan, 1968.

Swarupananda, Swami — *Shrimad Bhagavad Gītā*. Calcutta: Advaita Ashrama, 1967.

Tarkavachaspati, T. — *Vācaspatya*. Calcutta: Saraswati Press, 1883.

Telang, K.T. (tr.) — *The Bhagavadgītā with the Sanatsujātīya and the Anugītā*. Delhi: Motilal Banarsidass, 1965 [Also: Oxford Clarendon Press, 1908].

Thibaut, George — *The Vedānta-Sūtras with the Commentary of Rāmānuja*. Three parts. Oxford: Clarendon Press, 1904.

Thomas, E.J. — *The Bhagavad Gītā*. London: John Murray, 1959.

Thomson, J. Cockburn — *The Bhagavad-Gita*. Hartford: Stephen Austin, 1855.

Tilak, B.G. — *Gita Rahasya* (tr. B.S. Sukthankar). Poona: J.S. Tilak & S.S. Tilak, 1965.

Upadhyaya, Subhadra (ed.) — *Srīmadbhagavad-Gītāyāḥ BhagavadāśayānusaraṇābhidhānabhāṣyamBhagavadbhāskaraviracitam*. Varanasi: Varanaseya Sanskrit Vishvavidyalaya, 1965.

van Buitenen, J.A.B. — *Rāmānuja on the Bhagavad Gītā*. New Delhi: Motilal Banarsidass, 1968. Earlier edition: Ś-Gravenhage: H.L. Smits, 1953.

'The relative dates of Śaṁkara and Bhāskara' in *The Adyar Library Bulletin* XXV.

'A contribution to the critical edition of the Bhagavadgītā' in *Journal of the American Oriental Society* 85(1).

Vadekar, D.D. *Bhagavad-Gītā*. Poona: Oriental Book Agency, 1928.

Vidyālaṅkāra, Īśvaradatta *Rāmānuja's Commentary on the Bhagavadgītā*. Muzaffarpur, Bihar: Prof. Īśvaradatta, G.B.B. College, 1930.

Vidyasagar, Pandit Jibananda (ed.) *Dhatupadadarsha*, Calcutta: Sucharu Press, 1875.

Vireswarananda Swami *Srimad – Bhagavadgītā*. Mylapore. Madras: Sri Ramakrishna Math, 1948.

Vivekananda, Swami *Complete works of Swami Vivekananda*. Almora, 1948.

Yamunacharya, M. *Rāmānuja's Teaching in His Own Words*. Bombay: Bharatiya Vidya Bhavan, 1963.

Yogi, Maharishi Mahesh *Bhagavad-Gītā*. Harmondsworth, Penguin Books, 1969.

Zaehner, R.C. *The Bhagavad-Gītā*. Oxford: Clarendon Press, 1969.

Discordant Concord. Oxford: Clarendon Press, 1970.

Note

Readers of the Gītā in general may find the following two books bibliographically specially helpful:

J.C. Kapoor, *Bhagavad-Gītā: An International Bibliography of 1785-1979 Imprints* (New York and London: Garland Publishing Inc. 1983)

W.M. Callewaert and Shilanand Hemraj, *Bhagavadgitānuvāda: A Study in Transcultural Translation* (Ranchi: Satya Bharati Publication, 1983)

Index of Authors

Sanskrit Index